THE KNOWING ORGANIZATION

THE KNOWING ORGANIZATION

How Organizations Use Information to Construct Meaning, Create Knowledge, and Make Decisions

CHUN WEI CHOO

New York   Oxford
OXFORD UNIVERSITY PRESS
1998

Oxford University Press

Oxford   New York
Athens   Auckland   Bangkok   Bogota   Bombay   Buenos Aires
Calcutta   Cape Town   Dar es Salaam   Delhi   Florence   Hong Kong
Istanbul   Karachi   Kuala Lumpur   Madras   Madrid   Melbourne
Mexico City   Nairobi   Paris   Singapore   Taipei   Tokyo   Toronto   Warsaw

and associated companies in
Berlin   Ibadan

Library of Congress Cataloging-in-Publication Data
Choo, Chun Wei.
The knowing organization : how organizations use information to construct meaning,
create knowledge, and make decisions / Chun Wei Choo.
p. cm.
Includes bibliographical references (p.) and index.
ISBN 0-19-511011-0 (cloth : alk. paper). — ISBN 0-19-511012-9 (pbk. : alk. paper)
1. Communication in organizations.   2. Decision making.   3. Knowledge, sociology of. I. Title.
HD30.3.C46   1997
658.4'5—dc21   97-9034

1 3 5 7 9 8 6 4 2
Printed in the United States of America
on acid-free paper

To my wife Bee Kheng
and our children Ren Min and Ren Ee

TABLE OF CONTENTS

PREFACE

If recent history is any indication, one-third of the companies currently on the *Fortune* 500 list will disappear over the next five years. Yet there are organizations that have literally lived to be a hundred, continuing to thrive decade after decade. These organizations have survived not just because of their size or good luck. Many of them have demonstrated a capacity to adapt swiftly to changing conditions in the environment, to innovate continuously, and to take decisive actions that move their organization toward its goals. The design of these organizational capabilities is the theme of this book.

What is a *knowing organization?* At one level, the knowing organization possesses information and knowledge so that it is well informed, mentally perceptive, and enlightened—descriptions that may be found in the *Oxford English Dictionary*'s entry for "knowing." At a deeper level, the knowing organization possesses information and knowledge that confer a special advantage, allowing it to maneuver with intelligence, creativity, and, occasionally, cunning. This book suggests that the knowing organization is well prepared to sustain its growth and development in a dynamic environment. By sensing and understanding its environment, the knowing organization is able to prepare for adaptation early. By marshalling the skills and expertise of its members, the knowing organization is able to engage in continuous learning and innovation. By applying learned decision rules and routines, the knowing organization is primed to take timely, purposive action. At the heart of the knowing organization is its management of the information processes that underpin sense making, knowledge building, and decision making.

Purpose and Approach

This book brings together the insight developed from research in organization theory and information science into a general framework for understanding the richness and complexity of information use in organizations. Research in organization theory suggests that organizations create and use information in three strategic arenas. First, organizations interpret information about the environment in order to construct meaning about what is happening to the organization and what the organization is doing. Second, they create new knowledge by converting and combining the expertise and know-how of their members in order to learn and innovate. Finally, they process and analyze information in order to select and commit to appropriate courses of action. We combine these perspectives into a general model of organizations as "knowing" communities in which sense making, knowledge creating, and decision making are integrated in a cascade of information seeking and use that moves the organization from a broad interpretation of ambiguous environmental changes, through the replenishment of new knowledge for innovation and relearning, to converge upon the selection and implementation of a particular strategy or course of action. The knowing organization is effective because it continually evolves with its changing environment, refreshes its knowledge assets, and practices vigilant information processing in its decision making.

Research in information science on information needs and uses suggests that when people seek and use information, they are influenced by multiple levels of contingencies. At the cognitive level, different types of cognitive gaps lead to the activation of different information strategies to bridge those gaps. At the affective level, emotional and psychological states influence the preferences and methods of information seeking. At the situational level, characteristics of the work or problem situation determine the ways that information is used and assessed to be useful (or otherwise). We use this multitier approach to analyze information seeking and use in the organization's sense-making, knowledge-creating, and decision-making processes. We address the following questions: What are the cognitive strategies adopted to construct meaning, induce learning, and guide decision making? How do the affective or psychological states that characterize each of these modes sway information use? What are the situational dimensions that are salient in each mode and how do they constrain or modify information behavior?

Overall, the book has the following objectives. First, it analyzes and compares the principal modes by which an organization uses information strategically to make sense of its changing environment, create new knowledge for innovation, and make decisions that reflect past learning and ongoing adaptation. Second, it examines the structure and dynamics of information seeking and use in each of the three modes: sense making through the development of shared meanings; knowledge creation through the conversion and sharing of different forms of organizational knowledge; and decision making through the use of rules and routines that reduce complexity and uncertainty. Third, it proposes a new framework of the knowing organization, in which sense making, knowledge creating, and decision making are linked as a continuum of nested information activities that invigorate an organization with the information and knowledge to act intelligently.

Audience

As a textbook, reviewers indicate that *The Knowing Organization* will be of use in a variety of courses as a core text or supplement, especially in departments of organizational behavior within schools of business and in departments of management information systems. The text will also be useful in schools and departments of information management, information studies, or information science.

The material in this book will be of interest to researchers and students in the fields of information management and organization theory, and to people managing and working in organizations who share a common desire to acquire a clearer understanding of how organizations create, seek, and use information. It presents in a single volume a survey of the state of our knowledge about organizations as information-processing systems. By analyzing the connections and dependencies between various approaches, a unifying framework is developed that deepens our appreciation of the processes by which the organization creates meaning, knowledge, and action. The framework outlined is both a synthesis of contemporary perspectives on organizational learning and an invitation to further research on the management of information creation and use in organizations.

Our discussions will also interest the architects and designers of information systems and information services, including the management and staff of information system departments, libraries, information centers, and other groups who participate in the generation and processing of organizational information. As we clarify the role of information in organizations, we also clarify the conditions, patterns, and rules of use which render information meaningful and valuable. In the knowing organization, information systems and services go beyond simply *what* people want to know, to *why* and *how* they will use the information. Information systems and services would not just answer queries, but be designed as sets of activities that add value to information in order to assist users to make better decisions and better sense of situations.

Overview of the Contents

The book is divided into seven chapters. Chapter 1 sets the scene with brief introductions to theories of organizations as sense-making communities, knowledge-creating enterprises, and decision-making systems. It makes the case that these three apparently divergent points of view are in fact complementary pieces of a larger canvas, and that the information behaviors described in each model coalesce into a richer explanation of the nature of information use in organizations. The second half of the chapter previews the framework of the knowing organization and presents an example of such an organization in action.

Chapter 2 surveys the large body of research that has been completed since World War II on *information needs, information seeking,* and *information use.* Individuals first become aware of information needs as feelings of doubt and unease about the state of one's ability to make sense of one's experience. These vague feelings may congeal into better defined questions or topics, which can then initiate information seeking. Information seeking is the process of searching for information in a purposeful manner so as to be able to alter one's state of knowledge. Information use is when the individual selects and processes information, which leads to a change in the individual's capacity to make sense of an experience and to act or respond in light of that new understanding. Research suggests that the behavior of people seeking and using information should be analyzed at three levels. The situational level looks at how demands of the work-related context shape information needs and use. The cognitive level looks at how information is used to bridge different kinds of cognitive gaps. The affective level looks at how emotions and psychological states influence information seeking. Thus information needs, information seeking, and information use are all determined by the norms and demands of the work and social setting, by the individual's definition of the cognitive gap representing the information need and use, and by the emotional experience of seeking, selecting, and using the information encountered. This three-level framework is applied in subsequent chapters to explore the structure and dynamics of information use by people in organizations as they construct meaning, create knowledge, and make decisions.

Chapter 3 takes a closer look at the first of our three modes of strategic information use—*sense making.* Sense making is precipitated by a change or difference in the environment that creates discontinuity in the flow of experience, engaging the people and activities of an organization (Weick 1979). These discontinuities provide the raw data from the environment which have to be made sense of. The sense-making recipe is to interpret the environment through connected sequences of enactment, selection, and retention (Weick 1995). In enactment, people actively construct the environments which they attend to by bracketing, rearranging, and labeling portions of the experience, thereby converting raw data from the environment into equivocal data to be interpreted. In selection, people choose meanings that can be imposed on the equivocal data by overlaying past interpretations as templates to the current experience. Selection produces an enacted environment that is meaningful in providing a cause-and-effect explanation of what is taking place. In retention, the organization stores the products of successful sense making (enacted or meaningful interpretations) so that they may be retrieved in the future. Organizational sense making can be driven by beliefs or by actions (Weick 1995). In belief-driven processes, people start from an initial set of beliefs that are sufficiently clear and plausible, and use them as nodes to connect more and more information into larger structures of meaning. People may use beliefs as expectations to guide the choice of plausible interpretations, or they may argue about beliefs and their relevance to current experience, especially when beliefs and cues are contradictory. In action-driven processes, people start from their actions and grow their structures of meaning around them by modifying the structures in order to give significance to those actions. People may create meaning in order to justify actions that are visible, deliberate, and irreversible (committing actions), or they may create meaning in order to explain actions that have been taken to induce changes in the environment (manipulating actions).

Chapter 4 examines how an organization creates and makes use of new *knowledge*. As Peter Drucker has repeatedly observed in recent writings, the essence of management is about how existing knowledge can best be applied to produce new knowledge. This exhortation is elaborated and vindicated by the research of Nonaka and Takeuchi on large Japanese firms, the study by Leonard-Barton of U.S. manufacturing companies, and the work of Wikström and Normann on Swedish organizations. *Knowledge creating* is precipitated by a situation that reveals gaps in the existing knowledge of the organization or the work group. Such knowledge gaps stand in the way of solving a technical or task-related problem, designing a new product or service, or taking advantage of an opportunity. An organization possesses three kinds of knowledge: tacit knowledge embedded in the expertise and experience of individuals and groups; explicit or rule-based knowledge codified in organizational rules, routines, and procedures; and cultural knowledge expressed in the assumptions, beliefs, and norms used by members to assign value and significance to new information or knowledge. New knowledge is created by knowledge conversion (Nonaka and Takeuchi 1995), knowledge building (Leonard-Barton 1995), and knowledge linking (Badaracco 1991; Wikström and Normann 1994). In *knowledge conversion* (Nonaka and Takeuchi 1995) the organization continuously creates new knowledge by converting between the personal, tacit knowledge of individuals who produce creative insight, and the shared, explicit knowledge which the organization needs to develop new products and innovations. Tacit knowledge is shared and externalized through dialogue that uses metaphors and analogies. New concepts are created, and the concepts are justified and evaluated according to their fit with organizational intention. Concepts are tested and elaborated by building archetypes or prototypes. Finally, concepts which have been created, justified, and modeled are moved to other levels of the organizaton to spark new cycles of knowledge creation. In *knowledge building* (Leonard-Barton 1995) the organization identifies and nurtures activities that build up knowledge which strengthens the organization's distinctive core capabilities, enabling them to grow over time. These knowledge-building activities are: shared problem solving, experimenting and prototyping, implementing and integrating new processes and tools, and importing knowledge. Individuals with diverse signature skills work together on solving a problem. Through experimentation and prototyping, the organization extends its existing capabilities and builds new ones for the future. Successful implementation of new tools and processes requires users and technology to mutually adapt and to complement each other. Knowledge about the technology as well as the market is imported from outside the organization and absorbed. In *knowledge linking* (Badaracco 1991) the organization forms intimate learning alliances with other organizations in order to tranfer knowledge that is situated in the specialized relationships, work cultures, and operating styles of the partner organization. Wikström and Normann (1994) see an organization as a knowledge-creating value star at the center of many incoming flows of knowledge from suppliers, customers, and other partners. Knowledge is transformed into value not only within the organization, but also through knowledge-based interactions with its customers, suppliers, and other partners.

Chapter 5 discusses how decisions are made in organizations. *Decision making* is precipitated by a choice situation, an occasion in which the organization is expected to select a course of action. Completely rational decision making involves identifying alternatives, projecting the outcomes of each alternative, and evaluating the alternatives and their outcomes according to known preferences or objectives. These information-gathering and information-processing requirements are beyond the capabilities of any organization or any individual. Depending on the level of goal ambiguity or goal conflict, and the level of technical uncertainty, an organization copes with one of four modes of decision making. In the *boundedly rational mode,* when goals and technical clarity are relatively high, choice is simplified by performance programs (March and Simon 1993, 1958) and standard operating procedures (Cyert and March 1992, 1963), which codify the search and decision rules and routines that the organization has learned. In the *process mode* (Mintzberg, Raisinghani, and Théorêt 1976), when goals are strategic and clear but the technical methods to attain them are uncertain, decision making becomes a dynamic process marked by many interruptions and iterations. Nevertheless the process shows a general structure: it begins with the recognition and diagnosis of the problem, which is followed by the development of alternatives through searching for ready-made solutions or designing custom-made ones, and ends with the evaluation and selection of an alternative that has to be authorized or approved. In the *political mode* (Allison 1971), when goals are contested by various interest groups and technical certainty is high within groups, decisions and actions are the results of the bargaining among players pursuing their own interests and manipulating their available instruments of influence. Political decision making may then be likened to game playing, in which players take up positions, stands, and influence and make their moves according to rules and their bargaining strengths. In the *anarchic mode* (Cohen, March, and Olsen 1972), when goals and technical uncertainty are both high, decision situations consist of relatively independent streams of problems, solutions, participants, and choice opportunities. A decision happens through chance and timing, when problems, solutions, participants, and choices coincide; and when solutions are attached to problems, and problems to choices, by participants who have the time and energy to do so.

Chapter 6 examines the theory and process that underlie a *knowing organization.* We develop the perspective that organizational knowing is a social process in which knowing is tied to doing, and doing leads to the making of sense in the context of the organization and its environment. An activity view of knowing may be contrasted with a conventional view of organizational knowledge as "thing." The objectification of knowledge assumes that knowledge is universal and permanent, to be obtained by transferring it from experts or documents. The knowledge-as-object view concentrates on the question, "What knowledge does the organization need to acquire?" The activity view of knowledge asks a different question, "How are systems of knowing and doing changing, and how should the organization respond?" (Blackler 1995). Organizational knowing is the emergent property of the network of information use processes through which the organization constructs shared meanings about its actions and identity; discovers, shares, and applies new knowledge; and initiates patterns of action through search, evaluation, and selection of alternatives. Each mode of information use brings into play its distinctive set of cognitive, affective, and situational needs and resources. Organizational knowing occurs when the resources in each mode of information use are connected with and complement the resources of the other modes, and the organization is able to maintain continuous cycles of learning, innovating, and doing.

Finally, chapter 7 analyzes the contradictions that are inherent in the making of meaning, knowledge, and decision, and show how the resolution of these necessary tensions allows the organization to learn and adapt. Sense making attempts to reduce ambiguity, but a residual equivocality provides flexibility for future learning. Consensus about shared meanings enables coordinated activity, but divergent interpretations ensure robustness. In knowledge creation, exploitation of current expertise yields economies in the short run, but exploration of new areas develops new capabilities for long-term survival. In decision making, rules and preferences structure choice making, but individuals improvise and act with initiative so that the organization can discover new goals or deal with unfamiliar situations. Chapter 7 concludes with a discussion of the management of information resources, systems, and services required to vitalize a knowing organization. A process model is developed to address issues and challenges from the perspective of planning and designing information systems and services. The model is analyzed to develop principles of information management in the following areas: identifying information needs, information acquisition, information organization and storage, information products and services, information distribution, and information use.

By weaving together perspectives from organization theory and information science, the book offers a rich, multilayered representation of organizational learning and adaptation, and sets out the structure and dynamics of information creation and use, which constitute organizational knowing.

Acknowledgments

In researching and preparing this book, the author has had the good fortune of receiving assistance, advice, and encouragement from many generous individuals and groups. In the early days of the book's germination, Professor Ethel Auster at the Faculty of Information Studies (FIS), University of Toronto, fostered the growth of the ideas that came to be presented in this volume, and as the book progressed, she continued to supply guidance and support. I am grateful to Professor Tom Wilson of Sheffield University who graciously sent me copies of his recent articles, reports, and keynote speeches; Art Kleiner, for his insightful paper on scenario planning; Karl Sveiby, for a short but stimulating series of electronic mail exchanges about knowledge in organizations; and Rhoderick van der Wyck, for the copy of his master's thesis on strategic planning at the Royal Dutch Shell group of companies. Many parts of the book benefited directly and indirectly from presentations and discussions in the "Promise" group at FIS, an informal group focusing on information management, which includes my doctoral students Brian Detlor and Don Turnbull, a visiting scholar Professor Ricardo Barbosa, Ethel Auster, and the author. Two other doctoral candidates, Marija Dalbello-Lovric and Chris Halonen, read and commented on material in the last two chapters. A huge debt of thanks is owed to the three graduate student assistants who worked with me on the research and preparation of the book: Gillian Clinton, David McKenzie, and Elizabeth Chang. Over the past few years, students of the classes I taught on decision making and information management at FIS have through their case studies and discussions helped to sharpen several of the ideas presented here. The FIS Library staff has been nothing short of heroic in responding to my requests for books and papers, and the research would have been much more difficult without their assistance. Finally, a special note of appreciation goes to Ken MacLeod, my editor at Oxford University Press in New York, for his enthusiasm in supporting this project, and for his being so understanding about the pressures faced by a faculty member who is simultaneously trying to teach, supervise, conduct funded research, undertake consulting, and write a book. My hope is that the book would make a contribution to our understanding of information and organizations, for there could be no more appropriate way to express my gratitude.

University of Toronto
Toronto, Canada   C.W.C.
June 1997

(Readers are invited to visit the author's web site at http://choo.fis.utoronto.ca where additional resources on information and organizations related to the discussions in this volume may be found.)

THE KNOWING ORGANIZATION

1

THE KNOWING ORGANIZATION—
A HOLISTIC VIEW OF
HOW ORGANIZATIONS
USE INFORMATION

An organization is a body of thought thought by thinking thinkers.
—*Karl Weick 1979a, Cognitive Processes in Organizations, p. 42*

How *do* organizations use information? This question is much harder than it sounds. Information is an intrinsic component of nearly everything that an organization does, so much so that its function has become transparent. Yet the question is not facetious. Without a clear understanding of the organizational and human processes through which information becomes transformed into insight, knowledge, and action, an organization is unable to tap into the real value of its information resources and information technologies. In this chapter we preview a conceptual framework that brings together the principal ways in which an organization uses information strategically, and suggest how these processes are closely interconnected and could be managed to create a "knowing organization."

Current thinking in management and organization theory emphasizes three distinct arenas in which the creation and use of information play a strategic role in determining an organization's capacity to grow and adapt. First, the organization uses information to make sense of changes and developments in its external environment. Organizations thrive in a dynamic, uncertain world. A dependable supply of materials, resources, and energy must be secured. Market forces and dynamics modulate the organization's performance. Fiscal and legal structures define its identity and sphere of influence. Societal norms and public opinion constrain the organization's roles and reach. The critical dependencies between an organization and its environment require the organization to be constantly alert of changes and shifts in its external relationships. The organization that has developed early insight on how the environment is shaping will have a competitive edge. Unfortunately, messages and signals about events and trends in the environment are invariably ambiguous and subject to multiple interpretations. As a result, a crucial task of management is to discern the most significant changes, interpret their meaning, and develop appropriate responses. The immediate goal of sense making is for an organization's members to construct a shared understanding of what the organization is and what it is doing; the longer term goal is to ensure that the organization adapts and continues to thrive in a dynamic environment.

The second arena of strategic information use is when organizations create, organize, and process information in order to generate new knowledge through organizational learning. New knowledge enables the organization to develop new capabilities, design new products and services, enhance existing offerings, and improve organizational processes. Peter Drucker has called knowledge, rather than capital or labor, the only meaningful economic resource of the postcapitalist or knowledge society. For him, the right role of management is to ensure the application and performance of knowledge, that is, the application of knowledge to knowledge (Drucker 1993, 45). The creation and use of knowledge is a particular organizational challenge. Knowledge and expertise are dispersed throughout the organization, and are often closely held by individuals or work units. There have been numerous accounts of organizations having to reinvent the wheel unnecessarily and not being able to locate the expertise that exists somewhere in the organization. Another obstacle to learning is that organizations find it difficult to unlearn their past—to reexamine inherited assumptions and beliefs, or to question existing practices as the only viable alternatives. Senge (1990) has warned that many organizations are unable to fully function as knowledge-based organizations—they suffer from learning disabilities. To overcome these disabilities, the learning organization must develop the capacity for both generative and adaptive learning.

The third arena of strategic information use is when organizations search for and evaluate information in order to make important decisions. In theory, this choice is to be made rationally, based on complete information about the organization's goals, feasible alternatives, probable outcomes of these alternatives, and the values of these outcomes to the organization. In practice, rational choice making is muddled by the jostling of interests among organizational stakeholders, bargaining and negotiation between powerful groups and individuals, the limitations and idiosyncracies of personal choice making, the lack of information, and so on. Despite these complications, an organization must keep up at least an appearance of rational, reasoned behavior, both to sustain internal trust and to preserve external legitimacy. Although organizational decision making is a complex, messy process, there is no doubt that it is a vital part of organizational life: all organizational actions are initiated by decisions, and all decisions are commitments to action. Herbert Simon and his associates have maintained that management *is* decision making, so that the best way to analyze organization behavior is to analyze the structure and processes of decision making.

I. A PREVIEW OF THE KNOWING ORGANIZATION

Although they are often approached as distinct and separate organizational information processes, the central thesis of this book is that the three arenas of information use—sense making, knowledge creating, and decision making—are in fact highly interconnected processes, and that by analyzing how the three activities energize each other, a holistic view of organizational information use emerges.

At a general level, we can visualize sense making, knowledge creating, and decision making as representing three concentric layers of organizational information behaviors, with each inner layer building upon the information outputs of the outer layer (Fig. 1–1). Information flows from the external environment (outside the circles) and is progressively assimilated and focused to enable organizational action. First, information about the organization's environment is sensed, and its meaning is socially constructed. This provides the context for all organizational activity and in particular guides the knowledge-creation processes. Knowledge resides in the minds of individuals, and this personal knowledge needs to be converted into knowledge that can be shared and transformed into innovations. When there is sufficient understanding and knowledge, the organization is primed for action, and chooses its course rationally according to its goals. Organizational action changes the environment and produces new streams of experience for the organization to adapt to, thus beginning another cycle.

During *sense making,* the principal information process is the interpretation of news and messages about the environment. Members must choose what information is significant and should be attended to. They form possible explanations from past experience, and they exchange and negotiate their views in order to arrive at a common interpretation. During *knowledge creation,* the main information process is the conversion of knowledge. Members share their personal knowledge through dialogue and discourse, and articulate what they intuitively know through analogies, metaphors, as well as more formal channels. During *decision making,* the key information activity is the processing and analysis of information about the available alternatives in order to weigh their relative merits and demerits. Members are guided by rules, routines, and preferences that structure their information search and their design and evaluation of alternatives. All three modes of information use—interpretation, conversion, and processing—are dynamic, social processes that continuously constitute and reconstitute meaning, knowledge, and action.

The organization that is able to integrate sense making, knowledge creation, and decision making effectively may be described as a *knowing organi-*

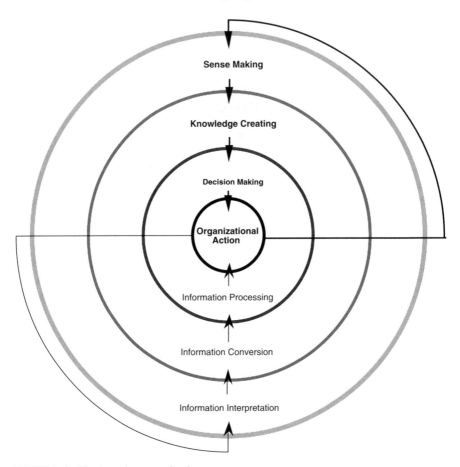

FIGURE 1–1. The knowing organization

zation. The knowing organization possesses information and knowledge so that it is well informed, mentally perceptive, and enlightened. Its actions are based on a shared and valid understanding of the organization's environments and needs, and are leveraged by the available knowledge resources and skill competences of its members. The knowing organization possesses information and knowledge that confers a special advantage, allowing it to maneuver with intelligence, creativity, and, occasionally, cunning. By managing information resources and information processes, the knowing organization is able to:

- Adapt itself in a timely and effective manner to changes in the environment

- Engage in continuous organizational learning, including the unlearning of assumptions, norms, and mind-sets that are no longer valid

- Mobilize the knowledge and expertise of its members to induce innovation and creativity

- Focus its understanding and knowledge on reasoned, decisive action

In the subsequent sections we will examine each of the three information use processes that make up the knowing organization. Although they apply different perspectives to explain different aspects of organizational behavior, the three information modes share important areas of overlap and mutuality. In fact, each process supplies essential elements that the other requires in order to function.

II. SENSE MAKING

People in organizations are continuously trying to understand what is happening around them. They first have to make sense of what is happening in their environments in order to develop a shared interpretation that can serve as a guide to action. In the model of sense making developed by Karl Weick (1979b, 1995) organizations are "loosely coupled" systems in which individual participants have great latitude in interpreting environmental change and enacting their own representations of external reality. The central information activity is to resolve the *equivocality* of information about the organization's environment: What is happening out there? Why is this taking place? What does it mean? This sense making is done retrospectively since we cannot make sense of events and actions until they have occurred, and we can then glance backward in time to construct their meaning. Current events are compared with past experience in order to construct meaning: "[T]he goal of organizations, viewed as sensemaking systems, is to create and identify events that recur to stabilize their environments and make them more predictable. A sensible event is one that resembles something that has happened before" (Weick 1995, 170).

An organization makes sense of its environment through four sets of interlocking processes: ecological change, enactment, selection, and retention (Fig. 1–2). Sense making begins when there is some change or difference in the

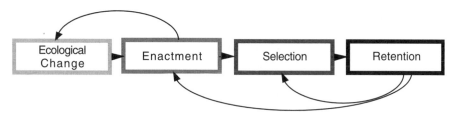

FIGURE 1–2. Sense-making processes in an organization (Weick 1979b)

organizational environment, resulting in disturbances or variations in the flows of experience affecting the organization's participants. This *ecological change* requires the organization's members to attempt to understand these differences and to determine the significance of these changes. In trying to understand the meaning of these changes, an organizational actor may take some action to isolate or bracket some portion of the changes for closer examination. Thus managers respond to equivocal information about the external environment by *enacting* the environment to which they will adapt. In creating the enacted environment, they attend to certain elements of the environment—they selectively bracket actions and texts, label them with nouns, and look for relationships. When managers enact the environment, they "construct, rearrange, single out, and demolish many 'objective' features of their surroundings. . . . they unrandomize variables, insert vestiges of orderliness, and literally create their own constraints" (Weick 1979b, 164). The result of this *enactment* is to generate equivocal raw data about environmental changes, raw data that will subsequently be turned into meaning and action.

The enactment process segregates possible environments that the organization could clarify and take seriously, but whether it actually does so depends on what happens in the selection process. In the *selection* process, answers are generated to the question, "What is going on here?" Selection involves the overlaying of various plausible relationship structures on the enacted raw data in an attempt to reduce their equivocality. These structures, often in the form of cause maps, are those that have proven sensible in explaining previous situations, and are now being superimposed on the current raw data to see whether they could provide a reasonable interpretation of what has occurred. The selection process therefore reaches into the past to extract history and select a reasonable scheme of interpretation.

In the *retention* process, the products of successful sensemaking are retained for future use. The product of organizational sense making is an enacted environment—"a sensible rendering of previous events stored in the form of causal assertions, and made binding on some current enactment and/or selection" (Weick 1979b, 166). As we have shown, the enacted environment is based on the retrospective interpretations of actions or events already completed. It is like a historical document, stored usually as a map of relationships between events and actions, that can be retrieved and superimposed on subsequent activities. In the sense making view, the reason for the existence of an organization is to produce stable interpretations of equivocal data about environmental change. Although the entire process operates to reduce equivocality, some equivocal features do and must remain if the organization is to be able to survive into a new and different future. Indeed, organizations can continue to exist only if they maintain a balance between flexibility and stability.

Weick illustrates the sense-making process with a field study of two jazz orchestras (Weick, Gilfillan, and Keith 1973). A jazz orchestra, with about twenty members, is a good example of a small organization. It has a leader, three section leaders, and each section has about five players. Its performance is judged by how well coordinated it plays as an ensemble, as well as how innovative the individual solos and group sections are. Once the orchestra starts to play, there is no turning back. The piece must be completed, even if numerous mistakes have been made and have to be covered up. At the end of the performance, feedback is immediate. Responsibility for errors or success is often difficult to place. In the field study, two jazz orchestras rehearsed three works by composers whose credibility was presented as either high or low. The orchestra that was told that it was to be playing music by a nonserious composer would be expected to make more errors due to doubts or indifference about the quality of the music. A comparable orchestra given the same piece of music but told that the writer was a serious composer would expend more effort to comprehend and perform it, and thus show fewer errors. This predicted difference in errors did occur on the first play-through, but disappeared on the second play-through, because members of the "nonserious" orchestra could now observe that the work was in fact purposeful. The orchestra rehearsal is an ideal setting in which to observe how an unfamiliar piece of music is made sensible. The music is equivocal because it is new and complex, and because there is uncertainty about how the music is to be performed and what the intentions of the composer are. The environment that the orchestra faces is not just the composition placed before them, but rather what they do with that composition when they play it through for the first time. In other words, the musicians *enact* rather than react to the environment. Each musician enacts the environment by bracketing it into discrete events such as "those twelve notes are thrilling," "these six bars require special care," "the composer is a serious musician," and so on. Once the musicians have labeled the stream of enacted music with reasonable nouns, they try to relate the nouns or variables in a reasonable manner. They infer that some of the variables covary together. For example, they may infer that as the composer's credibility decreases, the playing effort decreases and the tolerance for error increases, and this in turn affects the quality of the piece when judged retrospectively. After repeated exposures to a stream of experience, the musician summarizes variables and their connections into a cause map. These cause maps become available for retrieval or *selection* to be superimposed on new flows of experience. In summary, the process of sense making involves members to collectively reach some consensus about which portions of the environment should be labeled as variables and which connections among which variables are reasonable. The elapsed experience or environment becomes sensible when they can agree on what is consequential or trivial in their experience, and on the strength and direction of connections among these consequential elements. The outputs of the process are the enacted environments and the cause maps of variables and connections, and both are *retained* for imposition on future similar situations.

An important corollary of the sense-making model is that organizations behave as interpretation systems:

> Organizations must make interpretations. Managers literally must wade into the swarm of events that constitute and surround the organization and actively try to impose some order on them. . . . Interpretation is the process of translating these events, of developing models for understanding, of bringing out meaning, and of assembling conceptual schemes. (Weick and Daft 1983, 74)

What is being interpreted is the organization's external environment, and how the organization goes about its interpretation depends on how analyzable it perceives the environment to be and how actively it intrudes into the environment to understand it. Equivocality is reduced by managers and other participants who extensively discuss ambiguous information cues and so arrive at a common interpretation of the external environment.

III. KNOWLEDGE CREATION

According to Nonaka and Takeuchi (1995), the fundamental reason why Japanese enterprises have become successful is because of their skills and expertise at organizational knowledge creation. Knowledge creation is achieved through a recognition of the synergistic relationship between tacit and explicit knowledge in the organization, and through the design of social processes that create new knowledge by converting tacit knowledge into explicit knowledge. Tacit knowledge is personal knowledge that is hard to formalize or communicate to others. It consists of subjective know-how, insights, and intuitions that come to a person from having been immersed in an activity for an extended period of time. Explicit knowledge is formal knowledge that is easy to transmit between individuals and groups. It is frequently coded in the form of mathematical formulas, rules, specifications, and so on. The two categories of knowledge are complementary. Tacit knowledge, while it remains closely held as personal know-how, is of limited value to the organization. On the other hand, explicit knowledge does not appear spontaneously, but must be nurtured and cultivated from the seeds of tacit knowledge. Organizations need to become skilled at converting personal, tacit knowledge into explicit knowledge that can push innovation and new-product development. Whereas Western organizations tend to concentrate on explicit knowledge, Japanese firms differentiate between tacit and explicit knowledge, and recognize that tacit knowledge is a source of competitive advantage (Nonaka and Takeuchi 1995).

There are four modes of knowledge conversion (Fig. 1–3): from tacit knowledge to tacit knowledge through a process of socialization, from tacit knowledge to explicit knowledge through externalization, from explicit knowledge to explicit knowledge through combination, and from explicit knowledge to tacit knowledge through internalization.

Socialization is a process of acquiring tacit knowledge through sharing experiences. As apprentices learn the craft of their masters through observa-

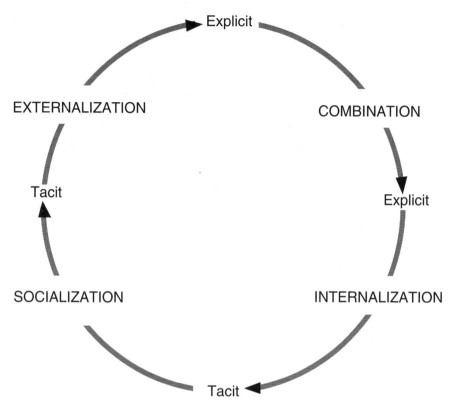

FIGURE 1–3. Organizational knowledge conversion processes (Nonaka and Takeuchi 1995)

tion, imitation, and practice, so do employees of a firm learn new skills through on-the-job training. When Matsushita was developing its automatic home bread-making machine in the late 1980s, a major problem was how to mechanize the dough-kneading process, a process that required the tacit knowledge of master bakers (Nonaka and Takeuchi 1995). When the doughs kneaded by a master baker and by a machine were x-rayed and compared, no meaningful differences were detected. The head of the software development team, together with several engineers, then decided to volunteer themselves as apprentices to the head baker of the Osaka International Hotel, who was reputed to produce the area's best bread. After a period of imitation and practice, one day she observed that the baker was not only stretching but also twisting the dough in a particular fashion, which turned out to be the secret for making tasty bread. This twisting-stretch movement was copied by the machine, and Matsushita's home bakery product sold a record-setting volume in its first year and became a highly successful export item worldwide.

Externalization is a process of converting tacit knowledge into explicit concepts through the use of metaphors, analogies, or models. The externalization of tacit knowledge is the quintessential knowledge-creation activity and is most often seen during the concept creation phase of new product development. Externalization is triggered by dialogue or collective reflection. When Canon was designing its Mini-Copier, a main hurdle was how to produce a low-cost disposable cartridge that would eliminate the need for expensive maintenance in conventional machines (Nonaka and Takeuchi 1995). The task force assigned to this problem debated vigorously about the production of photosensitive drum cylinders with a base material of aluminum drawn tube. One day, during one of these discussions, the leader of the task force sent out for some cans of beer. After the beer was consumed, he asked, "How much does it cost to manufacture this can?" The group then explored how the process of manufacturing aluminum beer cans could be applied to the fabrication of copier drum cylinders. By clarifying similarities and differences, the group discovered a process technology to manufacture a low-cost disposable aluminum drum cylinder that eventually helped Canon to establish its leadership position in the personal copier market.

Combination is a process of creating explicit knowledge by bringing together explicit knowledge from a number of sources. Thus individuals exchange and combine their explicit knowledge through telephone conversations, meetings, memos, and so on. Existing information in computerized databases may be categorized, collated, and sorted in a number of ways to produce new explicit knowledge. At Kraft General Foods, data from point-of-sales systems are analyzed not only to find out what does and does not sell, but also to develop new ways to increase sales (Nonaka and Takeuchi 1995). Kraft's own method of data analysis classifies stores and shoppers into six categories, so that the system can pinpoint who shops for which goods at what stores. This micromerchandizing system provides supermarkets with timely and detailed recommendations on merchandise mix and sales promotions.

Finally, *internalization* is a process of embodying explicit knowledge into tacit knowledge, internalizing the experiences gained through the other modes of knowledge creation into the individuals' tacit knowledge bases in the form of shared mental models or work practices. Internalization is facilitated if the knowledge is captured in documents or conveyed in the form of stories, so that individuals may reexperience indirectly the experience of others. For example, at GE's Answer Center in Louisville, Kentucky, all customer complaints and inquiries are documented into a huge database. Members of a new-product development team can then use this database to reexperience for themselves what the telephone operators had experienced (Nonaka and Takeuchi 1995).

As shown in Fig. 1–3, the four modes of knowledge conversion feed off each other in a continuous spiral of organizational knowledge creation. Knowledge creation typically begins with individuals who develop some insight or intuition into how to do their tasks better. This tacit know-how may be shared with others through socialization. However, as long as the knowledge stays tacit, the organization is unable to exploit it further. Thus the tacit know-how of the master baker's kneading technique has to be converted into explicit knowledge that is then used to design the kneading mechanism inside the bread-making machine. From the organization's perspective, externalization of tacit knowledge into explicit concepts is therefore pivotal. Drawing out tacit knowledge requires taking a mental leap, and often involves the creative use of a metaphor or analogy. (Recall the aluminum beer can in Canon's attempt to design a disposable copier cartridge.) An organization would have several bodies of explicit knowledge generated by different groups or units at different points in time. These disparate bodies of expertise may be combined and reconfigured into new forms of explicit knowledge. Finally, the new explicit knowledge created through the various modes would have to be reexperienced and reinternalized as new tacit knowledge.

IV. DECISION MAKING

When the organization has the understanding and knowledge to act, it must still choose from among available options or capabilities, and commit itself to a single strategy. Since all organizational behavior springs from decisions and since behavior is the unfolding of a series of decisions, the essential features of organizational structure and function may be derived from the characteristics of human decision-making processes and rational human choice (March and Simon 1993). In an ideal world, rational choice would require a complete search of available alternatives, reliable information about their consequences, and consistent preferences to evaluate these outcomes. In the real world, such demands on information gathering and processing are unrealistic. Instead of a comprehensive, objective rationality, Herbert Simon suggested that decision making in organizations is constrained by the principle of *bounded rationality:*

> The capacity of the human mind for formulating and solving complex problems is very small compared with the size of the problems whose solution is required for objectively rational behavior in the real world—or even for a reasonable approximation to such objective rationality. (Simon 1957, 198)

What constitutes the bounds that limit the capacity of the human mind for rational decision making? Simon identifies three categories of bounds: the individual is limited by his mental skills, habits, and reflexes; by the extent of knowledge and information possessed; and by values or conceptions of purpose which may diverge from organizational goals (Simon 1976, 40–41, 241). It is because individual human beings are limited in their cognitive ability that organizations become necessary and useful instruments for the achievement of larger purposes. Conversely, the organization can alter the limits to rationality of its members by creating or changing the organizational environment in which the individual's decision making takes place. Simon proposes that the organization influences its members' behaviors by controlling the *decision premises* upon which decisions are made, rather than controlling the actual decisions themselves (Simon 1976, 223). A fundamental problem of organizing is then in defining the decision premises that form the organizational environment: "The task of administration is so to design this environment that the individual will approach as close as practicable to rationality (judged in terms of the organization's goals) in his decisions" (Simon 1976, 240–41).

As a consequence of bounded rationality, the organizational actor behaves in two distinctive ways when making decisions. First, he or she *satisfices—* looking for a course of action that is satisfactory or good enough rather than seeking the optimal solution. The difference is between searching a haystack to find the sharpest needle in it and searching the haystack to find a needle sharp enough to sew with. A course of action is satisfactory if it exceeds some minimally acceptable criteria. For March and Simon (1993), "most human decision making, whether individual or organizational, is concerned with the discovery and selection of satisfactory alternatives" (p. 162). The search for a satisficing alternative, motivated by the occurrence of a problem, is concentrated near the symptoms or an old solution, and reflects the training, experience, and goals of the participants.

Second, organizations and organizational actors *simplify* the decision process—routines, rules, and heuristics are applied in order to reduce uncertainty and cope with complexity. There are many simplification strategies, and we will examine them and their implications in chapter 5, but perhaps the most important simplification is in the development of organizational action repertoires using *performance programs.* These programs are developed by organizations and individuals to deal with recurrent situations. By restricting the range of situations and the range of alternatives available, performance programs greatly reduce the cognitive and informational requirements of the decision-making process. For example, the sounding of the alarm in a fire station initiates a predefined action program, as does the appearance of a relief applicant at a social worker's desk, or the appearance of an automobile chassis in front of the work station of a worker on the assembly line (March and Simon 1993, 162). Most behavior in organizations is governed by performance programs.

Performance programs or organizational routines lie at the heart of organizational decision making and serve a number of valuable and visible functions. Routines reflect what the organization has learned from experience about how to deal with recurrent situations—organizations remember by doing, and action and decision routines become part of the organization's procedural memory. Planning, budgeting, and project evaluation procedures allow internal groups to compete for resources based on criteria and procedures that are open and nominally fair. Routines also allow the organization to project legitimacy externally to its community and stakeholders, since an organization following rational decision routines may be construed to have attempted to behave responsibly and accountably. Critics of routines and standardized procedures blame them as the cause of organizational stasis and inertia. Overly rigid routines can block organizational learning, stifle creativity, and forfeit organizational flexibility.

Organizational decision making is rational in spirit (and appearance) if not in execution: the organization is intendedly rational, even if its members are only boundedly so. Goals and objectives are set first, and when participants encounter problems in the pursuit of these objectives, a search for information on alternatives and consequences takes place, followed by evaluation of the outcomes according to the objectives and preferences. There is a linear, input–output flavor to the model, with a focus on the flow of information in the organization's decision-making processes (March and Simon 1993). The key features of organizations as decision-making systems are shown in Fig. 1–4. Organizations seek rational behavior in terms of actions that contribute to its goals and objectives. Unfortunately, the behavior of individual members is constrained by their cognitive capacity, information, and values. A way to bridge the gap between organizational rationality and the individual's bounded rationality is to design decision premises and decision routines that guide or direct individual decision behavior.

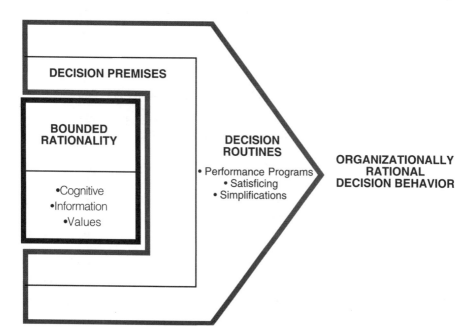

FIGURE I–4. Organizational decision making

For an illustration of how decision premises can mold organizational behavior, consider Johnson & Johnson, widely regarded as one of the world's most successful pharmaceutical companies. (In the 1995 *Fortune* magazine listings of America's top companies, J&J takes the lead as America's largest *and* most admired pharmaceutical company.) One of the reasons often suggested for its long-lived success is the universal accceptance within the company of the J&J credo. Several years ago, J&J showed how the decision premises contained in the credo were used to handle a major crisis. In 1982 seven people died after taking Tylenol capsules that had been laced with cyanide. Although the poisoning was not done on J&J premises and the victims were limited to the Chicago area, J&J took immediate action to withdraw all Tylenol capsules from the U.S. market at an estimated cost of $100 million. Simultaneously, J&J initiated with health-care communities a comprehensive communication program involving 2500 J&J employees. The Tylenol packaging was also redesigned into a tamper-proof container. J&J managers attributed this decisive action to their following the premises set out in the famous J&J credo (Aguilar 1988). The credo clearly ranks the responsibilites that J&J bears toward its stakeholders: "We believe our first responsibility is to the doctors, nurses and patients, to mothers and all others who use our products and services." Next comes responsibility to the employees, and then the community. The final responsibility is to the stockholders. As a result of taking tough action guided by these decision premises, the *Washington Post* wrote that "Johnson & Johnson has succeeded in portraying itself to the public as a company willing to do what's right, regardless of cost."

V. TOWARD THE KNOWING ORGANIZATION

There seems to be much that separates the three models of organizational information use (Table 1–1). The sense-making model sees the organization as trying to make sense of its equivocal environment. Members look back on their actions and experiences and enact or construct their own perceptions of the environment. Sense making is retrospective in that members can only interpret what they have already done or what has happened. The outputs of sense making are enacted environments or shared interpretations that guide action. The knowledge-creating model sees the organization as continuously engaged in knowledge conversion. Members' personal, tacit knowledge is to be leveraged into explicit knowledge that the organization can use to develop new products and services. The outputs of the process are new knowledge and the development of new organizational capabilities. The decision-making model sees the organization as a rational decision-making system. Decision behavior is precipitated by the recognition of a problem. Decision makers search for alternatives, evaluate consequences, and choose an acceptable outcome ac-

TABLE I–I. Three modes of organizational information use.

Mode	Central idea	Outputs	Main concepts
Sense making	*Enacting organization:* Environmental change → Interpret the equivocal data by enacting interpretations Information is interpreted	*Enacted environments* and shared interpretations for constructing meaning	Enactment, selection, retention
Knowledge creating	*Learning organization:* Existing knowledge → Create new knowledge through knowledge conversion and sharing Information is converted	New explicit and tacit knowledge for *innovation*	Tacit knowledge Explicit knowledge Knowledge conversion
Decision making	*Rational organization:* Problem → Search and select alternatives according to projected outcomes and preferences Information is analyzed	*Decisions* leading to rational, goal-directed behavior	Bounded rationality Decision premises Rules and routines

cording to their goals and preferences. Because individuals are limited by their information processing capacities, decision routines and search routines simplify their choice-making processes. The output of the process is the selection of courses of action that lead to rational, goal-directed behavior.

Of the three models, the rational decision-making framework is probably the most influential and widely applied. Yet there are some perplexing behavior patterns common in organizations that do not seem to fit this view. People gather information ostensibly for decisions but do not use it (Feldman and March 1981). They ask for reports but do not read them. Individuals fight for the right to take part in decision processes, but then do not exercise that right. Policies are vigorously debated but their implementation is met with indifference (March and Olsen 1976). Managers observed in situation to spend little time in making decisions, but are instead most often engaged in meetings and conversations (Mintzberg 1973, Kotter 1982). Such findings seem to suggest that decision making, apart from being an occasion for making choices, is also "an arena for developing and enjoying an interpretation of life and one's position in it. A business firm is a temple and a collection of sacred rituals as well as an instrument for producing goods and services. The rituals of choice tie routine events to beliefs about the nature of things. They give meaning" (Cyert and March 1992, 236). In other words, organizational life is not just about choice but also about interpretation, and the process of decision making must embrace the process of sense making even as it examines the behaviors of choice making. In their introduction to the 1993 edition of their 1958 classic, *Organizations,* March and Simon wrote:

> Some contemporary students of meaning in organizations would go further to assert that it is interpretation, rather than choice, that is central to life. Within such a view, organizations are organized around the requirement to sustain, communicate, and elaborate interpretations of history and life—not around decisions. Decisions are instruments to interpretation, rather than the other way around. Although we think an interpretive perspective yields important insights into organizations, we would not go that far, even in retrospect. But we suspect that a 1992 book on organizations, even while reaffirming that there is a real world out there to which organizations are adapting and which they are affecting, would need to pay somewhat more attention than a 1958 book did to the social context of meaning within which organizations operate. (March and Simon 1993, 18)

In the sense-making model the enacted environment is an output of the meaning-construction process, and serves as a reasonable, plausible guide for action. However, once the environment has been enacted and stored, people in the organization now face the critical question of what to do with what they know. These are what Weick (1979b) has called "the consequential moments." Furthermore, the shared interpretations are a compromise between stability and flexibility—some equivocal features do and must remain in the stored interpretations, so that the organization has the flexibility to adapt to a new and different future. People in organizations are therefore "people who oppose, argue, contradict, disbelieve, doubt, act hypocritically, improvise, counter, distrust, differ, challenge, vacillate, question, puncture, disprove, and expose. All of these actions embody ambivalence as the optimal compromise to deal with the incompatible demands of flexibility and stability" (Weick 1979b, 229). Where decision premises in the decision-making model control organizational choice making, shared assumptions and experiences in the sense-making model constrain the ways that people in an organization perceive their world. Both phenomena are aspects of *premise control,* and premise control becomes a useful concept that joins sense making with decision making (Weick 1995, 114). The central concern of sense making is understanding how people in organizations construct meaning and reality, and then exploring how that enacted reality provides a context for organizational action, including decision making and knowledge creating.

Commenting on the rational decision-making model, Nonaka and Takeuchi (1995) argued that this information-processing view has a fundamental limitation. For them, the decision-making model does not really explain innovation. The decision-making view is essentially conservative, where decision premises and performance programs are designed for control, and search biases inhibit radically innovative solutions. On the other hand, "when organizations innovate, they do not simply process information, from the outside in, in order to solve existing problems and adapt to a changing environment. They actually create new information and knowledge, from the inside out, in order to redefine both problems and solutions and, in the process, to recreate their environment" (p. 56). The key to innovation is in unlocking the personal, tacit knowledge of the organization's members. Tacit knowledge has two dimensions: the technical dimension and the cognitive dimension. The technical dimension is about the practical know-how of doing a task. The cognitive dimension consists of "schemata, mental models, beliefs, and perceptions" that "reflect our image of reality (what is) and our vision for the future (what ought to be)" (Nonaka and Takeuchi 1995, 8). These implicit models shape the way the people in an organization perceive the world around them—they create a shared understanding of what the organization stands for, where it is headed, what kind of world it wants to live in, and how to help make that world a reality. The knowledge conversion process has to be driven by this organizational intention, defined as the organization's aspiration to its goals. An organization's leadership must create a *knowledge vision* that "defines the 'field' or 'domain' that gives corporate members a mental map of the world they live in and provides a general direction regarding what kind of knowledge they ought to seek and create" (p. 227).

Although they adopt contrasting perspectives and grapple with different aspects of organizational behavior, the three modes of organizational information use are mutually supportive. The sense-making view shows how organizational members make sense of what is happening in the organization's environment. Such sense making must tap into the mental models and experiences of individual members of the organization. The resultant shared interpretation provides a framework for all organizational action. The knowledge-creating view shows how the personal, tacit knowledge of individuals may be unlocked and converted into explicit knowledge that moves organizational innovation. Innovation not only provides the organization with new goods and services, but also endows the organization with new capabilities and competences to pursue new possibilities. Finally, when understanding and knowledge converge on action, organizational members have to choose between available courses of action. The decision-making view shows how such choices are made, given that decision makers are limited in their cognitive and information-processing capacities. By designing rules, premises, and performance programs, organizations reduce the uncertainty and complexity of decision making and so simplify the decision process for the individual. Decision rules and routines are important for several reasons. First, they reflect sound or acceptable choice-making practices that the organization has learned over time. Second, they provide internal, procedural rationality to the extent that they make clear the steps and criteria in arriving at a choice, allowing organizational groups to compete fairly for resources. Finally, they establish external legitimacy, since an organization following rational decision routines may be thought to be able to behave responsibly and with accountability.

The three modes of information use complement each other by each supplying some of the missing pieces necessary for the other to function. Sense making provides enacted environments or shared interpretations that serve as meaningful contexts for organizational action. Shared interpretations help configure the organizational intent or knowledge vision necessary to regulate the knowledge conversion processes in knowledge creation. Knowledge creation leads to innovation in the form of new products and new competences. When it is time to select a course of action in response to an enactment of the environment, or as a result of knowledge-derived innovation, decision makers follow rules and premises to simplify and legitimitize their actions.

VI. THE KNOWING CYCLE

The knowing organization is one that links up the three strategic information processes of sense making, knowledge creating and decision making into a continuous cycle of learning and adaptation, a cycle that we may call the "knowing cycle" (Fig. 1–5).

Starting at the top of the diagram, streams of experience in the organization's environment are bracketed, labeled, and connected together in mental maps in order to make sense of the equivocal information. As a result of *sense making,* members enact the environment, and develop shared interpretations of what is happening to them and their organization. What emerges is a set of shared meanings or mental models that the organization uses to plan and make decisions. Shared interpretations are also helpful in defining the organization's intent or vision about what new knowledge and capabilities the organization needs to develop.

Generally, if sense making reduces equivocality sufficiently and reveals

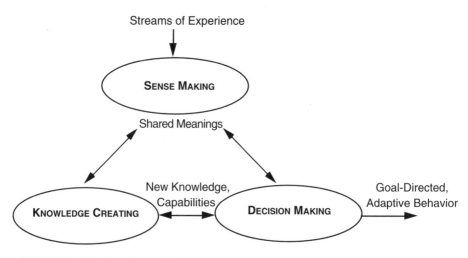

FIGURE I–5. The knowing cycle

the situation facing the organization to be a familiar one which the organization has learned to deal with before, then the organization can engage in *decision making* by selecting a pattern of action through invoking the appropriate learned rules or routines. In this case, the situation as rendered by the sense making will be used to select from the available decisional rules and premises. If, however, the situation is novel or unrecognized so that none of the existing rules appear relevant, then the organization would need to generate new decisional structures, including new rules and premises, from the enacted interpretation produced by the sense making.

On occasions, persistent decision failure may occur, as when no good enough solutions can be found, or when actions designated by existing decision rules do not bring about desired outcomes. There are of course many possible reasons for chronic decision failure, but often the symptom is the combined result of both faulty sense making and decision making. A case of obsolete shared interpretations used to sustain outdated decision premises seemed to have afflicted General Motors in the early 1980s. According to Mitroff and Linstone (1993), GM for many years had used the following retained assumptions to enact its competitive environment: "GM is in the business of making money, not cars;" "cars are primarily status symbols—style is therefore more important than quality;" "the American car market is isolated from the rest of the world;" "energy will always be abundant and cheap;" and so on. These assumptions were badly out of step with the reality of the new American automobile industry at that time. By 1985 GM was last in the industry in terms of product quality, manufacturing efficiency, and new product design (Ingrassia and White 1994).

The results of sense making may also indicate that the organization lacks some knowledge or capability to respond properly to the situation, perhaps to exploit an opportunity or to preempt a threat. *Knowledge creation* is achieved by converting between the internal, tacit knowledge that is held by individuals and the external, explicit knowledge that the organization can exploit. Recall how software engineers at Matsushita had to apprentice themselves to a master baker in order to learn the technique of simultaneously twisting and stretching the dough that was the secret to preparing tasty bread. This tacit knowledge, once externalized, had to be further massaged into designs for the kneading mechanism in the bread-making machine. The output of knowledge creation is thus fresh knowledge that leads to innovations, new products, and new organizational capabilities.

The results of sense making, in identifying knowledge gaps, also identify the initial criteria to evaluate the usefulness or value of new knowledge that is being developed. However, the creation of new knowledge may also suggest new products or services that can satisfy hitherto unmet market demands. Further sense making may then be necessary, for example, by gathering information about the potential market, or by testing whether the demand exists. Minnesota Mining and Manufacturing Company (3M) is a company whose history is decorated with stories of talented individuals who were able to invent new products or modify existing products that address latent consumer demand. A laboratory technician named Dick Drew invented masking tape and Scotch tape. John Borden, a sales manager, created a dispenser for Scotch tape with a built-in blade. More recently, Art Fry invented the Post-it sticky notepads. Fry sang in the church choir and wanted markers to stick to the pages of selected hymns that could be peeled off after use without damaging the hymn books. He used a weak adhesive that had been developed four years earlier to produce self-sticking sheets of papers. Following a gut feeling that there are many other uses for the sticky notes, Fry singlehandedly built a machine that would successfully apply the adhesive onto paper. Fry said, "Even though I felt that there would be demand for the product, I didn't know how to explain it in words. Even if I found the words to explain, no one would understand . . ." (Nonaka and Takeuchi 1995, 138). Fry distributed samples to 3M employees, and the rest was history. The development of new-product ideas has become a strong tradition at 3M, and researchers can spend up to 15 percent of their work time, or roughly one day a week, "pursuing their own dreams." 3M seems to be a company that recognizes that the seeds of innovations grow in the personal, tacit knowledge of creative individuals.

Having developed understanding and knowledge, the organization has to act. Choosing courses of action still requires coping with substantial equivocality and uncertainty. Sense making retains some equivocality in its interpretations in order to have the flexibility for future learning and adaptation. Knowledge creation produces new capabilities that are still untested, and innovations whose market acceptance may be hard to predict ("How many people will want to buy the home bread-making machine that Matsushita was building?"). Through its decision-making rules and routines, an organization reduces risk, uncertainty, and complexity by specifying the kinds of information to be sought and the satisficing criteria to evaluate options, and by clarifying goals and objectives. The output of decision making is therefore the selection of a pattern of actions that moves the organization closer to its goals but that is also an attempt by the organization to adapt to a changing environment as registered through its sense-making activity.

VII. THE KNOWING CYCLE IN ACTION

To understand how the three processes of sense making, knowledge creating, and decision making may be coalesced to achieve sustained organizational performance, we examine the Royal Dutch/Shell group of companies. Shell employs an organizational learning system ("scenario planning") that illustrates many of the properties of a knowing organization.

The Royal Dutch/Shell group is a century-old group of companies that has shown adaptiveness in anticipating and reacting to dramatic changes in its global environments. In the early 1970s Shell was able to discern differences between Iran and Saudi Arabia (while everyone else perceived the Arab oil nations as a homogeneous cartel) and thus anticipate the shortages that led to the 1973 oil shortage, which caused the price of oil to escalate from $2 to $13 per barrel in a year and a half. Oil prices continued to rise from 1973 onward, and most oil companies believed that the trend will persist. Shell, however, perceived that oil demand had been overestimated because consumers and industries had learned to be much more energy-efficient since the 1973 crisis. In 1981 Shell was able to sell off its excess reserves (while other companies were stockpiling following the Iran–Iraq war) before the glut caused the price collapse. In 1983, by recognizing the demographic and economic pressures on the Soviet Union (while Western politicians saw only an evil communist empire), Shell was able to anticipate perestroika and the appearance of a man like Gorbachev, who would bring about massive economic and political restructuring. Arie de Geus, head of planning of Shell for more than three decades, observes that "outcomes like these don't happen automatically. On the contrary, they depend on the ability of a company's senior managers to absorb what is going on in the business environment and to act on that information with appropriate business moves" (de Geus 1988, 70).

Being a large multinational corporation with interests all over the world, Shell faces a daunting task as it attempts to make sense of its highly complex and equivocal environment. Shell uses scenario planning as a means of reviewing experience and building mental maps (Galer and van der Heijden 1992). A scenario is an internally consistent account of how the business environment is developing. By using multiple scenarios, it is possible to make sense of a large number of diverse but intersecting factors in the environment. In this way, scenarios become tools for organizational perception, broadening the collective vision of the organization. Managers in most Shell companies "are trained to pay attention to world events, visualize what might happen next, and (in Shell parlance) 'adjust their mental maps' according to what they perceive. Then they base decisions on those mental maps, instead of on top-down policy" (Kleiner 1989, 7). Mental maps are stored interpretations retained from experience that people turn to first when trying to interpret new signals from the environment. Shell's scenario planning approach developed alternative stories about the future to stimulate its managers to reexamine their assumptions and to "think the unthinkable."

In trying to construct plausible interpretations of the external environment, Shell's planners differentiate between knowable "predetermined variables" and unknowable "key uncertainties," a process that is equivalent to *enacting* the environment. Predetermined variables are reasonably predictable (using, for example, demographic data) and set the boundaries of future scenarios. Key uncertainties are hard to predict and have high levels of ambiguity, but they also point out the most serious consequences of the decisions made. In selecting a reasonable interpretation, Shell's managers and planners plot out two or three scenarios and use them in extended conversations with managers to converge on a shared representation of the environment and a consensus on what Shell is to be in that new environment (van der Heijden 1996, Kleiner 1994).

Shell has evolved scenario planning into a system for *creating knowledge* that involves both the internalization and the externalization of knowledge. The objective of scenario planning is not to predict the future, but to reveal the nature and dynamics of the driving forces that are shaping the environment. Insight about driving forces is derived from both hard, analytical data and soft, intuitive hunches. Such knowledge is made explicit by weaving it into storylike scenarios of how these forces could interact to produce outcomes. Some of the scenarios would appear to contradict long-standing trends and may be difficult to accept initially. Provoked by the ideas in the scenarios, Shell managers spend many hours in face-to-face dialogue trying to understand the driving forces and how they may need to adjust their own mental models to take account of them. This conversion from explicit knowledge in the form of stories to tacit knowledge in the form of updated mental models is related to the process of *internalization* that Nonaka and Takeuchi described. Pierre Wack, one of the architects of Shell's scenario approach, describes the process:

> Scenarios deal with two worlds: the world of facts and the world of perceptions. They explore for facts but they aim at perceptions inside the heads of decision makers. Their purpose is to transform information into fresh perceptions. This transformation process is not trivial—more often than not it does not happen. When it works, it is a creative experience that generates a heartfelt "Aha!" from your managers and leads to strategic insights beyond the mind's previous reach. . . . It happens when your message reaches the microcosms of decision makers, obliges them to question their assumptions about how their business world works, and leads them to change and reorganize their inner models of reality. (Wack, cited in Kleiner 1989, 13)

To construct scenarios, Shell needed to be able to tap into the personal insights and experiences of its managers, who work in different countries all over the globe. It was important for knowledge sharing that managers operating in vastly different environments be encouraged to put forth candidly their concerns and perspectives. Extended conversations and special questions are employed to draw out the personal, tacit knowledge of managers and planners, and to *externalize* the knowledge into formal scenarios, which facilitate the creation of a shared interpretation of external developments (Wack 1985). Planners use an interviewing method with trigger questions and feedback which uncover the mental models, assumptions, and critical concerns of managers (van der Heijden 1994). Examples of the trigger questions include: "What two questions would you most want to ask an oracle?" "If you could go back ten years, what would have been a useful scenario then?" and "What do you want on your epitaph?" Managers' assumptions and concerns, together with the planners' projections, are then melded into a few scenarios that managers can use to deepen their understanding and uncover possiblities for action. This internalization of new knowledge derived from scenario analysis induced managers to consider new strategic options to prepare for the eventualities that their analysis indicated might develop. For example, in the 1970s Shell managers were able to use their knowledge about the possibility of an oil shortage to initiate *innovations* that would help them weather the crisis. Crude oil varies by geographical region, so that a refinery engineered to process crude from one source would not necessarily be able to handle crude from another source. Shell's innovation was "to convert its refineries so they could switch from Kuwait oil to Saudi or Iranian oil, and back again, depending on what was available and what product mix was needed at any moment" (Kleiner 1989, 11).

Over time, Shell evolved a "planning as learning" system in which the insight and the knowledge gained through scenario planning are able to ripple through various levels of organizational *decision making*. The highest level of global planning is the responsibility of a *Committee of Managing Directors* (CMD), which is generally composed of eight managing directors who have both functional and regional responsibilities (called "spheres of influence"). The CMD is described as being "like a small debating society, where the directors discuss global issues around the world" (van der Wyck and Hesseling 1994, 43). Shell's Group Planning Cycle begins with the first stage of developing scenarios for the review of the CMD. The second stage is The Business Planning Cycle (formerly known as The Programming and Investment Review). In this stage the CMD issues short-term guidelines derived in part from the global scenarios, called "premises" at Shell, that would help sectors, regions, and countries produce their business plans and, subsequently, their financial budgets. Shell saw the objective here as "implementing strategies in terms of specific medium-run actions, the assessment of financial and human resources required, and, most importantly, how much to commit to which action and when" (van der Wyck and Hesseling 1994, 48). The third and final stage is appraisal, in which the CMD monitors and reviews implementation and short-term targets. Graham Galer and Kees van der Heijden, long-time members of Shell's group planning, summarized the cycle thus:

> In Shell, scenario planning, understood as "corporate perception," is a means of internalizing and reviewing experience. Strategic planning workshops are a device for inferring conclusions, while business planning, project planning and budgeting are the means for planning new steps and taking action. Business appraisal provides feedback from the results of action. (Galer and van der Heijden 1992, 12)

At the operating company levels, more focused scenarios are developed to address a particular business issue concerning, for example, a market or an investment. In contrast with the global scenarios, these focused scenarios are generated quickly in one-day workshops, and are created by the managers themselves (van der Wyck and Hesseling 1994). Workshops are well structured, following predefined rules and a six-step routine: agree on objectives and purpose, identify most important and uncertain business variables (the critical uncertainties), write story lines, create the scenarios, assess implications for business, and agree on follow-up action.

Galer and van der Heijden (1992) illustrate the benefit of the scenario-based learning approach with the experience of one Shell operating company (opco):

> For example, in one Shell opco scenarios were used to make managers face the realities of an unstable political and economic regime, to prepare them for inevitable changes, to handle great uncertainty during the change process and to develop a joint vision of emerging as a strong player in a new world. This was done over a five-year period and helped among other things in changing the market profile away from profitable traditional businesses towards potential new markets and making the company financially robust for an uncertain future. (p. 9)

Shell's ability to make strategic sense of environmental signals, and to integrate its learning with its planning and decision-making processes, helped the group become one of the world's top performing oil companies. In the 1970s Shell's position did not seem strong—it did not have the huge Saudi Arabian reserves of Exxon, Chevron, Mobil, or Texaco, nor the exclusive relationship that Gulf or BP had with Kuwait. From a position of the least profitable of the seven large oil companies, Shell surged ahead to become the world's most profitable oil company in the late 1980s. Yet the transition into a learning organization was a long and gradual one, sustained by the momentum of the early successes of the scenario planning approach, and by the persevering efforts of a few individuals who understood sense making and planning as part of the continuum of organizational learning.

VIII. SUMMARY

This book presents a framework to reveal and analyze the interdependences between the three principal ways that an organization makes use of information strategically. By attending to and making sense of signals from its environment, the organization is able to adapt and thrive. By mobilizing the knowledge and expertise of its members, the organization is constantly learning and innovating. By designing action and decision routines based on what its members know and believe, the organization is able to choose and commit itself to courses of action.

Our discussion shows how the three modes of information use complement each other by supplying some of the missing pieces necessary for each mode to function. Sense making constructs the enacted environments and shared interpretations that serve as meaningful contexts and plausible guides for organizational action. The shared interpretations also define the organizational intent or knowledge vision necessary to motivate and direct the knowledge-creation process. A clear vision of what the organization is and what it wants to be in relation to its industry, market, or community will help the organization set its agenda for learning and knowledge building. The result is fresh knowledge that leads to innovation in the form of new products and new competences. When it is time to decide a strategy or a course of action, decision makers need to know which elements are most important to the organization, what options and capabilities are available, and how to disentangle a complex web of factors and contingencies to make an acceptable choice.

Sense making constructs meaning and so expresses what is vital to the organization and its members. Knowledge creating generates new innovations and competences that broaden the horizon of choice. In choice making, decision makers are channeled by routines, rules, and personal heuristics that both simplify and legitimize their actions.

In the following chapters we explore the relationships and interactions that cross-link the information processes and outputs of the knowing organization. In particular, we will examine the processes of information interpretation, information transformation, and information analysis that are exercised in sense making, knowledge creating and decision making. But before that, we need to avail ourselves of the insights from another rich area of research—information science. The next chapter presents an overview of the large number of studies on information needs and uses, and proposes an approach for analyzing and comparing information use behaviors in organizations.

C H A P **2** T E R

HOW WE COME TO KNOW—
A GENERAL MODEL
OF INFORMATION USE

When action grows unprofitable, gather information;
when information grows unprofitable, sleep.
  —*Ursula K. Le Guin 1969, The Left Hand of Darkness,* chapter 3)

We begin with a true story of wakeful information gathering. As an episode in scientific information seeking, few narratives have aroused our imagination as thoroughly as the discovery of the structure of DNA by James Watson and Francis Crick in 1953. For both Watson and Crick, the goal of finding the structure of DNA was "intertwined with the tormenting pleasures of competition, contest and reward. Absorption in the scientific problem alternated with periodic idleness, escape, play and girl-watching. Friendship and hostility between collaborators were expressed in a nagging yet productive symbiosis in which neither could really do without the special abilities of the other. And all this engaged not only the passion for creating new knowledge but also the passion for recognition by scientific peers and the competition for place" (Merton 1968, 1). The competition was for the ultimate prize of scientific achievement, the Nobel Prize, and the race was principally against Linus Pauling, a stellar figure who had already discovered the basic structure of the protein molecule. At the beginning of the race, little was known about the properties of DNA, except photographs produced by the diffraction of Xrays in Maurice Wilkins' laboratory at King's College, London, which suggested that the DNA molecule had the shape of a regular spiral. In fact, everyone's mind then was full of spirals because Pauling had recently built a model which showed that there is an underlying spiral in some proteins (Bronowski 1968).

In 1951, during an excursion to the Greek temples at Paestum in southern Italy, Watson was trying very hard to get close to Maurice Wilkins (who was then the main person working on DNA structure in England) in the hope of establishing a collaboration. Watson thought he had "a tremendous stroke of good luck" when "Maurice had noticed that my sister was very pretty, and soon they were eating lunch together. I was immensely pleased. For years I had sullenly watched Elizabeth being pursued by a series of dull nitwits. Suddenly the possibility opened up that her way of life could be changed. No longer did I have to face the certainty that she would end up with a mental defective. Furthermore, if Maurice really liked my sister, it was inevitable that I would become closely associated with his X-ray work on DNA" (Watson 1968, 24). However, Watson's hopes were soon dashed, for "neither the beauty of my sister nor my intense interest in the DNA structure had snared him."

Nevertheless, Watson did end up working alongside Crick in the Cavendish Laboratory at the University of Cambridge, an environment that was populated with scientific minds of the highest order, including three Nobel Prize winners in the Cavendish Laboratory itself. Thus Watson and Crick "entered the privileged inner circle of scientists among whom information is passed by a sort of beating of tom-toms, while others await the publication of a formal paper in a learned journal" (Medawar 1968, 5). Piecing together the DNA puzzle required single-minded information seeking that would from time to time bend the rules of conventional propriety: "As is now often the case at the forefront of science, only a part of the information needed by Watson and Crick came through formal channels of publications. Some of the salient information traveled on grapevines of personal relations giving fact and rumor about who was doing what might be pertinent to their own work" (Merton 1968, 44). One of the best remembered (and most notorious) incidents occurred when Watson and Crick had developed a configuration of the DNA backbone that needed to be verified with X-ray diffraction data. The diffraction data were being produced by Rosalind Franklin, Maurice Wilkins' crystallographer, with whom Watson and Crick were not exactly on the best of terms:

Rosy, of course, did not directly give us her data. For that matter, no one at King's realized that they were in our hands. We came upon them because of Max's [Max Perutz, Crick's boss] membership on a committee appointed by the Medical Research Council to look into the research activities of Randall's [J. T. Randall, Wilkins' boss] lab to coordinate Biophysics research within its laboratories. Since Randall wished to convince the outside committee that he had a productive research group, he had instructed his people to draw up a comprehensive summary of their accomplishments. In due time this was prepared in mimeograph form and sent routinely to all the committee members. The report was not confidential and so Max saw no reason not give it to Francis and me. Quickly scanning its contents, Francis sensed with relief that following my return from King's I had correctly reported to him the essential features of the B pattern. Thus only minor modifications were necessary in our backbone configuration. (Watson 1968, 105)

What enabled Watson and Crick to win the race was that they had one vital piece of information, the "one master key to the structure which other workers disregarded" (Bronowski 1968, 381). That key was the rule observed by the Austrian biochemist Erwin Chargaff working at Columbia University, namely, that the four chemical bases in DNA always showed up in pairs—the number of units of thymine seemed to be always the same as the number of adenine, and the number of units of cytosine the same as those of guanine. Off and on, this somewhat obscure evidence influenced the direction of their search until the moment when the double helical structure of the DNA was fully worked out:

Suddenly I became aware that an adenine-thymine pair held together by two hydrogen bonds was identical in shape to a guanine–cytosine pair held together by at least two hydrogen bonds. All the hydrogen bonds seemed to form naturally; no fudging was required to make the two types of base pairs identical in shape. . . . Chargaff's rules then suddenly stood out as a consequence of a double-helical structure for DNA. Even more exciting, this type of double helix suggested a replication scheme much more satisfactory than my briefly considered like-with-like pairing. Given the base sequence of one chain, that of its partner was automatically determined. Conceptually, it was thus very easy to visualize how a single chain could be the template for the synthesis of a chain with complementary sequence. (Watson 1968, 114–115)

This peek at the discovery of the structure of DNA introduces the main issues that we will address in this chapter: that information and insight are created in the hearts and minds of individuals, and that information seeking and use are a dynamic and disorderly social process that is enfolded in layers of cognitive, affective, and situational contingencies. The goal of this chapter is to draw upon the decades of research on information needs and uses (also known as user studies) in an attempt to develop a general model of how people seek and use information. In section I we present a broad-brushed survey of user studies, sketching a map that shows historical and current trends in the research focus and scope of these studies. The ensuing four sections develop a general, multiperspective model of information use.

I. MAPPING INFORMATION NEEDS AND USES RESEARCH

The study of how people behave as they seek and use information has a long history in information science, going back as far as the year 1948. At the Royal Society Scientific Information Conference of that year, two studies were presented—one on the information-seeking behavior of over 200 British scientists in government, university, and private research institutions, and the other on the use of the London Science Museum Library. The earliest studies were mostly sponsored by professional associations, which were designing their information programs to respond to the explosion of scientific information and new technology, or initiated by librarians or administrators of information centers or laboratories who needed data to plan their services. Information needs and uses studies grew significantly when government organizations began to support a number of studies on diverse groups, particularly scientific and technical groups, who were receiving funds from government agencies such as the U.S. Department of Defense and NASA. Over a fifty-year history, it is possible to count thousands of studies that in some significant way investigated the information needs and uses of particular groups of people. A very wide range of information users has been studied, including scientists, engineers, citizens of a community, special-interest groups, doctors, patients, people with health concerns, managers, administrators, small business people, government officials, lawyers, academics, students, library users, and so on. The seeking and processing of information is central to many social systems and human activities, and today the analysis of information needs and uses has become an increasingly important component of the research in disciplines such as cognitive psychology, communication studies, diffusion of innovations, information retrieval, information systems, decision making, and organizational learning.

What may be gleaned from decades of research on human information seeking? What are the goals and assumptions that have framed past research? What are some of the main findings, and what unifying perspectives, if any, have emerged? To answer these questions, it may be helpful to attempt to map the research terrain by locating past studies according to their scope and content, and using the map to detect movement toward promising destinations. Figure 2–1 plots a selection of important studies on information needs and uses along two axes that indicate research orientation and research scope. Studies are grouped together in clusters that are represented by black circles. The relative positions of the circles with respect to the axes indicate approximately their differences in research orientation and research scope. The relative sizes of the circles indicate approximately the number of studies in each cluster. (Any attempt to chart an area so rich in research necessarily requires large measures of subjective interpretation. The aim here is not to draw a definitive map of past endeavours, but to establish reference points for seeing patterns and trajectories.)

The horizontal axis of the map in Fig. 2–1 indicates the *research orientation* of the studies, which can range from being system oriented to being user oriented (Dervin and Nilan 1986). A *system orientation* views information as an external, objective entity that has a content-based reality of its own which is independent of users or social systems. Information exists a priori, and it is the task of the user to locate and extract the desired information. Each document or record contains information "about something," and that something may be determined objectively. Indeed, it is this specification of content that makes it possible to represent, organize, and store information. In the map the

System-Centered, Task-Directed Studies

These studies have been placed in the lower left-hand quadrant of the map of Fig. 2–1. Many of the earlier studies were largely concerned with the objective attributes of the information sources, channels, and systems utilized by particular groups of users in obtaining the information they require for scientific research or problem solving. For example, the U.S. Department of Defense in 1964 initiated a large-scale study of 1375 scientists and engineers selected from among 120,000 working for the department. Respondents were asked to recall their most recently completed tasks and to enumerate the "chunks" of information used to accomplish these tasks. The study found that in 52 percent of the searches, the first source used was a local source (typically a colleague); 42 percent of the information chunks consisted of performance characteristics and specifications; and there was little discrepancy between the depth of information desired and that obtained (Auerbach Corporation 1965; Menzel 1966; Bates 1971). Another large-scale study examined the information-seeking pattern of 1900 scientists and engineers in four very large U.S. corporations and 1200 IEEE members by asking participants to report on a recent instance of receiving information and on the sources of information utilized (Rosenbloom and Wolek 1970). A main conclusion was that the work of scientists involved to a greater extent the use of external information sources, while the work of engineers, with its more operational focus, involved more the use of internal sources. In more than half the cases examined, useful information was obtained from activity that was labeled "competence building," or was pointed out by others, and not from the outcome of specific searches.

One of the most comprehensive and unified studies of scientific communication and information use was the American Psychological Association's (APA) Project on Scientific Information Exchange in Psychology (Menzel 1966). In its first five-year period (1963–68), twenty-two reports were produced covering nearly every aspect of information use among psychologists, including information exchange activities associated with the attendance of conventions, the use of various types of information channels, and the effects of innovations in information exchange. One interesting innovation was the prepublication of papers that were to be presented at the annual APA convention. The studies found that, among other effects, the prepublication of papers stimulated greater audience participation, and that authors of prepublished papers were likely to delay or eliminate subsequent publication (Herner and Herner 1967). Today it has become the norm to publish a set of conference proceedings before the conference takes place. While the numerous studies are too rich to be briefly summarized, one of their major contributions has been to elucidate the differences in information and communication needs that exist among different disciplines, and to enable the professional societies to introduce or modify information channels and services that would best suit their members (Allen 1969).

In the United Kingdom a study of the Information Requirements of the

Social Sciences (INFROSS) was launched in 1969. The study surveyed over 2500 British social science researchers, and focused mainly on the information needs and uses of references, indexes, abstracts, library catalogs, and bibliographies, and on the use of books and libraries. The study concluded overall tha ere underdeveloped, and ide view articles, translation ser e 1971). Formal bibliogra ices were not well used, anc use them regularly. INFR ced many U.K. universities along the lines of those alre

Sys

The of the map of Fig. 2–1. Wh s, systems, and services, mar lude the broader context of l preferences, and information ormation needs of social ser n 1975 at the University of Sheffield as Project INISS (Information Needs and Information Services in local authority social services departments). Its basic goal was to understand the information needs of staff in social services departments and to design information services that would best respond to these needs. By observing the communication activities of staff in five departments, the study was able to relate the information behavior of the social services workers to their personal, work, and organizational characteristics. Staff strongly preferred personal, oral communications, such as face-to-face meetings or telephone conversations. Their workdays were highly fragmented so that most communication episodes were of short duration, and the functional specialization of the departments suggested specialized information services (Wilson and Streatfield 1977). The study led to the introduction of a number of successful innovations, including training courses, book collections chosen by office staff, abstracts bulletins, and indexes of expertise.

Mick et al. (1980) attempted to develop a generalized model of the environmental and situational variables (as distinct from individual attributes) influencing the seeking of scientific and technical information by scientists and engineers. By analyzing the information behavior of scientists and engineers working in a variety of organizational settings and environments, they identified key variables in five areas: perception of management attitudes toward informaton, general information orientation, specific task orientation, demographics, and perceived attributes of information sources. A number of hypotheses were tested on how these variables would influence information needs, access to information, and information satisfaction. The study revealed a few key organizational variables that management can control or modify in order to enhance the utilization of scientific and technical information.

A major research effort to define a comprehensive model of information seeking was that undertaken by Saracevic et al. (1988a,b,c). The goal of the large-scale, multiyear project was to formally enumerate all the important elements that would characterize information-seeking and retrieving activities. Forty users and thirty- searchers took part in the study. Forty questions were searched, each by nine searchers. The proposed general model of information-seeking and retrieving consisted of seven major events (with their accompanying classes of variables in parentheses): (1) User has a problem which needs to be resolved (user characteristics, problem statement). (2) User seeks to resolve the problem by formulating a question and starting an interaction with an information system (question statement, question characteristics). (3) Presearch interaction with a searcher, human or computer intermediary (searcher characteristics, question analysis). (4) Formulation of a search (search strategy, search characteristics). (5) Searching activity and interactions (searching). (6) Delivery of responses to user (items retrieved, formats delivered). (7) Evaluation of responses by user (relevance, utility) (Saracevic et al. 1988a, 164). Analysis of the empirical data showed that "the suggested models tested well, that is, the elements suggested by the models had by and large a significant relation with retrieval outcome." (Saracevic et al. 1988c, 213). For example, the context of a question was confirmed to be important, including the background leading to the question being asked, and the intended use of the information to be retrieved. Different types of questions—classified according to their clarity, specificity, complexity, and so on—may be expected to have different retrieval performance levels. Cycles in searching tended to improve outcome, since intermediate results may be reviewed and search strategies refined accordingly.

User-Centered, Task-Directed Studies

These studies are in the lower right-hand quadrant of the map of Fig. 2–1. As part of MIT's Research Program on the Management of Science and Technology, a number of studies on the information transfer behaviors of scientists and engineers were conducted by Thomas Allen and his associates over a ten year period (1963–73). The studies included the comparative evaluation of thirty-three project teams working on matched pairs of projects, and the analysis of communication networks in thirteen research laboratories (Allen 1977). In the matched-case method, Allen took advantage of the U.S. government's practice of awarding contracts to two or more laboratories simultaneously to perform the same design studies. Pairs of such projects were monitored, and the government agencies provided evaluations of each laboratory's performance. These evaluations were then related to the use of information channels by the individual laboratories. At the same time respondents were asked to track their use of information week by week through "solution development records." Each week respondents would estimate the probabilities of acceptance of a number of alternative solutions that would address a problem. Changes in the relative probabilities were then related to information channels and inputs. An interesting finding was that the choice of information channel or source was based on the cost associated with using the channel, balanced against the value or payoff expected of that source. Cost in this case is multifaceted and includes such important elements as physical accessibility and psychological cost (since asking for information is admitting ignorance, implying a loss of face or stature). Payoff is indicated by the technical quality or reliability of the source. In the communication network studies, Allen and associates identified the role of "technology gatekeepers" in introducing new information into the organization through a two-step process (that is, indirectly through the gatekeeper). Gatekeepers read more widely (including more refereed journals), continuously maintain a broad range of personal contacts, and can translate external information into terms that the average technologist in the organization can understand.

William Garvey, one of the heads of the American Psychological Association's Project on Scientific Information Exchange in Psychology, carried over the project's approach to examine information use in other scientific disciplines when he moved to the Johns Hopkins Center for Research in Scientific Communication. These studies adopted a psychological perspective of scientific communication which emphasized

> . . . the interaction between the scientist and his environment (a major element
> of this environment being other scientists). Each scientist brings to each situa-
> tion a particular cluster of psychological attributes (personality, skills, style, expe-
> rience, habits, etc.), which, combined with specific circumstances in the research
> process, gives the individual scientist a predisposition to perceive and detect, to
> assimilate, to associate, etc. what is happening with his research at any given
> moment. . . . his style, subjectivity, bias, etc. all play a part in his detection, se-
> lection, retention, and use of information encountered in the search. (Garvey
> 1979, 4)

It was precisely this variation in observation, selection, and interpretation among different individual scientists that allowed science to progress. The Johns Hopkins studies concluded that the scientific enterprise functioned as a social system, and that a key feature of the social system was the highly interactive process by which scientific communication took place.

Caplan et al. (1975) investigated the use of social science research information in the formulation of government policy. Two hundred and four upper level employees in the executive branch of the U.S. federal government self-reported 575 instances of the use of social science information. The study found that the political implications of research findings appeared to override all other considerations in determining whether the information is used or not. The nature and extent of information use were also influenced by the cognitive styles of the respondents. Three styles were identified. Those with a "clinical" style could analyze the scientific or objective internal logic of an issue as well as its value-laden or ideological implications. Those with an "academic" style concentrated on the internal logic of issues. Those with an "advocacy" style tended to ignore internal logic, but dealt mainly with political considerations.

Research and Practical Contributions So Far

Information needs and uses studies have added significantly to our appreciation of how people seek information. An abundance of field data has been collected and analyzed about the channels, methods, and sources used by various groups of scientists, technologists, professionals, government officials, citizens, and others as they seek information. Innovations were introduced to promote information exchange and simplify information access, including the prepublication of conference papers, customization of tools to help users locate and retrieve information, development of current awareness services, and so on. Data collection and analysis often leveraged upon methodologies from multiple disciplines, such as the critical incident technique to analyze information-receiving episodes, structured observations to log information activities, action research to introduce new tools or services, and special interviewing techniques that more fully unveil users' information needs.

In terms of theory construction, a number of general observations may be made:

1. Information needs and uses need to be examined within the work, organizational, and social settings of the users. Information needs vary according to users' membership in professional or social groups, their demographic backgrounds, and the specific requirements of the task they are performing.

2. Users obtain information from a wide range of formal and informal sources. Informal information sources, including colleagues and personal contacts, are frequently as important as and sometimes more important than formal information sources such as the library or on-line databases.

3. A large number of criteria can affect the selection and use of information sources. Research has found that many groups of users prefer sources that are local or close at hand, which are not necessarily the best regarded. For these users, the perceived accessibility of an information source is more important than its perceived quality.

(Choo and Auster 1993, 284–85)

While the number of user studies continued to proliferate, there was a growing unease about the lack of progress toward building up a unifying core of theoretical knowledge about information needs and uses. Generalization was thought to be difficult because many studies were limited to groups of users with special information requirements, and on their interactions with specific information channels, systems, and tools. There were no agreed upon definitions for the concepts of information needs, information use, and other important variables. This lack of a common framework made it difficult to compare and combine research findings, so much so that many user studies existed as isolated case studies and collections of empirical data which were peculiar to specialized and often small groups of users. Several studies also had a strong system focus, concentrating on the performance of selected information sources, information systems and communication channels—user needs and use of the information retrieved were not examined in detail.

User-Centered, Integrative Studies

These studies represent a relatively recent development and have been placed in the upper right-hand quadrant of the map of Fig. 2–1. An early call to examine information seeking from the point of view of the user (rather than that of the document or the information system) was made by Belkin (1980). People in problematic situations who are looking for information experience inadequacies in their state of knowledge—"inadequacies in a state of knowledge can be of many sorts, such as gaps or lacks, uncertainty, or incoherence, whose only common trait is a perceived 'wrongness' " (Belkin 1980, 137). Belkin named this condition an Anomalous State of Knowledge (ASK). The ASK hypothesis implies that information seekers are often unable to specify their information needs since they cannot readily express what they do not know or what is missing. Information retrieval systems that depend on users precisely specifying their information needs a priori are therefore unlikely to work well. Instead, the ASK hypothesis suggests that the information system should be designed to assist users in discovering and representing their knowledge of a problem situation, especially the anomalies that prevent specification of need. Belkin and his colleagues used a free-form interviewing technique that allowed users to describe problem situations with unstructured statements. The situation description was analyzed by computer according to statistical word occurrences and word associations in the text. A graph network was then drawn that represented the user's ASK. The same statistical profiling is used to represent each document in the database. Finally, the system applied different mechanisms to match the user's ASK structure with the word-association structures representing the documents in order to retrieve documents that would be relevant to the problem situation (Belkin et al. 1982).

Tom Wilson of the Department of Information Studies at the University of Sheffield (United Kingdom) has also advocated a user-centered approach to analyzing information needs and information seeking behavior. Adopting a phenomenological perspective, Wilson sees individuals as constantly constructing their own social worlds from the world of appearances around them. Information needs arise from these attempts to make sense of the world. Information seeking is "almost always frustrated in some degree because of the division between the meanings embedded in information systems and the highly personal meaning of the information-seeker's problem" (Wilson 1994, 32). He proposes a model in which information needs arise out of work setting and the roles the individual plays in social life, including work roles. Personal needs may be physiological, affective, or cognitive. Work roles and personal needs are influenced by the work setting and have sociocultural, politicoeconomic, and physical dimensions. As a result, in order to properly study information needs,

- Our concern is with uncovering the facts of everyday life of the people being investigated

- By uncovering those facts we aim to understand the needs that exist which press the individual toward information-seeking behavior

- By better understanding those needs we are able to understand better what meaning information has in the everyday life of people

- By all of the foregoing we should have a better understanding of the use and be able to design more effective information systems

(Wilson 1981, 11)

Our survey suggests that, over the years, information needs and uses studies have progressively broadened their research orientation and research focus. Going back to the research map, we can discern that on the horizontal axis of research orientation, studies have moved from an orientation that is primarily *system-centered* (in which information is objective, resides in a document or system, and where the main issue is how to get at this information) to an orientation that is also *user-centered* (in which information is subjective, resides in the users' minds, and is only useful when meaning has been created by the user). On the vertical axis of research scope, research has shifted from studies concentrating on particular information *tasks* or activities, such as literature searching, fact finding, or communications in a work group, to studies that go beyond the information-seeking activity itself by trying also to understand something of the personal, organizational, and social *situation* in which the information need arose and in which the acquired information will be put to use. Overall, then, we see a movement from the bottom left quadrant of the map to the top right quadrant—a movement from research that is primarily system and task oriented to research that is more user centered and integrative in approach.

II. TOWARDS A MULTIPERSPECTIVE MODEL OF INFORMATION USE

The study of information needs and uses is necessarily cross-disciplinary, linking cognate areas such as cognitive psychology, communication studies, diffusion of innovations, economics, information retrieval, organization theory, and social anthropology. At the same time this diversity presses for a unifying perspective that would bring coherence to the bounty of research on how humans seek and use information. After years of decrying the lack of a general theoretical framework, there is an emerging convergence on what constitutes the defining elements in an analysis of information needs and uses. While information often has a physical manifestation such as a document or record, the context and meaning of the information therein are created afresh each time it is taken up by a user. Information is fabricated by individuals, who cut new cloth from the fabric of their past experience and tailor the cloth according to the exigencies of the particular situation in which the information is to be used. A general model of information use must embrace the totality of human experience that is information seeking—the thoughts, feelings, actions, and the environment in which these are played out. Our starting position is that the information user is a sentient, cognitive person; that information seeking and use is a dynamic process extending over time and space; and that the context of information use determines in what ways and to what extent the received information is useful. While individual information behavior may exhibit infinite variety, order may be found by unraveling the cognitive, affective, and situational layers that enfold information seeking and use.

The development of our model of information seeking and use proceeds in three stages. In section III we examine the environment for information seeking, where we are concerned with both the internal environment for information processing, which is internal to the individual, and the external environment for information use, which is part of the individual's work or social milieu. The *information processing environment* consists of the individual's cognitive needs and affective responses, while the *information use environment* includes attributes such as organizational structure and work-related cultures. In section IV we examine three sets of information behaviors: information needs clarification, information seeking, and information use. We assume that information seeking and use is purposeful, that is, the individual requires information in order to move from the current state to a desired end state. Movement may be problematic because the individual lacks the knowledge or means to do so. The individual first becomes aware of or recognizes a problematic situation, and clarifies or defines *information needs* in terms of important entities or concepts, their attributes and relationships, available options, desirable outcomes, and so on. *Information seeking* then is the process in which the individual searches for information in order to change his or her state of knowledge. During information seeking, typical behaviors include identifying

Table 2–1. Theoretical framework of information seeking and use.

Environment Behaviors	Information-processing environment		Information use environment
	Cognitive needs	*Affective responses*	*Situational dimensions*
Information needs			
Information seeking			
Information use			

and selecting sources; articulating a query, question, or topic; extracting the information; evaluating the information found; and extending, modifying, or repeating the search. *Information use* is the selection of relevant messages from the larger space of information encountered during the search, and the processing of the information so that it leads to a change in the state of the individual's knowledge or capacity to act. In section V we examine the interactions between the information-processing and use environments and each of the information behaviors. The overall approach is previewed in Table 2–1. The specific effects of the interactions vary across individuals and particular problem situations, so the cells in the matrix are left empty for the moment. In the ensuing chapters of the book we will use the matrix as a framework to analyze how participants in organizations seek and use information in strategic ways.

III. COGNITIVE, AFFECTIVE, AND SITUATIONAL DIMENSIONS OF INFORMATION USE

Over the next three subsections we outline the cognitive sense making approach developed and applied by Brenda Dervin, the affective responses accompanying an Information Search Process identified by Carol Kuhlthau, and the situational dimensions of the information use environment proposed by Robert Taylor. All three perspectives share the common stance that information is constructed in the thoughts and feelings of users, and that information is deployed in work and life settings whose conditions determine the use and usefulness of information. All three perspectives contribute to a fuller understanding of the human experience of information seeking and use. Each perspective sheds its own light on choice and action in the principal stages of information use behavior: information needs, information seeking, and information use.

Cognitive Needs in Information Seeking and Use

Since information is constructed in the mind of the individual, the study of information use should include an analysis of how the human actor recognizes an inability to act or comprehend a situation because of a lack of information, and so proceeds to find information to fill this want. While this subjective, person-by-person analysis could yield prodigious data sets, it begs the larger question of whether one could then derive generalizable categories that characterize human information seeking. The theoretical and empirical work of Dervin (1983a, 1983b, 1992) in developing a sense making model suggests an approach.

In the sense making metaphor the person is moving through space and time, taking steps through experiences (Dervin 1992). A new step is taken in each new moment. Even though the step may be a repetition of past action, it is a new step because it takes place at a new moment in space and time. Movement is accompanied by the person continually making sense of his or her actions and the environment. For as long as the person is able to construct meaning, movement ahead is possible. However, from time to time movement is blocked by a perceived discontinuity. The person is stopped in a situation where movement forward is prevented by the perception of some kind of cognitive gap. The person has run out of internal sense and needs to create new sense. The person defines the nature of the gap and, based on this interpretation, selects tactics to bridge the cognitive gap. Finally, the person crosses the cognitive bridge she has constructed in order to continue on the journey. The essence of the sense making approach is understanding how the individual defines a gap situation and attempts to bridge the cognitive gap. Information seeking and use are analyzed in terms of the triangle of "situation— gap— use," exemplified by these questions: (1) What in your situation is stopping you? What is missing in your situation? (2) What questions or confusions do you have? (3) What kind of help do you hope to get? (Dervin and Clark 1987). The results of field studies applying the sense making approach show that gap-defining and gap-bridging strategies account for individual information behavior better than factors such as system characteristics, message content, or user demographics.

More than forty different sense making studies have been conducted over two decades in a number of institutions, such as the California State Library, the National Cancer Institute, and the Ohio Department of Health, and on a range of populations, including blood donors, cancer patients, college students, computer software users, immigrants, and library users (Dervin and Nilan 1986; Dervin 1992). The principal research methodology is the micromoment time-line interview. Each respondent is asked to reconstruct a situation in terms of the events and steps that make up the time-line development of the situation. The respondent then describes each step in detail in terms of how the respondent saw the situation, the gap, and the help wanted. A general finding of these studies is this: The ways in which people *perceive their cogni-*

tive gaps and the ways that they *want information to help* are good predictors of their information seeking and use behaviors. Better yet, the ways in which people perceive their cognitive gaps and the ways in which they want information to help can be coded into universal categories that are applicable across different groups of information users:

> Much of the quantitative work of sense-making studies, to date, has also focused on developing generic categories to describe needs, barriers, and helps wanted— categories which are universal in the sense that they pertain to gap-bridging and gap-defining across situations while at the same time they capture important aspects of particular situations. Across studies, these category schemes have stabilized. (Dervin 1992, 75)

For example, a set of categories, labeled *situation stops,* has been developed to describe the ways in which humans see their way ahead being blocked. These situation stop or gap-defining categories include the following (adapted from Dervin 1992):

- *Decision stop:*   Where the human sees two or more roads ahead
- *Barrier stop:*   Where the human sees one road ahead but something or someone stands on the road blocking the way
- *Spin-out stop:*   Where the human sees self as having no road
- *Wash-out stop:*   Where the human sees self as on a road that suddenly disappears
- *Problematic stop:*   Where the human sees self as being dragged down a road not of his or her own choosing
- Other situation categories that depend on how the human judges perceptual embeddedness (how foggy is the road), situational embeddedness (how many intersections are on the road), and social embeddedness (how many people are also traveling)

People who perceive themselves as being in these situation gaps will ask questions in their attempts to bridge the gap. A second set of categories has been developed to relate these gap-bridging questions to: the timing and location of events; understanding causes; projecting outcomes; and identifying characteristics of self, others, events, and objects. Finally, to capture how people put the information obtained to use, a third set of help categories has been developed: creating ideas, finding directions or ways to move; acquiring skills; getting support or confirmation; getting motivated; getting connected to others; calming down or relaxing; getting pleasure or happiness; and reaching goals (Table 2–2).

In summary, the sense making approach provides a cognitive metaphor for information-processing and use in which information needs are compared with

Table 2–2. Sense making model (Dervin 1992)
(Situation and information use categories).

Situation	Information use (help)
Decision stop	Creating ideas
Barrier stop	Finding directions
Spin-out stop	Acquiring skills
Wash-out stop	Getting support
Problematic stop	Getting motivated
Perceptual embeddedness	Getting connected
Situational embeddedness	Calming down
Social embeddedness	Getting pleasure
	Reaching goals

gap perceptions, information seeking with gap-bridging strategies, and information use with the help in crossing the gap. Research using the approach has revealed general categories by which people perceive and bridge their cognitive and information gaps, and has found that the way the individual perceives a gap is a good predictor of how the individual will go about bridging the gap and wanting the information to help.

Affective Responses in Information Seeking

Cognitive needs are draped in affective responses so that they are as much felt as they are thought about. Recent research in neurobiology shows that emotions play a crucial role during information seeking and processing by directing attention to potentially important new or confirmatory information, and by marking out options that, based on past experience, could be dangerous or favorable (Damasio 1994; LeDoux 1996). Information uses studies recognize that information needs are both affective and cognitive in origin, so that emotional responses often regulate information seeking by channeling attention, pointing out doubt and uncertainty, indicating likes and dislikes, and motivating effort. From her studies of the information-seeking behaviors of library users and college students, Kuhlthau (1991, 1993a, 1993b) observed common patterns in the users' experience as they search and use information. She postulates that the Information Search Process is composed of six stages: initiation, selection, exploration, formulation, collection, and presentation (Table 2–3). Each stage in the search process is characterized by the user's behavior in three realms of experience—the affective (feelings), the cognitive (thought), and the physical (action). During *initiation* the user first recognizes a need for more information. Feelings of uncertainty and apprehension are common. Thoughts center on contemplating the problem and relating it to past experience. Actions involve discussing possible topics and approaches with others.

Table 2–3. Information search process (Kuhlthau 1991, 1993a, 1993b).

Stages	Appropriate Task	Feelings common To each stage
1 Initiation	Recognize information need	Uncertainty
2 Selection	Identify general topic	Optimism
3 Exploration	Investigate information on general topic	Confusion, frustration, doubt
4 Formulation	Formulate focus	Clarity
5 Collection	Gather information pertaining to focus	Sense of direction, confidence
6 Presentation	Complete information search	Relief, satisfaction, disappointment

During *selection* the user identifies the general area or topic to be investigated. Feelings of uncertainty are replaced by optimism and a readiness to search. Thoughts are on choosing a topic most likely to "succeed" and best able to satisfy the criteria of personal interest, information available, and time allocated. Actions involve seeking background information on the general topic area. During *exploration* the user expands personal understanding of the general area. Feelings of confusion and doubt may increase. Thoughts are on becoming sufficiently informed and oriented in order to formulate a focus or a personal point of view. The fourth stage of *formulation* is the turning point of the process in which the user establishes a focus or perspective on the problem that can guide searching. Feelings of uncertainty fall as confidence rises. Thoughts become clearer and more directed. During *collection,* the user interacts with information systems and services to gather information. Confidence increases and interest in the project deepens. With a clear sense of direction, the user is able to specify and look for particular, relevant information. In the final stage of *presentation* the user completes the search and resolves the problem. There is a sense of relief, accompanied by satisfaction if the search is thought to have gone well, or disappointment otherwise. Thoughts are on closing the search with a personal understanding of the issues investigated. Kuhlthau's extended field work on college students and library users found that the participants' feelings and thoughts matched those predicted by the model. However, at the task or action level, most participants began to gather information before they had explored background or developed a focus or perspective. In most stages of the search process, the dominant activities were information gathering and attempting to complete the search.

Central to Kuhlthau's model of the information search process is the notion that uncertainty—experienced both as a cognitive state and as an affective response—rises and falls as the search process progresses. Kuhlthau captions this "a principle of uncertainty for information seeking":

Uncertainty due to a lack of understanding, a gap in meaning, a limited construct initiates the process of information seeking. Uncertainty is a cognitive

state that commonly causes affective symptoms of anxiety and lack of confidence. Uncertainty and anxiety can be expected in the early stages of the Information Search Process. The affective symptoms of uncertainty, confusion, and
frustration are associated with vague, unclear thoughts about a topic or question.
As knowledge states shift to more clearly focused thoughts, a parallel shift is
noted in feelings of increased confidence. (Kuhlthau 1993a, p. xxiii)

The implications of the uncertainty principle are elucidated through a set
of six corollaries (Kuhlthau 1993a, 1993b). First, information search is a process of constructing understanding and meaning. The user constructs meaning
from the information encountered, and in doing so, moves from uncertainty
and vagueness to confidence and clarity as the search progresses. Second, the
formulation of a focus, guiding idea, or point of view is the pivotal point in
the search process. Formulation is an act of thoughtful reflection, the result of
relating and interpreting the information encountered in order to select a defined area to concentrate searching on. Unfortunately, many users bypass the
formulation activity altogether, beginning to gather information without first
forming a sufficiently clear focus. Third, information encountered may be redundant or unique. Redundant information fits into what the user already
knows or believes in, and is readily recognized to be relevant or not. Unique
information is new and extends knowledge, but it may not match the user's
constructs, requiring reconstruction. Too much redundant information leads to
boredom, while too much unique information causes anxiety. Fourth, the range
of possibilities pursued in a search is influenced by the user's mood or attitude
towards the search task. A user in an invitational mood would tend to take
more expansive, exploratory actions, whereas a user in an indicative mood
prefers conclusive actions that lead to closure (Kelly 1963). Computer-based
information systems assume an indicative mood, and therefore try to provide
information with speed and specificity. In reality, a user's mood changes during the search process, from perhaps an invitational, exploratory mood in early
stages to a more indicative mood as the search progresses. Fifth, the search
process is a series of unique, personal choices based on the user's predictions
or expectations about what sources, information, and strategies will be effective or expedient. Thus users make predictions or develop expectations about
the sources used or not used, the sequence of source use, and the information
selected from the sources as relevant or irrelevant. Relevance is not absolute
nor constant, but varies considerably from individual to individual. Finally, the
user's interest and motivation levels grow as the search progresses. Interest is
higher in later stages when the user has defined a search focus and has enough
understanding of the topic to become intellectually engaged. Interest may also
be enhanced by introducing the notion of fun and play, but most information
systems ignore this need.

In summary, the cognitive gap or uncertainty that drives the information
search process is accompanied by distinct emotional states. In the early stages
of information search, uncertainty or lack of understanding causes affective

symptoms of anxiety, confusion, frustration, and doubt. As the information search progresses, feelings shift toward increased confidence and satisfaction if the search has been successful. These affective states motivate and direct the individual's information-processing and information use experience. Affective responses influence, and are influenced by, the user's ability to construct meaning, focus the search, balance redundant and unique information, manage moods and expectations, and deepen personal interest in the search.

Situational Dimensions of Information Needs and Uses

Information behavior may be defined as the sum of activities through which information becomes useful (Taylor 1991). The usefulness or value of information is based not only on the subject matter or how well the information content matches a query or topic, but also on the requirements, norms, and expectations that are contingent upon the user's work and organizational contexts. These contexts are what Taylor calls *information use environments* (IUEs), which consist of "those elements that (a) affect the flow and use of information messages into, within, and out of any definable entity; and (b) determine the criteria by which the value of information messages will be judged" (Taylor 1986, 24). The elements of the information use environment may be grouped into four categories (Table 2–4): sets of people, problem dimensions, work settings, and problem resolution assumptions (Taylor 1991).

Sets of people share assumptions and attitudes about the nature of their work that act on their information behaviors. These assumptions may be learned formally through education or professional training, or assimilated informally through, for example, membership and participation in a group. Tay-

Table 2–4. Information use environments (Taylor 1991).

Sets of people	Typical problems	Work settings	Problem resolution
1 Professions 2 Entrepreneurs 3 Special interest groups 4 Special socio-economic groups	• Problems are *dynamic* • *Discrete classes of problems* are created by requirements of profession, occupation, social condition, etc. • *Problem dimensions* determine the criteria for judging the value of information	• Organization structure and style • Domain of interest • Access to information • History, experience	• Assumptions about what constitutes the resolution of a problem • *Classes of information use* • *Traits of information* anticipated to resolve problem

lor identifies four sets of people based on patterns of information behavior (Taylor 1991, 222): the professions (engineers, lawyers, social workers, scientists, teachers, managers, physicians, etc); entrepreneurs (farmers, small-business people, etc.); special-interest groups (consumers, citizen groups, hobbyists, political action groups, ethnic cultural groups, etc.); and special socioeconomic groups (information-poor, the disabled, minorities, the elderly, etc.). Demographic and nondemographic characteristics help describe these sets of people. (Taylor was initially most interested in testing his framework by examining the professionals and entrepreneurs.) From the wide range of demographic variables that might be applicable, education appears to be the most significant. Among the nondemographic characteristics, the more important appear to be preferences for channels and media; use of social networks; and attitudes toward new technology, education, risk taking, and innovation. Scientists and engineers, for example, make heavy use of print media such as journals and books, whereas managers prefer face-to-face meetings or telephone conversations. Doctors tend to rely on their social networks of colleagues for information on the efficacy of new drugs. As for attitudes toward information and innovation, scholars and policy makers may value background and context, whereas teachers and engineers may favor specific information addressing practical concerns.

Problem dimensions are the characteristics of the typical problems that a set of people are concerned with. Taylor asserts that "each of the definable IUEs has a discrete class of problems, spawned by its particular setting and by the exigencies of its profession, occupation, or life style" (Taylor 1991, 225). Problems change over time as new information is received and people alter their perceptions. Problems act as surrogates of the information use environment, and because they encapsulate enough of the more salient demands of the use environment, defining problem dimensions enables information needs to be inferred in a more systematic way (MacMullin and Taylor 1984). MacMullin and Taylor identify eleven problem dimensions that define information need and serve as criteria by which the relevance of information to a problem will be judged. These dimensions position problems as lying on a continuum between each of the following pairs:

- Design and discovery
- Well structured and ill structured
- Simple and complex
- Goals are specific and goals are amorphous
- Initial state understood and initial state not understood
- Assumptions agreed upon and assumptions not agreed upon
- Assumptions explicit and assumptions not explicit
- Familiar pattern and new pattern

- Magnitude of risk not great and magnitude of risk great
- Susceptible to empirical analysis and not susceptible to empirical analysis
- Internal imposition and external imposition

Collectively, these dimensions provide a detailed representation of the information use environment surrounding problem situations, and suggest ways of elaborating information needs that include both subject-related needs and situation-related demands.

Work settings are the social and physical attributes of the organization or unit that a set of people work in—attributes that influence attitudes toward information, the types and structures of information required, and the flow and availability of information. The style and culture of the organization, including its goals and reward and recognition systems, help mold members' perceptions about the role and value of information. The content of the work to be performed, whether it be designing a skyscaper or decoding a software program, will set its own information demands peculiar to the domain. Work-setting features such as organizational hierarchy and the location of information sources can affect the flow and availability of information. Perceived accessibility of a source is an important variable governing the decision whether to use the source. Accessibility is a function of source proximity, physical effort required, as well as the psychological cost of using the source. An organization that has specialized in a particular area for many years may become set in its ways and may tend to attenuate the effect of new information. Confident in its history and experience, such an organization may absorb large amounts of information without conceiving the need to rethink its behavior.

Problem resolution assumptions are the perceptions shared by a set of people about what constitutes the resolution of their typical problems. These assumptions guide information seeking and use in several ways. They provide a frame of reference to view and structure problems; and they create expectations about the traits of information required to resolve the problem. For Taylor, the ways in which people view their problems and what they anticipate as resolution constitute a built-in although unconscious means of controlling the amount of information used. Thus people's perceptions and anticipations indirectly control the breadth and depth of their information search—including the time and effort to spend on searching, where to search, how information encountered is to be filtered, and how much and what kinds of information are required. Managers, for example, do not attempt comprehensive searches or look for optimal solutions. Instead, they search for information locally, using familiar sources, often seeking solutions in the vicinity of the problems. Problems are considered resolved when a good enough solution has been found, that is, a manager "satisfices" as she "looks for a course of action that is satisfactory or 'good enough' " (Simon 1976, p. xxix).

Rosenbaum (1993, 1996) introduces structuration theory (Giddens 1984) to clarify the interactions between Taylor's information use environment and information behaviors. In structurational terms, the information use environment is that part of the organizational structure which contains the rules and resources that affect the information behaviors of organizational members. As users engage in information behaviors,

---

. . . they intentionally and unintentionally draw upon and make use of the IUE, simultaneously reproducing these elements as conditions which allow them to engage in information behaviors. . . . By drawing upon and using these rules, users transform them from virtual to actual existence, making possible the information behavior of valuing and reproducing the rules in the actions of using them. (Rosenbaum 1993, 242)

As people interact with one another or with organizational information systems, they draw upon the resources of the information use environment, and through their interaction information becomes useful. Thus the information use environment and information behaviors mutually and simultaneously constitute each other, so that the information use environment is both an essential resource for as well as a product of situated information behaviors.

In summary, the information use environment consists of sets of people who share assumptions about the nature of their work and the role of information in it; whose work is concerned with problems characterized by dimensions that are applied to judge the usefulness of information; whose work settings influence their attitude toward information as well as the availability and value of information; and whose perceptions about problem resolution regulate the intensity of their information search and their expectations about the kinds of information they need. Taylor suggests that the informationu use environment "can become a generalizable model, a fruitful means for organizing, describing, and predicting the information behavior of any given population in a variety of contexts" (Taylor 1991, 251).

IV. INFORMATION-SEEKING AND USE BEHAVIORS

Having elaborated on the influence of cognitive needs, affective responses, and situational dimensions on information use in the previous section, we now take a closer look at the information seeking activity itself. Information seeking is the human and social process through which information becomes useful to an individual or group. Information use is an elusive concept to define. Much of this book is given to a discussion of the three arenas in which organizations use information strategically (meaning construction, knowledge building, decision making). For the moment we take a finer grained view of information use at the level of the individual—we regard information use as the individual selecting messages to act upon from the larger body of information found during information seeking. Conceptually, information seeking may be thought of as comprising three stages—the recognition of information needs, which leads to information seeking, and then information use. In practice, these stages tend to fold into each other, so that each activity itself is a microcosm of one or more of the other activities. For example, the clarification of information needs itself requires information seeking and use, the gathering of information switches between sources and strategies as new information is received, and so on. Nevertheless, a conceptual partitioning into stages facilitates analysis of the structure and dynamics of information-seeking behavior. We do this over the next three subsections, and then sketch a general model of information use that shows how each information-seeking stage combines cognitive, affective, and contextual elements into human experience.

Information Needs

Information needs are often thought of in terms of a person's cognitive needs—gaps or deficiencies in the state of mental knowledge or understanding that may be represented by questions or topics that could be posed to an information system or source. Satisfying the cognitive need then involves retrieving information whose subject matter matches that of the inquiry. However, because information is sought and used in social situations, information often has to satisfy not just cognitive needs, but also affective or emotional needs (Wilson 1994). While the performance of organizational tasks, including planning and decision making, is the main generator of cognitive needs, "the nature of the organization, coupled with the individual's personality structure, will create affective needs such as the need for achievement, for self-expression and self-actualization. . . . In such a wider view the individual would be perceived not merely as driven to seek information for cognitive ends, but as living and working in social settings which create their own motivations to seek information to help satisfy largely affective needs" (Wilson 1981, 9, 10). Furthermore, information needs do not emerge fully formed but grow and evolve over time. Initially the individual may experience a vague sense of unease about some general concern or inadequacy in her knowledge. She may or may not embark on information gathering at this point, but she is likely to be sensitive to information encountered about that issue. Gradually she forms an assessment about the importance of that concern and is able to articulate the information voids that have to be filled in order to develop understanding or enable action. Awareness of an information need does not always lead to search—the individual may decide to accept or suppress the problem. Acceptance or suppression is influenced by the individual's perception of the importance or appropriateness of the problem, her knowledge of the domain, and her assessment of the cost and effort of doing the search (Marchionini 1995). With acceptance, the individual then attempts to understand and define the problem by limiting its boundaries, labeling key concepts and entities, and anticipating what form and format of information is required. By developing a focus and an anticipation of how the information is to be helpful, the person is well prepared to commence information seeking.

Taylor (1968) suggests that human beings experience four levels of information needs—visceral need, conscious need, formalized need, and compromised need. At the *visceral* level, the person experiences a vague sense of dissatisfaction, a gap in knowledge or understanding that is often inexpressible in linguistic terms. The visceral need may become more concrete and pressing as more information is encountered and its importance grows. When this occurs, the visceral need enters the *conscious* level, where the person develops a mental description of the area of indecision. Such a mental description is likely to be in the form of rambling statements or a narrative that reflect the ambiguity that the person still experiences at this level. To develop a focus, the person may consult with colleagues and friends, and when ambiguity is sufficiently reduced, the conscious need moves to the *formalized* level. At the *formalized level,* the inquirer is able to construct a qualified, rational statement of the information need, expressed, for example, in the form of a question or topic. Here the formal statement is made without the user necessarily having to consider what sources of information are available. When the user interacts with an information source or system, either directly or through an intermediary, she may recast the question in anticipation of what the source or system knows or is able to deliver. The formalized question is thus modified or rephrased in a form that could be understood or processed by the information system. In this sense the question finally presented represents the information need at the *compromised* level. Taylor's conceptualization of levels of information need is supported and reinforced in the literature of library and information science, especially in the area of the reference interview (Markey 1981).

Looking at information needs as emerging through multiple levels emphasizes the principle that satisfying information need goes beyond finding information that matches the apparent subject matter expressed in the individual's questions or topic descriptions. A statement of need at the compromised or formalized levels does not retain the nuance and innuendo that give color and complexion to a bald statement of a question or topic. The better that the information found is able to connect with these conscious and visceral needs, the more the individual will feel that the information is pertinent, meaningful, or useful in a personal way. Thus whether the information is assessed to be valuable depends on whether it satisfies or resolves the visceral state of unease that precipitated the information need in the first place. From the cognitive perspective, the representation of information need as visceral and conscious is akin to Belkin's (1980) treatment of information need as an anomalous state of knowledge, in which the individual is unable to readily express her information needs since she cannot specify what she does not yet know or what is presently missing. In terms of emotional states, Kuhlthau's (1993a,b) uncertainty principle predicts that feelings of uncertainty and confusion would dominate in early stages of search due to ambiguities in the information need, and that confidence increases as the search progresses. For Kuhlthau, feelings of uncertainty begin to ebb when the individual is able to formulate a focus or theme around which information seeking can then take place. As for situational demands, Taylor (1991) has identified elements of the information use environment that could modify the visceral, conscious, and formal expressions of information need. For example, the degree to which the situation is new or familiar, simple or complex; and the extent to which participants agree or disagree on assumptions, goals, and options, are all likely to influence the nature and intensity of the information need across its various levels.

Information Seeking

Information seeking is the process in which humans purposefully engage in the search for information so as to change their state of knowledge (Marchionini 1995). It is part of a larger human and social activity through which information becomes useful to an individual or group. For the same information need, each of us would seek information somewhat differently, depending on our knowledge about sources, past experiences, personal preferences, and so on. Research suggests that underlying this variety is a broadly applicable sequence of categories of information-seeking behaviors. We have seen one such sequence in Kuhlthau's division of the information search process into six stages: initiation, selection, exploration, formulation, collection, and presentation. Marchionini (1995) analyzes the information-seeking process in an electronic environment as made up of eight subprocesses, which call on each other and develop in parallel: recognize and accept an information problem; define and understand the problem; choose a search system; formulate a query; execute search; examine results; extract information; and reflect/iterate/stop.

Ellis (1989a,b) and Ellis et al. (1993) derive a general behavioral model of information seeking from an analysis of the information-seeking patterns of social scientists, research physicists, and chemists. The model describes eight categories of information-seeking activities as generic: starting, chaining, browsing, differentiating, monitoring, extracting, verifying, and ending. *Starting* comprises those activities that form the initial search for information— identifying sources of interest that could serve as starting points of the search. Identified sources often include familiar sources that have been used before as well as less familiar sources that are expected to provide relevant information. The likelihood of a source being selected depends on the perceived accessibility of the source, as well as the perceived quality of the information from that source. Perceived accessibility, which is the amount of effort and time needed to make contact with and use a source, has been found to be a strong predictor of source use for many groups of information users (such as engineers and scientists [Allen 1977]). However, in situations when ambiguity is high and when information reliability is especially important, less accessible sources of perceived high quality may be consulted as well (see, for example, the environment scanning behavior of chief executives in Choo [1994]). While searching the initial sources, these sources are likely to point to, suggest, or recommend additional sources or references. Following up on these new leads from an initial source is the activity of *chaining*. Chaining can be backward or forward. Backward chaining takes place when pointers or references from an initial source are followed, and is a well established routine of information seeking among scientists and researchers. In the reverse direction, forward chaining identifies and follows up on other sources that refer to an intial source or document. Although it can be an effective way of broadening a search, forward chaining is much less commonly used, probably because people are unaware of it or because the required bibliographical tools are unavailable. Having located sources and documents, *Browsing* is the activity of semidirected search in areas of potential interest. The individual often simplifies browsing by looking through tables of contents, lists of titles, subject headings, names of organizations or persons, abstracts, and summaries, and so on. Browsing takes place in many situations in which related information has been grouped together according to subject affinity, as when the user views displays at a conference or exhibition, or scans periodicals or books along the shelves of a bookshop or library. Chang and Rice (1993) define browsing as "the process of exposing oneself to a resource space by scanning its content (objects or representations) and/or structure, possibly resulting in awareness of unexpected or new content or paths in that resource space" (p. 258). They regard browsing as a "rich and fundamental human information behavior" that could lead to outcomes such as serendipitous findings, modification of information needs, learning, enjoyment, and so on. During *Differentiating,* the individual filters and selects from among the sources scanned by noticing differences between the nature and quality of the information offered. For example, social scientists were found to prioritize sources and types of sources according to three main criteria: by substantive topic; by approach or perspective; and by level, quality, or type of treatment (Ellis 1989a,b). The differentiation process is likely to depend on the individual's prior or initial experiences with the sources, word-of-mouth recommendations from personal contacts, or reviews in published sources. Taylor (1986) points out that for information to be relevant and consequential, it should address not only the subject matter of the problem but also the particular circumstances that affect the resolution of that problem. He identifies six categories of criteria by which individuals select and differentiate between sources: ease of use, noise reduction, quality, adaptability, time savings, and cost savings. *Monitoring* is the activity of keeping abreast of developments in an area by regularly following particular sources. The individual monitors by concentrating on a small number of what are perceived to be core sources. Core sources vary between professional groups, but usually include both key personal contacts and publications. For example, social scientists and physicists were found to track developments through core journals, on-line search updates, newspapers, conferences, magazines, books, catalogs, and so on (Ellis et al. 1993). *Extracting* is the activity of systematically working through a particular source or sources in order to identify material of interest. As a form of retrospective searching, extracting may be achieved by directly consulting the source, or by indirectly looking through bibliographies, indexes, or online data-bases. Retrospective searching tends to be labor intensive, and is more likely when there is a need for comprehensive or historical information on a topic. For some groups or in some situations, the accuracy of the information is critical, and requires the activity of *Checking* for correctness or absence of obvious errors. Ellis found that the majority of the chemists he studied attempted to verify all their information, especially sources perceived to be unreliable (Ellis et al. 1993). Finally, Ellis observed that a small number of the chemists performed the bulk of their searching at the end rather than a the beginning of a project. Thus, some would return to the literature again at the writing up stage, when they needed to relate their findings to other published work. Ellis named this activity *Ending.*

Although the Ellis model is based on studies of academicians and researchers, susbsets of the categories of information-seeking behaviors may be applicable to other groups of users as well. For example, Sutton's (1994) analysis of the information-seeking behavior of attorneys noted that the three stages of legal research he identified (base-level modeling, context-sensitive exploration, and disambiguating the space) could be mapped into Ellis's categories of starting, chaining, and differentiating. The identification of categories of information-seeking behavior also suggests that information retrieval systems could increase their usefulness by including features that directly support these activities. Ellis thought that hypertext-based systems would have the capabilities to implement these functions (Ellis 1989a,b). If we visualize the World Wide Web as a hyperlinked information system distributed over numerous networks, most of the information-seeking behavior categories in Ellis' model are already being supported by capabilities available in common web browser software. Thus a user could use the browser to reach a search engine to locate sources of interest (starting); follow hypertextual links to related information resources—in both backward and forward linking directions (chaining); scan the web pages of the sources selected (browsing); bookmark useful sources for future reference and visits (differentiating); subscribe to e-mail-based services that alert the user of new information or developments (monitoring); and search a particular source or site for all information on that site on a particular topic (extracting).

Information Use

Perhaps because it is so much a subconscious part of everyday experience, information use as a concept has been difficult to define satisfactorily. To develop our model, we regard information use pragmatically as the individual making a choice or selection of messages from a larger pool of messages to attend to or to act on (Taylor 1986). Presumably this choice is based on the individual perceiving some meaningful relation between the message content and the task or problem at hand. A discussion of this "meaningful relation" is outside the scope of this book, but this relation is perceived and determined by the individual, based on factors such as the content and form of the message, and the individual's knowledge and frame of reference. The outcome of information use is a change in the individual's state of knowledge or capacity to act. Thus, information use typically involves the selection and processing of information in order to answer a question, solve a problem, make a decision, negotiate a position, or understand a situation.

Whether a chunk of information is selected or ignored depends to a large extent on the perceived *relevance* of the information encountered to the question being pursued and to the problem situation in which that question is enveloped. Information relevance is generally believed to be a good predictor of information use, and the relationship between relevance and use has been explored in different ways, from both a system perspective and a user perspective. The system view is based on the assumption that the content of a document or information item may be represented objectively and that this representation may then be matched with a query. Thus a document is said to be relevant to a query when it is objectively judged to be so by a consensus of those practicing in a field (Harter 1986). The system view leads to the practical application that an information retrieval system could be designed to compute the amount of match between terms in a user's query and terms from a document in order to measure the degree that the document is "about" the topic of the query. The difficulty here is that any single representation of a document or query conveys different content and meaning to different people. In contrast to the system view, the user-centered view sees relevance not as an objective, inherent property of the information item, but as a relationship between information and query that is constructed or determined by the user. From a human judgment perspective then, relevance is assumed to be:

- Subjective, depending on human judgment and thus not an inherent characteristic of information or a document
- Cognitive, depending ultimately on human knowledge and perceptions
- Situational, relating to individual users' information problems
- Multidimensional, influenced by many factors
- Dynamic, constantly changing over time
- Measurable, observable at a single location in time

(Schamber 1994; Harter 1992; Saracevic 1970, 1975)

To distinguish the user view, some authors have suggested the term *pertinence* to indicate the ability of an information item to go beyond "topic relatedness" to satisfying some personal, visceral need of the individual. (See our earlier discussion of Taylor's levels of information needs.) Pertinence goes deeper than relevance by connecting with personal cognitive and affective needs, and by addressing particular demands of the situation in which the information need arises.

Taylor (1991) proposes a taxonomy of eight classes of information uses, generated by the information need perceived by users in particular situations, and derived in part from the classification scheme developed by Dervin (1983) which was reviewed earlier. The categories are not mutually exclusive, so that information used in one class may also address the needs of other classes.

1. *Enlightenment:* Information is used to develop a context or to make sense of a situation. Information is used to answer questions such as: "Are there similar situations? What are they? What is the history and experience of corporation X in making product Y, and how is this relevant to our intent to manufacture Y?"

2. *Problem Understanding:* Information is used in a more specific way than enlightenment—it is used to develop a better comprehension of a particular problem.

3. *Instrumental:* Information is used so that the individual knows what to do and how to do something. Instructions are a common form of instrumental information. Under some conditions, instrumental information use requires information use in other classes.

4. *Factual:* Information is used to determine the facts of a phenomenon or event, to describe reality. Factual information use is likely to depend on the actual and perceived quality (accuracy, reliability) of the information that is available.

5. *Confirmational:* Information is used to verify another piece of information. Confirmational information use often involves the seeking of a second opinion. If the new opinion does not confirm existing information, then the user may try to reinterpret the information or choose between sources to trust.

6. *Projective:* Information is used to predict what is likely to happen in the future. Projective information use is typically concerned with forecasts, estimates, and probabilities.

7. *Motivational:* Information is used to initiate or sustain personal involvement, in order to keep moving along on a particular course of action.

8. *Personal or Political:* Information is used to develop relationships; enhance status, reputation, personal fulfillment. Dervin (1983b, 62) associates this information use with phrases such as "Got control," "Got out of a bad situation," and "Got connected to others."

(Adapted from Taylor 1991, 230)

Among the most important elements influencing information use are the individual's attitudes toward information and information seeking, which are the results of education, training, past experience, personal preferences, and so on. The risk here is adopting an oversimplified assumption of the information user as either wanting to extract specific, definitive information in the minimum time, or willing to invest the effort to browse and explore. The truth is more likely to be that people vacillate continuously between extracting and exploring, and that information use is a messy, disorderly process subject as much to the vagaries of human nature as any other human activity:

> Humans are, by their nature, contradictory: drawn to make quick decisions that reduce uncertainty but struggling to understand clearly enough to make a good decision; striving for order, but enjoying the intellectual challenge of disorderly facts and unconventional ideas; needing the familiar, but craving the risk of the unknown; unable to express what is needed, but nonetheless perpetually asking questions; highly knowledgeable but unable to transfer that knowledge. This is the user whom we wish to serve. (Morris 1994, 29)

V. A GENERAL MODEL OF INFORMATION USE

Over the last two sections we presented the stages of information seeking and the various elements that establish the context of information use. Together they provide a palette for sketching a general model of how individuals need, seek, and use information. Figure 2–2 shows that cycles of information seeking and use are embedded in an information processing environment composed of the individual's internal cognitive structures and emotional dispositions, and a larger information use environment determined by the conditions of the work or social setting in which the information use takes place.

The model highlights three important properties of human information seeking and use. First, *information use is constructed,* for it is the individual who breathes meaning and energy into bloodless information. The way that information is given form and purpose depends on both the cognitive and the affective structures of the individual. Cognitively, the individual frames a problem situation by specifying boundaries, goals, means, events, objects, relationships, and so on, in order to delineate an information space in which to search and act. Affectively, emotions alert the individual to mark certain cues and signals as being especially important, and to prefer or select certain sources, messages, and information-seeking tactics based on feelings that are the result of past experience with similar sources and methods. Second, *information use is situational.* The individual's belonging to a work or social group, the structure of the typical problems faced by the group, the setting in which the groups work or live, and the modes of defining problem resolution all combine to establish a context for information use. The context defines norms, conventions, and practices that constitute the information behaviors through which information becomes useful. Thus norms and expectations are transmitted about the traits and attributes of the kinds of information that would be required. Assumptions are shared about how and when a problem is considered to be resolved. Information seeking may be limited by constraints imposed by the amount of available time and resources, and by the degree of access to required information and advice. Third, *information use is dynamic,* in two complementary senses. Information needs, seeking, and use proceed in repeated, recursive cycles that interact in no predetermined order, so that outwardly, the process often appears chaotic and meandering. Information seeking and use is also dynamic in the manner that it interacts with the cognitive, affective, and situational elements that compose its environment. These elements continuously animate the information seeking process by altering the individual's perception of appropriate information roles and behaviors, and by varying the criteria by which information value is to be judged. At the same time, the information use context is constantly being reshaped by the effects of the individual's action and sense making that are the outcomes of information use. In this section we elaborate on the structure and dynamics of information seeking and use suggested by our general model.

As shown in Fig. 2–2, *information needs* may be analyzed in terms of their cognitive, affective, and situational elements. Information needs percolate through several levels of an individual's consciousness, from the visceral through the conscious to the formal. It may begin with the individual experiencing a vague sense of unease about the state of her knowledge or understanding about the situation she is in. This visceral need is progressively clarified through conversations with others, observation, and reflection until the individual is able to express the information need in the form of a narrative or a number of rambling statements. Taylor (1968) calls this the user's conscious need, which is given substance and form when it is cast into a formal question or topic that could adequately represent the information need, and that could then be presented to an information system. Cognitively, Dervin (1992) uses the metaphor of a person making the journey through life being stopped in gap situations when the ability to make sense has run out. An analysis of the gap situation provides a rich representation of the individual's information needs. Dervin identifies a number of generic information gaps such as decision stops (the person faces two or more roads ahead), barrier stops (one road ahead but the way is blocked), and spin-out stops (no road ahead). People who perceive themselves as being in these situation gaps will ask questions in their attempts to bridge the gap. The perception of the information gap in turn depends on the work and social setting of the individual. Important features of the information work setting that might influence gap perception include variables such as membership in a particular community or profession, and the classes of problems that are typical of the social group or occupation. Problems may be characterized by dimensions that reflect both their subject-related needs and situation-related demands. For example, they may be well or ill structured, simple or complex, familiar or new; their assumptions may or may not be agreed upon; their goals may be specific or amorphous (MacMullin and Taylor 1984). Thus well-structured problems require formal, quantitative data, whereas ill-structured problems need information on how to interpret or proceed. Again, problems with specific goals require information that operationalizes or measures the goals, while problems with amorphous goals would first need information to clarify preferences and directions. In terms of affective responses, the recognition, clarification, and elaboration of information needs is a stage during which the individual experiences high levels of uncertainty accompanied by feelings of anxiety, doubt, and confusion. This is particularly evident when the need is first felt at the visceral level. The nature and the intensity of these affective responses are likely to influence the individual's choice of which vague notions of an area of interest are to be addressed as personalized concerns. Kuhlthau (1993b) suggests that the concept of information need may be expanded to include "vague notions, hunches, and hints of interest" (p. 161). Information systems and services may thus be designed to assist users to clarify and explore their concerns and interests during the early stages of the information search process.

Information seeking is the next conceptual stage of the model that becomes important after the individual has developed a sufficiently clear understanding of the information need, and is able, for example, to articulate the need as questions or topics that can guide information search. Information seeking thus concentrates on the behaviors of individuals as they actively search for information. Ellis et al. (1993), for example, categorizes information-seeking activities into starting, chaining, browsing, differentiating, monitoring, extracting, checking, and ending. The framework in Fig. 2–2 again suggests that information seeking is influenced by cognitive, affective, and situational requirements. Characteristics of the work or social setting of the individual can induce or constrain certain patterns of information-seeking behaviors. The culture and structure of the organization or work group will affect the individual's attitudes toward information and information gathering. Thus starting or the identification of sources is likely to be constrained by the accessibility to information sources, and the flow of information in the organization. Browsing depends on the amount of time available in the work process for information scanning, and on whether the successful completion of a task requires a thorough search of potential sources. Differentiating between sources again is a function of whether the organization values or is indifferent to the use of high-quality information and reliable sources. Monitoring and extracting vary according to the demands of the task or the task domain, and again require the availability of tools or services that support these activities. Generally the attitudes toward information, the information demands of the task domain, and the access to sources, tools, and services are dimensions of the work setting that could significantly influence information seeking. From the cognitive perspective, Dervin (1992) sees information seeking as human attempts to bridge information gaps. According to her sense making theory, the ways in which people perceive and define their cognitive gaps (as, for exam-

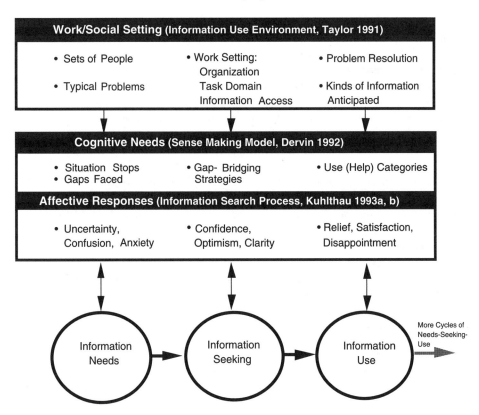

FIGURE 2-2. General model of information use

ple, decision stops, barrier stops, spin-out stops) are good predictors of the ways in which they try to bridge them, that is, the way they seek information to fill the information need. The kinds of questions that people then ask in their gap-bridging attempts may be categorized according to questions about "characteristics of self, characteristics of others, characteristics of objects or events, the reasons or causes of events, the consequences of actions or events, and the connections between things" (Dervin 1992, 75). In terms of affective responses, Kuhlthau (1993b) describes how uncertainty rises and then falls in the course of information search, and how initial feelings of anxiety and confusion could be replaced by feelings of increased confidence as the search progresses. A corollary of the uncertainty principle is that people should embark on a search only after they have formulated a sufficiently clear focus, guiding idea, or point of view that could guide the search. The individual's mood toward the search may also influence the breadth and depth of the information seeking—a person in an invitational mood would explore more sources while a person in an indicative mood would seek information that leads to closure or action. The individual may be affected by the amount and uniqueness of information found. She may be bored by too much redundant information, but become confused and anxious by too much unique information. If the information found enables the individual to see the problem more clearly and to develop a sense of direction, she will experience increased optimism and confidence as the search progresses.

Information use is the final stage of the model when the individual acts on the information selected during the search to, for example, answer a question, resolve a problem, make a decision, negotiate a position, or make sense of a situation. The outcome of information use is therefore a change in the individual's state of knowledge and capacity to act. As we have noted, information use is continuous and recursive throughout the information-seeking process. During the information needs stage, the development and clarification of needs are manifestly information use; and again during the information-seeking stage, movement between sources and selection of information both take into account the information encountered thus far in the search. Most cases of search come to some form of closure when active information seeking stops or falls to a low level, and when the individual perceives that there is sufficient information for action or sense making. Whether information encountered is actually used depends on the individual's personal assessment of the cognitive and affective relevance of the information received as well as on the non-subject-related attributes of the information that would determine its pertinence to the requirements of a particular problem situation. Individuals are more likely to use information that confirms or supports their existing cognitive structures. When they confront information that contradicts their existing beliefs and assumptions, they experience a sense of conflict or tension. People reduce or relieve this *cognitive dissonance* (Festinger 1957) by one of several defensive maneuvers, such as avoiding the new information, rejecting its validity, explaining away the differences, reconstructing new cognitive structures, and so on. Taylor (1991) emphasized that different sets of people have developed different notions of what constitutes the *resolution of a problem,* and that these norms will influence their patterns of information use. Scientists reporting research results, for example, build upon retrospective information about past related work, and have to show that they have collected and analyzed data according to accepted rules and standards of objectivity. On the other hand, most managers deal with problems by making do with incomplete information, filling in gaps with their own intuition and judgment, and settling on solutions that are less than optimal but good enough to keep the work activity moving ahead. Norms and conventions about practices that lead to acceptable problem resolution are developed through education and training, professional preparation, and experience from working in a task domain. Taylor (1991) also categorized eight classes of information use: enlightenment, problem understanding, instrumental, factual, confirmational, projective, motivational, and personal or political. The particular mode of information use depends on the social and physical attributes that specify the information use environment, attributes such as the familiarity of the situation, the amount of time available to deal with the problem, and the interests of stakeholders. From the cognitive perspective, Dervin (1992) views people as using information to bridge their cognitive gaps in order to cross to the other side and continue on their life journeys. Information use is seen in the ways in which people put answers to use, and this depends on the ways that people want the information to help. Based on her field work, Dervin classified *help categories* into "creating ideas, finding directions or ways to move, acquiring skills, getting support or confirmation, getting motivated, getting connected to others, calming down or relaxing, getting pleasure or happiness, and reaching goals." (Dervin 1992, 75). In terms of affective responses, what the individual experiences during the use stage depends on the perceived quality of the search process and outcomes (Kuhlthau 1993b). If the search is thought to have been successful, the individual may feel a sense of satisfaction and pride in now being able to base actions or decisions on sufficient reliable information. Conversely, if the search had been truncated or compromised in some way, the individual may experience disappointment, frustration, and diffidence. The individual may take a negative emotional response as a signal to avoid acting on the information or to attempt expanding or repeating the search.

VI. SUMMARY

The general model of information use presented in this chapter is an attempt at identifying and relating the major elements that influence the behavior of the individual when seeking and using information. The model is based on a number of guiding ideas. Information needs arise when the individual recognizes gaps in his or her state of knowledge and ability to make sense of an experience. Information seeking is the process in which the individual then purposefully searches for information that can change his or her state of knowledge. Information use occurs when the individual selects and processes information or messages, which leads to a change in the individual's capacity to make sense of the experience and to act or respond in the light of that new understanding. Information seeking and use is part of a larger human and social activity through which information becomes useful to an individual or group. Information seeking and use is situated action, so that the way the process develops depends on changing conditions in the individual's context of information use, and this in turn depends on the changes in the context induced by the individual's actions. Although information seeking and use is a dynamic, nonlinear process that often appears disorderly, the model suggests that there is underlying structure in the ways people look for and use information. The model provides a framework for analysis by conceptually partitioning the information use process into three stages: information needs, information seeking, and information use. Within each stage, the model examines the effects of the individual's cognitive needs, affective responses, and situational demands.

Information needs do not emerge fully formed but are clarified and defined over a period of time. Information needs are first felt at the visceral level as a vague sense of unease and uncertainty. The feeling of uncertainty diminishes as the information need progressively takes shape as conscious and then formalized questions or topics. The nature of information needs depends on the perception of the cognitive gap in which the individual's ability to make sense of her situation has run out. The model identifies categories of these situation gaps and they have been found to be important predictors of how individuals then seek and use information to bridge the gaps. The information required also depends on the norms and expectations of the group or community the individual belongs to, and the dimensions of the typical kinds of problems faced by them.

Information seeking is analyzed in the model as eight categories of generic information-seeking behaviors: starting, chaining, browsing, differentiating, monitoring, extracting, verifying, and ending. The activities of starting, chaining, and browsing are important in assisting the individual to develop a focus to guide the search and a strategy for executing the search. The development of a focused strategy increases the individual's feeling of confidence and control. The amount of browsing, differentiating and monitoring of information and sources is influenced by properties of the individual's work or social setting, including the structure and culture of the organization, and the availability or access to information. Information that is extracted typically answers questions about the characteristics of and relationships between persons, objects, and events; as well as the consequences of and reasons for actions or events.

Information use is the selection and processing of information resulting in new knowledge or action. Information is often regarded as being used to answer a question, resolve a problem, make a decision, negotiate a position, or make sense of a situation. What constitutes the resolution of a problem depends on the expectations developed by sets of people as a result of their education, professional training, and cultural background. The model identifies eight classes of information use: enlightenment, problem understanding, instrumental, factual, confirmational, projective, motivational, and personal or political. In the gap-bridging/sense making metaphor, information use is seen as the way that the individual wants information to help in order to allow her to continue on her life journey. The individual feels satisfaction and confidence when the search has been successful in producing usable information, and disappointment or frustration otherwise.

The model developed in this chapter examines information seeking and use at the level of the individual. The next three chapters of the book will investigate how organizations, as social systems of people, structures, and processes, use information to make sense of the environment, create new knowledge for learning and innovation, and make decisions that enable action. We will adopt the general model of information use presented in this chapter as a framework for analyzing information processes in organizations. Our goal is to give face and voice to the many roles that information plays on the organizational stage.

3

THE MANAGEMENT OF

AMBIGUITY—

ORGANIZATIONS AS

SENSE-MAKING COMMUNITIES

. . . man is an animal suspended in webs of significance he himself has spun.
   —*Clifford Geertz 1973, The Interpretation of Cultures, p. 5*

If you want to know the taste of a pear, you must change the pear by eating it yourself. . . . All genuine knowledge originates in direct experience.
   —*Mao Zedong 1937, speech given in Yenan, China, July 1937*

Many people believe that some of the world's best wines are produced in France. Any firm aspiring to become a significant player in the world wine market must consider on what grounds it wishes to be compared with the established cachet of the French wine producers. The anthropologist Mary Douglas provides an interesting account of how the California wineries effectively reinvented the market environment by creating their own classification system, which in turn defined how the Californian wine producers were to make sense of their businesses. Historically, French wine producers have developed a classification system based on geography, with each geographical location maintaining a tradition for a certain quality of wine. For example, within the Bordeaux region are the smaller regions of Médoc, St. Emilion, Graves, Côtes; and within these are the individual chateaux. Médoc uses a classification system derived from the average price fetched by its wine over the one hundred years preceding 1855, and it was this classification that selected the best land for vineyards. The classification divides quality into several levels of a hierarchy: the first, second, third, and fourth growths at the top, the *Cru Bourgeois* at the bottom, and lastly the unclassed growths. Somewhat differently in St. Emilion, quality is checked by a committee, which required that its most celebrated chateaux, the *Premiere Grands Crus,* requalify for their exalted positions every ten years, while lesser chateaux, the *Grands Crus,* had to submit each vintage for tasting. Each chateau therefore produced its own unique wine. By referencing the established labels of quality, "the chateau is not considered as a plot of land so much as a brand name of whose reputation the owner is extremely careful. . . . Naming the wine after the region and the chateau is to condense information that can only be unpacked by connoisseurship. The name encapsulates a tried process, a traditional blend of grapes, a soil, the slope of a valley, and a climate" (Douglas 1986, 105–6). The net result is that the regional classification system erected a monopolistic guild that protected the French wine producers. The chateau and regional names were the property rights of the French producers, and these names could not be transferred or shared by wine producers in California (Californian wines could only go as far as calling themselves Bordeaux type or Burgundy type.) However, the Californian wine producers elected not to pursue a "Napa Valley type," which would in any event have had a hard time in challenging the reputed French regions. Instead of a geographical classification, the Californian producers adopted a classification system that was based on the type of grape. As a result, each winery could and did produce a range of wine products using several varieties of grape. Douglas observed that among six well-known Napa County wineries, one (Hetz) used twelve kinds of grapes to produce twelve wines, another (Joseph Phelps) used eight grapes, two used five or six grapes, and the remaining two each used three. This diversification extends to methods of viticulture, treatment of the wine at various stages, and techniques of bottling or corking. By acting to implement their own classification, the Californian wine producers were making possible the strategy of diversification where "each winery is seeking a diverse range of specialized wines within a highly diversified market" (Douglas 1986, 108). The success of the Californian wine industry leads Douglas to observe wryly that publications like Hugh Johnson's popular *World Atlas of Wines,* which uses place for explaining French wines, is largely irrelevant to the Californian scene. Although she was writing about how institutions can impose their own classifications on people, Mary Douglas has also described an instance of how organizations can enact their external environment and in doing so, influence their own sense making and action making. Rather than passively treating the environment as a given text to be read and interpreted, enacting organizations make sense of the environment by creating or reconfiguring parts of it.

Today's organizations have their eyes fixed perpetually on the horizon, watching markets shift from day to day, firms jostle with one another for position, technological innovations open up new terrain, and government policies fold and refold boundaries. More than ever, organizations are keenly aware that their ability to survive and evolve is determined by their capacity to make sense of or influence their environments and to constantly renew meaning and purpose in the light of new conditions. Adaptability in a dynamic environment presents a twofold challenge, for it requires organizations to be skilled at both sensing and making sense. Sensing, or noticing potentially important messages in the environment, is problematic because the organization is simultaneously immersed in multiple streams of interaction with many different parts of the environment, and because almost every part of the environment is interconnected with other parts in complex and unpredictable ways. Organizations scan the environment broadly in order to have sufficient information to recognize trends and developments that will impact the organization, and to identify significant issues that need to be analyzed further. A detailed analysis of the theory and practice of how organizations scan the environment concluded that scanning can be made more effective if it is systematic, thorough, participatory, and integrative (Choo 1995a). The core process of scanning is information management—casting a wide information net by involving as many participants as possible to act as sensors, and systematically processing and integrating the gathered information into a usable knowledge base.

Making sense, or constructing meaning from what has been sensed about the environment, is problematic because the information about the environment is ambivalent, and therefore subject to multiple interpretations. Selecting an appropriate interpretation is hard because each person sees different parts of the environment as interesting, depending on the individual's values, history, and experience. Whereas sensing or scanning is gathering sufficient information to reduce environmental uncertainty, sense making involves choosing and agreeing on a set of meanings or interpretations to reduce ambiguity in environmental cues. Unlike scanning, which can be designed as a systematic and structured activity, sense making is inherently a fluid, open, disorderly, social process. The basic mode of sensemaking is discourse, for it is through talk that organizational members find out what all others think, and it is through talk that people persuade, negotiate, and reshape their points of view. Sense making is further complicated by the possibility that the organization can or wishes to intrude actively into the environment (as in the example of the Californian wineries) in order to produce, influence, or modify parts of it. In a manner of speaking, the organization that enacts its environment is involved in giving rather than making sense, although the modified elements become absorbed into the overall environment that the organization then needs to comprehend and respond to.

Organizational sense making has been defined in various ways by different researchers. March and Olsen (1976) saw sense making as part of experiential learning in which "individuals and organizations make sense of their experience and modify behavior in terms of their interpretations" 56). Starbuck and Milliken (1988b) observed that "sensemaking has many distinct aspects—comprehending, understanding, explaining, attributing, extrapolating, and predicting, at least. . . . What is common to these processes is that they involve placing stimuli into frameworks (or schemata) that make sense of the stimuli" (p. 51). Sense making is sometimes thought of as belonging to a larger process of organizational adaptation that also includes scanning the environment, interpreting, and developing responses. In this vein, Thomas, Clark, and Gioia (1993) write that sense making "involves the reciprocal interaction of information seeking, meaning ascription, and action" and that "each element of this sense making process is presumed to have some relationship to performance" (p. 240).

This chapter is divided into four sections. Section I explores the nature of organizational sense making, identifying the properties that distinguish sense making as a unique process. Section II describes the belief- and action-driven processes that result in sense making as well as the interlocking behaviors of enactment, selection, and retention that form the sense making recipe. Section III discusses the cognitive, cultural, and communication strategies that create shared meaning and consensus in organizations so that collective action is possible and purposeful. Section IV focuses on how information is acquired, processed, and used in sense making in terms of cognitive, affective, and situational variables.

I. THE NATURE OF ORGANIZATIONAL SENSEMAKING

Drawing together the various discussions of sense making in the research literature, Weick (1995) identifies seven distinguishing properties of sense making as an organizational process. In his view, sense making is understood as a process that is:

1. Grounded in identity construction

2. Retrospective

3. Enactive of sensible environments

4. Social

5. Ongoing

6. Focused on and by extracted cues

7. Driven by plausibility rather than accuracy

(Weick 1995, 17)

We now paraphrase Weick's explanations of each of these properties.

Sense making is grounded in identity construction. Sense making is necessary for the individual to maintain a consistent self-conception and is often initiated when the individual fails to confirm self-identity. The environment is like a mirror into which people project themselves and observe the consequences in order to learn about their identities. This projection is not one-way nor passive, for people simultaneously try to shape and react to the environments they face—even as they deduce their identity from the behavior of others toward them, they also try to influence this behavior. Thus what the situation means is determined by the identity that the individual adopts in dealing with it.

Sense making is retrospective. The sense making individual attends to events that have already taken place. She does so from a specific point in time, so that what is occurring at that moment will affect what she is likely to notice as she casts this backward glance. Furthermore, because the event has already elapsed, the individual has to rely on a memory trace of the event, which may or may not be accurate. In retrospective sense making, the main problem is to select a plausible meaning from several alternative meanings in order to make sense of past events. For this, the individual needs values and priorities to clarify what is important and therefore meaningful in the elapsed experience.

Sense making is enactive. In sense making, people in organizations often produce part of the environment that they face. Weick calls this process enactment. One way people enact is by breaking up streams of experience into packets which they then label with categories. By bracketing experience, people endow objects and events with cognitive value in their minds, thus providing the raw material for sense making. Another way that organizations enact is to undertake actions that actually result in physical or structural changes in the environment that they are relating to, as in the case of the Californian wineries. Enactment implies that action is a precondition for sense making as, for example, "when the action of saying makes it possible for people to then see what they think" (Weick 1995, 30).

Sense making is social. All sense making is done in social groups of more than one individual. Even when a person appears to be alone, his sense making will take into account the reactions of others not physically present, but who will be affected or whose reactions will be important. More often than not, sense making occurs in groups of people engaged in talk, discourse, and conversation, which become the media for social construction.

Sense making is ongoing. Sense making never starts or stops, but is continuous in the flow of activities and projects that constitute organizational life. From this continuous stream, people isolate packets of experience for labeling and reflection, and the way they do this selection is based on the perceived salience induced by the particular activities or projects they are working on at the time. Although sense making does not stop, it can be interrupted. Interruptions invoke emotional responses, which then influence the sense making process (see section IV).

Sense making is focused on and by extracted cues. Extracted cues are "simple, familiar structures that are seeds from which people develop a larger sense of what may be occurring." (Weick 1995, 50). They provide points of reference or starting nodes from which ideas may be linked and connected into networks of meaning. The extraction of cues is the result of scanning, searching, or noticing. The interpretation of cues depends on the organizational context—a context that can bind people to actions, determine the relevance of information, and impose norms and expectations on what explanations are acceptable (Salancik and Pfeffer 1978).

Sense making is driven by plausibility rather than accuracy. People behave pragmatically when sense making, favoring plausibility over accuracy when they construct accounts of what is going on. The reason is that "in an equivocal, postmodern world, infused with the politics of interpretation and conflicting interests and inhabited by people with multiple shifting identities, an obsession with accuracy seems fruitless, and not of much practical help, either" (Weick 1995, 61). Besides, whenever organizational action is time constrained, managers would tend to trade off accuracy for speed.

As a terse summary, one may say that sense making is a continuous, social process in which individuals look at elapsed events, bracket packets of experience, and select particular points of reference to weave webs of meaning. The result of sense making is an enacted or meaningful environment, which is a reasonable and socially credible rendering of what is taking place. The central problem in sense making is how to reduce or resolve ambiguity, and how to develop shared meanings so that the organization may act collectively.

There are general similarities between the organizational sense making described here and the sense making metaphor of Brenda Dervin that we discussed in the last chapter. Dervin (1992) sees the individual as continually making sense as she moves through time and space in an ongoing life journey. From time to time, movement is blocked by a gap in the path she is traveling on when she is temporarily unable to make sense of her situation. Information is then sought and processed in a manner that is influenced by her perception of the gap and how she wants the information to help. Using the organizational sense making language, we may say that in Dervin's model, the individual encounters a break or gap in the flow of organizational experience which requires new sense to be made. The individual then constructs new meaning by selecting from the information she has available; that the information selected depends on her enactment or perception of the cognitive gap; and this is in turn influenced by her retrospective recall of past experience and by the particular conditions, or extracted cues that define the current gap. In Dervin's model that information use is pragmatic where the ability to continue on the journey is often sufficient or even more important than securing the most accurate information.

Over a period of three years, Isenberg (1984, 1986a, 1987) studied the thinking processes of managers by analyzing data from many sources: managers' think-aloud protocols collected while they were at work, managers' and students' think-aloud protocols in solving a business case, in-depth interviews with managers, and on-the-job observations. Eighteen senior managers, including three chief executives and thirteen divisional general managers from ten corporations, were studied in depth, with an additional number of senior managers participating in the interviews only. Overall, the studies led Isenberg (1986a,b) to conclude that managers develop plausible, as opposed to necessarily accurate, models of their situations, and that managers develop and efficiently use knowledge structures that guide how they recognize, explain, and plan. *Plausible reasoning* is a central thinking process for managers because they function in an environment of continuous change and uncertainty, and they are often required to act in order to ensure the ongoing viability of the organization. Isenberg gives an instance from his field observations:

For example, one general manager received a phone message from a product expediter in a sister division that purchased products from the general manager's
own division. The general manager surmised that the expediter could have been
calling for one of two reasons: to say something about either price or delivery
time on a specific production run. The surmise was based on previous experience with the particular expediter, knowledge that the run was late, and the general manager's impression that he had never interacted with the expediter around
any other issue. Before returning the call, the general manager walked by his
marketing manager's office and asked a marketing person why he thought the expediter called. He received the answer "price." The general manager then returned the call. Note that the reasoning process rapidly limited the number of
hypotheses for the general manager to test and that although the answer constituted a weak test of his hypothesis, the answer considerably increased the manager's certainty with minimal effort and minimal risk. The increase in certainty
was enough for him to go back and return the phone call with an idea already
developed for how to discuss price with the expediter. It is this latter point that
is the critical one: plausible reasoning helps the manager increase his or her certainty to the point of feasible action. (Isenberg 1986a, 247)

Again, there are close similarities between the enactment process and the
model of plausible reasoning developed by Isenberg (1986a,b). Like Weick,
Isenberg emphasizes that managerial thinking and action are not separate or
sequential activities. Rather than thinking first before doing, many managers
think *while* doing, so that thinking is inextricably tied to action in what Isenberg has called *"thinking/acting cycles"* (Isenberg 1984). This allows managers
to act when information or understanding is incomplete, and furthermore, by
reflecting on the results of their action, managers can often derive new insight
and reduce uncertainty. Based on his field studies, Isenberg conceptualized the
plausible reasoning process used by managers in planning and implementing
action as a sequence of four steps:

1. The manager needs to develop a different understanding of a phenomenon, often due to an experience of surprise.

2. The manager tries to take advantage of the data he or she already has
   in order to speculate about the new situation. Each speculation is tested
   against data and assumptions that already exist, and the search for new
   data at this point is confined to search in long-term memory.

3. A very selective external search for information is engaged in, particularly in order to confirm one or more of the speculations, although
   disconfirmation may also occur. The goal of the search at this point is
   to achieve a degree of certainty that will allow the manager to proceed
   to step 4 at minimal cost and minimal risk.

4. The manager engages in action in the face of incomplete but tentative
   understanding of the situation and uses the feedback of his or her actions to complete the understanding.

(Isenberg 1986a, 247–48)

As we shall see, these steps fit well with the enactment–selection framework proposed by Weick, which we introduce next.

II. ORGANIZATIONAL PROCESSES OF SENSE MAKING

In this section we describe the processes by which organizations make sense of their environments, their identities, and their actions. We begin with a discussion of the enactment process by which people in organizations bracket experience, select meanings, and retain sensible interpretations. We then illustrate the enactment process with a case study of the Scottish knitwear industry. The ensuing subsections discuss two other sets of organizational sense making processes that are complementary—belief-driven processes and action-driven processes.

The Enactment Process

Weick (1979b) encapsulates the main sense making recipe in this question: "How can I know what I think until I see what I say?" (The quote is from Graham Wallas' *The Art of Thought,* in which the author wrote "The little girl had the making of a poet in her who, being told to be sure of her meaning before she spoke, said: 'How can I know what I think till I see what I say?' " [Wallas 1926, 106]). The recipe suggests that people in organizations are continually engaged in talk in order to find out what they are thinking and to construct interpretations of what they are doing. The recipe is executed in connected sequences of enactment→selection→retention (ESR). We briefly introduced these processes in chapter 1, but because they constitute the main routines of sense making, we elaborate here on how they work and illustrate them with an example. We unpack each process by examining its inputs, transformation processes, and outputs (Table 3–1).

Enactment is the process by which individuals in an organization actively create the environments that they face, and which they then attend to. The enactment process begins as a result of noticing some change or discrepancies in the flow of experience. (Weick [1979b] included another process that precedes enactment called "ecological change," which refers to breaks or changes in the flow of experience that provide the occasion for sense making.) Raw data about these environmental changes form the input to the process. Individuals isolate some of these changes for closer attention by bracketing and labeling portions of the experience, or by taking some action to create features of the environment to attend to. In this way, "managers construct, rearrange, single out, and demolish many 'objective' features of their surroundings. .. people, often alone, actively *put* things out there that they then perceive and nego-

TABLE 3–1. The sense making recipe.

	Inputs	*Processes*	*Outputs*
Enactment	Raw data from the environment	• Bracket raw data • Act or create features of the environment to attend to	Equivocal data as raw data for sense making
Selection	• Equivocal data from enactment process • Enacted interpretations that worked before	Select and impose meanings or interpretations on equivocal data	Enacted or meaningful environment
Retention	Enacted environment from selection process	Storage of enacted environment as product of successful sense making	Enacted interpretations for use in future ESR sequences

tiate about perceiving. It is that initial implanting of reality that is preserved by the word *enactment.*" (Weick 1979b, 164–65, italics in original). The output of enactment is a set of equivocal, uninterpreted raw data, which supply the base material for the other sense making processes.

Selection is the process by which people in an organization generate answers to the queston, "What's going on here?" (Weick 1979). What the selection process chooses are the meanings that can be imposed on the equivocal data from the enactment process. Possible meanings come from meanings and interpretations that have proven sensible in the past, as well as from "patterns implicit in the enactments themselves" (Weick 1979, 175). Past interpretations are used as templates that are laid over current data in order to reveal plausible configurations. Selection, based on an assessment of the degree of fit, is necessary because many of the possible meanings would be inapplicable or inconsistent with the current data. The result of the selection process is an enacted environment that is meaningful in that it provides a cause-and-effect explanation of what is taking place.

Retention is the process by which the products of successful sense making, that is, enacted or meaningful environments, are stored so that they may be retrieved on future occasions as possible meanings to be imposed on new equivocal situations. Retained meanings are stored as enacted environments that are "a punctuated and connected summary of a previously equivocal display" (Weick 1979b, 131), or as cause maps that identify and label variables, and connect the variables in causal relationships (p. 132).

We can now see how the sense making recipe of "how can I know what I think until I see what I say?" is mirrored in the enactment–selection–retention sequence. Enactment may be compared with "saying" or doing; selection with "seeing"; and retention with "thinking" or remembering. The three processes embrace each other in cycles, where feedback between processes amplify or attenuate the salience of changes observed in the external environment, and accelerate or constrain the movement of information cues that influence the choice of meaningful interpretations and the retention of enacted meanings.

Sense Making in the Scottish Knitwear Industry

In the mid-1980s Scottish knitwear manufacturers accounted for nearly half of total British exports in knitted outerwear, and enjoyed significantly higher profitability levels than other British knitwear producers (Baden-Fuller et al. 1987). The Scottish knitwear manufacturers included companies such as Ballantyne, Cooper & Rowe, Dalkeith/Jaeger, Lyle & Scott, and Pringle, which produced knitted outerwear under their own brand names using high-quality Scottish or cashmere yarn. They manufactured knitwear by combining various colored yarns into garments whose sizes and shapes were determined on the knitting machine. This labor-intensive technique produced "fully-fashioned" knitwear and was quite different from the "cut-and-sew" technique, which allowed larger scales of production but resulted in lower quality products and more unused yarn, so that it was unsuitable for the expensive cashmere material. The 1980s saw all the companies greatly extending their product ranges, with most producers manufacturing thousands of varieties of sweaters.

Although a few of the larger firms had small internal design departments, all the firms hired outside design consultants to help create new products. Independent agents who received commissions brokered the sale of the finished garments to retail stores all over the world. These agents were contractually barred from representing other competing brands of knitwear. Retail stores were typically large department stores and specialty boutiques which sold classic, expensive clothing to the carriage trade. Through extensive interviews with top managers from more than a third of the Scottish knitwear manufacturers located in the border region of Scotland, Porac, Thomas, and Baden-Fuller (1989) were able to uncover some core beliefs underlying the mental models used by the top managers to understand their firms' competitive environment. One set of beliefs concerned how the firms established their own distinctive *market identity,* another set determined how they dealt with other parties in the *transactional network* (the producers, agents, retailers, and consumers).

Making sense of market identity. Sense making was the process by which the firms studied, discovered or invented their self-identities, their collective identity, and the perceived identities of their customers and competitors. The firms defined their business as the production of top-quality cashmere pullover and cardigan sweaters, and perceived that their customers were individuals in the top 2–5 percent income bracket of any given country (Porac et al. 1989). Three managing directors expressed this belief thus (quoted in Porac et al. 1989, 406):

We're top-end. We're not interested in Marks & Spencer's or anybody other than the top 2 percent in any country.

If people are looking for knitwear, the top 5 percent, we are the segment they will look to.

We are in the market where customers imply want the best. Pure and simple. People must want the best.

This emphasis on exclusiveness and high quality also colors their perception of the competition (quoted in Porac et al. 1989, 407):

Quite honestly, there is not a lot of competition. The Italian industry is a different industry from ours. The Asian industry is a different industry from ours. . . . Basically it's pullovers and cardigans. It's classic type garments. In my opinion, it is quite clearly defined that people expect to buy the best cashmere pullovers from Scotland.

The majority of our competitors are either within our own group, or within our own town. . . . We don't try to be high fashion like the Italians. We call ourselves "classical elegance."

The collective market identity shared by the group of knitwear manufacturers was therefore based on the following core beliefs: that they made the best cashmere knitwear in the world, that their customers were high-income earners who bought premium quality, and that they had no significant competition from outside the group because of their unique capabilities. Their collective competitive strategy was to focus narrowly on a small segment of the market that wanted established quality and classical appeal. This strategy was evolved rather than the result of deliberate planning or detailed market research, as we shall see.

Enacting the transactional network. The transactional network consists of the producers, agents, retailers, and customers who make up the value chain of the knitwear business. The highly interdependent and mutually reinforcing relationships between these groups constrained the generation and flow of information as well as the exploration of meanings and choices. As a result, the transactional network also became an enactment network through which participants created and confirmed a shared interpretation of their competitive position. The Scottish knitwear producers secure contracts with retail shops through agents. Agents are selected because their non-knitwear-product representations fit in well with the "classical elegance" image that the Scottish manufacturers wish to project. Selected agents then negotiate with retail shops that sell classically designed clothing. These retail shops are in turn patronized by customers whose tastes are inclined toward traditional knitwear products. Notice how the participants in this transactional network preselect each other as compatible business partners, and by doing so mutully reinforce and sustain the collective belief that the Scottish knitwear manufacturers sell garments of classical elegance. The self-defining and self-reinforcing interactions of the network clearly illustrate the dynamics of the enactment–selection–retention sequence of the sense making recipe:

> The self-definition as a producer of "high quality fully-fashioned knitwear" leads to the selection of agents selling classically designed clothes, who are suppliers of shops merchandising classic garments to consumers with a limited range of preferences for "classical elegance." Market cues from consumers are filtered back through informal network channels and provide the Scottish firms with information primarily about preferences for variations on classically designed garments. Such filtered information is assimilated into the existing business definition, and focuses the attention of managers on a limited set of possible product offerings. In doing so, both the business definition and the competitive space it implies are reinforced, and the Scottish firms use their finite psychological and material resources to compete with each other in the fully-fashioned classic knitwear sector. (Porac et al. 1989, 409)

Enactment takes place as the producers, agents, retailers, and customers act and think together to bracket, label, and influence their environment and experience. Labels used to bracket salient experience included phrases used by the managers such as "friendly competition," "Scottish quality," "classical elegance," "crowd in Hong Kong that manufactures for Ralph Lauren," and so on. Enactment is ongoing as it feeds on filtered information generated by like-minded others in the transaction network. Selection takes place when the participants choose and maintain the interpretation that has been sensible for that industry for many years—that they are in the business of selling high-quality knitted outerwear to discerning high-income customers. Retention takes place as the participants continue to store, retrieve, and reapply interpretations that they have enacted to make sense of any changes in their business environment. For example, the Scottish manufacturers have historically used the traditional but labor-intensive methods of hand finishing, partly because they produced high-quality sweaters, but also because the manufacturers had available a pool of workers skilled in hand finishing. Unfortunately hand finishing was not as efficient as the more modern manufacturing techniques that were increasingly being adopted by many domestic and foreign competitors to produce lower cost garments. In deciding to continue with the use of the less-efficient method of hand finishing, the Scottish manufacturers were reselecting and retaining their enacted interpretation that they were producers of high-quality knitwear which was sold to customers wanting premium quality garments. The sense making cycle invoked here shows that enactment is the result of the simultaneous blending of action making and meaning making.

Belief- and Action-Driven Processes

The enactment–selection–retention sequence begins as a personal routine by which people in organizations create or isolate portions of their experience in order to construct meaning. Given that each individual sees different parts of the environment as interesting, and overlays different interpretations on these data, the question now is, how do people in organizational groups grow and link their thoughts and perceptions together so that some form of collective action is possible? Weick (1995) suggests that organizations achieve this through belief-driven processes and action-driven processes:

Sensemaking can begin with beliefs and take the form of arguing and expecting. Or sensemaking can begin with actions and take the form of committing or manipulating. In all four cases, people make do with whatever beliefs or actions they start with. Sensemaking is an effort to tie beliefs and actions more closely together as when arguments lead to consensus on action, clarified expectations pave the way for confirming actions, committed actions uncover acceptable justifications for their occurrence, or bold actions simplify the world and make it clearer what is going on and what it means. In each of these cases, sensemaking involves taking whatever is clearer, whether it be a belief or an action, and linking it with that which is less clear. These are fundamental operations of sensemaking. Two elements, a belief and an action, are related. The activities of relating are the sensemaking process. The outcome of such a process is a unit of meaning, two connected elements. And the connected elements are beliefs and actions tied together by socially acceptable implications. (Weick 1995, 135)

Belief-Driven Processes: Belief-driven processes are those in which groups of people spin webs of meaning around an initial set of sufficiently clear and plausible cues and predispositions by connecting more and more small pieces of information into larger structures of meaning (Table 3–2). When cues appear "similar" in their fit with each other and with existing frames of reference, the process is likely to be one based on "expecting." When cues and beliefs are contradictory, the process may be based on "arguing." *Arguing* is a process by which people move from one initial idea to the selection of another, through reasoned discourse that involves drawing inferences from existing beliefs, and justifying those inferences in the face of other competing claims (Brockeriede 1974). This process of developing, presenting, comparing, and evaluating explanations in a group often leads members to discover new explanations or to deepen their insights on existing ones. Arguing provides people with a socially acceptable procedure to debate the ambivalence and contradiction that is inherent in most issues. Arguing as reasoned debate does not imply flaring tempers and pounding fists, the occurrence of which would in fact undermine discussion. The most common forum for the work of arguing is in meetings. Schwartzman (1987, 1989) views meetings as "sense makers" that define and represent the social entities and relationships that establish meaning and identity for its participants. Arguing as sense making allows people in organizations to resolve or reduce ambiguity, discover new goals, enhance the quality of available information, and clarify new ideas.

Expecting is the other belief-driven process by which people in organizations apply beliefs as expectations to guide and constrain the selection of salient information and the choice of plausible interpretations. Whereas arguments typically are tentative proposals that need to be elaborated or tested with others, expectations are often more strongly held than arguments, and people tend to be more interested in confirming than in contradicting them. In many cases expectations can have a powerful effect on the way individuals filter information and interpretations, so much so that self-fulfilling prophecies become a fundamental act of sense making (Weick 1995). Initially, prophecies provide the minimal structures around which new information can coalesce. People then actively connect data with their prophecies based on the beliefs that they hold. In doing so, people tend to seek out confirmatory evidence, ignore or devalue contradictory news, and cling as far as possible onto their initial hypotheses. Expecting and expectations thus provide people with a sense of stability and social order, and with a set of cognitive structures within which they can find and construct meaning.

Action-Driven Processes: Action-driven processes are those in which groups of people grow webs of meaning around their actions, commitments or manipulations by creating or modifying cognitive structures that give significance to these behaviors (Table 3–2). Two kinds of action can drive sensemaking— "committing" actions for which a person or group is responsible, and "manipulating" actions taken by a person or group that make an actual change in the environment (Weick 1995). *Committing* becomes important if, in situations when behaviors and beliefs contradict each other, it is easier to change the beliefs than the behaviors. Behavior becomes binding and hard to change when the behavior is explicit (evidence exists that the act took place), public (witnesses saw the act), and irrevocable (act is irreversible) (Kiesler 1971). Furthermore, if the person was also seen to have performed the action deliber-

TABLE 3–2. Organizational sense making processes.

Belief-Driven Processes	**Arguing** Creating meaning by connecting the contradictory
	Expecting Creating meaning by connecting the similar
Action-Driven Processes	**Committing** Creating meaning to justify actions high in choice, visibility, and irrevocability
	Manipulating Creating meaning to explain actions taken to make things happen

ately, with substantial effort and few external demands, then the act occurred because the person chose to do it, and is therefore responsible for it. Commitments form a convenient framework for organizing information and perceptions. An instinctive reaction is to pigeonhole incoming information according to whether it supports the committed action, opposes it, or is irrelevant to it. In this way, committing influences sense making by directing attention, noticing new features, and selecting data.

Manipulating is the other action-driven process by which people in the organization take actions that lead to changes in the environment, which, in turn become some of the constraints for their own sense making. Common methods of manipulation include constructing desirable niches, negotiating domains, forming coalitions, educating clients and employees, advertising to potential clients and customers, and resolving conflicts (Hedberg, Nystrom, and Starbuck 1976). Manipulating brings clarity to sense making, since by making things happen, people can latch onto these created events and explain them as a way to make better sense of what is taking place. Whereas committing makes new sense by justifying the action itself, manipulating does the same by explaining the meanings of the consequences of the action taken.

The belief- and action-driven processes of sense making are compared in Table 3–2. Arguing is a belief-driven process that creates meaning by connecting and resolving contradictory information and perceptions. Expecting also uses beliefs embedded in anticipations or prophecies to create meaning by connecting and selecting information that is compatible with expectations. Committing is an action-driven process that creates meaning through justifying actions that have been taken which are deliberate, visible, and hard to reverse. Manipulating creates meaning by explaining the consequences of actively intruding into and changing the environment. It is clear that both beliefs and actions can serve as reference points for meaning generation, and that once again the essence of sense making is in the blending together of cognitive structures and active choices to construct reality.

III. SHARED MINDS: CONSENSUS AND CULTURE

Sense making in organizations creates a structure of shared meanings and understandings based on which concerted action can take place. A network of shared meanings and interpretations provides the social order, temporal continuity, and contextual clarity for members to coordinate and relate their actions. As a cognitive framework, it presents criteria for selecting, valuing, and processing information. Where information is lacking or equivocal, shared beliefs and assumptions can fill in the gaps or reduce the ambiguity sufficiently in order for organizations to be able to act. As a framework of meanings and values, it presents benchmarks for relating and evaluating actions and results, and defines communal membership and commitment to purpose. Although order and stability are essential for coordinated action, organizations must also be able to continuously assess the validity of assumptions and beliefs, unveil opportunities or threats hidden in new information, and stimulate innovation through inquiry and experimentation. More than order and stasis, organizations need variation and diversity in points of view to ensure flexibility and adaptiveness for long-term growth and development. The basic structure of shared meanings needs to be sufficiently loose and to retain enough residual equivocality to provide the space for new ideas to breed and new responses to be enacted. How might this fine balance between order and venturism be struck? Research has found that organizations and managers employ a number of meaning-making and meaning-sharing mechanisms to simultaneously build consensus and accommodate diversity.

Managing Consensus through Shared Meaning

Given that individuals and groups differ in their histories, values, and sense making styles, how do shared meanings then emerge from such heterogeneity? While much research is still needed, the available evidence suggests two general strategies that organizations use to achieve an actionable level of consensus—tapping into shared *cognitive structures* or collective knowledge bases that guide the processing of information as well as the making of action; and engaging in *communication behaviors* that establish agreement on action implications, but at the same time retain a residual amount of ambiguity to accommodate differing interpretations. As examples of shared cognitive structures, we present research on the concepts of cognitive consensus, industry recipe, and dominant logic. As examples of communication behaviors, we discuss the ideas of equifinal meanings and interpretation framing.

Cognitive Consensus: Some researchers have suggested that organizations develop a certain level of *cognitive consensuality* that makes possible a reasonable degree of common understanding for collective action. Consensuality in this case does not imply complete agreement, but that "individuals have achieved a certain similarity in the way they process and evaluate information" (Gioia and Sims 1986, 8). It does imply that "there is a reasonable amount of implicit agreement among organization members as to the appropriate meaning of information or events. This leads to consensual cognitive scripts prescribing behavior and action (which are also implicitly agreed to as appropriate by organizational members)" (Finney and Mitroff 1986, 320). In an attempt to determine whether cognitive scripts underlie common organizational events, Gioia, Donnellon and Sims (1989) analyzed videotaped data collected from ninety-six simulated appraisals conducted by twenty-four experienced middle-level and upper level managers interacting with four different subordinates drawn from a group of business administration students. The results revealed a common behavioral script that suggested the existence of a consensual cognitive script for enacting the appraisal interviews. The use of consensual structures and scripts still allows for differences in individual behavior based on personal styles and preferences. For example, a general cognitive script in an organization may require that business plans be supported by statistical data and analysis. One manager may choose to prepare the business plan working alone, another manager may prefer to delegate the plan to subordinates; in both cases, a business plan bolstered by statistical analysis is produced that is in line with the script. The individual managers themselves have in fact superimposed their personal behavioral scripts over the general script of how to prepare statistical business plans: "The result is schemas and scripts super-imposed on schemas and scripts—that is, meaning and action superimposed on meaning and action. This complex and interactive set of meanings directs the enactment of behavior by the individual, the group, and ultimately the organization" (Finney and Mitroff 1986, 322). At the same time, consensuality and concerted action are enacted for a common purpose—they are necessarily tenuous constructions that are subject to revision or dissolution when the perception of reality changes (Gioia 1986).

Industry Recipe: In order to develop meaning and draw conclusions from unclear and uncertain information, members of the organization do not directly use the methods of logical analysis or decision making to process information, but must first exercise human judgment and creative thinking to deal with the information uncertainty. From his field study of three industries, Spender (1989) observed that firms in the same industry share a body of knowledge and beliefs that is used to cope with uncertainty. Following Alfred Schutz, who saw individuals using "recipes," or shared patterns, of beliefs to make sense of everyday experience, Spender called the shared knowledge the *industry recipe:*

I suggest that the burdens and risks of exercising judgement cause managers to cast around for guidance. I hypothesize that they draw their primary support from other managers operating in the same industry. There is no simple imitation involved here. These managers do not seek support that is substantive, detailed or prescriptive, a specific formula which tells them precisely what to do. They know well enough that other firms are in different circumstances and may well be pursuing different policies. I hypothesize that the imitation is at an extremely intellectual level, a sharing of those judgements which give organizational data their meaning. In this way the managers adopt a way of looking at their situations that is widely shared within their industry. I call this pattern of judgements the industry's "recipe." I argue that the recipe is an unintended consequence of managers' need to communicate, because of their uncertainties, by word and example within the industry. The recipe develops a context and experience bound synthesis of the knowledge the industry considers managers need to have in order to acquire an adequate conceptual grasp of their firms. (Spender 1989, 188)

From his study of seven major dairies in London and Manchester in the United Kingdom, Spender identified fourteen constructs that composed the dairy industry recipe. For example, the recipe indicates that the dairymen need to increase the volume demand of milk in the distribution network (construct 1—increasing gallonage), that gallonage can be increased by supplying milk to smaller retailers as well as bottled milk buyers who purchase in bulk (2—expanding the business), that friendly relations be maintained with the buyers which are family-owned businesses (3—awareness of other retailers' positions), that gallonage can also be expanded by increasing the length and the number of drop points in the milk rounds (4—improving the rounds), and by increasing either the number of customers or the amount of milk delivered to existing customers (5—increasing the drop density), and so on. For an individual firm, the industry recipe enables collective action while accommodating interpretive variations, because while it offers general guidance about what is important and appropriate behavior, the recipe is ambiguous enough for individual firms to adapt to their particular situations and preferences.

Dominant logic: Organizations are inundated with information, but find it difficult to interpret and act on the flood of information. Organizations are information-rich but interpretation-poor systems awash in raw information, which must be channelled and converted into organizational intelligence. Bettis and Prahalad (1995) suggest that organizations use a *dominant logic* to function as an information filter or funnel that focuses organizational attention:

> Organizational attention is focused only on data deemed relevant by the dominant logic. Other data are largely ignored. "Relevant" data are filtered by the dominant logic and by the analytic procedures managers use to aid strategy development. These "filtered" data are then incorporated into the strategy, systems, values, expectations, and reinforced behavior of the organization. (Bettis and Prahalad 1995, 7)

The dominant logic is embedded in the shared mind-sets, belief structures, and frames of reference that have been developed based on past experience, and which the managers of an organization use to conceptualize the business and make critical decisions (Prahalad and Bettis 1986). IBM, for example, was for many years guided by the dominant logic that computer mainframes are central to its business. This logic was entrenched in IBM's development of business strategies, reward systems, promotion preferences, and resource allocation priorities. (In recent years, with the growing use of smaller computers in client-server networks, IBM has updated the role of large mainframe computers as enterprise "super-servers" capable of supporting numerous clients in large networks.) Bettis and Prahalad (1995) maintain that the dominant logic is an emergent property of the organization as a complex, adaptive system, that is, it is not the property of any particular constituency, but appears as the dynamic result and shared property of the interactions between the various groups and subsystems of the organization.

Equifinal Meanings: In order to reconcile diversity with coordination, organizations develop communication behaviors that allow members of a group to broaden their ideas to accommodate multiple interpretations that are nevertheless consistent with each other in their behavioral implications. For example, Donnellon, Gray, and Bougon (1986) found that "in the absence of shared meaning, organized action is made possible by the shared repertoire of communication behaviors group members use while in the process of developing *equifinal meanings* for their joint experience. . . . Equifinal meanings, then, are interpretations that are dissimilar but that have similar behavioral implications" (p. 44). Donnellon et al. identified four communication mechanisms for achieving equifinal meanings: metaphor, logical argument, affect modulation, and linguistic indirection. Metaphors can reconcile differences in meaning because it allows people to understand and experience one kind of thing in terms of another, and so give new meaning to their actions and beliefs (Lakoff and Johnson 1980). Logical arguments can be used in situations of disagreement to move another party to agreement through incremental steps. Affect modulation evoke feelings through the use of voice, gesture, and emotion-laden words to cause the redefinition of a situation. Linguistic indirection employs the passive voice and broad or imprecise language to create equivocality and so play down sources of dissent. Donnellon et al. (1986) observed that metaphors are particularly effective in generating equifinal meanings because their vagueness allow the different parties to maintain their own interpretations while providing common ground for communal behavior. The study found that in a simulated organization, members of one department eventually agreed to a strike action as a response to planned layoffs only after the meaning of striking was enlarged through the use of the metaphor "Striking is principled behavior." In the same study, group members used logical argument and affect modulation to garner support for a selected interpretation of another department's actions, while linguistic indirection helped motivate the search for equifinal meanings.

Interpretation framing: Just as the process of sharing meaning is a complex communication activity with many patterns of behavior, the concept of shared meaning itself can have more than one dimension. If shared meaning is multifaceted, then collective action can take place as long as there is consensus around one or more (but not necessarily all) of the multiple dimensions. Fiol (1994) suggests that shared meaning can reside in the *content* of the interpretation as well as in the *framing* of the interpretation. Content is reflected in the categories or labels that people use to define what is expressed (labels such as "threat" or "opportunity"), while framing refers to how people express their viewpoints, regardless of its content. Fiol noted that framing differs in the breadth of the frame (for example, the number or scope of issues attended to, the number of constituencies or functional areas perceived as relevant) and in the rigidity of the frame (such as the degree of certainty conveyed, the stability of opinions over time). While people may maintain diverse interpretations about the content of an issue, they may nevertheless show agreement about how the issue is being broadly framed. Fiol (1994) studied how a Fortune 100 financial services company made sense of and evaluated a new venture project over a period of two years. The new venture team consisted of eleven managers ranging from division CEO to group vice presidents covering functions in finance, law, marketing, operations, and systems. The CEO required that all major communications in the group be recorded in a new venture log, which eventually ran to more than 2000 pages of entries spread over three volumes, reflecting the three phases of the project. In the first phase, which lasted six months, the team failed to see a need for the new venture, especially how it could add to or be integrated with existing products, and decided to reject the proposal. In the second phase (seven months) the new-venture idea was reintroduced, this time as a totally new business, separate from the division's current offerings. This new form gained the tentative support of top managers in the team, and the idea was then pursued as a "new business proposal." In the third phase (nine months) the subgroups worked to flesh out and operationalize the project. Eventually, "the 'New Business' concept that emerges from the third notebook is almost identical to the idea that the (project) Champion had presented more than a year earlier and that had been soundly rejected" (Fiol 1994, 409). Data analysis revealed that over the course of the project, there was a general progression from less to greater certainty about their positions (frame rigidity), and a clear convergence toward the perceived scope of the project (frame breadth) as encompassing internal systems, customer needs, and marketing issues. While there was convergence in framing, team members continued to the end to maintain their divergent perceptions about the controllability of the issues raised (interpretation content), with the subgroups perceiving different levels of control over project outcomes. In the final analysis it was the agreement on how the new venture is to be framed that provided the unifying premise for the new venture to proceed.

Consensus in Organizational Culture

The sharing of meaning in a group based on a common set of beliefs and values that leads to similar patterns of behavior within the group is seen as evidence of the existence of a group culture. Indeed, the consensual sharing of beliefs and behaviors among members of a group is regarded as the essence of culture: "If there is no consensus or if there is conflict or if things are ambiguous, then, by definition, that group does not have a culture in regard to those things. It may have subcultures, smaller groups that have a shared something, a consensus about something, but the concept of sharing or consensus is core to the definition, not something about which we have an empirical choice" (Schein 1991, 246). This view, though not uncommon, is not shared universally by students of organizational culture, and we will also present a more diffracted image of culture that encompasses both consensus and multiplicity.

Integrated View of Organizational Culture: What then is culture? Schein's (1985, 1991, 1992) definition is well known and germane to our discussion. According to him, culture is:

1. A pattern of shared basic assumptions
2. Invented, discovered, or developed by a given group
3. As it learns to cope with its problems of external adaptation and internal integration
4. That has worked well enough to be considered valid, and therefore
5. Is to be taught to new members of the group as the
6. correct way to perceive, think, and feel in relation to those problems

(Schein 1991, 247)

In Schein's conceptualization, culture is the result of the organization's efforts to simultaneously adapt to external environments and manage its internal integration. All groups need to face the tasks of external adaptation and internal integration, and both tasks involve building consensus on collective identity, function, and allowable behaviors. In the process of *external adaptation,* members develop consensus on: the core mission and functions of the organization; the specific goals to be pursued; the basic means to be used to attain the goals (including structure, reward, and authority systems); the criteria to be used for measuring results; and the appropriate remedial strategies if goals are not achieved (Schein 1992, 52). In the process of *internal integration,* members develop consensus on: a common language and conceptual categories to be used so that members can communicate with and understand each other; the group boundaries and criteria for inclusion; the criteria for the distribution of power and status; the norms of intimacy, friendship, and love; the criteria for the allocation of rewards and punishments; and the concepts for explaining the unexplainable (ideology and religion) that members can fall back on to cope with and respond to what they cannot understand (Schein 1992, 70–71). To illustrate the dynamic process by which an organization learns its shared assumptions, Schein outlines this scenario of how organizational culture grows from the seeds of the founder's beliefs:

Basically the founder of the new group starts with some beliefs, values, and assumptions about how to proceed and teaches those to new members through a variety of mechanisms. What is for him or her a basic reality becomes for the group a set of interim values and beliefs about which they have limited choice. The group then behaves in a certain way based on the founder's beliefs and values, and either succeeds or fails. If it fails, the group eventually dissolves and no culture is formed. If it succeeds, and this process repeats itself, what were originally the beliefs, values, and assumptions of the founders come to be validated in the shared experiences of the group. (Schein 1991, 249)

Over time, the learning and validation of a set of shared assumptions becomes constituted in the culture of the organization and provides a shared framework of cognitive, behavioral, and affective responses. Within this framework, members can continuously make sense of and adapt to the external environment, and continuously develop and maintain internal relationships among themselves.

Multiperspective View of Organizational Culture: While Schein's treatment of culture, as a prescription of organization wide consensus that brings about clarity, stability, and unity of action, is certainly a desirable state of affairs, many organizations in practice do not enjoy the level of integration and consistency that it prescribes. An alternative view suggests that organizational culture should be examined simultaneously through multiple lenses, with each lens bringing into focus special features that are missed by the others. Martin (1992) proposes that three interpretive perspectives are needed, which she calls the integration, differentiation, and fragmentation views (Table 3–3). The *Integration* perspective is defined by organizational members experiencing a high level of consensus, consistency, and clarity. All members share a set of basic assumptions, values, common concerns, or "content themes". These

TABLE 3–3. Three perspectives of organizational culture (From the *Cultures of Organizations: Three Perspectives* by J. Martin. Copyright © 1992 by J. Martin. Used by permission of Oxford University Press, Inc.).

Perspective	Integration	Differentiation	Fragmentation
Consensus (orientation to consensus)	Organizationwide consensus	Subcultural consensus	Multiplicity of views (no consensus)
Consistency (relation among manifestations)	Consistency	Inconsistency	Complexity (not clearly consistent or inconsistent)
Clarity (orientation to ambiguity)	Exclude it	Channel it outside subcultures	Focus on it
Metaphors	Clearing in jungle, monolith, hologram	Islands of clarity in sea of ambiguity	Web, jungle

themes are enacted consistently in a variety of cultural manifestations (actions, stories, rituals, jargon, and other symbols); and members know what they are to do and why, so that there is no place for ambiguity. In many respects, Schein's (1985, 1992) conceptualization of organizational culture portrays such a unifying, integrative perspective. Instead of a single, seamless culture, the *Differentiation* perspective assumes that organizations consist of a number of subcultures based on differences in power, areas of interest, and work or professional practices. Its defining features are that consensus exists only locally within subcultures; inconsistent interpretations of content themes are common; and clarity is preserved within subcultures while ambiguity is channeled outward. The differentiation perspective acknowledges that conflict and power are important elements of cultural behavior, and assumes that collective action based on consensus is most likely within subcultures. Finally, the *fragmentation* perspective sees organizations as "webs of individuals" who are loosely and sporadically connected as "new issues come into focus, different people and tasks become salient, and new information becomes available" (Martin 1992, 150–51). The organization lacks a center and its boundaries are blurred as part-time employees, contractors, suppliers, and customers move in and out of the organization. There is no organizationwide or subcultural consensus, any local consensus is temporary and limited to particular issues. Neither consistencies nor inconsistencies are clear. Constant flux and ambiguity is the rule of the day. In this view, collective action is still possible because individuals form temporary coalitions to tackle specific issues and concerns:

> When a particular issue becomes salient, one pattern of connections becomes relevant. That pattern would include a unique array of agreements, disagreements, and domains of ignorance. A different issue would draw attention to a different pattern of connections—and different sources of confusion. Whenever a new issue becomes salient to cultural members or researchers, a new pattern of connections would become significant. (Martin and Meyerson 1988, 117)

Meyerson and Martin (1987) applied the three perspectives to analyze cultural change in the Peace Corps/Africa during the Kennedy and Nixon administrations. From the integration perspective, the volunteers and staff of Peace Corps/Africa during the Kennedy administration were all seen as sharing the same core values espoused by Kennedy and the top administrators—the importance of international volunteer work, altruism, the excitement of living in new environments, and the ability to change the world through their work and ideals. The differentiation perspective focused on the behaviors of several subculture groups, including the top staff (the Africa director, country directors); volunteers assigned to particular countries; and volunteers assigned to specific projects such as sanitation, agriculture, and teaching English. The fragmentation perspective concentrated on the consequences of the short two-year tenures of most volunteers and the high turnover of country directors. As a result, "transient issue-specific interest groups" often developed, establishing informal alliances around issues such as an epidemic in a particular country or the relative importance of English instruction. Furthermore, since most volunteers worked in isolated settings, Peace Corps members had to be tolerant of confusion and to be able to live with ambiguity. When Nixon became President, the integration view focused on the new kinds of Peace Corps volunteers he deemed desirable: people with practical skills in construction and farming so that the corps could do more infrastructure building and less English teaching. The differentiation view saw how environmental factors, including a severe dought that caused famine, outflows of refugees, and changes in several national governments, influenced the composition of subcultures. In addition, new country members, the termination of sanitation projects, and the introduction of drought-resistant crops and irrigation projects all led to new subcultural configurations. The fragmentation view showed temporary alliances coalescing on concerns such as effective education techniques for introducing innovations (new sewage disposal methods, cooking untraditional grains), and political violence in a particular country. Budget cuts in Washington DC and uncertainty about the Corps' future further increased the feeling of anxiety and ambiguity. Overall, the integration view focused on the creation of an organizationwide consensus based on policies initiated by the corps leadership; the differentiation view focused on local consensus in subcultures formed by people working in the same countries or projects; while the fragmentation view focused on the experiences of individuals who were working in fast-changing and isolated settings. Martin explains the value of adopting a three-perspective analysis of organizational culture:

> At any point in time, a few fundamental aspects of an organization's culture will be congruent with an Integration perspective—that is, some cultural manifestations will be interpreted in similar ways throughout the organization, so they appear clear and mutually consistent. At the same time, in accord with the Differentiation perspective, other issues will surface as inconsistencies and will generate clear subcultural differences. Simultaneously, in congruence with the Fragmentation viewpoint, still other issues will be seen as ambiguous, generating unclear relationships among manifestations and only ephemeral issue-specific coalitions that fail to coalesce in either organization-wide or subcultural consensus. Furthermore, individuals viewing the same cultural context will perceive, remember, and interpret things in different ways. (Martin 1992, 168–69)

IV. INFORMATION SEEKING AND USE IN SENSE MAKING

The managed reduction of information ambiguity lies at the heart of organizational sense making. When ambiguity is excessively high, organization members lack a clear and stable frame of reference within which their work and behavior have meaning and purpose. When ambiguity is unnecessarily suppressed, organization members feel unduly complacent and unchallenged to learn or innovate. Each organization finds its own balance between ambiguity and certainty, and this locus depends on the business of the particular organization, its relationships with other organizations and stakeholders, the turbulence of its operating environment, and the beliefs, assumptions, and values held by its members. Through the sense making process equivocal information is interpreted and negotiated so that members share some basic understandings upon which collective action can be taken. In this section we detail the information-seeking and use processes that constitute sense making and meaning construction in organizations. As we do so, we will draw together many of the principles, concepts, and techniques that we encountered earlier. The sequence of presentation follows the conceptual framework developed in chapter 2: we will examine (1) information needs, (2) information seeking, and (3) information use, each in terms of cognitive needs, affective responses, and situational dimensions (Table 3–4).

TABLE 3–4. Information needs, seeking, and use in sense making.

	Information needs	*Information seeking*	*Information use*
Sense Making	• Needs are unclear • "What's happening here?" • "Which interpretation to choose?"	• Scanning the environment • Noticing significant, reliable information • Developing interpretations through verbal discourse	• Reduce but not eliminate ambiguity • Build consensus or shared meanings for collective action
Cognitive needs	• Frames of reference • Plausible interpretations • Information to decide on values, priorities	• Clarity and quality of information • Information reliability and accuracy • Retrieval from organizational memory	• Reduce equivocality • Use schemas to process information • Prefer information that confirms expectations
Affective responses	• Interruptions invoke emotional responses • Positive and negative emotions • Uncertainty, doubt, tension, stress	• Emotions help recall of memory • Nonverbal communication through rich information media • Affective moods	• Tension between self-beliefs and group consensus • Feeling of confidence or trust in information • Perception of threat or challenge
Situational dimensions	• Perceived environmental uncertainty • Ill-structured problems • Unclear goals	• Environmental analyzability and organizational intrusiveness • Access to information: systems, structures, people, values, experience	• Organizational cultures as meaning systems • Commitment to visible actions • Enacted environments

Information Needs in Sense Making

During sense making, information needs are unclear. The lack of clarity revolves around two basic questions: In the flood of signals indicating change in the environment, which messages and cues are important and need to be focused on? Given that the information is ambivalent, which interpretation is the most plausible and should be used to understand what the cues mean? The central issue is therefore the management of ambiguity. Whereas uncertainty refers to the lack of information about an issue, ambiguity refers to the equivocality of the information available, where the same information can support multiple and sometimes conflicting interpretations. The lack of information may be addressed by gathering more data that are relevant to an issue, but the lack of clarity has to be met by constructing the most reasonable interpretation that makes sense of the available information. The initial attempt to reduce ambiguity is to try and fit the information with existing assumptions, beliefs, and expectations.

Information Needs and Cognitive Needs: Organizations develop cognitive *frames of reference* to define the boundaries of a domain of inquiry, suggest appropriate methods of inquiry, and allocate significance, value, and priority to information. These organizational frames of reference consist of "cognitive elements, cognitive operators, and reality tests that select, organize, and validate information." (Shrivastava and Schneider 1984, 796). *Cognitive elements* "determine the type of information and data that the organization prefers to use," as well as "represent the intellectual commitments and cognitive interests or motives of inquiry in organizations" (Shrivastava, Mitroff, and Alvesson 1987, 96). Some organizations treat subjective, personal experience as valid sources, others prefer objective, formal data. Cognitive elements also reflect vocabularies for expressing features important to the organization: an organization stressing service quality would use a vocabulary different from another stressing financial performance. *Cognitive operators* are "methods by which information is ordered and arranged to make meaning and sense out of large amounts of data that organizations continuously receive. . . . They essentially consist of guidelines for perceiving and formulating problems, descriptions of acceptable solutions, and criteria for evaluating solutions" (Shrivastava and Schneider 1984, 798). By specifying methods for ordering information, they also specify the acceptable methods for studying organizational problems. *Reality tests* validate the elements of the frame of reference, as well as the information that results from organizational inquiry, by comparing current situations with critical past experiences. Overall, the frame of reference sets the boundaries of the scope of any organizational inquiry, and provides the information-organizing principles that "shape information acquisition and processing patterns in organizations. . . . information selectively enters the system in patterns based on its nature, source, timing, and consistence with cognitive elements. Rudimentary organization is implicit in this selective perception.

Cognitive operators classify and categorize information allowing the formation of concepts/constructs" (Shrivastava and Schneider 1984, 801).

Within this cognitive frame of reference, the need is for information that will reduce ambiguity and increase clarity by pointing toward a *plausible interpretation* that can be used to make sense of what is going on: "The problem is that there are too many meanings, not too few. The problem faced by the sense maker is one of equivocality, not one of uncertainty. The problem is confusion, not ignorance. . . . = [people =] need *values, priorities, and clarity* about preferences to help them be clear about which projects matter. Clarity on values clarifies what is important in elapsed experience, which finally gives some sense of what that elapsed experience means" (Weick 1995, 27–28). The search for meaning thus requires having the information to (1) notice what is important in the organization's experience, and (2) select or develop a plausible interpretation of what that experience means. For managers coping with ambiguity the main task is seeking answers to the questions, " 'what information do you notice?' and 'how do you interpret it?' The most significant informational problem for these managers was to find the right problem to address and to structure the related information search and information processing in a productive way" (McCaskey 1982, 158).

Information Needs and Affective Responses: Emotions play an important role in sense making. When information is confusing and incomplete, when different subjective points of view clash, and when there is nevertheless a need to quickly converge on some basic shared understanding of what is going on, feelings of stress, tension, and uncertainty are likely to be common. Specifically, these affective states are aroused in the individual when there is an interruption or disruption in the flow of work, and when the information encountered has to be processed to establish a fit (or otherwise) with interpretations and schemas remembered by the organization. Work disruptions therefore create the occasions requiring sense making and information seeking. *Work interruptions* can invoke both *positive and negative emotional responses:*

> If the interruption slows the accomplishment of an organized sequence, people are more likely to experience anger. If the interruption has accelerated accomplishment, then they are likely to experience pleasure. If people find that the interruption can be circumvented, they experience relief. If they find that the interruption has thwarted a higher level plan, then the anger is likely to turn into rage, and if they find that the interruption has thwarted a minor behavioral sequence, then they are likely to feel irritated. (Weick 1995, 49)

As Kuhlthau (1993b) has observed, the initiation of the information-search process is characterized by feelings of "uncertainty due to a lack of understanding, a gap in meaning, a limited construct" (p. xxiii). Because the human mind prefers order, simplicity, consistency and stability, it experiences feelings of *stress and tension* when confronted with a high level of ambiguity brought about by equivocal information from confusing situations. Feelings can act as *markers* (Damasio 1994) to indicate mismatches between the available information and the cognitive categories or schemas the individual is using to make sense. One way to investigate and try to restore the match is to look for more information to corroborate, refute, or amplify the initial evidence, so feelings of doubt and stress can lead to the recognition of information needs. (Other ways of resolving the mismatch are to adjust either the data or the schemas, which we will discuss in our section on information use.) Emotions also shape information needs by influencing the perception and prioritization of a problem situation. For example, managers become personally and emotionally involved during problem recognition:

> Thus, managers are not cool and detached observers of their organizational scenes. They are invested in their points of view, policies, and ways of doing things, and they are identified with the fate of their people and their organizations. To contemplate a problem is not a cool mental act but "hot cognition." (McCall and Kaplan 1990, 29)

Information Needs and Situational Dimensions: Information need situations may be described by a small set of problem dimensions, which are "those characteristics that, beyond specific subject matter, establish the criteria for judging the relevance of information to a problem or to a class of problems" (Taylor 1986, 42). Of the eleven problem dimensions that have been identified (Macmullin and Taylor 1984), five are particularly relevant to understanding information needs during sense making. (1) Sense making problems tend to be *discovery* rather than design problems—information for discovery concentrate on a small, detailed set of data perceived to be important in order to discover its meaning. (2) Sense making problems tend to be *ill-structured* and require information on how to interpret or proceed. (3) Sense making problems tend to be *complex,* involving many variables that interact with each other. (4) Sense making problems tend to have *amorphous goals,* so that information is required to clarify preferences and directions. (5) Sense making problems tend to be those in which *assumptions are not agreed* upon. Assumptions may be contradictory or contested, and information is needed to explain underlying perceptions, define terms and concepts, and so on.

In the research literature of how organizations scan their external environments, *perceived environmental uncertainty* is the omnibus variable that represents the external environment's perceived complexity and changeability. Duncan (1972) infers two dimensions of the environment that would determine its perceived uncertainty: the simple–complex dimension (the number of environmental factors considered in decision making) and the static–dynamic dimension (the degree to which these factors change over time). Duncan found that decision makers in environments that are dynamic and complex experienced the greatest amount of perceived environmental uncertainty. Perceived environmental uncertainty itself is conceptualized as (1) lack of information on environmental factors associated with a decision situation; (2) lack of knowledge about the outcome of a specific decision; and (3) inability to assign probabilities with confidence on how environmental factors affect success or failure. There is general agreement in the findings of scanning studies that managers who experience higher levels of perceived environmental uncertainty tend to do a larger amount of information seeking or environmental scanning (see for example, Kefalas and Schoderbek 1973; Nishi et al. 1982; Daft et al. 1988; Auster and Choo 1993). In terms of information needs, research suggested that the external business environment may be divided into *environmental sectors,* such as the customer, competition, technological, regulatory, economic, and sociocultural sectors (Choo and Auster 1993). Again, there is agreement in the research findings that information scanning tends to be focused on the market-related sectors, with information on customers, suppliers, and competitors appearing to be the most important (see for example, Ghoshal 1988, Lester and Waters 1989; Choo 1993; Olsen et al. 1994).

Information Seeking in Sense Making

Three related activities constitute the information-seeking process in organizational sense making: scanning, noticing, and interpreting. *Scanning* involves sweeping the external information environment broadly and systematically in order to monitor developments that could impact the organization. From this broad sweep, specific events or discontinuities are *noticed,* and information about them is isolated for closer scrutiny. Such information tends to be equivocal, so the main task then becomes *interpreting* the meaning of noticed events by talking about and negotiating disparate perceptions in verbal discourse. Organizations scan using a variety of methods, ranging from the irregular, ad hoc scan to continuous, proactive information gathering as part of an institutionalized scanning-planning system. The size of the organization, the industry it is in, the organization's dependence on and perception of the environment, and its experience with scanning and strategic planning are some of the factors that affect the choice of scanning method (Choo 1995a).

Information Seeking and Cognitive Needs: From an information perspective, every change or development in the external environment creates signals and messages that organizations may need to heed (Dill 1962). Some of the signals would be weak (difficult to detect), many would be confusing (difficult to analyze), and others would be spurious (not indicative of a true change). The information seeker would have to attend selectively to numerous signals created by a dynamic environment, interpret often confusing messages, and make sense of cues in relation to existing frames of reference. A basic cognitive need of information seeking in sense making is thus to subjectively increase the *clarity and quality of information* about ambiguous situations. Unfortunately information comes rarely directly from the scene. More often than not it travels a circuitous route, flowing through many intermediate channels. The risks of failure in gathering reliable information become real:

> Sources of failure are legion: even if the initial message is accurate, clear, timely, and relevant, it may be translated, condensed, or completely blocked by personnel standing between the sender and the intended receiver: it may get through in distorted form. If the receiver is in a position to use the message, he may screen it out because it does not fit his preconceptions, because it has come through a suspicious or poorly regarded channel, because it is embedded in piles of inaccurate or useless messages (excessive noise in the channel), or, simply, because too many messages are transmitted to him (information overload). (Wilensky 1967, 41)

Because sense making situations are those in which ambiguity is high and action is consequential, organizational members seeking information may be particularly sensitive to the *reliability* of a source and the *accuracy* of its information. Studies on source use in scanning have found that managers do not just rely on the most accessible sources (a common heuristic that characterized how many groups of users seek information, see chapter 2), but that they also use heavily sources they perceived to be dependable or authoritative (see Culnan 1983; Auster and Choo 1993). A source is more likely to be seen to be credible when it has a good track record of supplying accurate data, when the individual has used it before, or when another well-regarded source has recommended it. Based on available research,

> . . . the general pattern of source usage for scanning suggests that although managers use a wide range of sources in scanning, they prefer personal sources that communicate information personally rather than impersonal sources that communicate information formally or to broad audiences. This preference for live information from personal sources is particularly strong when seeking information about market-related environmental sectors which are highly fluid and equivocal. There is some evidence to indicate that source selection for scanning is influenced by the perceived quality of the source, and not just its perceived accessibility. (Choo 1995a, 96)

Since sense making involves overlaying existing meaning structures on the new information, sources that provide access to what sense the organization has made in the past become important in constructing interpretations. Interpretations of the past can be embedded in the minds of individuals as well as in systems and artifacts that make up the *organizational memory* (Walsh and Ungson 1991). Walsh and Ungson postulate that organizational memory is held in five "storage bins": individuals, culture, transformations, structures, and ecology. Individuals "store their organization's memory in their own capacity to remember and articulate experience and in the cognitive orientations they employ to facilitate information processing" (Walsh and Ungson 1991, 63). Also, individuals maintain their own files and collections of data. Because retrieving from memory is not simply a matter of literal recall but also involves subjective reconstruction, the other components of organizational memory actively modulate the selection and processing of information. Thus culture "embodies past experience that can be useful for dealing with the future" (p. 63), transformation procedures convert inputs into outputs and so encode the logic and rules of work, structures are the definitions of individual roles "which provide a repository in which organizational information can be stored" (p. 65), and ecology is the physical structure of the workplace that reflects hierarchy and affects the flow of feedback and information.

Information Seeking and Affective Responses: Emotions can assist the search and *recall of information from memory.* When past experiences are retained in memory, their contents are associated with the individual's affective responses at that time. Memory is colored by emotion:

> People remember events that have the same emotional tone as they currently feel. Anger at being interrupted should encourage recall of earlier events where feelings of anger were dominant. These earlier moments of anger should stand out when people look back over their past experience to discover 'similar' events and what those previous events might suggest about the meaning of present events. Past events are reconstructed in the present as explanations, not because they look the same but because they feel the same. (Weick 1995, 49)

A large part of information seeking during sense making is comparing experiences and interpretations among organizational members. Since recollections fade with time and the current situation is ambiguous, such information sharing is marked by feelings of doubt and uncertainty. In conversing about ill-defined situations, formal and explicit language is inadequate. Hunches, intuitions, and judgments are better carried through nonverbal rather than verbal channels: "Nonverbal messages are themselves more ambiguous and, very importantly, can be disowned. The use of an ambiguous channel of communication can help a manager convey the subjectivity and nuance of meaning that are crucial in an ambiguous situation" (McCaskey 1982). Organizational members reduce equivocality by using information sources and communication channels of different *information richness:*

> Information richness is defined as the ability of information to change understanding within a time interval. Communication transactions that can overcome different frames of reference or clarify ambiguous issues to change understand-

ing in a timely manner are considered rich. Communications that require a long
time to enable understanding or that cannot overcome different perspectives are
lower in richness. (Daft and Lengel 1986, 560)

Rich information media use multiple cues, feedback, and language variety.
Managers and others will turn to rich information channels such as face-to-
face discussions when they are dealing with ambiguous, complex, ill-defined,
or conflict-laden situations. Face-to-face meetings are the richest information
medium because they provide instant feedback, include multiple cues such as
voice inflections and body gestures, add a personal touch, and use language
variety. The use of rich information media helps participants to interpret a
fuzzy situation and come to an acceptable agreement. Because managers must
confront ambiguous and conflicting cues about the environment, and then create and maintain a shared interpretation among themselves, they use rich media to talk about the environment and negotiate an understanding.

Affective mood can influecnce the breadth of the information search. Following Kelly (1963), a mood is thought of as "a stance or attitude that the
individual assumes which opens or closes the possibilities in a search" (Kuhlthau 1993a, 350). A person in an "invitational" mood would search more
sources, and take more exploratory actions, while a user in an "indicative"
mood would prefer a short search that comes to a closure quickly. Weick
(1995) also suggests that affective states can signal to the individual when
information search may be stopped. In his view, since the feeling of order and
clarity is an important goal of sense making, information seeking can end once
this feeling is achieved.

Information Seeking and Situational Dimensions: Organizations differ in
their modes of scanning interpretation, depending on their beliefs about the
analyzability of the external environment, and the extent to which the organization *intrudes* into the environment to understand it (Daft and Weick 1984).
An organization that believes the environment to be analyzable, in which
events and processes are determinable and measurable, would seek to discover
the "correct" interpretation through systematic information gathering and analysis. Conversely, an organization that perceives the environment to be unanalyzable would create or enact what it believes to be a reasonable interpretation
that can explain past behavior and suggest future actions. An organization that
actively intrudes into the environment would allocate resources for information
search and for testing or manipulating the environment. A passive organization
on the other hand, takes whatever environmental information comes its way,
and tries to interpret the environment with the given information. Four possible
modes of scanning interpretation result: undirected viewing, conditioned viewing, enacting, and discovery. *Undirected viewing* takes place when the organization perceives the environment to be unanalyzable and so does not intrude
into the environment to understand it. Information seeking is opportunistic,
relying more on irregular contacts and casual information from external, per-

sonal sources. *Conditioned viewing* takes place when the organization perceives the environment to be analyzable but is passive about gathering information and influencing the environment. Information seeking is based on passive detection, using internal, impersonal sources, with a significant amount of data coming from records and information systems. *Enacting* takes place when the organization perceives the environment to be unanalyzable but then proceeds to actively intrude into the environment in order to influence events and outcomes. Information seeking is from external, personal sources and emphasizes feedback about the actions that the organization has taken. *Discovery* takes place when the organization perceives the environment to be analyzable and it actively intrudes into the environment to collect information extensively in order to find the correct interpretation. Information seeking is based on active detection, collecting information extensively and intensively through a variety of sources, including internal, impersonal (formal) sources.

Within the organization, the flow of information and the *access to information* sources influence the information seeking patterns of its members. McCall and Kaplan (1990) suggest that, at least for managers, there are four important sets of sources: "(a) systems and structures set up to keep them appraised of ongoing events, (b) the people around them who volunteer information and can be approached in search of trouble signs, clues, and missing pieces of puzzles, (c) the values of the organization, which point people in certain directions and define the critical variables in a complex array of possibilities, and (d) the manager's own direct experience" (p. 16). Systems and structures refer to information systems and organizational structure. Although computer-based *information systems* increase the general availability of information, the access to large amounts of data can result in information overload or in users selectively drawing upon the database to find information that supports a desired position while ignoring information that goes against it (Hogarth and Makridakis 1981). *Organizational structures* define information domains within which some sources are accessible while others are not. Hierarchy and specialization also constrain and direct the flow and availability of information. *Other people* within the organization are among the most important and often used information sources, yet their accessibility and willingness to provide information cannot be taken for granted. For example, people are highly sensitive to the way that their information is being received, and the likelihood of passing on information depends on their perception of the effect of the information on the recipient as well as the sender. Subordinates are known to withold from their superiors information that prejudices their position, or conversely, to expedite information that enhances their cause. As a result, blocking, delaying, hiding, or even distorting information is not uncommon. The *values of the organization* can have pervasive effects on what information is considered relevant; what data are collected systematically, who gets to see the data, and who cares about them (McCall and Kaplan 1990). Thus a firm stressing customer service as a main organizational value is more likely to recognize, collect, and make available data on service elements. Finally, the manager's own *direct experience* is also important because concrete information based on personal, firsthand experience is more accessible and more vivid to the individual than secondhand information (Hogarth and Makridakis 1981).

Information Use in Sense Making

During sense making, information is processed to reduce situational ambiguity and to develop a consensus of shared meanings that enable organizational members to act. Both are partial objectives—ambiguity cannot and should not be completely removed, and consensus is rarely and need not be universal throughout the organization. By maintaining a residual level of equivocality and accommodating a diversity of interpretations the organization stays nimble and vigorous. People in organizations reduce ambiguity by parsing current experience and selecting interpretations from past experience to impose meanings. They progressively construct networks of meanings by starting from some existing beliefs or some sequence of actions that have been taken. The process may be belief driven (Weick 1995), where organizational members construct meaning by connecting similar pieces of information based on expectations, or by connecting contradictory information through argumentation. The process may be action driven, in which case they create meaning to justify visible actions they are committed to, or they create meaning to explain actions they took to make things happen. People in organizations develop shared meanings by tapping into shared cognitive structures or collective knowledge bases in order to establish some level of cognitive consensus that can be the foundation for collective, purposeful action. Developing consensus is aided by a number of communication behaviors that allow a diversity of interpretations or points of view to coexist or to be reconciled. The nature and extent of the consensus depend on the properties of the organizational culture, which can simultaneously be integrated, differentiated, and fragmented (Martin 1992).

Information Use and Cognitive Needs: Organizational members begin to *reduce equivocality* by selectively comparing the information they have on hand with the information they have retained in their mental knowledge structures. A knowledge structure is "a mental template that individuals impose on an information environment to give it form and meaning," so that "an individual's knowledge structure orders an information environment in a way that enables subsequent interpretation and action" (Walsh 1995, 281). Bartlett (1932) introduced the idea of *schemas* as mental structures that control attention and reconstruction of memory by providing a "knowledge base that serves as a guide for the interpretation of information, actions, and expectations" (Lord and Foti 1986, 22). Schemas are used to reduce equivocality in a number of ways: "Schemas guide the rapid recall of remembered data and solutions, the instantaneous categorization and evaluation of new data, and the default filling in of missing data and solutions via inference" (Isenberg 1986a, 252). First, schemas help make inferences about otherwise ambiguous events by suggesting cause–effect explanations. For example, a schema could suggest that an early product announcement by a competitor is intended to preempt similar introductions by others. Second, schemas guide the categorization as well as the normative appraisal of events, people, and objects (Isenberg 1986a,b). For example, particular organizations such as GM and IBM may be categorized as "prototypical business organizations," and the U.S. automotive industry's difficulties in the 1970s may be construed as cases of complacent management. Third, "schemas fill in missing data by supplying default options" and "they fill in missing solutions to problems through the recall of past instances" (Isenberg 1986a, 249). Thus once a particular schema is activated, the particular features and responses that are part of the schema are easily recalled and preferentially used in the absence of further information. Examples of organizational schemas include the cognitive maps that members infer from their organizational experience (Bougon, Weick, and Binkhorst 1977; Huff 1990; Eden 1992), standard operating procedures, as well as the dominant logic and industry recipes that we discussed earlier in the chapter. Schemas play a vital role in sense making, so much so that "sensemaking will tend to be schema driven rather than evidence driven" (Weick 1995, 153).

Because people favor order, consistency, and stability, they tend to cling on to the *expectations* generated by their schemas. This cognitive need is strong and induces a keen bias for information that confirms expectations, resulting in their selectively using only supportive information while rejecting or destructing contradictory data (Hogarth 1987). Since sense making is about finding a plausible, believable explanation, a preferential use of confirmatory data according to strong expectations may well be a practical heuristic that allows the individual to construct an interpretation that is sufficiently clear and sufficiently accurate for the purpose at hand (Snyder 1984; Weick 1995). If confirmatory evidence is available or found, the information is selected for processing or retention. This could then lead to the making of inferences or interpretations implied by the expectations. Such an apparent "validation" reinforces the expectations, which become even more strongly held. In cases when events and expectations diverge, both events and expectations may be modified to create situations leading to *self-fulfilling prophecies.* Self-fulfilling prophecies operate when initial expectations lead to the taking of certain actions that in turn produce results that reinforce the original expectations. This mutually confirming cycle is self-amplifying:

As the actions increase in frequency, the original expectation is strengthened, and as the original expectation is strengthened, there is an even further increase in actions in an ever-increasing, nonlinear cycle. . . . Because of the nonlinear nature of this circular interaction, the original expectation needs only enough initial credibility to start the ball rolling. Actions then lead to outcomes that heighten the original expectation. That is why a weak initial belief can lead to a huge nonlinear effect. . . . actions that confirm the original belief increasingly amplify the belief. (Goldstein 1994, 72, 77)

While self-fulfilling prophecies can distort perceptions and outcomes, again they may be seen as practical strategies by which people make use of the available information:

. . . self-fulfilling prophecies are a fundamental act of sensemaking. Prophecies, hypotheses, anticipations—whatever one chooses to call them—are starting points. They are minimal structures around which input can form as the result of some kind of active prodding. That prodding is often belief-driven, and the beliefs that drive it are often expectations. (Weick 1995, 148)

Self-fulfilling prophecies can also induce equilibrium that blocks off new information from outside its own self-sufficient structure. Organizations can unblock information flow by techniques such as connecting work groups with their environments, questioning differences in beliefs and points of view, contrasting the original purpose of a group with its current functioning, challenging assumptions creatively, using nonverbal methods to represent groups and systems, and so on (Goldstein 1994).

Information Use and Affective Responses: Sense making is an emotion-laden process, in which "the anxiety and fear of disorder, of not having a social place, seems to drive people to don masks, seek alliances, accept the prescriptions of others, and generally pick up whatever cultural pieces seem to fit together" (Fineman 1993, 13). Emotional arousal is particularly evident when organizational groups and members negotiate a general framework of shared meanings to coordinate action. Given that groups and members have different beliefs, values, and histories, developing a set of shared meanings usually requires resolving the tension between wishing to follow one's beliefs on the one hand and building consensus by including other points of view on the other. While complete agreement on what something means is rarely attainable, a desirable end result is for members to construct jointly an overarching set of understandings and to feel a sense of commitment to the goals and behaviors that are implied by their shared interpretations. Commitment and trust are more likely when:

1. Participants have had adequate opportunity to explain their own points of view and to influence the discourse on plausible interpretations
2. Participants understand the logic behind the selection of the shared interpretation and how it can further the organization's overall goals

3. Participants recognize that the shared interpretation can be revised or even replaced when warranted by new evidence.

Communication behaviors that are invoked in the interpretive discourse can also help relieve tension between self-values and shared consensus. For example, metaphors are used to allow parties to maintain their own interpretations while creating common understanding (Donnellon et al. 1986); voice, gesture, and emotion-laden words allow participants to modulate affective responses and cause the reconsideration of a situation (Donnellon et al. 1986); and interpretations may be expressed or framed in ways that permit agreement (Fiol 1994).

As we have noted, feelings of doubt and stress are induced when the available information does not harmonize with the individual's mental schemas or expectations. Because people hang on to their expectations, an initial response is to try to "retrofit" deviant information into existing schemas or categories. Sometimes more search is undertaken to gather information to confirm or reject the out-of-place data. Rarer still would be the occasions when the individual becomes convinced of the veridicality of the new information and therefore decides to revise her mental schemas and anticipations. When a large change in the individual's belief and knowledge structures appears necessary, feelings of stress and excitement lead the individual to appraise the disruption as *a threat or a challenge:* "The disruption is appraised as primarily threatening or challenging according to personal beliefs, predispositions, and one's sense of whether his or her personal resources are adequate to the demands of the disruption" (McCaskey 1982, 75). If perceived as a threat, the coping response may be to not engage the problem at all by avoiding, denying, or distorting the available information. If seen as a challenge, the response would be to engage the ambiguity directly through vigilance, further information gathering, and bold action (McCaskey 1982).

Information Use and Situational Dimensions: Taylor (1991) suggested that a defining feature of the information use environment of a group of users is what the members regard as the *resolution of a problem.* In the case of managers making meaning, the problem of reducing situational ambiguity is considered solved when they can agree on or accept a plausible interpretation, an interpretation that is credible and reasonable but not necessarily very accurate. Such sense making is embedded in *organizational cultures* as systems of shared meanings (Smircich 1983). As we discussed earlier, organizational culture is best analyzed as being simultaneously integrated, differentiated, and fragmented. In the integrated perspective, the organization enjoys organizationwide consensus about basic values and assumptions which are consistent in content and in the ways they guide action and give rise to cultural symbols. Integrated cultures therefore provide cognitive clarification, helping individuals to make sense retrospectively of their activities, and increasing their awareness of role expectations and the organization's history (Martin 1992). In the differentiation perspective, subcultures, rather than the entire organization, form "islands of localized lucidity," with each subculture creating its own "coherent meaning system," and "providing clear solutions to problems shared by a group" (Martin 1992, 93). To preserve subcultural clarity and cohesiveness, ambiguous or contradictory information is channeled outside the boundaries of the group. In the fragmented perspective, a multiplicity of interpretations coexist and do not coalesce into a stable consensus (Martin 1992). Organizational cultures are temporary webs of individuals loosely connected by the issues they are interested in. Information use is highly selective and focused on specific issues. Individuals' participation and positions in these interest networks are constantly changing, and rather than pushing ambiguity away, they confront and deal with it directly.

We saw earlier that sense making may be belief driven or action driven. When actions are hard to change, people may instead modify their beliefs. Belief adjustment is more likely when the individual is highly committed to a course of action: "People try hardest to build meaning around those actions to which their commitment is strongest. *Commitment* in other words, focuses sensemaking into binding actions" (Weick 1995, 156). According to Salancik (1977) and Kiesler (1971), individuals are likely to become committed or bound to a behavior when the following situational dimensions apply:

1. The individual's acts are explicit or unambiguous.
2. The behavior is irrevocable or easily undone.
3. The behavior has been entered into freely or has involved a high degree of volition
4. The act has importance for the individual.
5. The act is public or is visible to others.
6. The act has been performed a number of times.

(Staw and Ross 1987, 52)

In short, individuals are likely to be bound to a current course of action when their prior behaviors in pursuing that course have been explicit, freely chosen, visible to others, irrevocable, repeated, and important (Staw and Ross 1987). Behavioral commitment introduces order into the sense making process by noticing features that justify the behavior, and by imputing value to the incoming information. When commitment is strong, individuals notice or look for features in a situation that others may miss in order to have the justification to support the continuance of the behavior. Available information and diverse interpretations are categorized into those that support, oppose, or are irrelevant to the behavior. On the whole, "commitment affects sensemaking by focusing attention, uncovering unnoticed features, and imposing value" (Weick 1995, 159).

Organizations also *enact their own environments,* which then influence their selection and use of information. Recall our earlier discussion of how the Scottish knitwear manufacturers enacted their own transactional network of producers, agents, retailers, and customers. The knitwear producers hired agents to canvass contracts with retailers, and selected agents who fit in well with their classical elegance image. These selected agents then negotiate with retailers that sell classically designed clothing and whose customers are inclined toward traditional knitwear. By preselecting each other as compatible partners, the participants in the transactional network are mutually reinforcing the collective belief that Scottish knitwear producers sell garments of classical elegance. The partners have essentially enacted their own business environment, and in doing so, have set up situational constraints on the generation, flow, and use of information. Thus little market research was done, and there was a dearth of statistical data about market trends or consumer preferences. Market information was sampled only from sources that confirmed the producers' self-definition as purveyors of classically elegant knitwear.

V. SUMMARY: THE MANAGEMENT OF ORGANIZATIONAL SENSE MAKING

The central information problem in organizational sense making is to reduce ambiguity in messages about the environment and to develop shared meaning among members in order for collective, purposeful action to take place. Organizations cannot and do not attempt to eradicate ambiguity totally or to establish consensus throughout the organization. By maintaining a level of information equivocality and by accommodating a diversity of interpretations, an organization provides the cognitive white space for its members to inquire, experiment, and discover. The principal information activities in sense making are scanning, noticing, and interpreting. Scanning is sweeping the environment broadly and systematically in order to watch developments that can be important to the organization. Noticing is isolating significant events for closer scrutiny, and the process of noticing may involve acting on the environment, thereby changing parts of it. Interpreting is selecting plausible interpretations and developing a set of shared beliefs and perceptions that can guide action. The main medium of sense making is face-to-face conversations between different sets of people who engage simultaneously in talking, thinking, and seeing. The output of sense making is a network of shared meanings that provides plausible explanations and assigns significance to ambiguous cues. Shared meanings and assumptions define an information processing framework that sets criteria and values for the selection, seeking, and use of information, as well as suggesting ways to simplify the gathering and analysis of data.

Overall, the sense making organization uses information to reduce equivocality and develop shared meaning, while at the same time allowing dissimilar interpretations to coexist so that the organization can test the validity of old assumptions, see opportunities or threats brought forward by new information, and stimulate inquiry and improvisation.

C H A P T E R

4

THE MANAGEMENT OF LEARNING—
ORGANIZATIONS AS KNOWLEDGE-
CREATING ENTERPRISES

Knowledge, a rude unprofitable mass,
The mere materials with which wisdom builds,
Till smoothed and squared and fitted to its place,
Does but encumber whom it seems to enrich.
Knowledge is proud that he has learned so much;
Wisdom is humble that he knows no more.
    —*William Cowper 1785,* The Task, *book 6*

Knowledge in an organization is widely dispersed and assumes many forms, but its quality is revealed in the range of capabilities that the organization possesses as a result of this knowledge. While most of the organization's knowledge is rooted in the expertise and experience of its individual members, the organization provides a physical, social, and cultural context so that the exercise and growth of this knowledge takes on meaning and purpose. Knowledge is also the outcome of the relationships that the organization has nurtured over time with its customers, suppliers, and partners. These relationships are often strategic to the focal organization, accelerating its learning and broadening its reach. Because organizational knowledge is both highly personal and widely distributed, organizations are designing social and technical structures to promote the internal sharing of expertise among its individual members, while simultaneously forging partnerships with other organizations and groups to exchange and jointly create new knowledge.

As long as knowledge remains personal to individual members so that it cannot be shared easily, organizations cannot multiply the value of this expertise. On the other hand, the formalization of personal knowledge may impede learning and creativity. Consider a modern-day consulting firm whose employees move from client to client, helping the client company to solve problems or implement new systems and procedures. Over time, the employee consultants develop insight about the special requirements of clients in particular industries, and accumulate knowledge about the kinds of solutions and implementation strategies that are likely to work well for certain categories of clients. Although this personal knowledge is critical to the operation and success of the consulting firm, it is also knowledge that is hard to extract and externalize. Wanda Orlikowski (1988) studied how one such firm resolved this dilemma for her doctoral research. The firm is among the largest of the Big 8 accounting firms, with one of the biggest management consulting practices in terms of revenues and personnel. Founded in 1913, the firm has offices in major cities around the world, with headquarters in a large U.S. city in the Midwest. The research focused on the management consulting practice (MCP) division of the firm, whose primary business is the design and building of computer-based information systems. The MCP's New York City office consisted of three branches, one in Manhattan, Connecticut, and New Jersey, employing a total of some 750 consultants. MCP's main consulting practice is to custom-build application software for its clients by sending in project teams who remain and work on the client site for months or even years to produce a computerized information system. Building software for clients is a highly complex, knowledge-intensive activity that is fraught with uncertainty. Over its history, MCP evolved two innovations to manage its internal knowledge and to cope with the task-related uncertainty—a standardized system development methodology and a suite of computer-aided software engineering (CASE) tools. Orlikowski explains how MCP's standardized methodology (Modus) came to be:

> When the MCP division first started developing information systems for clients some thirty years ago, the only written "knowledge" of systems development in the Firm was extracted post hoc from the documentation generated for each project. These so-called "client binders" served as the Firm's information expertise about the systems development production process during the initial years of the consulting practice. As the practice grew, some attempt was made to systematize this varied and highly idiosyncratic knowledge. During meetings partners would review the project documentation, trying to extract general procedures, and identify the common factors that made some projects successful, others mediocre, and still others failures. Over time these generalized "rules of thumb" became more extensive and more sophisticated as the MCP division gained more experience. Eventually the informal guidelines about how to run a successful systems development project and what factors constitute good systems practice evolved into the formal, standardized methodology that "Modus" is today. (Orlikowski 1988, 166–67)

Thus MCP's system development methodology grew out of the daily activities of consultants working on projects. By analyzing and reflecting on this practical know-how, MCP partners were able to generalize and formalize their experiences into a methodology which specified the sequence of tasks to be performed at each stage of the system development life cycle, and defined the standards for documentation, control, scheduling, and project estimation. The institutionalization of a standard methodology was also in line with the firm's "one-firm" philosophy, which required all partners to follow a common approach in the ways they dealt with clients' problems and communicated about them. From its earliest days, the firm had espoused the policy of speaking with one professional voice, and abiding and upholding the official viewpoint of the firm.

The formalization of the Modus methodology made possible the next major innovation in MCP's consulting practice—the introduction of a standard set of computer-aided software engineering (CASE) tools, which MCP called "productivity tools," to support and implement the methodology. This integrated tool environment included software to capture ongoing documentation of the new system into a data dictionary, project estimating aids, the project control system, screen and report design aids, data and program design aids, installation tools, and prototyping facilities. The tools "implemented the standard software engineering design philosophy and project management method articulated in Modus." In fact, "the tools were deliberately based on the methodology as it was recognized that production technology logic had to be compatible with that of the production process, else inconsistency and discontinuity would disrupt the systems development process" (Orlikowski 1988, 183). The use of the methodology and the CASE tool set was mutually reinforcing. Since the tools were based on Modus, their use ensured compliance with the methodology. At the same time, Modus was also constantly being updated to better reflect the tool environment. This reciprocal interdependence characterized the codevelopment of the tool and the methodology. Furthermore, the use of computerized tools enhanced the aura of professionalism in the consultants' normal work activities:

Tools render an image of a room of consultants all seated in front of their personal workstations, all bent over their keyboards, flashing through complicated-looking screens, performing sophisticated cut and paste procedures, and all done to the accompaniment of the reassuring whir of the disk drives, the steady tapping of keys, and the regular sigh of the laser printer emitting its professional-looking documents. It certainly looks industrious. (Orlikowski 1988, 403)

As a result of employing the tool methodology, MCP reported savings of 30 to 50 percent in code generation, and an elimination of between 50 and 70 percent of the systems installation phase. The use of tools "dramatically" increased MCP's profitability, and allowed it to reap the benefits of operating economies of scale. The competitive position has been improved by enabling the firm to bring the price of its services down, to lower its bids on contracts, to go after larger projects, and to increase the income contribution of each partner.

Besides productivity and profitability gains, there were other important and somewhat surprising benefits derived from the use of the CASE tools and methodology. As a professional services firm, MCP is expected to provide customized solutions to each of its clients. Indeed, each client will have its own data-processing environment that made customization mandatory. Although this might appear incompatible with MCP's standardized production process, the software utilities in the CASE tool set were in fact relatively easy to modify so that they could work well with a client's hardware and software configurations. Each client company therefore was provided with tools that were customized to the project and technical characteristics of the site. At the same time, since the underlying process logic may not change that much from project to project, MCP is able to reuse significant portions of their development outputs:

> With the deployment of productivity tools it is able to adapt a set of system designs and documentation developed for one project for use in selling a similar system to another client. By being able to customize the visible features of the design to the potential client's needs while leaving the essential logic of the systems design intact, the Firm can exploit the power of the tools in saving time by not having to design another system or generate new documentation. It can use the logic of the existing system to customize the labels, change the screen and report headings, and change client references in the documentation, and have a new comprehensive systems proposal to present to a potential client. And if the client accepts the proposal and the project gets underway, many of the tools, shells, macros can be directly transferred to the new project site, hence avoiding reinvention of the wheel. (Orlikowski 1988, 352)

The standardization process thus extends beyond tools and methodology to the "industry standard solutions" that MCP is able to offer to its clients, who receive tested solutions that have been optimized for their local computing environments. (The success of its integrated CASE tool environment prompted MCP to sell the tool set as a generalized productivity tools package to the clients themselves and to other data-processing companies.)

The experience of MCP highlights several of the themes that will be developed in this chapter.

1. *Valuable organizational knowledge resides in individuals who build up their knowledge by working on the job over extended periods of time.* MCP's consultants worked with many clients and through many projects before they acquired insights about which development practices are likely to lead to system success.

2. *To the extent that this knowledge remains personal to the individual, the organization is limited in its ability to leverage this expertise.* MCP was able to externalize the skills of its consultants and convert them

into standardized tools and methods, which allowed the firm to handle more projects and to train new staff more quickly.

3. *To the extent that this knowledge remains within the organization, the organization's customers and partners are limited in their ability to maximize the value-adding contribution of this knowledge.* MCP's consultants worked one on one with its clients in teams that included the client's own systems staff and end users to develop solutions that were based on tested logic, but were tailored to the client's computing environment.

The formalization of knowledge also had important negative consequences. Orlikowski (1988) emphasized that the use of automated tools in MCP resulted in the deskilling of the system development tasks:

. . . the tools in their design and implementation deskill the functional production tasks of systems development. The requirement for technical skills has been eliminated through the routinization of the tasks, detaching the execution of a task from the knowledge underlying it. The requirement for functional skills has been reduced to some extent through the rationalization of tasks which makes much of the development work an exercise in filling in standardized forms and using abstracted design techniques. Deskilling the tasks has generated a number of unintended consequences that have raised some problems in the Firm. The tools seem to be breeding a generation of relatively unskilled consultants, whose long-term systems development performance is suspect. The tools create among analysts a dependence on tools and a lack of understanding of programming that sometimes hinders project progress. . . . through formalizing, abstracting and reifying tasks, tools limit individual discretion, eliminate creativity and flexibility, generate shallow designs, encourage passivity, and discourage reflectiveness. (Orlikowski 1988, 241, 250)

The danger here is that the widespread use of standardized tools and methods is likely to increase reliance on the tools and reduce the motivation to probe more deeply and creatively into the underlying assumptions and rules. Without this constant stretching and testing of existing theory, the creation of new knowledge will be stymied. The dilemma before an organization is therefore to externalize knowledge so that it can be shared, but to do so without compromising the impetus to learn and innovate.

This chapter is divided into six sections. Section I and II discuss the three classes of organizational knowledge, with an elaboration on the nature of tacit knowledge at various levels of the organization. Section III and IV examine the phases and activities of the knowledge-creating process in an organization, attempting a synthesis of the recent work of Nonaka and Takeuchi (1995), Leonard-Barton (1995), and Wikström and Normann (1994). Section V describes a special but strategic mode of knowledge creation—the sharing and transfer of knowledge with other organizations outside the parent institution through knowledge links. Section VI describes information seeking and use in the knowledge-creating process.

I. ORGANIZATIONAL KNOWLEDGE

In this chapter we are primarily concerned with the knowledge in organizations that leads to technical innovation, that is, knowledge that enables or results in the development of new competences, products, or services, or the improvement of important organizational work activities. We are especially interested in the processes that transport and transform knowledge across different levels of the organization, and between a focal organization and its partners. Knowledge that can be formalized or codified in some way diffuses more quickly and more extensively than knowledge that cannot. Thus Boisot (1995) classifies types of knowledge based on whether the knowledge is codified and whether it is readily diffused. Codified knowledge is "knowledge that can be stored or put down in writing without incurring undue losses of information," such as stock market prices, software code, and legal statutes; while uncodified knowledge is "knowledge that cannot be captured in writing or stored without losing the essentials of the experience it relates to," such as recognizing a face, operating complex machinery, or playing the piano. Diffused knowledge is shared with others, such as radio broadcasts, published reports, and press releases, while undiffused knowledge "stays locked inside one's head whether because it is hard to articulate or because one decides to keep it there," such as company secrets, childhood memories, and personal fantasies (Boisot 1995, 145). Using the dimensions of codification and diffusion, Boisot devises a typology of knowledge pertinent to our discussion here (Table 4–1).

Public knowledge is codified and diffusible. It is what we conventionally regard as knowledge in society, and can be found structured and recorded in textbooks, research journals, and other formal and informal printed sources. The utility and value of public knowledge can be enhanced by well-designed coding procedures: "Well-chosen codes bestow upon their data valuable powers of combination, allowing them to form novel patterns either on their own or by linking up with existing items of codified knowledge." However, codi-

TABLE 4–1. Typology of knowledge (Boisot 1995, 146).

Codified	Proprietary knowledge	Public knowledge
Uncodified	Personal knowledge	Commonsense knowledge
	Undiffused	Diffused

fied public knowledge "slowly gets woven into a dense impermeable tissue of facts, categories, and concepts that may subsequently prove hard to modify— i.e., over time it acquires inertia" (Boisot 1995, 147). ***Commonsense knowledge*** is widespread but much less codified. A person acquires commonsense knowledge gradually over a lifetime through personal experiences and encounters with family, friends, peers, and other members of the person's community. What becomes internalized as common sense depends on the person's social situation or membership in groups, and on the extent of influence others have over what she learns and perceives. ***Personal knowledge*** is even more idiosyncratic and hard to articulate. Since personal knowledge by definition grows out of the individual's own experience that is not accessible to others, a shared context for discourse does not exist, thus preventing the diffusion of the knowledge. The communication of personal knowledge generally requires the parties to be copresent and to jointly share in the concrete experiences. ***Proprietary knowledge*** is knowledge that a person or group develops and codifies on its own in order to make sense of particular situations. Although proprietary knowledge is codified and is therefore technically diffusible, it may not be meaningful to do so because its relevance is bound to the specific circumstances and needs of the originator.

In Boisot's classification, personal, proprietary, and commonsense knowledge are particularly relevant to an analysis of the organization's internal knowledge. Personal knowledge based on personal experience is the basis of all organizational knowledge. Proprietary knowledge is knowledge unique to the organization, which the organization has developed in response to its specific circumstances. Commonsense knowledge is shared by members of the organization to establish a sense of identity and meaning. Following on from Boisot's classification, we propose that the knowledge of an organization may be usefully differentiated into

1. Tacit knowledge
2. Explicit knowledge
3. Cultural knowledge

Tacit knowledge is the implicit knowledge used by organizational members to perform their work and to make sense of their worlds. As in Boisot's personal knowledge, it is knowledge that is uncodified and difficult to diffuse. Tacit knowledge is hard to verbalize because it is expressed through action-based skills and cannot be reduced to rules and recipes. It is learned through extended periods of experiencing and doing a task, during which the individual develops a feel for and a capacity to make intuitive judgments about the successful execution of the activity. Pulp and paper mill operators, photocopier repair technicians, ship navigators, bank account officers, town planners, doctors, and managers are but a few examples of professions where tacit knowledge has been observed to play an instrumental role. Tacit knowledge is vital to the organization because organizations can only learn and innovate by somehow levering on the implicit knowledge of its members. The most advanced computer-based information systems on their own do not generate new knowledge, only human beings led by tacit know-how have the capability to do so. Since tacit knowledge underlies organizational knowledge, we elaborate on tacit knowledge in the next section.

Explicit knowledge is knowledge that can be expressed formally using a system of symbols, and can therefore be easily communicated or diffused (Nonaka and Takeuchi 1995). Explicit knowledge may be object based or rule based. It is object based when the knowledge is codified in strings of symbols (words, numbers, formulas) or in physical objects (equipment, documents, models). Object-based knowledge may be found in examples such as product specifications, patents, software code, computer databases, technical drawings, tools, prototypes, photographs, and so on. Explicit knowledge is rule based when the knowledge is codified into rules, routines, or standard operating procedures. A large part of an organization's operations is controlled by rules and standard procedures. Although all organizations operate with standard procedures, each organization would have developed its own repertoire of routines, based on its experience and the specific environment it operates in. Cyert and March ([1963]1992) distinguish between four major types of rule-based procedures: task performance rules, rules for maintaining organizational records, information-handling rules, and planning rules. *Task performance rules* specify methods for accomplishing organizational tasks. They form the bulk of the organization's rules and procedures and are important because they embody and facilitate the transfer of past learning. Performance rules also have a coordinating function, so that a solution implemented by one group is consistent with a large number of other solutions and tasks being performed elsewhere in the organization. *Record-keeping rules* specify what records and how such records should be maintained by the organization. In the short term, records (such as financial statements or cost records) have a control effect. In the longer term, records are used to predict the environment by suggesting "simple hypotheses about the relation between the past and the future" (Cyert and March [1963]1992, 126). *Information-handling rules* specify the organization's communication system in terms of the characteristics of the information to be taken into the firm, the rules for distributing and summarizing internal and external information, and the characteristics of the information leaving the firm. *Planning rules* specify the periodic planning process as a standard procedure and produce intended allocation of resources among the activities of the organization (Cyert and March [1963]1992).

Cultural knowledge consists of the cognitive and affective structures that are habitually used by organizational members to perceive, explain, evaluate, and construct reality. Cultural knowledge includes the assumptions and beliefs that are used to describe and explain reality, as well as the conventions and expectations that are used to assign value and significance to new information. These shared beliefs, norms, and values form the framework in which organizational members construct reality, recognize the saliency of new information, and evaluate alternative interpretations and actions. As in Boisot's commonsense knowledge, cultural knowledge is uncodified and broadly diffused over the links and relationships that connect a group. Sackmann (1991, 1992) identifies four kinds of cultural knowledge in an organization: dictionary knowledge, directory knowledge, recipe knowledge, and axiomatic knowledge. *Dictionary knowledge* comprises commonly held descriptions, including expressions and definitions used in the organization to describe the "what" of situations, such as what is considered to be a problem, or what is considered to be success. *Directory knowledge* refers to commonly held practices and is knowledge about sequences of events and their cause-effect relationships that describe the "how" of processes, such as how a problem is solved or how success is to be achieved. *Recipe knowledge* comprises prescriptions for repair and improvement strategies that recommend what action "should" be taken, for example, to solve a problem or to become successful. *Axiomatic knowledge* refers to reasons and explanations of the final causes or a priori premises that are perceived to account for "why" events happen. Sackmann's categories of cultural knowledge are closely related to the schemas, scripts, cause maps, and basic assumptions that we presented in our discussion of organizational culture in the last chapter. In the context of knowledge creating, cultural knowledge plays the vital role of providing a pattern of shared assumptions (Schein 1991) so that the organization can assign significance to new information and knowledge. Cultural knowledge supplies values and norms that

> . . . determine what kinds of knowledge are sought and nurtured, what kinds of knowledge-building activities are tolerated and encouraged. There are systems of caste and status, rituals of behavior, and passionate beliefs associated with various kinds of technological knowledge that are as rigid and complex as those associated with religion. Therefore, values serve as knowledge-screening and -control mechanisms. (Leornard-Barton 1995, 19)

Garud and Rappa (1994) propose that the development of new knowledge based on technology is a sociocognitive process which rests on three definitions of technology: "technology as beliefs, artifacts, and evaluation routines" (p. 345). Technology development is guided by beliefs about what is possible, what is worth attempting, and what levels of effort are required. Technology as physical artifact specifies the technology's form (such as shape or material of construction) and function (such as uses and applications). Technology as evaluation routines defines testing routines and normative values that "filter data in a way that influences whether or not researchers perceive information as useful. Researchers with different beliefs attempt to sway each other with respect to the routines utilized to judge the technology" (Garud and Rappa 1994, 346). Evaluation routines also facilitate communication about the technology and allow the new technology to gain legitimacy in the eyes of researchers. Beliefs, artifacts, and evaluation routines interact with each other to shape the evolution of new technology. Garud and Rappa suggest that beliefs guide the creation of artifacts that in return raise commitment in the technology; beliefs are externalized as testing routines and standards; and routines legitimize and select the form that the technology takes. Overall, an organization's beliefs regarding the feasibility and value of technology or new knowledge would influence the direction, content, and intensity of the knowledge development effort. As part of the cultural knowledge of the organization, these beliefs would also shape the routines and norms by which new information and knowledge would be evaluated.

The three types of organizational knowledge are interdependent. Tacit knowledge is embedded in the skills of an individual or the shared practices of a group. Rule-based knowledge is dispersed across multiple participants and groups who act in a coordinated manner according to rules and routines. Insofar as the performance of routines involves the exercise of the personal skills of individuals, tacit knowledge is ensconced in rule-based knowledge. Cultural knowledge is shared by many members of the organization in order to give meaning and value to information, events, and actions. Insofar as rules and routines are manifestations and codifications of organizational culture, rule-based knowledge is ensconced in cultural knowledge.

II. TACIT KNOWLEDGE

Michael Polanyi begins his consideration of human knowledge by "starting from the fact that *we can know more than we can tell*" (1966, 4; italics in original). Thus we can almost instantly recognize a face from among a thousand, but we usually cannot explain how we recognize a face that we know. Tacit knowledge permeates our personal and work lives, enabling us to drive the automobile, enjoy a poem, or deal with a problem situation. In all such cases of personal knowing, *"the aim of a skilful performance is achieved by the observance of a set of rules which are not known as such to the person following them"* (Polanyi 1962, 49; italics in original). Tacit knowledge is hard to transfer or verbalize partly because it cannot be broken down into particular rules or elements, and partly because it exists as an emergent quality of knowing something as a whole:

> The skill of a driver cannot be replaced by a thorough schooling in the theory of the motorcar; the knowledge I have of my own body differs altogether from the knowledge of its physiology; and the rules of rhyming and prosody do not tell me what a poem told me, without any knowledge of its rules. (Polanyi 1966, 20)

Tacit knowledge may be likened to *knowing that is in our action,* "implicit in our patterns of actions and in our feel for the stuff with which we are dealing" (Schön 1983, 54). Schön defines this "knowing in action" with the following properties:

- There are actions, recognitions, and judgments which we know how to carry out spontaneously; we do not have to think about them prior to or during their performance.

- We are often unaware of having learned to do these things; we simply find ourselves doing them.

- In some cases, we were once aware of the understandings which were subsequently internalized in our feeling for the stuff of action. In other cases, we may never have been aware of them. In both cases, however, we are usually unable to describe the knowing which our action reveals.

(Schön 1983, 54)

From her up-close analysis of the work of operators in pulp and paper mills, Zuboff observed how the operators relied on action-centered skills that are based on tacit knowledge:

When operators in Piney Wood and Tiger Creek discuss their traditional skills, they speak of knowing things by habit and association. They talk about "cause and effect" knowledge and being able to see the things to which they must respond. They refer to "folk medicine" and knowledge that you don't even know you have until it is suddenly displayed in the ability to take a decisive action and make something work. . . . The body is an instrument, actively registering information and, in turn, expressing what it learns in action. Inferential linkages between actions and their consequences need not be made explicit in order for skill to be learned or enacted. Action-centered skills are so called in part because their development, execution, and memory can remain confined to the sphere of tacit knowledge. (Zuboff 1988, 71, 187)

Tacit know-how is not limited to technical skills, but is just as important in undergirding the actions of professionals in architecture, engineering, management, psychotherapy, and so on (Schön 1983). Zuboff again provides an example of how bank account officers in the Global Bank Brazil made their credit decisions:

Our credit decisions have been more related to feeling than to technical skill. For big loans, the officer knows the client and the client's environment. He spends time with that person. They dine together, play golf together. That is why we specialize by industry and company size. This is why the officer comes to know things that are not written. Credit is given by the feeling in one's stomach. (Quoted in Zuboff 1988, 164)

Cognitive psychologists distinguish between declarative or *semantic memory,* which stores information such as facts, concepts, and associations that represent our general knowledge of the world, and *procedural memory,* which allows us to learn skills and know-how to do things, and stores information on the components of individual skilled action (Schacter 1996; Squire and Knowlton 1995; Singley and Anderson 1989). With this distinction, Cohen and Bacdayan (1994) suggest that tacit knowledge resides in procedural memory rather than declarative memory: "Procedural memory has close links to notions of individual skill and habit. It is memory for how things are done that is relatively automatic and inarticulate, and it encompasses cognitive as well as motor activities" (p. 554). Furthermore, studies have shown that "procedural knowledge is less subject to decay, less explicitly accessible, and less easy to transfer to novel circumstances" (p. 557). Cognitive scientists Varela, Thompson, and Rosch (1991) regard human cognition as *embodied action* that "depends upon the kinds of experience that come from having a body with various sensorimotor capacities," and that "these individual sensorimotor capacities are themselves embedded in a more encompassing biological, psychological, and cultural context." In other words, "sensory and motor processes, perception and action, are fundamentally inseparable in lived cognition" (p. 173).

Tacit knowledge incorporates "knowledge of the particular circumstances of time and place" (Hayek 1945, 521). Tacit knowledge is the capacity to take action, where "actions are always situated in particular social and physical circumstances," and such *situated action* is based on local properties of the task environment that "orient or position us in a way that will allow us, through local interactions, to exploit some contingencies of our environment, and to avoid others" (Suchman 1987, 178, 188). Brown (1993) believes that situated action often exerts a powerful influence: "By participating, by interacting with the world, the world often suggests what to do next. It affords actions" (p. 90). To demonstrate this *situational affordance,* he cited an account based on actual observation of how people in a supermarket chose between two brands of cheese in a cheese barrel. They did not attempt to divide the weight by the price of each brand to calculate and compare their prices per unit weight. Instead, people simply grabbed a chunk of each, placed them on top of each other to see that they were the same size, then turned them over to read the price. The lower price was the one they chose—"No division was needed. The world did the dividing for them" (Brown 1993, 91; story also attributed to Jean Lave). Brown concluded that:

> The story showed people fully engaged in activity within the world. They participated and used the situation as an aid in getting the job done and found clever ways to register the situation or context in a way to let it, itself, do some of the work for them. They found a way to let the context carry some of the representational and computational load. (Brown 1993, 91)

In summary, tacit knowledge, elusive as it may be, has a number of defining features. It is hard to verbalize or to be codified using symbols such as in formulas or written-down rules. It is hard to break down into elements or steps because tacit knowledge is distributed in the totality of the individual's action experience. It is action centered, relying on tactile cues registered by the human body interacting with its environment. Such action is situated in the social and physical dimensions of the setting in which it is applied. Despite it being uncodified, tacit knowledge can be and is regularly taught and shared. Tacit knowledge can be learned by example. Thus apprentices learn their craft by following and copying their masters; professionals develop expertise through periods of internship; and new employees are immersed in on-the-job training. Professionals reflect on what they know during the practice itself (for example, when they encounter an unusual case) as well as afterward (for example, in a postmortem), and in doing so test and refine their own tacit knowledge (Schön 1983). Tacit knowledge can also be shared. Although not completely expressible in words or symbols, tacit knowledge may be alluded to or revealed through rich modes of discourse that include the use of analogies, metaphors, or models, and through the communal sharing of stories.

The Tacitness of Communal Knowledge

While tacit knowledge is a personal resource, researchers have found that teams as well as whole organizations can be usefully thought of as possessing knowledge that has the characteristics of tacit knowing, that is, knowledge which is hard to document but is dispersed among multiple actors who interact with each other and with the physical, cultural, and social dimensions of their task and organizational setting. Studies such as those of Brown and Gray (1995), Brown and Duguid (1991), Wenger (1991), and Orr (1990) challenge the traditional assumptions that learning and knowing implies individual mastery, and that everything that is knowable can be made explicit:

> Why is it, then, that we always think of learning in individualistic terms of acquisition of information? . . . We think of individual capabilities, judged in standard terms of intelligence. And we think of books, assuming that information exists on paper or in words, there to be acquired by individual minds. This mentalistic view is pervasive: The myth of the acquisition of information and the myth of the individual learner are both central to our culture. .. As valuable as information is, information by itself is meaningless. . . . Information only takes on meaning in the context of the social practices of the communities that give it cultural life. (Wenger 1991, 7)

Instead of treating knowledge as being explicit and individually acquired, knowledge in organizations is often tacitly shared by members of social groups: "With individuals, tacit knowledge means intuition, judgment, common sense—the capacity to do something without necessarily being able to explain it. With groups, tacit knowledge exists in the distinct practices and

relationships that emerge from working together over time—the social fabric
that connects communities of knowledge workers" (Brown and Gray 1995,
80). Research suggests that a group holds this tacit knowledge as a community
that forms around a shared practice. Members of such *communities of practice*
participate in a shared practice informally but legitimately. The community of
practice provides a context in which the meaning of objects, problems, events,
and artifacts gets constructed and negotiated, and in which people live, work,
communicate, and understand the environment and themselves (Brown 1993).
Communities of practice emerge naturally from the organization's web of interactions, and need not be formally controlled or designed. By reconceiving
organizations as comprising communities of practice, working, learning, and
innovation are integrated in a unified view (Brown and Duguid 1991).

Badaracco (1991) also suggests that just as individual craftspersons have
tacit knowledge, so do successful teams, small groups, and departments in
companies. The team's knowledge resides in the relationships that bind together "a group of individuals, the coordinated accomplishment of several
tasks, and the use of a variety of tools" (Badaracco 1991, 84). Specifically,
each team member possesses partial but complementary knowledge, so that
only the team working together as a whole has the full body of knowledge.
Moreover, members of successful teams know how to work with each other.
They have "a tacit understanding of how the people in the group can work
together with the resources they have to accomplish particular tasks" (p. 86).

Evolutionary economic theory addresses the question of where does organizational knowledge reside, and how this knowledge relates to that of others
and the knowledge environment in general (Winter 1994; Nelson and Winter
1982). The theory claims that *organizations remember by doing,* and that the
most important form of storage of an organization's operational knowledge is
in its routines and the memory of its members: "In the sense that the memories
of individual members do store so much information required for the performance of organizational routines, there is substantial truth in the proposition
that the knowledge an organization possesses is reducible to the knowledge of
its individual members" (Nelson and Winter 1982, 104). According to evolutionary economic theory, "much of the knowledge that underlies organizational
capabilities is tacit knowledge" (Winter 1994, 473), and this may be elaborated
from more than one perspective:

Knowledge possessed by an organization may be tacit knowledge in the sense,
first, that the possession arises from the association with the organization of an
individual for whom the knowledge in question is tacit. Related articulable
knowledge may be possessed by other members of the organization, to the effect
that 'We have someone who knows about (or can do) that.' Second, the fact that
the myriads of relationships that enable the organization to function in a coordinated way are reasonably understood by (at most) the participants in the relationship and a few others means that the organization is certainly accomplishing its
aims by following rules that are not known as such to most participants in the or-

ganization. Third, in a metaphorical sense an organization's knowledge is tacit to the extent that its top decisionmakers are uninformed regarding the details of what happens when their decisions are implemented. (Winter 1987, 171)

Organizational innovations germinate from the seeds of tacit knowledge. Although tacit knowledge develops initially in the skills and intuitions of individuals, this personal knowledge is progressively socialized. Thus the individual participates in a community where knowledge is shared, and the group then modulates this personal knowledge through its network of roles, relationships, and tools to invent new knowledge. The new group-based knowledge is still tacit, because it is embedded in the structure and practices of the group; it cannot be easily codified; and it is revealed through the shared behavior of the group that enables it to solve problems and innovate. In this sense, therefore, tacit knowledge may be said to exist at the group and organizational levels. Tacit knowledge is potentially valuable because it is unique expertise acquired by individuals working in the particular environment of an organization. Tacit knowledge becomes substantively valuable when it is turned into new capabilities, products, or services. Innovations materialize when implicit knowledge is surfaced and shaped into objects or systems. Implicit knowledge generates new value when it is made explicit. The next section discusses the organizational processes by which tacit knowledge is transformed into explicit knowledge.

III. KNOWLEDGE CONVERSION

The recent history of numerical control machines provides an instance of a somewhat ingenious way of converting tacit knowledge into explicit computer programs, and furthermore, turning this capability into a competitive advantage (Sabel 1982, Noble 1984). Numerical control machines are machine tools, each equipped with a built-in computer that controls its operations. They are used widely in many large-scale manufacturing industries. The computer of the numerical control machine has to be programmed individually for each component that the machine is to fabricate. This programming could be done by an engineer coding the operations on a central computer, or it could be done by "recording" the activities of a human operator. In Germany and Japan numerical control users and machine designers opted for the latter, recording the movements and tasks of their most skilled tool operators, in effect externalizing the operators' tacit knowledge and converting it into machine-readable code. The recording process also allowed the operators to make corrections or improvements to recorded sections as they learned to do a particular task more efficiently. In the United States many managers and engineering departments programmed the numerical control machines themselves, partly because they believed that programming by engineers was superior to machinist programming, and partly because they did not want to be dependent on unionized tool operators, should they become the only ones able to run the machines. This difference in the knowledge conversion method has "long-term" consequences: " . . . nowadays most of the machines are being programmed by less expensive skilled workers rather than by senior engineers who, much more expensively, know both the abstract language of numerical-control programming and the concrete routines of metal working. This means that now the Japanese and the Germans control the international sales of most machine tools, whereas thirty or so years ago the United States was the dominant force in that market. Obviously, someone in the United States made a big mistake in what kind of skill system to build numerical control into . . ."(Stinchcombe 1990, 53).

Managing human knowledge and converting it into useful products and services is fast becoming a critical skill for organizational survival (Quinn, Anderson, and Finkelstein 1996). As long as skills and expertise remain internalized in the individual, the organization is limited in its ability to parlay that knowledge in some larger, strategic sense. Kogut and Zander (1992) observed that: "unless able to train large numbers of individual or to transform skills into organizing principles, the craft shop is forever simply a shop. The speed of replication of knowledge determines the rate of growth; control over its diffusion deters competitive erosion of the market position. For a firm to grow, it must develop organizing principles and a widely held and shared code by which to orchestrate large numbers of people and, potentially, varied functions" (p. 390). While the energy for innovation—the creative spark—can only be lit by the insightful individual, organizations must supply the fuel and the environment for the spark to catch, and nourish the flame into something the organization can use. Organizational knowledge creation is therefore "a process that 'organizationally' amplifies the knowledge created by individuals and crystallizes it as a part of the knowledge network of the organization" (Nonaka and Takeuchi 1995, 59). According to Nonaka and Takeuchi, there are two sets of dynamics that drive the process of knowledge amplification: (1) converting tacit knowledge into explicit knowledge; and (2) moving knowledge from the individual level to the group, organizational, and interorganizational levels. The process grows like a spiral as the interaction between tacit and explicit knowledge takes place dynamically at higher and higher levels of the organization.

The basis of organizational knowledge creation is therefore the conversion of tacit knowledge into explicit knowledge and back again. Explicit knowledge is knowledge that "can be expressed in words and numbers, and easily communicated and shared in the form of hard data, scientific formulae, codified procedures, or universal principles" (Nonaka and Takeuchi 1995, 8). Examples of explicit knowledge include chemical formulas, market forecasts, operations procedures, product specifications, software code, and technical standards. Nonaka and Takeuchi do not view tacit knowledge and explicit knowledge as mutually exclusive but as complementary entities. Over time, human knowledge shifts between the tacit and the explicit through a process of social interaction between individuals, which also produces new knowledge and expands its use. There are four modes in which organizational knowledge is created through the interaction and conversion between tacit and explicit knowledge: socialization, externalization, combination, and internalization (Nonaka and Takeuchi 1995). (Data from a survey of 105 Japanese middle managers were factor analyzed and found to support the hypothesis that knowledge creation is indeed comprised of these four conversion modes [Nonaka et al. 1994].)

Socialization

Socialization is the process of sharing experiences that creates tacit knowledge such as shared mental models and technical skills. Apprentices learn their craft—both physical and cognitive skills—through socialization by observing, assisting, and copying the behaviors of experienced practitioners. Socialization thus transfers tacit knowledge through the medium of shared experience. The work of Lave and Wenger (1991) suggests that apprenticeship is effective when novices observe and learn through *legitimate peripheral participation.* The novice starts by staying safely on the periphery of practice as a participant observer. When she feels sufficiently comfortable or when the mentor feels she is ready, the learner can move from the periphery to the centre to engage the task, and then move back out again. In this sense the learner is also a legitimate participant who can move to the centre of practice from time to time. Being legitimately on the periphery also means that learners have access to the various modes of communication used by the competent practitioner (mail, meetings, stories, reports) so that they can pick up valuable know-how on technique and nuance.

We can discern some interesting features of the mode of apprenticeship in the Big 8 management consulting practice (MCP) studied by Orlikowski (1988). The firm's standardization of its system development methodology (Modus) defined a set of vocabulary to refer to concepts such as entity, data item, database, data flow, and so on, and a grammar of rules to represent allowable relationships among these concepts. This vocabulary and grammar together constitutes a "language of systems development," which is used by the consultants to understand and interpret the organizational realities they are trying to automate. Furthermore, by encoding the systems development language into the CASE tools, consultants collaborating or communicating via these tools are required to use the language. The result is that "the uniform language of systems development plays a very significant role in sustaining the one-firm culture, informing the production process of the Firm, serving as the basis for consultants' indoctrination and training, and differentiating the Firm from its competitors" (Orlikowski 1988, 341). Thus MCP's new recruits learn to be systems developers not only by acquiring the skills of programming and analysis, but also by learning to understand and use the language that represents the firm's specific interpretation of systems development. Recruits spend six weeks in training before their first assignment. Recruits come from all over the world to the "Center for Professional Education" in the U.S. Midwest to receive instruction from trainers who are the firm's consultants specially flown in from their local offices. The objective of the training is as much to "indoctrinate everyone into our way of doing work" (senior manager's quote) as it is to teach technical skills. Recruits then work for two years as staff analysts with experienced consultants in project teams at the clients' sites, where they do mostly installation tasks such as programming, testing, and documentation. It is during this period of on-the-job experience that the new staff analysts learn the skills of business problem analysis and systems design from the experienced consultants.

Nonaka and Takeuchi (1995) provide two examples of socialization at Japanese companies. At Honda, "brainstorming camps" are held at resort inns, where participants meet informally to discuss and solve difficult problems in development projects while drinking sake, sharing meals, and bathing together in a hot spring. At Matsushita Electric Industrial Company, the head of software development of the bread-making machine project apprenticed herself to the chief baker at a leading hotel in order to observe and learn the secret of simultaneously stretching and twisting the dough to produce tasty bread.

Externalization

Externalization is the "quintessential" knowledge-creation process in which tacit knowledge becomes explicit through the sharing of metaphors, analogies, models, or stories. It can be triggered by dialogue and often takes place during collective reflection.

The case study of the Big 8 management consulting practice (MCP) showed how the firm's development of a model of the systems development life cycle captured and codified the tacit knowledge of its consultants. Thus "the informal, context-specific systems development knowledge generated through the interaction of consultants involved in building particular information systems for clients became in time and through repeated use available for institutionalization" (Orlikowski 1988, 217). As we saw near the beginning of this chapter, the model of the systems development process emerged gradually out of the daily activities of consultants working on projects. Consultants documented their projects in client binders, which were then reviewed by the partners to extract the common success and failure factors, and to generalize rules of thumb for good systems practice. Over time, these informal guidelines evolved into MCP's standardized methodology model, which defines in detail the sequence of tasks in each stage of the development life cycle as well as the conceptual framework within which information systems are to be developed for all clients. In the formalization of the standard methodology, we are witnessing the externalization of the tacit knowledge of experienced consultants into the explicit knowledge of the systems development model.

Nonaka and Takeuchi (1995) recount how Honda engineers used metaphors and analogies during their collective discussions on designing a new urban car. In 1978 Honda, concerned that its Accord and Civic models were becoming too familiar, launched the development of a new-concept car with the slogan, "Let's gamble." The project team leader introduced the metaphor of "Automobile Evolution" to challenge the "reasoning of Detroit" and to ask the question, "what will the automobile eventually evolve into?" After discussion, the concept of a tall (in height) and short (in length) car was hatched through an analogy between the idea of "man-maximum, machine-minimum" and the image of a sphere containing the maximum volume within minimum space. The concept led to the development of the Honda City automobile, nicknamed the Tall Boy. Although it contradicted the conventional low and long design principle, tall and short cars like the Honda City are now quite prevalent in Japan. In this case, the use of attractive metaphors and analogies had helped to spur enthusiasm and focus energy on the creative process.

War stories, or anecdotes of experience, can be effective vehicles for sharing and transferring otherwise hard-to-articulate collective wisdom. In an ethnographic study of photocopier repair technicians, Orr (1990) found that the technicians used stories to preserve knowledge and to explore it in subsequent diagnoses. In one incident, a sophisticated new machine had been installed recently but had never worked reliably. Changing the component indicated by the error code did not rectify the problem. According to Orr, a dozen stories were exchanged between the assigned technician and the team's technical specialist,

as the two searched their memories for possible culprits, looking for the key perspective which would integrate their random facts. . . . They are faced with a failing machine displaying diagnostic information which has previously proved worthless and in which no one has any particular confidence this time. They do not know where they are going to find the information they need to understand and solve this problem. In their search for inspiration, they tell stories. (Orr 1990, 176, 178–179)

The shared story telling eventually developed the correct diagnosis that the initial error code (E053) should not be believed, but this code may then be followed by a second error code (F066), indicating the true source of the failure, a shorted dicorotron. This new insight, not found in the field repair manuals, is then communicated to other technicians as a shorter version of the story. By including technical details and emotional coloring, stories deepen the listener's understanding and affective response, which facilitates subsequent retrieval and evaluation. By providing more details than are necessary, stories also supply additional information that might turn out to be important for a different problem: "The apparent object is to keep all knowledge as closely connected as possible, so that if a new problem connects to any known facts at all, it connects to an understanding of the system with known failures and solutions on which to base a diagnostic strategy" (Orr 1990, 184). In this way stories become carriers of knowledge, carriers that can transfer general principles through the telling about particular situations (Brown 1993).

Combination

Combination is the process of combining or reconfiguring disparate bodies of existing explicit knowledge that leads to the production of new explicit knowledge. This is a common form of knowledge transfer that typifies the learning in schools and instructional programs. In organizations, members combine their explicit knowledge by exchanging reports, memos, and a variety of other documents. Businesses are also using computer-based data management and analysis tools to reveal trends and patterns that would otherwise remain buried in their huge operational databases.

The experience of the MCP consulting practice again illustrates the process of recombining explicit knowledge. With the adoption of a standard system development methodology, it became practical to develop utilities that would simplify the work required by some stages of the methodology. Most of the tools were developed initially on projects by team members to facilitate system development for a particular client. After a few high-profile early successes with the use of these tools, MCP decided to promote their use and to combine the diverse utilities into an "integrated development environment" of computer-aided software engineering tools. The generalized tools package was later made available for purchase as a product in its own right, and could be purchased by any organization in the data-processing community. While the tools of the development environment were based on MCP's system development methodology, the use of the tools also induced changes in the methodology, so that the methodology was constantly updated to more appropriately reflect the tool development environment (Orlikowski 1988).

For many organizations their on-line transaction-processing systems record a continuous stream of operational and competitive data, which become potentially a vast and valuable source of intelligence about customers and clients, buying and service patterns, and so on. Unfortunately, because such databases are traditionally designed and structured to ensure the reliable and speedy completion of transactions, decision makers lack the tools to query the database in order to obtain the insight they need. In recent years, new data management technology is increasingly being used to replicate data from operational production systems into "data warehouses" that end users can access and analyze without affecting transactional performance and data integrity. A data warehouse sets up a separate cleaned-up version of the operational data specifically to support end user query and decision making. It draws together data from multiple sources throughout the enterprise and structures them according to subjects and data models that are meaningful to end users such as knowledge workers and decision makers. They then access and manipulate warehoused data through decision-support tools such as spreadsheets, statistical analysis programs, and executive information systems. In order to do more refined analysis, forecasting, and trend spotting, end users need to be able to look at the data from many vantage points. Software for on-line analytical processing provides this capability, allowing users to create multidimensional views of large amounts of data as they slice and dice the data in various ways to discover patterns and trends.

Internalization

Internalization is the process of learning and socializing by repetitively doing a task so that the explicit knowledge of the applied principles and procedures becomes absorbed as the tacit knowledge of the individual's style and habit. For this to happen, the explicit knowledge needs to be "lived" or experienced by the individual, either personally by going through the experience of performing an activity, or vicariously by participating in simulations, role-playing exercises, or by listening to oral stories that bring the experience sufficiently to life.

In the training program of the MCP management consulting practice, new recruits join the "Computers in our Practice School" (CPS), which consists of a simulation of an actual systems development project: "Recruits work in teams and have to conduct the actual installation of a system for a client— usually the order entry system—from detailed design through to the implementation. By all accounts these three weeks are intensive and pressured. During their three week participation in CPS, the recruits continue their learning of "Modus" [MCP's development methodology] begun in the self-study course, and learn the more specific tasks of programming (COBOL) and testing. They work an average of twelve hours a day, five days a week, and eight hours a day on Saturdays and Sundays. The intent of CPS is to simulate as much as possible the working conditions of real projects . . . '' (Orlikowski 1988, 398–99). A staff analyst who had recently completed CPS had this to say: "You go there not for the skills you learn, but for the indoctrination. Spending three weeks in the same room with the same hundred people doing things you can't see the need for—you quickly get to know the way the Firm does things, and realize if that's what you want to do" (Quoted in Orlikowski 1988, 399). The firm's training school also houses a "Cultural Center," which includes a museum that presents the firm's history through a display of artifacts and memorabilia. An interactive video system in the center allows users to select and play videotapes of the partners discussing the firm's history, goals, and values. The video system is like an electronic storyteller which passes on the traditions, anecdotes, and norms that give meaning to the professional life of the firm consultants. Nonaka and Takeuchi (1995) suggest that the internalization of explicit knowledge can be helped if the knowledge is documented to facilitate study and assimilation. At MCP, its standard development methodology is documented in detail, and is available in three formats—as a set of ten three-ring binders, a package of fourteen computer diskettes, and a textbook (Orlikowski 1988).

IV. KNOWLEDGE CREATING

Organizations create and exploit knowledge to develop new capabilities and innovations through three overlapping activities: (1) generating and sharing tacit knowledge, (2) testing and prototyping explicit knowledge, and (3) linking and tapping external knowledge. Tacit knowledge, although personal and difficult to codify formally, may nevertheless be informally shared and revealed through the use of rich communication devices such as metaphors, analogies, models, and stories. Through a process of combination, testing, and refinement, tacit knowledge is progressively transformed into more explicit, tangible forms, such as innovations, enhanced products or services, or new capabilities. A work group may also develop new knowledge by absorbing knowledge from outside the group or organization, or conversely by transferring its own knowledge to other departments or organizations. Since knowledge conversion is as much a social as a technical process, the pace and scope of knowledge mobilization depends on the culture of the organization, that is, the cultural knowledge that influences behaviors such as the sharing of information, willingness to experiment, and working with outsiders. In this section we elaborate on these themes by comparing and extending the research findings of Wikström and Normann (1994), Nonaka and Takeuchi (1995), and Leonard-Barton (1995).

Organizational Knowledge Processes (Wikström and Normann 1994)

Wikström and Normann (1994) distinguish three kinds of knowledge processes in organizations: (1) generative processes, (2) productive processes, and (3) representative processes. *Generative processes* are those in which "new knowledge is created largely in activities which are geared to the solving of problems" (p. 107). First produced in the course of problem solving, generative knowledge is important for increasing the overall pool of knowledge resources in the organization, and for providing the organization with the capabilities to enter new businesses or bring forth better products. *Productive processes* are those in which new knowledge is accumulated and used by the organization to produce customer offerings. Productive processes thus yield knowledge that is manifest and used: "A drill is manifest knowledge deriving from the knowledge processes of a manufacturing company. A headache tablet is manifest knowledge deriving from the knowledge processes of a pharmaceutical company" (Wikström and Normann 1994, 14).

Productive knowledge and processes are also reproductive in the sense that they are applied repeatedly. *Representative processes* are those in which the organization conveys its manifest knowledge to the customer, so that its knowledge is made available to the customers for their own value-creating processes. For example, "when a machine is sold it becomes a representative outside the company of all the knowledge processes within the company which led to its existence" (p. 108). Through representative processes, a price tag is attached to manifest knowledge. The three knowledge processes (generative, productive, and representative) overlap and are to some extent synchronous and reciprocal. As Wikström and Normann explain:

Let us take an example. The method of production for making drills, say, has changed, and this opens up the possibility of making new and better products. The productive processes have thus given rise to generative processes. Or perhaps discussion with a customer about the qualities of the drill and the customer's special requirements lead not only to new products but also to new business ideas. The representative processes can thus trigger important spin-offs into the generative processes. . . . At different times or in different places at the same time one piece of knowledge can be part of generative, productive or representative processes. The technical principle on which the drill is based may be tested in a new type of tool; this is a generative process. At the same time the drill is being manufactured as part of a batch; this is a reproductive process. And at the same time, again discussions are being held with customers about the purchase of drills; this is a representative process. (Wikström and Normann 1994, 108, 114)

Phases of the Knowledge-Creation Process (Nonaka and Takeuchi 1995)

Nonaka and Takeuchi (1995), based largely on their analysis of innovative Japanese companies, propose a model in which the knowledge-creation process develops through five phases: (1) sharing tacit knowledge, (2) creating concepts, (3) justifying concepts, (4) building an archetype, and (5) cross-leveling knowledge. In the first phase of *sharing tacit knowledge,* individuals from different functional areas share their skills and experiences in working together toward a common goal. They typically interact with each other through face-to-face dialogue in self-organizing teams in order to jointly develop shared tacit mental models. For example, the team at Honda that evolved the "Tall Boy" concept for the Honda City car often exchanged their ideas while informally sharing sake away from the office. This first phase corresponds to the knowledge conversion mode of socialization that we discussed in the last section. In the second phase of *creating concepts,* the continuous dialogue in the self-organizing team intensifies as members collectively reflect on the shared tacit mental model developed in the first phase, and attempt to verbalize the model into words and explicit concepts. Making tacit knowledge explicit is aided by the use of multiple reasoning and communication methods such as deduction, induction, dialectic reasoning, contradictions and para- doxes, metaphors, analogies, and war stories. The process is iterative, with team members employing figurative language to creatively brainstorm ideas and possibilities. The second phase corresponds to the knowledge conversion mode of externalization. In the third phase of *justifying concepts,* the newly created concepts are evaluated at the organizational level to determine whether the concepts are in line with organizational intention and meet the needs of society at large. The screening process applies justification criteria such as cost, profit margin, and the degree to which a product can contribute to the firm's growth. Justification criteria are typically formulated by top and middle management, based on their understanding of the overall organizational vision or strategy. In the fourth phase of *building an archetype,* "the justified concept is converted into something tangible or concrete, namely, an archetype" (Non- aka and Takeuchi 1995, 87). An archetype may be a physical prototype in the case of new-product development, or a "model operating mechanism" in the case of service or organizational innovation. An archetype is built by combin- ing the newly created explicit knowledge with existing explicit knowledge (about components or technologies already in use, for example). This fourth phase therefore corresponds to the knowledge conversion mode of combina- tion. In the fifth phase of *cross-leveling of knowledge,* the concepts that have been created, justified, and modeled are used to activate new cycles of knowl- edge creation. Within the same organization, knowledge that has been made tangible as an archetype can trigger more knowledge creation in other units or departments, as well as at different levels of the organization. This new knowl- edge can also initiate knowledge creation in customers, suppliers, competitors, and others affiliated with the organization. For example, the implementation of point-of-sale systems may precipitate changes in the way suppliers collect and process their data, making new market information available that enables both organizations to become more responsive to customer needs.

Knowledge-Building Activities (Leonard-Barton 1995)

Leonard-Barton's analysis of knowledge management focuses on organizations whose core capabilities are technology based, and where "the primary engine for the creation and growth of technological capabilities is the development of new products and services" (Leonard-Barton 1995, p. xiii). An organization's core technological capabilities embody proprietary knowledge that is unique to the organization and that is superior to the knowledge of its competitors. Core technological capabilities give the organization its distinctive competitive edge, because they have been developed over time, and are hard to transfer or imitate. To create and maintain core technological capabilities, the organization needs to understand what dimensions constitute these capabilities, and to know how to manage the activities that create knowledge (Leonard-Barton 1995). Core technological capabilities are the result of the synergy between four inter-dependent dimensions—employees' knowledge and skills; physical technical systems such as equipment, databases, and software; managerial systems that include education, reward, and incentive systems; and values and norms that determine what kinds of knowledge are sought. Leonard-Barton identifies four main activities carried out in the course of developing new products and pro-cesses through which an organization builds its knowledge and extends or creates new capabilities: (1) shared, creative problem solving; (2) implement-ing and integrating new methodologies and tools; (3) experimentation and pro-totyping; and (4) importing knowledge from outside. In the activity of ***shared problem solving***, employees with different specializations and problem-solving approaches are brought together so that the diversity of their knowledge and backgrounds can be channeled toward creative problem solving. According to Leonard-Barton, as people become highly skilled, they develop individual "signature skills," which are formed from their specializations, cognitive style preferences, and preferences for particular tools or methods. Bringing people with diverse signature skills together to work on a problem generates the cre-ative abrasion that, when managed properly, can be a source of innovative solutions. To tap this creative energy productively, managers and employees need to develop integrative skills and use techniques such as defining clear shared visions of the project outcome and constructing physical prototypes to bridge different realms of specialization. In the activity of ***implementing and integrating new methods and tools***, proprietary knowledge is introduced into process tools and methods that improve internal operation. Leonard-Barton (1995) stresses that "the implementation of such tools must be managed as an innovation project" (p. 110). To ensure successful implementation, user involvement is essential since the future users of the tools will have critical information that must be integrated during design. At the same time, both the technology and the user environment need to adapt to each other mutually so that users and the new tools complement together effectively. Through the activity of ***experimentation and prototyping***, the organization extends its ex-isting capabilities, as well as building new capabilities for the future. Leonard-Barton believes that continuous and widespread experimentation develops a diverse portfolio of technological options for the organization, and that the act of experimentation itself "sets up a virtuous cycle of innovation" (p. 114). Experimentation must be properly managed to ensure that learning does take place. For example, "intelligent failures" which provide valuable lessons should be encouraged, and feedback channels that facilitate learning from ex-perimentation (such as project audits) should be established. In discussing the activity of ***importing knowledge from outside***, Leonard-Barton distinguishes between external knowledge that is technological in nature, and knowledge about the market. The key to importing technological knowledge is for the organization to expand its "absorptive capacity" by scanning broadly and con-tinuously for technological opportunity, and by identifying employees who can act as technological gatekeepers and boundary spanners. Importing knowledge about the market presents a special challenge when the technological potential outstrips users' ability to understand it. In such situations, the organization can seek new-product opportunities through market experimentation and qualitative techniques such as "emphatic design," which is "the creation of product or service concepts based on a deep (emphatic) understanding of unarticulated user needs" (Leonard-Barton 1995, 194) obtained by observing actual customer behavior, interacting directly with those who understand the organization's capabilities and potential user needs, and redirecting existing capabilities to new products or markets. In summary, Leonard-Barton emphasizes the continuous interaction between knowledge-building activities and the core capabilities of the organization. While core capabilities are created and expanded through knowledge-building activities, these activities are themselves dependent on and enabled by the organization's core capabilities. The central theme is therefore the creation of knowledge by "managing the interaction between activities pursued in the course of developing new products and processes, and the organization's core technological capabilities" (Leonard-Barton 1995, 17).

A Comparison of Knowledge-Creating Processes

Our brief review of the knowledge-creating processes described by Wikström and Normann (1994), Nonaka and Takeuchi (1995), and Leonard-Barton (1995) suggests broad similarities, as presented in Table 4–2.

TABLE 4–2. Knowledge-creating processes.

Knowledge Processes (Wikström and Normann 1994)	Knowledge Conversion Phases (Nonaka and Takeuchi 1995)	Knowledge Building Activities (Leonard-Barton 1995)
Generative Processes Generating new knowledge	Sharing tacit knowledge	Shared problem solving
	Creating concepts	Experimenting and prototyping
Productive Processes operationalizing new knowledge	Justifying concepts	Implementing and integrating new processes and tools
	Building an archetype	
Representative Processes Diffusing and transferring new knowledge	Cross-leveling knowledge	Importing knowledge

Generative processes are those which create new knowledge in the course of problem solving, with the new knowledge extending the organization's capabilities to offer improved products or services or to move into new areas. Since the phases of "sharing tacit knowledge" and "creating concepts" described by Nonaka and Takeuchi are also concerned with the generation of new knowledge in the activities of problem solving and new-product development, they may be considered as generative processes. Moreover, Leonard-Barton's discussion of individual signature skills suggests that they are related to personal tacit knowledge, and the "shared problem solving" activity she describes is similar to the "sharing tacit knowledge" phase of Nonaka and Takeuchi in that both emphasize a sharing of ideas and insights by people with a diversity of skills and experiences. The goal of Leonard-Barton's 'experimenting and prototyping' activity is to extend the organization's current and future capabilities through continuous and managed experimentation. Leonard-Barton believes that experimenting and prototyping, by executing and trying out tentative designs on a small scale, are in fact occasions for generating new knowledge. Her description of "experimenting and prototyping" as a knowledge-building activity aligns it with the "creating concepts" phase of Nonaka and Takeuchi, and both activities are "generative processes."

Productive processes are those that develop and apply the generated knowledge in operational processes to produce new or enhanced customer offerings. The phases of "justifying concepts" and "building an archetype" described by Nonaka and Takeuchi are concerned with operationalizing the newly created concepts that have been converted from sharing tacit knowledge. The new concepts are justified according to pragmatic criteria such as their efficiency, cost-effectiveness, and contribution to profits and growth. Justified concepts are then converted into tangible archetypes to test their practicability and operational readiness. Similarly, since the activity of "implementing and integrating new methods and tools" described by Leonard-Barton introduces proprietary knowledge into process tools and methods that improve internal operation, it may be considered part of the productive processes of applying new knowledge in the internal operations of the organization to produce customer offerings.

Wikström and Normann (1994) describe representative processes as those that convey the organization's manifest knowledge to the customer, typically in the form of a finished good or a service. For our discussion here, we may broaden the concept to include the diffusion of knowledge across internal organizational boundaries (so that a recipient department receiving new knowledge is like a customer of the department that originated the knowledge), as well as the transfer of knowledge to and from customers, the market, suppliers, partners, and so on. Within this wider conceptualization, the "cross-leveling of knowledge" phase described by Nonaka and Takeuchi, in which new knowledge spreads across organizational levels and departmental lines, may be regarded as a representative process. Likewise, Leonard-Barton's discussion of "importing knowledge" from the market and external technology sources suggests that it is also a representative process, except that representative knowledge from an outside source is being transferred into the organization rather than the other way around.

In summary, we highlight these observations in the management of organizational knowledge:

1. *An organization generates new knowledge that extends its capabilities by sharing and converting the tacit knowledge of its members.* To do this, people engage in face-to-face dialogue and work together in groups to reflect on and solve problems collectively.

2. *An organization operationalizes new concepts so that they can be applied to produce new or enhanced offerings, or to allow the organization to function more efficiently.* To do this, new concepts are evaluated and justified according to criteria derived from organizational goals, and their practical feasibility and usefulness are tested in realistic settings. The application of new knowledge in process tools and methods needs to be managed as an innovation project of its own, requiring user participation and continuous adaptation.

3. *An organization diffuses and transfers new knowledge into as well as out of the organization, moving knowledge across departmental boundaries and organizational peripheries.* As new knowledge is spread to other departments and to higher levels of the organization, new cycles of learning are generated. New knowledge from external sources as well as the market are combined with and used to expand the organization's existing capabilities.

A Culture of Innovation

Knowledge creation needs to be sustained in a conducive social and cultural environment. Nonaka and Takeuchi (1995) discuss five enabling conditions as being particularly important. First, since the knowledge spiral is driven by **organizational intention** or aspirations, the organization needs to clearly conceptualize a vision about what kind of knowledge would be most valuable to realizing the organizational intention, and to apply this vision as the principal yardstick for judging the usefulness of new knowledge. Second, organizational members, either on their own or in self-organizing teams, should be given the freedom to act with **autonomy** so that they would motivate themselves to experiment and discover new knowledge. Third, the organization can stimulate the knowledge creation process by inducing **fluctuation and creative chaos** by, for example, introducing breakdowns of set routines or habitual frameworks, evoking a sense of crisis, and stating ambiguous visions and goals. Fourth, information should be made available to organizational members which goes beyond their immediate operational requirements. **Information redundancy** promotes the sharing of tacit knowledge and the exchanging of ideas. Fifth, according to the principle of **requisite variety,** an organization's internal diversity must match the variety and complexity of its external environment. This implies that organizational members should have prompt access to a wide range of information so that they can cope with fast-changing contingencies. There are echoes of these five enabling conditions throughout Leonard-Barton's discussion of management strategies to support organizational knowledge building (Table 4–3). She emphasizes that organizations need to have a clear understanding of their core capabilities and strategic intent; that members be enouraged to experiment continuously; that creative abrasion is an effective way of parlaying members' cognitive diversity and variety of signature skills; and that group boundaries should be kept porous so that information can be broadly diffused.

To illustrate how putting in place these enabling conditions can spur creativity, consider the case of 3M (Minnesota Mining and Manufacturing Company), a company with an impressive track record of successfully developing and commercializing widely used innovations. Over its history, 3M staff invented a number of well-known and well-used products, such as masking tape, Scotch tape, and Post-it notes, as well as some other sixty thousand products in wide-ranging categories, such as bioelectronic ears, computer storage media, overhead projection systems, reflective highway signs, and video recording tape. In 1990, 3M had 42 separate product divisions, each with average sales of about $200 million and employing a relatively small median number of 115 people. 3M's core ideology embraces the following principles: Innovation— "thou shalt not kill a new product idea"; absolute integrity; respect for individual initiative and personal growth; tolerance for honest mistakes; product quality and reliability; and "our real business is solving problems" (Collins and Porras 1994, 68). With the ideology defining the organizational and strategic intent, 3M implemented a number of mechanisms to encourage innovation and

TABLE 4–3. Conditions to promote knowledge creation.

Enabling Conditions (Nonaka and Takeuchi 1995)		Management Strategies (Leonard-Barton 1995)
Organizational intention	←——————→	Strategic intent Core capability
Autonomy	←——————→	Signature skills
Fluctuation and creative chaos	←——————→	Creative abrasion Continuous experimentation
Information redundancy	←——————→	Information-porous boundaries Importing knowledge
Requisite variety	←——————→	Cognitive diversity

knowledge building that gave substance to its credo. We outline some examples below (from Collins and Porras 1994, 156–58), indicating in parentheses the enabling conditions that each mechanism supports:

- The 15 percent rule, by which technical staff are encouraged to spend up to 15 percent of their time on projects of their own choosing. (autonomy, continuous experimentation)
- The 30 percent rule, by which each division is expected to generate 30 percent of annual sales from new products and services introduced in the previous four years. (fluctuation and creative chaos, continuous experimentation)
- A "dual ladder" career track that allows technical and professional staff to advance without giving up their research or professional interests. (cognitive diversity)
- Staff who successfully champion a new product get the chance to run it as her or his own project, department, or division. (signature skills)
- New product forums at which all divisions share and show their new products, and technical forums at which staff present technical papers and exchange ideas and findings. (information redundancy, information sharing)
- Technology sharing awards given to those who develop a new technology and successfully share it with other divisions. (porous boundaries, exporting/ importing knowledge)
- "Problem-solving missions" of small "hit teams" despatched to customer sites to deal with particular, idiosyncratic customer problems. (shared problem solving)

Through a variety of exhortatory policies and concrete measures, 3M created an organizational environment that is conducive to innovation and experimentation. 3M sought to be an organization that constantly evolves, driven forward by employees stretching their individual initiative and creativity. This belief is reflected in some of the expressions often cited as representative of the 3M culture: "Encourage, don't nitpick. Let people run with an idea." "Hire good peole, and leave them alone." "If you put fences around people, you get sheep. Give people the room they need." "Encourage experimental doodling." "Give it a try—and quick" (Collins and Porras 1994, 152).

V. KNOWLEDGE LINKING

The creation of knowledge is no longer the activity of an organization working in isolation, but the collaborative result of its members working closely in internal groups and in partnerships with other organizations. The migration of knowledge between organizations continues to pose many challenges. To be sure, a significant amount of knowledge is still being transacted in the form of specific pieces of equipment, software, blueprints, documents, and the like. However, such prefabricated knowledge tends to have short life spans and is often exchanged for operational or tactical reasons. The strategic knowledge of any organization lies in its long-term knowledge-generating capabilities, which it has built up over time. These capabilities are the result of the quality of its internal network of people, skills, communications, information resources, and cultural norms, and the quality of its external network of relationships with customers, suppliers, distributors, information sources, and other associates. In this section we amplify the idea of knowledge as organizational capability that is distributed over its knowledge networks, and discuss strategies by which organizations enhance their knowledge-building capability by enhancing the knowledge-density of their networks.

Knowledge Links

Organizations can expand their knowledge and capabilities relatively quickly by acquiring new knowledge directly from other organizations. However, the expertise of most organizations is unique to that institution, and takes the form of "embedded knowledge" that "resides primarily in specialized relationships among individuals and groups and in the particular norms, attitudes, information flows, and ways of making decisions that shape their dealings with each other" (Badaracco 1991, 79). To transfer embedded knowledge from another organization therefore requires the parties to design work and social structures that develop both technical and personal empathy. What is being learned is not just the nuts and bolts of an activity, but also the color and texture of the social and technical milieu in which that activity makes sense. Time is required for know-how and nuance to be revealed and to work their way through organizational and cultural differences. Badaracco (1991) calls such learning alliances *"knowledge links,"* which are defined by four traits. First, the central objective of knowledge links is learning and creating knowledge. This may be contrasted with product links, where the main goal is typically to provide access to a new product or to open up a wider distribution for an existing product. A knowledge link is not focused on any particular product, but is concerned with developing longer term capabilities that can generate a stream of products. Second, knowledge links are more "intimate" than product links. Since the partner organizations are working toward sharing and jointly creating capability, they each have a significant stake in the relationship. Moreover, in order for the partners to learn, create, or strengthen their specialized capabilities, their personnel need to be given the opportunity to work together closely. Third, knowledge links can be established with a wide range of partners. Links need not be confined to being with other organizations in the same industry or sector. Mutually beneficial links can be formed between buyers and suppliers, university researchers and companies, labor unions and their companies, and so on. Fourth, knowledge links have greater strategic potential than product links. Knowledge links can extend or enhance an organization's basic capabilities whereas product links tend to be more tactical, allowing the organization, for example, to catch up or defend its position.

When General Motors was trying to learn the Toyota production system, it established the NUMMI (New United Motor Manufacturing, Inc.) plant in 1984 as a joint venture with Toyota in order to facilitate the learning of "intimate, embedded knowledge." NUMMI took over a General Motors facility at Fremont, California, that had been described by one GM manager as the "worst plant in the world." NUMMI began production in 1984 with the same union leadership and approximately 85 percent of the work force comprised of former GM Fremont employees. Within two years, NUMMI was more productive than any other General Motors plant and had quality that rivaled its sister Toyota plant in Japan. NUMMI is generally recognized as an outstanding "natural experiment" that demonstrated the benefits of high-performance work organization and cooperative labor relations. Work at NUMMI is organized based on Toyota's lean production system that seeks to utilize labor, materials, and facilities as efficiently as possible. The system is guided by the principles that quality should be assured in the production process itself with no defects overlooked or passed on, and that team members should be treated with consideration, respect, and as professionals ("full utilization of workers' abilities"). The NUMMI system combines employee involvement and continuous improvement processes. In order to ensure that each job is done in the most efficient way, the performance of the work is specified explicitly by sequences or procedures. NUMMI team members themselves are responsible for setting the work standards and continuously improving the job standards for maximum efficiency. (The old GM Fremont plant had 82 industrial engineers while NUMMI had none.) NUMMI also used production leveling in an attempt to produce no more vehicles and parts than can be sold. Through production leveling, NUMMI was able to implement just-in-time scheduling and to maintain employment stability.

Badaracco (1991) observed that through NUMMI, GM had the chance to learn firsthand Toyota's collaborative approach to worker and supplier relationships, just-in-time inventory management, and efficient plant operations; while for Toyota, the project helped it learn about managing U.S. workers, suppliers, and logistics, and about cooperating with the unions and the state and local governments: "Scores of GM managers and thousands of workers have worked at NUMMI or at least visited the operation. It would have been much simpler for GM to buy from Toyota the manual *How to Create the Toyota Production System,* but the document does not exist and, in a fundamental sense, could not be written. Much of what Toyota 'knows' resides in routines, company culture, and long-established working relationships in the Toyota Group" (Badaracco 1991, 100).

Knowledge-based Value Stars

More and more of today's organizations do not just offer a product or service per se—they offer a package that is a combination of products and services in which the defining feature is that the package helps customers to create value for themselves. This is a knowledge-based conceptualization of economic value, where value is in the knowledge or competences of an organization, and in the customer relationships that provide access to the customer's ongoing value-creating activities (Normann and Ramirez 1993). Value has become *knowledge dense,* and Normann and Ramirez suggest that we think of this density as

> . . . a measure of the amount of information, knowledge, and other resources that an economic actor has at hand at any moment in time to leverage his or her own value creation. Value has become more dense in that more and more opportunities for value creation are packed into any particular offering. . . . the goal of business is not so much to make or do something of value for customers as it is to mobilize customers to take advantage of proffered density and create value for themselves. . . . Companies create value when they make not only their offerings more intelligent, but their customers (and suppliers) more intelligent as well. (Normann and Ramirez 1993, 69, 70)

As a corollary, the relationship with any customer should also be reconceptualized from a linear sequence of value-adding activities (Porter's [1985] value chain) to a *value star,* in which the customer's value-creating processes receive contributions from many different sources, including suppliers, the suppliers' suppliers, the customers own customers, its customers' customers, and so on (Normann and Ramirez 1993; Wikström and Normann 1994). The flow of knowledge may be drawn as a star where the organization's value-creating processes take place at the point of convergence of many incoming flows of knowledge from many sources. This knowledge may be conveyed in the form of new modes of collaboration, training and education, and information sharing through networks of users, suppliers, and others.

The value-star concept is combined with our earlier classification of organizational knowledge processes as generative, productive, and representative processes to represent the organization as a knowledge system in which knowledge is not only transformed into value within the organization, but that value is also created through knowledge-based interactions and offerings with the "customer's value star" on the output side and the "supplier's value star" on the input side (Fig. 4–1). Wikström and Normann (1994) elaborate on the value star model:

> The model, which is now complete, includes not only the transformation of knowledge but also two value stars. The first is the customer's value star, in

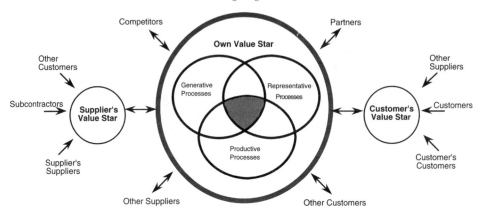

FIGURE 4–1. The Organization as Knowledge-Creating Value Star (Reprinted from *Knowledge and Value: A New Perspective on Corporate Transformation* by Wikström and Normann 1994, 112 by permission of Routledge.)

> which the company's output represents an important value-creating input. The other value star, on the company's input side, works on the same principle but in reverse, the company in the model now represents the supplier's customer, and the knowledge-generating capacity of the suppliers contributes significantly to the company's own value-creating capacity . . . The [knowledge] processes are merging with one another; there is much mutual giving and taking. Contact with customers yields new ideas and stimuli for the generative processes, for example, while productive knowledge and skill can indicate possible ways of developing new customer offerings, and so on. . . . when the company system makes a contribution to the customer's value star in the shape of its various offerings, it receives at the same time knowledge from the customer's value star— knowledge from and about the customer and knowledge from and about other parts of the value star. The value star is thus based on the idea of mutual exchange of knowledge, which automatically leads to more value being created for all those involved. (pp. 111, 113, 114)

The experience of McKesson, a U.S. wholesaler of pharmaceutical products to drugstores, illustrates how an organization can expand the value constellation of itself as well as its customers, suppliers, and other partners. In the early 1970s McKesson found that while the company itself was among the most efficient in the industry, its customers, which were the retail drugstores, were being acquired and their operations streamlined by the large retail chains. In response to these competitive pressures, McKesson changed its role from that of simply supplying products to that of supplying knowledge inputs to the customers' value-creating activities (Wikström and Normann 1994). The new strategy was to create a new offering which complemented product supplies with services and information that improved the drugstores' internal efficiency as well as the level of service they could provide to their customers. Thus the retail pharmacists were offered management training, store layout consulting services, and an advanced computerized ordering system called Economost, which allowed the retailer to operate more rapidly, reliably, and cost-effectively, while at the same time dramatically increasing the productivity of warehouse staff and expanding McKesson's share of the retailer's business (Clemons and Row 1988). A new charge card also made it possible for the retailer to identify and target different customer categories with customized services and marketing. McKesson's innovations had a dramatic effect on the wholesale drug distribution industry, reshaping cost structures, relationships with customers, and the way that distributors do business. From 1975 to 1987 McKesson increased its sales over four times while expenses only rose 86 percent (Clemons and Row 1988).

VI. INFORMATION SEEKING AND USE IN KNOWLEDGE CREATION

As knowledge-creating enterprises, organizations may be usefully thought of as repositories of capabilities, capabilities that are the result of the knowledge of the organizational individuals and groups being given form and coherence through the relationships, processes, and tools that define the organization. The management of organizational knowledge is therefore the management and nurturing of the organization's capabilities.

In this section we are primarily concerned with the gathering and use of information in organizational processes of knowledge creation that generate knowledge for product or process development, spawn new innovations, and enable the movement of knowledge across organizational boundaries. We consider information seeking and use in the context of how knowledge is converted between the tacit and the explicit through processes of externalization and combination, how experimentation and scanning the market help identify and clarify opportunities, and how knowledge from outside sources is transferred, combined, and absorbed to create new products and capabilities. As suggested by the framework developed in chapter 2, we examine (1) information needs, (2) information seeking, and (3) information use in terms of cognitive needs, affective responses, and situational dimensions. A summary outline of the ensuing discussion is given in Table 4–4.

Information Needs in Knowledge Creation

In knowledge creation, information needs arise from gaps in the organization's existing knowledge, understanding, or capabilities. Such gaps may stand in the way of the organization's being able to solve a problem or take advantage of an opportunity. To initiate information gathering, the needs pertaining to a problem or opportunity situation have to be identified and elaborated. To reduce the high levels of uncertainty and ambiguity inherent in the search for new knowledge, the information-seeking process is guided by beliefs and as-

TABLE 4–4. Information needs, seeking, and use in knowledge creation.

	Information Needs	*Information Seeking*	*Information Use*
Knowledge Creation	• Identify gaps in existing knowledge, capabilities • Criteria to design, evaluate new knowledge • Information about sources of knowledge, capabilities	• Intensive information sharing and searching • Wide range of sources and knowledge-sourcing mechanisms	• Mobilize internal knowledge • Exploit external knowledge • Knowledge use as social process
Cognitive Needs	• Defining and framing the problem • Innovations as social systems • Locus and level of knowledge	• Porous information boundaries • Gatekeeping and boundary spanning • Information stickiness	• Absorptive capacity • Cognitive diversity • Combinative capability
Affective Responses	• Uncertainty, doubt, tension, stress • Use intuition to develop a focus or feasible idea	• Emotional attachment to signature skills • Redundant or unique information • Resistance to new ideas	• Not-invented-here syndrome • Emotional knowledge • Creative abrasion, creative chaos
Situational Dimensions	• Design versus discovery • Complex problems with amorphous goals • New product definition situation: technology and market factors	• Information politics • New or established markets and technologies • Access to external sources of knowledge	• Organizational intention • Technological utopianism • Initiation stages of the innovation process

sumptions about what areas of knowledge development would be advantageous for the organization, which areas are feasible and which are not, as well as what levels of effort would be required. These beliefs give shape and direction to the specification of information needs, and provide the criteria by which new information and knowledge would be evaluated as they are encountered in the information-seeking process. Gaps in knowledge, understanding, or capability may be filled in a number of ways—by locating expertise or experience within the organization, by learning or developing the desired capabilities, or by transferring knowledge from outside the organization. An important part of the elaboration of information needs is therefore to discover sources and develop strategies for acquiring the specific know-how.

Information Needs and Cognitive Needs: The creation of organizational knowledge takes place when organizations solve problems, develop new products or processes, or transfer technologies and methods across their boundaries. In problem-solving and new-product-development situations, information is needed in the first instance to introduce sufficient clarity and definition in order to set a general direction for the process to begin. *Defining and framing the problem* is a necessary part of the knowledge creation process, and often involves members participating in dialogue and reflection to clarify as much as is initially possible questions concerning the nature and limits of the problem situation, goals and performance criteria of the new-product development, technologies that may be relevant, and the resources and expertise available and required. Countervailing this desire for clarity is the need to deliberately introduce a certain level of obfuscation in the initial goals and objectives, partly because management lacks the knowledge to be specific, and partly because vague goals give room for participants to experiment. Nonaka and Takeuchi (1995) identify this as an important enabling condition for promoting the growth of organizational knowledge, citing many examples of Japanese top management supplying only ambiguous product visions in order to generate the "fluctuation and creative chaos" that encourages members to be creative and to actively seek out and try new possibilities.

The introduction of an innovation in an organization must be accompanied by the development of a social system that supports the innovation (Stinchcombe 1990). Information needs therefore are not limited to technical concerns but must also reflect the social and economic requirements that have to be addressed. Stinchcombe (1990) structures the *social requirements of an innovation* around six elements (which he also calls theories), with each element identifying the information that needs to be processed: (1) a core theory of the innovation, or what is technically involved in the design of the innovation; (2) a theory of the investment in the innovation, or what are the risks and profits that justify the innovation; (3) technical-costs of the innovation, or what it will cost to produce the innovation; (4) the market or benefits of the innovation, or who will want the goods, at what price, and how can the organization reach them; (5) a theory of the division of benefits, or how benefits are to be distributed, and what promises of future returns can attract investors; (6) a personnel part of the theory, or what are the levels of competence, trustworthiness, motivation, and so on of the personnel involved (Stinchcombe 1990, 167–68).

Knowledge in organizations exists in many forms and at many levels. Organizational knowledge may be *tacit* in the implicit expertise of the individual or in the skills, experience, and relationships of the members of a group. Individuals or groups can skillfully perform an activity without being able to articulate the rules or theory that describe the activity. Organizational knowledge may also be *explicit* and readily observable. For example, equipment configurations, customer databases, maps and blueprints, standards and specifications, documented rules and procedures, all clearly manifest knowledge in physical formats. Because of the tacit/explicit spectrum of organizational knowledge, the identification and selection of information sources to approach become an important element of establishing information needs. This generally requires an appraisal of the *locus and the organizational level* at which the required information may be found. In a situation where technological knowledge is being imported from outside an organization or group, "the challenge remains to determine just where the know-how resides. In equipment? Software? Procedures? The heads of a few key individuals?" (Leonard-Barton 1995, 170). It is also necessary to draw the distinctions between know-how that exists at various levels of the organization, such as skills and experience possessed by the individual, recipes or methods adopted by the group, rules and routines applied by the organization, and relationships and information dissemination mechanisms shared by a network of organizations (Kogut and Zander 1992).

Information Needs and Affective Responses: Feelings of uncertainty and doubt are characteristic of the intial stages of information seeking when organizational members are trying to clarify the information needs that should guide their knowledge exploration processes. As Kuhlthau (1993a,b) has observed, the state of uncertainty about the nature of information needs causes affective symptoms of anxiety and lack of confidence during early phases of the information search. The feeling of uncertainty begins to ebb once the individual is able to formulate some kind of focus or guiding idea which can be used to steer further search. Kuhlthau regards this formulation of a theme as a pivotal point in the search process, and suggests that it is an outcome of the individual reflecting thoughtfully on the information encountered thus far in the search. During the first phases of the knowledge creation process, information needs are progressively answered through information scanning, knowledge sharing, and participative dialogue. By a process of collective reflection, members of a project team develop a shared mental model which can be verbalized into explicit concepts using words, expressions, as well as metaphors and analogies. It is through the activities of "sharing tacit knowledge" and "creating concepts" (Nonaka and Takeuchi 1995) that the initial feelings of uncertainty and doubt give way to a heightened sense of direction, confidence, and optimism about what is desirable and achievable. The early feelings of stress and anxiety can be channeled to increase motivation and foster creativity. For example, corporations are known to have tackled hard R&D problems by forming "skunk works" of small research teams which are set outside the main organization structure, and are given the mandate to work intensively and uninhibitedly on complex problems and challenging goals.

Intuition may play a significant role in situations when information needs are unclear or when a guiding theme does not readily crystallize. Since intuition generally refers to a form of knowing or sensing without the use of rational processes, it is helpful to differentiate between expert intuition and emotive intuition (Simon 1987). Emotive intuition is based on emotional responses, often precipitated by conditions of stress. For example, managers in stressful situations are known to behave in nonproductive ways to allay feelings of guilt, anxiety, and embarassment (Simon 1987). Expert intuition is based on accumulated knowledge and experience that results in a capability to recognize and retrieve patterns from memory. Leonard-Barton (1995) describes companies which deliberately create industry experts and technologists who have developed a fine "intuition" of what the market wants now and will need in the future. Such expert intuition is built upon the individuals' immersion in a rich and sizable pool of personal knowledge about customers, competitors, markets, technologies, standards, and so on. Emotions are not absent in the exercise of expert intuition, but they are used to signal to the experts the affective values of current options, affective values that recall their past experience in working with similar options.

Information Needs and Situational Dimensions: Information needs may also be clarified by examining the problem dimensions that characterize the situation in which those needs arise. Of the eleven problem dimensions identified by MacMullin and Taylor (1984), four are particularly relevant to understanding information needs in organizational knowledge creation. (1) The problem to be solved can lie on a continuum between ***design and discovery.*** Design problems may be solved by applying existing knowledge in new ways, while discovery problems may require information and expertise about new technologies and markets. (2) The problem is likely to be ***complex,*** with many variables interacting simultaneously, so that information is needed to reduce the problem to simpler tasks. (3) The problem's goals are likely to be ***amorphous*** and challenging, requiring information to give substance and priority to design objectives and preferences. (4) The problem is likely to be of a ***new pattern*** or unfamiliar, so that information is required to clarify and understand what is possible and what would constitute a significant advance. Generally, because problem solving and knowledge creation often involve thinking broadly and making surprising connections, organizational members can benefit from access to information that goes beyond their immediate operational requirements. In other words, a certain level of information redundancy (Nonaka and Takeuchi 1995) in the organization is likely to encourage information sharing and cross-pollination that stimulates innovation.

In ***new-product-development situations,*** two sets of factors determine the kinds of information that are needed: "the maturity of the technological design underlying the product line and the degree of alignment beween the proposed product line and the current customer base" (Leonard-Barton 1995, 180). When the maturity of the technological design is low, the product will be new to the world, so the developer's questions revolve around whether they can solve the problems to make the product work. When the technological maturity is high, the product incorporates incremental improvements to a well-established or "dominant design" (Utterback 1994). When the market alignment is high, the product is intended for current customers, so the main issue is understanding what features are most desirable to the existing customers.

When the market alignment is low, the product is attempting to create a new market, so the major concerns are identifying who the customers will be and how they will use the product. Depending on the degree of technological maturity and market alignment in a particular new-product situation, an organization can adopt the appropriate product definition strategy. For example, when both technological maturity and market alignment are high, explicit customer demands often drive technological enhancements along known performance parameters for current products (Leonard-Barton 1995). Conversely, when both technological maturity and market alignment are low, the technology and the market coevolve together, with technological potential attempting to match or better respond to market need (which may have to be revealed or discovered).

Information Seeking in Knowledge Creation

Information seeking in the pursuit of new knowledge needs to be simultaneously broad and narrow. Generally, the process begins by scanning broadly and sharing information extensively, connecting with many sources inside and outside the organization. The initial objectives are to assess the state of development of an area, to understand the range of possibilities, and to identify new opportunities or market needs. At some stage, when the problem is sufficiently defined and the areas where critical information is lacking are apparent, information gathering becomes more narrowly focused and even more vigorous. Throughout, information is accessed in a variety of modes, such as attending conferences, conversing with individuals, visiting sites, and reading up on an area. Information seeking during knowledge creation is therefore characterized by intensive information seeking and sharing, and by the use of a number of information channels that introduce expertise from outside the group or organization. Two sets of difficulties are commonly encountered in the scanning and focusing of information: the difficulties of sourcing and transferring information from outside the organization or group, and the difficulties of retrieving and making explicit the tacit knowledge of the experienced and the expert.

Information Seeking and Cognitive Needs: Organizations that are effective at knowledge creation constantly expose their members to new ideas and innovations from outside the organization. The sources of innovation vary greatly. In some fields, as expected, the current product manufacturers are the typical innovators, but in many other fields, users are found to develop the most innovations, and in others yet, suppliers of innovation-related components and materials are the typical sources of innovations (von Hippel 1988). Organizations need to recognize that more than ever, knowledge is a widely distributed resource that is shared and jointly created by many groups of participants, including customers, suppliers, competitors, consultants, researchers, scientists, and so on. To tap into the abundance of information that is in the external environment, organizations scan broadly and maintain ***porous organizational boundaries*** (Leonard-Barton 1995) that facilitate the absorption of external information. Leonard-Barton also recommends that in the case of technological knowledge the following sources be monitored: other companies (competitors and noncompetitors), universities, vendors, national laboratories, customers, and consultants. Research suggests that environmental scanning improves organizational performance (Choo 1995a). Several studies show that scanning is associated with higher levels of organizational achievement, and this is the case for large companies as well as small businesses across a wide range of industries, and for nonprofit organizations such as educational institutions and hospitals. The general result is that scanning organizations outperformed organizations that did not scan or scanned inadequately.

It is well known that certain individuals perform catalytic roles in the movement and assimilation of information across organizational peripheries. Allen (1977) found that in science and engineering organizations, information from the outside world does not move directly into the organization. Instead, the information flow is indirect and involves two or more steps. External information passes through ***technological gatekeepers,*** who read more, including the more research-oriented journals, and who have a broad range of personal contacts both outside and inside the organization, which they maintain on a continuing informal basis. It is the gatekeepers who keep their colleagues informed, and who are often consulted about current, external developments. Tushman and Scanlan (1981) noticed a similar phenomenon. Because organizations limit their scope and specialize in certain activities, they evolve local norms, languages, and conceptual frameworks. While this specialization increases the efficiency of internal information processing, it also sets up obstacles to information transfer from the external environment. As a result, it becomes necessary to recode information messages at the firm's boundaries. Boundaries can be spanned effectively only by individuals who understand the coding schemes used on both sides of the perimeter, enabling them to recognize significant information on one side and disseminate it on the other side: Tushman and Scanlan name this process ***informational boundary spanning.***

The phenomenon of information gatekeeping or boundary spanning is not limited to scientific organizations, but can be found in a wide spectrum of social communication patterns, including voting behavior and the diffusion of innovations. (In both cases, opinion leaders influenced the votes of friends, or the adoption of innovations such as hybrid seed corn and new drugs.) Allen summarizes:

The phenomenon of the gatekeeper is not an isolated one. Rather it is one example of a much more general class of phenomena. There will always be some people who, for various reasons, tend to become acquainted with information sources outside their immediate community. They either read more extensively than most or develop personal contacts with outsiders. A large proportion of these people in turn attract colleagues from within the community who turn to them for information and advice. (Allen 1977, 150)

The information required for technical problem solving is often hard to acquire and transfer, necessitating significant expenditures of cognitive effort, time, and money. To reflect the costs of information transfer, von Hippel (1994) defines the "stickiness" of a unit of information as "the incremental expenditure required to transfer that unit of information to a specified locus in a form usable by a given information seeker" (p. 430). *Information stickiness* is a function of the attributes of the information itself as well as the attributes and choices made by the information seeker and information providers. Thus stickiness increases when the information to be transferred is part of the tacit knowledge of a skilled individual, or when the user is unfamiliar with or untrained in acquiring a type of information, or when the provider charges for access to its databases. Information may be made easier to transfer by "unsticking" it, as when tacit knowledge is made explicit through narrating or recording procedures, or when gatekeepers filter and selectively introduce outside information.

Information Seeking and Affective Responses: Information seeking in the context of knowledge creation is likely to be influenced by the individual's attitudes and preferences about the types of information and the style of information gathering. This may be especially true in the case of sharing information that is based on personal, tacit knowledge. In Kuhlthau's (1993a,b) model of the information search process that we presented in chapter 2, she drew a few corollaries from the affective responses of uncertainty and anxiety that characterize stages of the search process. Among these corollaries, two are particularly pertinent to our discussion here, and they concern the effects of redundant information, and the searcher's personal choices about how and where to gather information. Kuhlthau (1993a,b) observed that *redundant information* fits into what the individual already knows or recognizes, and its relevance and usefulness is easily judged. Redundant information can therefore build confidence and reduce the level of uncertainty. Unique information is new and can extend knowledge, but it may not match the individual's current cognitive framework, requiring the individual to reconstruct meaning and significance. Too much redundant information leads to boredom, whereas too much unique information causes anxiety. Nonaka and Takeuchi (1995) extend the notion of redundant information in an interesting way. They define redundant information somewhat differently, and then show that redundant information can be used to generate a sense of creative tension. For them, redundant information is information that goes beyond the immediate operational requirements, coming from the intentional overlappping of information about other functional areas that are not one's own. The effect is that "sharing redundant information promotes the sharing of tacit knowledge, because individuals can sense what others are trying to articulate. . . . redundant information enables individuals to invade each other's functional boundaries and offer advice or provide new information from different perspectives. In short, redundancy of information brings about 'learning by intrusion' into each individual's sphere of perception" (Nonaka and Takeuchi 1995, 81).

Kuhlthau (1993a,b) also concluded that the search process is a series of unique, personal choices about what sources and information-seeking strategies will be effective or expedient. Beliefs and expectations about what sources to use or not to use, about the sequence of sources to be approached, and about the information selected from the sources as relevant or irrelevant, are based on the individual's own experience, training, and cognitive style. Information relevance is therefore a matter of personal judgment and preference. Leonard-Barton (1995) makes a similar but more general argument in her discussion of the *signature skills* that people use in problem solving. She observes that the skilled individual becomes emotionally attached to a particular style of problem solving and information seeking, a style by which the individual establishes her own professional identity. Signature skills are the result of three interacting influences—the individual's preferred type of task, preferred cognitive approach to problem solving, and preferred technology (tools and methods) for performing the task. Specialists tend to pursue their signature skills in depth, and the signature skills become "emotionally tied to people's egos and identities" (Leonard-Barton 1995, 63). This is partly the reason why many experts resist new ideas. Starbuck (1992) attributes this resistance to five factors: clients or peers may view the expert's need to learn as evidence of deficient knowledge; experts account carefully for their use of time and are reluctant to spend it on learning something new or unproven; experts' specialization necessarily reduces versatility and flexibility; experts protect their niches as partial monopolies; and experts' perceptual filters keep them from noticing some social and technological changes.

Information Seeking and Situational Dimensions: The sharing of information is a necessary condition of organizational knowledge creation. Ironically, the more information intensive an organization is, the less likely it is that its members would share their information freely: "As people's jobs and roles become defined by the unique information they hold, they may be less likely to share that information—viewing it as a source of power and indispensability—rather than more so. When information is the primary unit of organizational currency, we should not expect the owners to give it away" (Davenport, Eccles, and Prusak 1992, 53). From their analysis of more than twenty-five organizations, Davenport and associates found that the major reason for the inability to create information-based organizations was the failure to manage the politics of information use. Among the organizations studied, five models of information politics were observed: technological utopianism, anarchy, feudalism, monarchy, and federalism (Davenport, Eccles, and Prusak 1992). The most common political model of information sharing was a form of *information feudalism,* in which individual managers and their departments control information acquisition, storage, distribution, and analysis. Managers act as powerful feudal lords, who not only rule over the creation and circulation of information, but also determine the meanings and interpretations that should be attached to the information. This fragmentation of information integrity undermines the organization's efforts to consolidate and cross-fertilize its knowledge assets so that the organization as a whole can learn and adapt. Instead of feudalism Davenport et al. recommend a form of *information federalism* as being the most appropriate model in today's environment. Federalism recognizes that politics is a necessary and legitimate activity for people with divergent interests to work out a collective purpose and the means for realizing it. Under federalism, managers negotiate among themselves the use and definition of information. Managers bargain with each other to cede some of their information assets in return for producing a larger pool of knowledge that they can tap into and exploit to advantage.

In new-product or new-service development situations, the activity of gathering information to learn about the market depends on whether ***the market and the technology are new or well established.*** Specifically, information seeking varies according to how mature the product or service technology is and how well the product or service matches with current customer needs (Leonard-Barton 1995). When the new product is an extension of an established product line, an appropriate information-gathering strategy is to make use of traditional market research techniques such as conducting surveys and focus group discussions; and interacting with "lead users," "whose present strong needs will become general in a marketplace months or years in the future" (von Hippel 1988, 107). When either the technology is immature or the market is likely to be a new or unknown set of customers, traditional market research techniques work less well because no analogous product exists, and users and developers cannot easily visualize the new product. In this situation, Leonard-Barton (1995) suggests the use of data collection techniques based on "emphatic design," which she defines as "the creation of product or service concepts based on a deep (emphatic) understanding of unarticulated user needs" (p. 194). This deep understanding is achieved by collecting data about actual observed customer behavior, allowing product developers and users to interact directly so that market and technological potential can be assessed, and redirecting existing technical capabilities imaginatively toward new products or services. When neither the technology nor the market is certain, market research and emphatic design techniques are not applicable because it is not clear how the technology will shape the product and who the customers will be. In this situation, new markets are being evolved, and information seeking may involve extrapolating current trends, planning scenarios about the future, and conducting market experiments (Leonard-Barton 1995).

Information Use in Knowledge Creation

The organization evaluates new knowledge in relation to its beliefs about how the application of the knowledge will enhance its competitive position, its interpretations about how the market will react to new products or services, and its expectations about how the new capability matches its longer term goals and vision.

These beliefs are embedded in evaluation routines and norms that determine the usefulness of new information, and appraise the value of new knowledge. Then people, resources, tools, and processes have to be brought together to turn the knowledge into physical products or actual capabilities. An organization seeks to mobilize knowledge from internal as well as external sources, but each category of information use has to grapple with different management issues. Internal knowledge creation has to balance focus, speed of response, and harmonious communications on the one hand with cognitive diversity and creative abrasion on the other. External knowledge transfer requires the organization to be at a stage of technical readiness to absorb the new knowledge, and to be able to address acceptance issues such as dealing with the not-invented-here syndrome. In either case, the creation, absorption and exploitation of new knowledge is not just a technical activity, but a social process that needs to be managed according to the culture and context of the organization. We discuss some of these concerns next.

Information Use and Cognitive Needs: The ability to recognize the potential value of new, external knowledge, assimilate it, and then exploit the knowledge is vital to the knowledge-creating enterprise. The organization's ***absorptive capacity*** to evaluate and utilize outside knowledge is largely a function of the level of prior related knowledge that the organization already possesses (Cohen and Levinthal 1990). Absorptive capacity is generated and increased when the organization conducts its own R&D, is directly involved in manufacturing operations, sends its personnel for advanced technical training, and so on. Cognitive research on individual learning suggests that the accumulation and richness of the preexisting knowledge increases the ability to put new knowledge into memory as well as the ability to recall and use it. Thus learning is cumulative, and learning capability is greatest when what is to be learned is related to what is already known (Cohen and Levinthal 1990). The implication here is that the existence of a diversity of knowledge and knowledge structures possessed by members of the organization would increase the probability of relating new incoming knowledge to what is already known. This call for knowledge diversity is in line with the entreaty by Leonard-Barton (1995) that innovating organizations should maintain a ***diversity of cognitive styles*** in order to benefit from an eclectic mix of different signature skills among its members. In practical terms, Cohen and Levinthal suggest that the organization requires an existing internal staff of technologists and scientists who are not only competent in their fields but also familiar with the organization's idiosyncratic needs, procedures, routines, complementary capabilties, and external relationships. They also note that:

> . . . firms may conduct basic research less for particular results than to be able to provide themselves with the general background knowledge that would permit them to exploit rapidly useful scientific and technological knowledge through their own innovations or to be able to respond quickly—to become a fast second—when competitors come up with a major advance. . . . we may think of basic research as broadening the firm's knowledge base to create critical overlap with new knowledge and providing it with the deeper understanding that is useful for exploiting new technical developments that build on rapidly advancing science and technology. (Cohen and Levinthal 1990, 148)

An interesting corollary of the need for an organization to invest in absorptive capacity is that when an organization intends to acquire and use knowledge that is relatively unconnected to its current activities and capabilities, then the organization may need to first work at or invest in creating the absorptive capacity (by, for example, R&D or specialized training) to assimilate and exploit the new knowledge.

A related view is the idea that organizations learn new skills by recombining their current capabilities, so that:

> Creating new knowledge does not occur in abstraction from current abilities. Rather, new learning, such as innovations, are products of a firm's *combinative capabilities* to generate new applications from existing knowledge. By combinative capabilities, we mean the intersection of the capability of the firm to exploit its knowledge and the unexplored potential of the technology . . . (Kogut and Zander 1992).

This view would be consonant with Schumpeter's (1934) argument that innovations generally are combinations of existing knowledge and incremental learning. Kogut and Zander (1992) suggest that the main reason why organizations tend to learn in areas that are cognate to their existing practice is because the introduction and exploitation of innovations occur by building on the social relationships that currently exist in the organization, since "a firm's capabilities cannot be separated from how it is currently organized" (p. 392).

Information Use and Affective Responses: The introduction of new knowledge from outside the organization may meet with resistance. One of the most well-known forms that this resistance could manifest itself is in the phenomenon of the *not-invented-here (NIH) syndrome.* This syndrome is defined as "the tendency of a project group of stable composition to believe it possesses a monopoly of knowledge of its field, which leads it to reject new ideas from outsiders to the likely detriment of its performance" (Katz and Allen 1982, 7). Such behavior may be a natural consequence of individuals who, over time, increase order and stability in their work environments so as to reduce the amount of stress and uncertainty that they need to face. As a result, the longer the individuals' tenure in a group, the stronger their emotional attachment to strategies and decisions that they were (perhaps partly) responsible for, and the more resistant they become toward outside new ideas that upset the familiarity and confidence of their work environments. In their study of 345 R&D professionals working on fifty projects in a large corporate research facility, Katz and Allen (1982) found that project performance increases up to 1.5 years' tenure, stays steady for a time, but by 5 years has declined noticeably. The performance decline is best explained by

> a project team's tendency to ignore and become increasingly isolated from sources that provide more critical kinds of evaluation, information, and feedback. . . . Thus overall performance will suffer when research teams fail to pay sufficient attention to new advances and information within their relevant external R&D community, when technical service groups fail to interact among themselves, or when development project members fail to communicate with individuals from other parts of the organization, particularly R&D, marketing, and manufacturing. (Katz and Allen 1982, 16)

When scouting for external knowledge, organization members sometimes rely on their gut feel or emotional response to assess and evaluate the significance of new, unfamiliar information. Similarly, when sharing knowledge internally, members reveal and often stick to their affective preferences, even when they are unable to account for their existence. In both cases, what is being activated is not just technical knowledge about how to do things, but also *emotional knowledge* (Plotkin 1994) about how one feels and thinks about the factual knowledge. Emotions are mental and physiological signposts that signal the possible presence of significant events or information, their significance having been learned over long periods of time. Plotkin (1994) suggests that "whatever the emotion being signalled, one of its functions is to tell us what to attend to, what to learn about" (p. 208). Emotion therefore supports cognition in at least two ways: "It informs our intelligence what to learn and think about. And it also serves as a reliable signalling system of how we are going to behave towards others, or how they are going to treat us" (p. 209). Both Leonard-Barton (1995) and Nonaka and Takeuchi (1995) recognize that shared problem solving and knowledge sharing are vigorous processes where creativity is stimulated by the exchange of emotional energies. Thus Leonard-Barton writes of the positive effects of managed *creative abrasion,* whereas Nonaka and Takeuchi identify *fluctuation and creative chaos* as an enabling condition for knowledge creation.

Information Use and Situational Dimensions: The innovation process in organizations may be divided into two general stages: *initiation,* which includes "all of the information gathering, conceptualizing, and planning for the adoption of an innovation, leading up to the decision to adopt," and *implementation,* which includes "all of the events, actions, and decisions involved in putting an innovation into use" (Rogers 1983, 363). During initiation, the organization "sets its agenda" by identifying problems or performance gaps that create a need for innovation, or scanning the environment for new innovations of potential value. The organization then "matches" a problem from its agenda with an innovation to assess how well they are likely to fit. In agenda setting and matching, new information is processed with reference to the organization's intention and core capabilities. *Organizational intention* is the organization's goal aspirations and conceptualizes a vision of what kind of knowledge should be developed (Nonaka and Takeuchi 1995). *Core capabilities* comprise the employee knowledge and skill, physical technical systems, managerial systems, and values and norms that set an organization apart and give it a unique edge (Leonard-Barton 1995). During implementation, the organization "redefines" the innovation as it is modified to fit the situation of the organization and the demands of the problem. The organization may also "restructure"how work is organized around the new innovation. As the innovation becomes more widely used, the relationship between the innovation and the organization is "clarified." Eventually the innovation is "routinized" and loses its separate identity (Rogers 1983).

Turning an organizational innovation into a going concern that regularly produces benefits for the innovating organization is tantamount to creating a new *social system* (Stinchcombe 1990). Such a social system has "to nurture technical ideas, to make investments in risky situations, to build a production system that can produce effectively and can come down the learning curve rapidly, to reach the market that can afford the innovation while it is still expensive, and to arrange the division of benefits so that both investors and personnel will be motivated to develop the competencies needed to all these things and then do them" (Stinchcombe 1990, 192). Unfortunately, many organizations overlook the social requirements of producing an innovation, and confine themselves instead to technical matters and to administrative structures that support technical problem solving. Organizations implicitly subscribe to a theory of innovation that Stinchcombe calls *technological utopianism,* in which "the theory is merely describing the technical way to achieve some end, with no analysis of the social and economic forces needed to bring the innovation into being" (p. 174). In informational terms, the introduction of an innovation involves a higher level of uncertainty than the making of established products, and uses information in different ways to, for example, enhance or better apply the innovation, determine or penetrate markets, and coordinate the information and work flow between engineering, production, and marketing units. Stinchcombe (1990) concludes that "innovations should tend to create pressures for divisional decentralized administration [Chandler 1962], such that the innovation has a separate but integrated news-collecting, information-processing, and decision-making structure. . . . such a division is likely to have a higher skill mix than a division with an equally complex product or service that is no longer an innovation" (p. 24).

VII. SUMMARY: THE MANAGEMENT OF KNOWLEDGE CREATION

Knowledge creation extends the organization's capabilities by leveraging the expertise of its own members, and by learning from and with others outside the organization. In mobilizing internal knowledge, information processes are managed to promote the sharing of information, conversion of tacit knowledge, experimentation and prototyping, and the migration of knowledge to other parts of the organization. In importing external knowledge, the flow of information from outside is facilitated by the communication function of gatekeepers and boundary spanners, while its assimilation is influenced by the range, diversity, and depth of the related knowledge that already exsists in the organization. Both modes of knowledge creation take place in a larger organizational context defined by an appraisal of the new knowledge in relation to the organization's strategic intention, an appreciation of the organization's core capabilities, an assessment of the market and technology potential, and a recognition that operationalizing innovations requires the support of new social and information systems.

5

THE MANAGEMENT OF UNCERTAINTY— ORGANIZATIONS AS DECISION- MAKING SYSTEMS

Reason sits firm and holds the reins, and she will not let the feelings burst away and hurry her to wild chasms. The passions may rage furiously, like true heathens, as they are; and the desires may imagine all sorts of vain things: but judgement shall still have the last word in every argument, and the casting vote in every decision.
  —*Charlotte Brontë 1847,* Jane Eyre, *chapter 19*

The essence of ultimate decision remains impenetrable to the observer— often, indeed, to the decider himself . . . . There will always be the dark and tangled stretches in the decision-making process—mysterious even to those who may be the most intimately involved.
  —John Fitzgerald Kennedy, Preface to Decision-Making in the White
    House *by Theodore Sorensen 1963*

Formal decision making in organizations is structured by procedures and rules that specify roles, methods, and norms. The assumption is that rules and routines would lighten the information processing required of complex problems, embody efficient or reliable techniques learned from experience, and coordinate the actions and results of disparate organizational groups. When the decisions to be made are highly consequential and visible, when, for example, safety and public opinion are at stake, the organization may attempt to manage the process more closely through an elaborate system of checks and controls. Following routines and procedures over time can institutionalize certain ways of viewing the world, form habits about the acquisition and passing on of information, and in general establish values and norms that influence how the organization copes with choice and uncertainty. The intended result of this combination of culture, communication, and consensus is to improve decision efficiency and to help ensure a greater level of rational choice behavior. The unintended effect of such a tightly coupled system could be the rigidification of decision routines and decision values, and a collective desire to maintain the interlocking system of culture and communication that has been built up over time. In some cases, both effects could actually work against the original goals of enhancing decision behavior, and may instead stand in the way of organizational members accurately interpreting new information and acting on the information in a rational manner.

On January 28, 1986, at 11:38 A.M. EST, the space shuttle Challenger was launched from Cape Canaveral, Florida. The mission ended 73 seconds later when the Challenger disintegrated into a billowing cloud of fire and smoke. All seven crew members, including Christie McAuliffe ("America's teacher in space"), were killed in the explosion. The Presidential Commission investigating the accident subsequently concluded that Challenger was destroyed after hot propellant gases flew past the aft joint of the shuttle's right solid rocket booster, burning through two synthetic rubber seal rings, called O-rings, and vaporizing the seal. The commission also concluded that "the decision to launch the Challenger was flawed," and faulted the project management structure for not allowing information about the recent history of O-ring problems to flow to the decision makers (Bell and Esch 1987). The House of Representatives conducted its own hearings and also concluded that "the fundamental problem was poor technical decision-making over a period of several years by top NASA and contractor personnel."

Why was it that, despite the elaborate procedures and standards that were put in place to control how risks were assessed and launch decisions were taken, despite the availability of information and data about the technical problems that eventually led to the explosion, and despite the warnings and objections about the risks and uncertainties presented by the particular conditions of the Challenger launch, the decision was made to proceed with the mission? On the tenth anniversary of the disaster, Diane Vaughan produced a probing analysis of the reasons and forces that led to the error. Contrary to conventional accounts that pointed to managerial neglect and defective decision making, Vaughan argued that the Challenger accident

. . . is a story that illustrates how disastrous consequences can emerge from the banality of organizational life. It is a story of rather ordinary influences on decision making that operate inconspicuously but with grave effect. No fundamental decision was made at NASA to do evil; rather, a series of seemingly harmless decisions were made that incrementally moved the space agency toward a catastrophic outcome. (Vaughan 1996, 410)

Morton-Thiokol Inc. had engineered the space shuttle's solid rocket booster (SRB) based on the Air Force's Titan III design because of its reliability. The SRB's steel case was divided into segments that were joined and sealed by rubber O-rings. Although the Titan's O-rings had occasionally been eroded by hot gases, the erosion was not regarded as significant. A second, redundant O-ring was added to each joint to act as backup should the primary O-ring fail. As early as 1977, a test of the SRB case showed an unexpected rotation of the joints, which decompressed the O-rings, making it more difficult for them to seal the joints. In 1980 a review committee concluded that safety was not jeopardized and the joints were classified as criticality 1R, denoting that joint failure could cause loss of life or shuttle (the 1 in the rating), and that secondary O-rings provided redundancy (the R in the rating). During 1983 the SRBs were modified to use thinner walls, narrower nozzles, and more powerful fuel, which worsened the joint rotation. Tests showed that the rotation could be so large that a secondary O-ring could not seal a joint and provide redundancy. The R rating was consequently removed from the joints' criticality classification. Nevertheless, many NASA and Thiokol documents produced over the next three years continued to list the criticality as 1R, and seemed to suggest that neither management thought that a secondary O-ring could really fail to seal a joint (Starbuck and Milliken 1988a). In a flight readiness review of March 1984, NASA's top managers discussed and accepted the idea that some O-ring erosion was "acceptable" because the rings embodied a safety factor. The incidence of heat damage at the SRB joints was growing—three of the five 1984 flights showed heat damage, eight of the nine 1985 flights, and the flight on January 12, 1986, just two weeks before Challenger. In spite of these signals, the management of the SRB project at Marshall Space Flight Center (SFC) and at Thiokol remained confident that the erosion was "allowable" and an "acceptable risk." The April 1985 flight showed significant damage at one primary O-ring, with a substantial amount of hot gas blowing by this ring, which in turn eroded the secondary O-ring (Bell and Esch 1987). This led Lawrence Mulloy, SRB project manager at Marshall, to place a "launch constraint" on all subsequent flights, acknowledging that a problem of criticality 1, 1R, 2, or 2R might occur. However, Mulloy "waived" the launch constraint for all subsequent flights up to the last one:

Since the risk of O-ring erosion was accepted and indeed expected, it was no longer considered an anomaly to be resolved before the next flight . . . I concluded that we're taking a risk every time. We all signed up for that risk. And the conclusion was, there was no significant difference in risk from previous launches. We'd be taking essentially the same risk on Jan. 28 that we have been ever since we first saw O-ring erosion. (Quoted in Bell and Esch 1987, 43, 47)

In early December 1985, Thiokol was told to "close out" long outstanding problems, including O-ring erosion problems, and the relevant problem reports were subsequently marked as "contractor closure received." O-rings were no longer listed as a launch constraint for the flight readiness review of January

15, 1986, and O-rings were not mentioned in the flight readiness review documentation of the Challenger (Starbuck and Milliken 1988a).

On the afternoon of January 27, 1986, the eve of the launch, the weather forecast predicted unusually cold weather for Florida, with temperatures in the low 20s in the early hours of January 28. Thiokol engineers expressed concern that at such cold temperatures, the O-rings would harden and not seal the joints against the hot ignition gases. Two telephone conferences were held at three sites (Thiokol, Marshall SFC, and Kennedy Space Center) on the evening of January 27 to discuss whether the launch should be delayed. Thirty-four engineers and managers participated in the second conference, where Thiokol engineers warned that at the forecast temperatures, the O-rings would seal more slowly than on the coldest launch to date, a January 1985 mission, when the temperature was 53°F, at which a primary O-ring was eroded so that it failed to seal, allowing hot gases to "blow by" to the secondary ring. Although the secondary ring did seal the joint then, the engineers argued that a more extensive blow-by could damage the secondary ring so that it would not seal. Someone then pointed out that one of the Thiokol data points showed blow-by at 75°F, suggesting that temperature was not the only factor. Roger Boisjoly, a Thiokol staff engineer, was asked what evidence existed to show that O-ring damage was the result of cold temperatures. Boisjoly replied that he could not quantify his concerns, that he had no data to quantify it, but that he knew "it was away from goodness in the current database" (Presidential Commission Report 1986, vol. 4, 791). Lawrence Mulloy, manager of the SRB project at Marshall, asked Thiokol management for a recommendation. Thiokol's Joseph Kilminster, the vice president of space booster programs, replied that he could not recommend a launch at any temperature below 53°F. Mulloy said that since booster joint temperatures had never been set as launch criteria, Thiokol was effectively trying to create new launch commit criteria on the eve of the launch. He then exclaimed, "My God, Thiokol, when do you want me to launch, next April?" (Presidential Commission Report 1986, vol. 5, 843). George Hardy, Marshall's deputy director of science and engineering, added that he was "appalled" at the Thiokol recommendation, that the data presented did not conclusively support a correlation between temperature and O-ring erosion, but that he would not agree to a launch against Thiokol's recommendation. The challenges from both Mulloy and Hardy, worded in strong language, put pressure on the Thiokol engineers. Kilminster then asked for permission for Thiokol engineers and managers to go off line for a few minutes. All participants who were asked why the caucus was called thought that it was because Thiokol's engineering analysis was weak:

Thiokol's recommendation for 53°F as the baseline temperature for decision making was central to the controversy. . . . In the absence of a formalized, test-derived rule about O-ring temperature that also took into account pressure and sealing time, uncertainty prevailed. Thiokol created a rule, using the experience

base: do not launch unless O-ring temperature is 53°F or greater. But people at
Marshall and Kennedy were surprised at the choice of this number. First, it was
contradicted by data from tests done at 30°F presented in Thiokol's own charts
. . . Second, it contradicted other temperature guidelines. There were serious differences about which ones applied. (Vaughan 1996, 308, 309)

During the off-line caucus, which lasted for about half an hour, Thiokol's
senior vice president Jerry Mason stated that the possibility of blow-by and
erosion had always been present in the earlier flights, and had been considered
as acceptable risks. They should therefore consider the temperature issue sepa-
rately on its own. Mason reaffirmed the belief in redundancy, that the primary
O-ring would perform properly, but if it sealed slowly and blow-by occurred,
then the secondary O-ring would be in position and would seal. Boisjoly and
another engineer (Arnold Thompson) defended the engineering position that
based on the data they had, they did not know what the secondary O-ring
would do in these cold temperatures. After several minutes of discussion Mason noted that they were starting to go over the same ground again and again
and said: "Well, it's time to make a management decision." Mason, Kilminster,
Wiggins (VP & GM Space Division), and Lund (VP Engineering) then con-
ferred among themselves, effectively excluding the engineers from the decision making. Mason, Kilminster, Wiggins supported a launch recommendation,
but Lund hesitated. Mason said to Lund: "It's time to take off your engineering
hat and put on your management hat." Lund then voted with the rest. When
they were later asked why they had reversed their initial recommendation and
changed their minds about the danger of a low-temperature launch, "all said
that they were influenced by facts not taken into account before their initial
recommendation. These facts supported redundancy: thus, they believed that
the secondary [O-ring] would seal the joint" (Vaughan 1996, p. 319).

When the teleconference resumed, Kilminster summarized Thiokol's position. Although temperature effects were a concern, the data predicting blow-
by were inconclusive. Erosion tests had indicated that the primary O-ring
could sustain three times more erosion than that experienced in the previous
worst case. Furthermore, even if the primary failed, the secondary as backup
would still seal the joint. Stanley Reinartz, manager of the shuttle projects
office at Marshall, then asked all participants of the teleconference whether
there were disagreements or comments about Thiokol's recommendation. No
one said anything. As part of normal NASA procedures, Mulloy asked Kilminster to fax a copy of the flight-readiness rationale and recommendation to
Marshall and Kennedy. The teleconference ended. At 11:38 A.M. the following
morning the Challenger was launched. The ambient temperature was 36°F.
Seconds later, the shuttle exploded, killing all on board.

In the end, the Challenger disaster was the result of an organizational and
social process that had its origins in "routine and taken-for-granted aspects of
organizational life that created a way of seeing that was simultaneously a way
of not seeing" (Vaughan 1996, 394). In this process, information initially

viewed as indicating potentially dangerous deviance is reinterpreted as being within the norms of acceptable joint performance, and therefore officially within the limits of acceptable risk. According to Diane Vaughan, this ***normalization of deviance*** was the outcome of three social forces: the production of culture in the SRB work group, the culture of production, and structural secrecy.

In the ***production of culture,*** the SRB work group repeatedly used a decision-making sequence to develop norms, values, and procedures that supported their central belief about redundancy, and which allowed them to reinterpret deviant information. The decision sequence consisted of five steps: (1) signals of potential danger; (2) official act acknowledging escalated risk; (3) review of evidence; (4) official act indicating the normalization of deviance: accepting the risk; and (5) shuttle launch (Vaughan 1996, 65). The decision sequence was evident from the first shuttle launch. As we noted, the space shuttle improved on the already reliable Titan design by adding a second O-ring to back up the first, thereby providing redundancy. Unfortunately, tests showed that the rocket booster joints rotated on ignition, so much so that the secondary O-ring would not be in position to seal (step 1: danger signal). The rotation problem was taken seriously, and Marshall SFC authorized an engineer's trip to manufacturing firms to examine the problem and allocated resources for more testing (2: official acknowledgment). More test results and some corrective action convinced the engineers that the O-rings were an acceptable risk, and that the secondary rings would perform their redundant function (3: review evidence). The joint was then officially certified as flightworthy and classified as criticality 1R (R for redundancy) at each of the four levels of flight readiness review (4: official normalization of deviance). The successful launch and completion of the first mission confirmed the engineers' and managers' assessment that the rocket booster joint was safe (5: shuttle launch). This decision sequence was subsequently repeated many times, creating precedents that established a normative standard for future decisions, right up to the launch of the Challenger:

> On January 27, 1986, the five-step decision sequence was enacted once again. The predicted cold weather was a signal of potential danger, creating uncertainty about the relationship between O-ring resiliency and redundancy. Arranging the teleconference was an official act of acknowledging escalated risk. There followed a review of the evidence, culminating in an official act indicating the normalization of deviance: accept risk. The decision was followed by the destruction of STS 51-L [Challenger's official designation] . . . (Vaughan 1996, 379)

The incremental and repeated use of the decision sequence over time generated the social and technical affirmation of the SRB work group's actions and beliefs, appearing to validate the dominant logic that the design of the booster joint was redundantly safe and therefore an acceptable risk.

The work group's beliefs and norms were reinforced by a *culture of production,* which consisted of the institutionalized belief systems of the engineering profession, NASA, and the Marshall Space Flight Center, and which was dominated by three cultural imperatives: the original technical culture, bureaucratic accountability, and political accountability (Vaughan 1996). As members of the engineering profession, the group regarded deviations from specifications as common in innovative designs. Problems and discrepancies were the norm, and to proceed with anomalies was acceptable when certain conditions were met. Furthermore, the interpretation of data generally involved flexibility and personal judgment, so that some level of ambiguity and disagreement usually remained even after group deliberations. As they went along, the engineers crafted their own ad hoc rules to deal with issues of design, testing, and risk evaluation, which was again consistent with the engineering practice of "debugging through use." The engineering profession was also a bureaucratic profession, which institutionalized the norms of the legitimacy of bureaucratic authority relations and conformity to rules, and the need for compromise between cost, schedule, and safety. Thus the SRB engineers adhered to the strict reporting procedures of the flight readiness review, which spanned four levels of project management, and the balancing of cost, schedule, and safety was the criterion by which NASA approved change processes. At NASA the original technical culture inherited from the Apollo era espoused "a commitment to research, testing and verification; to in-house technical capability; to hands-on activity; to the acceptance of risk and failure; to open communications; to a belief that NASA was staffed with exceptional people; to attention to detail; and to a 'frontiers of flight' mentality" (McCurdy 1989, 302). This technical culture was the source of NASA's "can do" image, that NASA can accomplish any challenge that is put to it. For the SRB work group, the source of the can-do attitude was in their rule following: "rigorous adherence to the engineering methods, routines, and lessons of the original technical culture and to the bureaucratic proceduralism of the organization" (Vaughan 1996, 234). After Ronald Reagan became U.S. president, NASA, along with other government agencies, was urged to increase its use of external business contractors. This required NASA to create and expand administrative structures to coordinate and control complicated contractor relationships, causing NASA to acquire the characteristics of bureaucratic accountability. At about the same time, political accountability became necessary to garner support for funding the space shuttle program. The program was approved on the promise of providing economical, routine spaceflight, and the program was to be developed on a commercial, pay-its-own-way basis. In the ensuing years, NASA continued to push a production schedule that perpetuated this promise, although a wide gap separated this vision and the realities of the program's technical uncertainty and rising costs. The workload increased with the number of launches per year, and made the goals of the original technical culture more difficult to realize. The overall effect of the culture of production was that the decisions from 1977 to 1985 were "to those in the work group making the technical decisions, normal within the cultural belief systems in which their actions were embedded. Continuing to recommend launch in FRR [Flight Readiness Review] despite problems with the joint was not deviant; in their view, their conduct was culturally approved and conforming" (Vaughan 1996, 236).

The third organizational factor that resulted in the normalization of deviance was the hiding of information about the seriousness of the O-ring problem through *structural secrecy,* which Vaughan (1996) defines as "the way that patterns of information, organizational structure, processes, and transactions, and the structure of regulatory relations systematically undermine the attempt to know and interpret situations in all organizations" (p. 238). At NASA, structural secrecy affected information use by three groups: the SRB work group, NASA top management, and the safety regulators. For the work group members, the repetition of the five-step decision process in dealing with anomalies meant that signals initially seen as deviant were reinterpreted in the context of past decision streams, which had construed similar signals as acceptable risks. Vaughan noted that these signals accumulated incrementally over time, and their significance was unclear because the signals were mixed, weak, and repeated so that they became routine. For NASA's top managers, information was systematically censored through the effects of official organizational practices, specialization, and the reliance on signals. It was the official practice to progressively reduce the package of data charts and materials for management review as it worked its way through the four levels of flight readiness review—typically, the package first presented to level IV FRR would be about a half-inch thick, but this would be shrunk to 10–15 pages by the time it reached level I FRR (Vaughan 1996). For the information that did get through, the ability of level II and I administrators to interpret the information was constrained by the fact that though they were also trained as engineers, they now had broad administrative responsibilities, which were more administrative than technical. Although information had been condensed, time to read the packages was limited, and some level II and I administrators relied totally on oral presentations and the signals they received during the FRR sessions themselves. The third group affected by structural secrecy were the safety regulators. NASA had both internal and external safety units. Internal units were dependent on NASA for staff, information, and resources, and this interdependence undermined their ability to monitor and surface safety problems. Of the two internal regulators, NASA cut 71 percent of the staffing of one unit between 1970 and 1986, and discontinued the other unit when the space shuttle became operational. The external advisory panel consisted of nine aerospace industry leaders who theoretically would have been able to assess safety issues with autonomy. Unfortunately the panel's breadth of responsibilities and lack of time meant that it could not be expected to uncover all potential problems.

In Vaughan's analysis, the three forces of production of culture, culture of production, and structural secrecy work together to explain the history of meaning and choice making that led to the decision to launch the Challenger. The production of culture, through repeated decision routines that normalized deviant information, developed and maintained the group's belief in redundancy—that the secondary O-ring will back up the primary. This belief in redundancy provided the frame of reference for processing information. The culture of production, expressed in the norms of the engineering profession and the culture of NASA organizations, legitimized the decision process as conforming to acceptable practices of engineers and managers who have to exercise interpretive flexibility, develop ad hoc rules, and follow bureaucratic procedures in dealing with complex, innovative, risky technical systems. Structural secrecy blocked information flow and attenuated signals about the O-ring problem, hiding and diluting the information so that the signals of potential danger lost their ability to overturn the dominant belief about redundancy. The three forces converged on the eve of the launch in a final denouement of the history and style of decision making that has characterized the space shuttle program: "It can truly be said that the Challenger launch decision was a rule-based decision. But the cultural understandings, rules, procedures, and norms that always had worked in the past did not work this time. It was not amorally calculating managers violating rules that were responsible for the tragedy. It was conformity" (Vaughan 1996, 386).

Relating to the modes of organizational information use presented in this book, the analysis of the Challenger accident reveals failures and lapses in sense making, knowledge creating, decision making, and information management. In sense making, the NASA and Thiokol engineers and managers maintained a self-image and a dominant ideology that allowed them to continue to select and retain schemas and rules that enacted interpretations which were no longer valid. With twenty-five successful shuttle launches behind them, the belief that the secondary O-rings provided redundancy seemed sufficiently vindicated. In terms of knowledge, the engineers never really understood all of the contingencies that could lead to a failure of the O-rings, so that on the eve of the launch, there were no data to quantify the concerns about ring behavior in cold temperatures. Roger Boisjoly, a staff engineer knowledgable about the O-rings, had warned that the quality of the damage on the January 1985 launch was worse because "the putty looked different than in other instances of blow-by" (Vaughan 1996, 355). NASA management saw this as an intuitive argument that was not substantively supported. Thiokol engineers acknowledged that their argument was subjective and based on engineering feel. Because of the inability to convert and share this tacit knowledge, the warning signals remained weak and confused, and could not raise doubt about the assumption of O-ring redundancy. In decision making, the process was preoccupied with rules, norms, and conformity that allowed engineers and managers to incrementally normalize warning signals as acceptable risks. Through a repetitive pattern of decision making and weaving of self-crafted rules, engineers and managers reconstructed their decision premises of what constituted acceptable risks. Information flow was blocked and information was concealed as an outcome of the organization's structural attributes, including the bureaucratic decision and review procedures that stressed conformity and compromise, and the functional specialization that limited information flow to top administrators. We will return to some of these issues in this chapter and the next.

I. BOUNDED RATIONALITY

Imagine a decision situation in which an individual has to select a course of action. In order to make a completely rational choice, the decision maker would have to identify all available alternatives, predict what consequences would be produced by each alternative, and evaluate these consequences according to goals and preferences. The information requirements of a purely rational mode of decision making are daunting. First, information is needed about the present state—what alternatives are currently available or should be considered. Second, information is needed about the future—what are the consequences of acting on each of the various alternatives. Third, information is needed about how to move from the present to the future—what are the values and preferences that should be used to choose between the alternatives that will, according to the set criteria, best achieve the desired results. The information-seeking and information-processing demands implied here are unrealistic. In most situations we do not have complete information about all feasible alternatives, or we cannot afford the time and cost of attaining this complete knowledge. Whichever the alternative, acting on it always creates both intended and unintended consequences, and the unanticipated consequences may well turn out to be highly significant. We rarely have a well-defined or completely consistent set of preferences or criteria by which we can, for example, rank the available alternatives in order to choose the most desirable one. Herbert Simon suggests instead that humans are only "boundedly rational" so that while they attempt to be rational, their rational behavior is limited by their cognitive capabilities and by constraints that are part of the organization. The rationality of the organizational decision maker is bounded in at least three ways:

1. Rationality requires a complete knowledge and anticipation of the consequences that will follow on each choice. In fact, knowledge of consequences is always fragmentary.

2. Since these consequences lie in the future, imagination must supply the lack of experienced feeling in attaching value to them. But values can only be imperfectly anticipated.

3. Rationality requires a choice among all possible alternative behaviors. In actual behavior, only a very few of all these possible alternatives ever come to mind.

(Simon 1976, 81)

In order to cope with their bounded rationality and the complexity of the problems they have to deal with, people in organizations adopt a number of reductionist strategies, which allow them to "simplify" their representation of the problem situation by selectively including the most salient features rather than attempting to model the objective reality in all its complexity (March and Simon 1993,1958). In general terms, people in organizations "satisfice" rather than maximize, that is, they choose an alternative that exceeds some criteria rather than the best alternative; and they follow "action programs" or routines that simplify the decision-making process by reducing the need for search, problem solving, or choice:

1. Optimizing is replaced by satisfying—the requirement that satisfactory levels of the criterion variables be attained.
2. Alternatives of action and consequences of action are discovered sequentially through search processes.
3. Repertories of action programs are developed by organizations and individuals, and these serve as the alternatives of choice in recurrent situations.
4. Each specific action program deals with a restricted range of situations and a restricted range of consequences.
5. Each action program is capable of being executed in semi-independence of the others—they are only loosely coupled together.

(March and Simon 1993,1958, 191)

Satisficing

As a result of bounded rationality, decision making is driven by the search for alternatives that are good enough rather than the best possible: "Most human decision-making, whether individual or organizational, is concerned with the discovery and selection of satisfactory alternatives; only in exceptional cases is it concerned with the discovery and selection of optimal alternatives" (March and Simon 1993,1958, 162). An alternative is considered optimal if it is superior to all other alternatives when a single, consistent set of criteria is used to compare all the available alternatives. An alternative is considered satisfactory if it meets or exceeds a set of criteria that defines "minimally satisfactory alternatives." Such a limited search for good enough alternatives Simon and March called "satisficing." The difference between optimizing and satisficing is likened to "the difference between searching a haystack to find the sharpest needle in it and searching the haystack to find a needle sharp enough to sew with" (p. 162). For example, the owner of a retail store could set prices optimally by determining how demand would vary with price across all her potential customers, and then choosing the price that maximizes sales, or she could satisfice by applying a simple markup over cost that would provide an acceptable level of profit. In the Challenger case, technical decision making follows the norms of satisficing, as engineers and managers constantly struggle to respond to the criteria of cost, schedule, and safety, which act simultaneously as goals and as constraints. In the aerospace industry, the task of risk management is defined as the ability to make the technical changes necessary to enhance the safety and performance of flight systems while controlling costs and schedule. According to Vaughan (1996, 226), "satisficing where cost, schedule, and safety were concerned was institutionalized in the criteria for NASA's own change approval process" where NASA compares the performance improvement of the change with its impacts on cost, schedule, and safety.

Neither satisficing nor maximizing is likely to be observed in pure form. Depending on the situation and the nature of the goals, decision makers sometimes attempt to maximize on some dimensions of the problem while satisficing on others (March 1994). When universities consider granting tenures to professors, for instance, both satisficing rules (such as "does this person meet the university's standards for satisfactory performance?") and maximizing rules ("is this person likely to be the best possible person to be found?") may be invoked at the same time. Satisficing evaluates the positions of alternatives relative to a baseline or target, while maximizing compares the positions of alternatives relative to each other. Satisficing behaviors "simplify a complex world. Instead of having to worry about an infinite number of gradations in the environment, individuals simplify the world into two parts—good enough and not good enough" (March 1994, 21).

Because only limited amounts of time, information resources, and, above all, intellectual energy are available to identify alternatives, predict their consequences, and clarify preferences, attention becomes the scarce resource that affects participation in a decision as well as the quantity and quality of information that is brought to bear on a decision:

> The information-processing systems of our contemporary world swim in an exceedingly rich soup of information, of symbols. In a world of this kind, the scarce resource is not information; it is processing capacity to attend to information. Attention is the chief bottleneck in organizational activity, and the bottleneck becomes narrower and narrower as we move to the tops of organizations . . . (Simon 1976, 294)

Thus because the decision maker's capacity to attend is limited, he may overlook some significant news, fail to be present at a decision meeting, or respond hurriedly to set deadlines and the actions of others. The capacity to attend also depends on the language or vocabulary that the organization has developed for recording, retrieving, and transferring information. An organization that emphasizes presenting a high level of service to its customers may develop a rich vocabulary for differentiating many aspects of service quality, thereby making it easier for members to attend to and communicate about customer service dimensions that are relevant for decision making. Conversely, where service is not stressed, subtle distinctions about service are uncoded and may not be attended to at all in choice making.

Satisficing is more than a rule about how decisions take place in organizations, it is also a rule about how organizations search for information. The criterion of satisficing specifies that search is often induced by failure, so that search is started when performance falls below an acceptable target level, and stops or decreases when performance achieves its target. March (1994) identifies three principal features of satisficing as a theory of search. First, search is thermostatic. Search is turned on and off when performance falls below and rises above a desired level. Second, targets are considered sequentially: "A satisficing search process is serial rather than parallel; things are considered one at a time—one target, one alternative, one problem" (March 1994, 28). Furthermore, alternatives in the neighborhood of the problem symptom are searched first (a solution to a problem in the production department is searched first in the production department). Third, search is active in the face of adversity. When faced with a set of poor alternatives, which all fail to meet the target, the satisficing decision maker will try to find better ones by changing the problem constraints, whereas the maximizing decision maker will select the best of the poor lot.

Since satisficing is essentially a "first-past-the-post" strategy, the criteria or standards that define minimal acceptability are not static but are adjusted over time, so that who gets to control the standards becomes an important question: "These standards go up and down with positive and negative experience. As solutions are easier to find, the standards are raised; as they are harder to find, the standards fall. *The organization can control these standards, and it defines the situation;* only to a limited extent are they up to individuals" (Perrow 1986, 122).

Lindblom (1959) describes a variation of satisficing that he observed in public policy decision making. When formulating policy on a complex issue (such as controlling inflation), an administrator does not attempt to go to the root of the matter to consider the myriad economic, social, and political variables that affect and are affected by inflation. The information required would have been enormous, and even if the information were available, the administrator would have to learn and apply theoretical principles to evaluate the alternatives and outcomes. Instead, the administrator contents herself with a relatively simple goal (such as maintaining a period of stable prices), compares a limited range of already familiar alternatives, and avoids having to go back to theory. Lindblom suggests that the prevalent mode of decision making by administrators is a strategy of ***disjointed incrementalism,*** which is to proceed by making *successive limited comparisons.* Changes are made in small increments by processes that seem disconnected. These small changes appear to be made to move away from current ills rather than to move toward defined goals. Selection of goals and analysis of needed action are closely intertwined, so that means and ends adjust to each other, and objectives are reconciled with policies as much as policies to objectives. Choice is simplified by considering changes at the margin, and evaluating few alternatives and a few outcomes of each alternative. A succession of incremental changes reduces the risks of serious mistakes. Policies are not made once and for all, but are made and remade endlessly. The result is that decision making begins to look like a 'science of muddling through' (Lindblom 1959).

Cognitive Simplifications

Rationality requires looking ahead into the future, since the consequences of actions are all necessarily in the future, and in this sense all rationality is based on predictions of one kind or another (Stinchcombe 1990). Rational decisions are therefore based on beliefs and expectations about the likelihood of uncertain events or outcomes that lie in the future. In dealing with uncertainty, people rely on a limited number of heuristic principles to reduce the complex task into simpler judgmental operations (Tversky and Kahneman 1974; Hogarth and Makridakis 1981; Kahneman et al. 1982; Schwenk 1984; Hogarth 1987; Sutherland 1992; Piatelli-Palmarini 1994). These heuristics are two-edged, for while they reduce mental effort in decision making, their use can also lead to systemic biases or errors in judgment. Tversky and Kahneman (1974) identify three sets of heuristics that are used to assess likelihoods and predict values: representativeness, availability, and anchoring and adjustment.

People use heuristics of *representativeness* when they are assessing the likelihood that an event or object belongs to a certain category. They do so by judging the similarity of the event or object to stereotypes that they believe to be representative of category members. Managers, for example, may quickly categorize a price-lowering action by a competitor as an attempt to gain market share; supervisors may select someone based on the perception of certain traits that they believe to typify a desirable worker. Representativeness heuristics may capture learning from experience, but can lead to systemic errors when they do not take into account the size of the sample, prior or base probabilities of the various categories in the population, the distinction between events that are independent or related, the tendency for extreme events to regress to a mean, and so on. Schwenk (1984) observed that strategic decision makers are insensitive to sample size when making predictions, especially since they are often unable to collect data on a large number of past strategies and must generalize from a small base of experience. They tend to view strategic decisions in terms of simple analogies, assuming that the analogy is representative of their decision situation, and glossing over important differences between the two. They also overestimate the extent to which the past is representative of the present, including the extent to which solutions used for problems in the past will continue to work for present problems. This appears to have been the case for some of the managers and engineers at NASA and Thiokol, who continued to believe that the secondary O-rings on the Challenger were still adequate backups in the event of primary O-ring failure, even when contradictory evidence was presented and when different launch conditions were being considered.

People use heuristics of *availability* when they are assessing the likelihood or plausibility of a particular development. They do so by recalling familiar, recent, and vivid instances. Consumers, for example, base their buying decisions on past satisfactory use rather than on results of objective evaluations; air travelers worry for their own safety after learning about recently publicized accidents. Availability heuristics can save time and effort in searching for relevant precedents, but can lead to biases when they are unduly limited to instances that are easy to recall or information that is easy to retrieve. Nisbett and Ross (1980) suggested that decision makers may give excessive weight to one or a few vividly described cases, basing their assessment of the likelihood of a future event on this readily retrieved example. Thus Schwenk (1984) noted that "a single vivid description of a new venture's failure in a particular industry may influence the decision about entering the industry more than volumes of statistical data indicating high success rates in the industry" (p. 121).

People use heuristics of *anchoring and adjustment* when they are trying to estimate the value of a quantity. They do so by starting from an initially presented value (the anchor) and adjusting it to arrive at a final estimate. The size and direction of the adjustment depends on the locus or magnitude of the initial value. Managers, for example, may estimate sales and budgets for the next period by simple extrapolations of values obtained in the previous period. Decision makers who are monitoring organizational strategies may accurately recognize important changes in the environment but fail to revise their strategies or performance targets sufficiently as justified by the new information. Anchoring heuristics may be useful in providing ballpark estimates, but can lead to errors when the adjustment is insufficient or when the adjustment fails to consider the interdependency of related events (as is the case when the overall probability of success of a sequence of steps can be greatly lower than the success probability of each individual step).

Hogarth (1987) summarizes the major consequences of limited human information-processing capacity as follows:

1. Perception of information is not comprehensive but *selective.*

2. Since people cannot simultaneously integrate a great deal of information, they process information in predominantly *sequential* manner.

3. Information processing is necessarily dependent upon the use of operations that *simplify judgmental tasks* and *reduce mental effort.*

4. People have *limited memory* capacity.

(Hogarth 1987, 208)

From our experience we may recall instances when decision makers selectively attend to striking cases; pay greater attention to more recently encountered incidents that are still fresh in their minds; or overlook or forget important information because of memory overload. While the heuristics we have discussed can systematically introduce error in judgment and choice, the boundaries separating the rational and the nonrational are often not at all clear-cut. Human information processing embraces a broad repertory of cognitive strategies, ranging from logical, reasoning methods to intuitive, heuristic-based modes, and which approach is activated depends on the requirements of the particular problem situation:

> The main lesson to be drawn from experimental research in this domain is that these strategies coexist in our mind, thus justifying, at least to a certain degree, both the sweeping claim that we are naturally rational and the opposite sweeping claim that we are naturally irrational. . . . Depending on the exact formulation of the task at hand, specific reasoning strategies are reproducibly elicited in our mind, and even slightly different formulations can sometimes produce a switch, shifting the delicate balance between coexisting intuitions and strategies, between spontaneous rationality and spontaneous irrationality. (Piatelli-Palmarini 1994, 5)

II. MODELS OF ORGANIZATIONAL DECISION MAKING

In the following sections we present and compare four important models of the organizational decision-making process: the rational model, the process model, the political model, and the anarchic model. The rational model, developed initially by Simon, March, and Cyert, conceptualizes decision making as goal directed and problem driven, and choice behavior as regulated by rules and routines so that the organization acts in a manner that is intendedly and procedurally rational. The process model, exemplified by the work of Mintzberg, Raisinghani, and Théorêt (1976), elucidates the phases and cycles that give structure to apparently complex and dynamic decision-making activities. The political model, developed by Allison (1971), sees politics as the mechanism of decision choice when different players occupy different stands and exercise different amounts of influence, so that decisions are less the result of rational choice than the pulling and hauling that is politics. The anarchic model is discussed with reference to the garbage can model proposed by Cohen, March, and Olsen (1972), in which organizations are likened to garbage cans where problems and solutions are dumped by participants, and decisions are the outcomes of the meeting of independent streams of problems, solutions, participants, and choice situations. Whichever the decision mode, the organizational environment of decision making is defined by at least two properties: the structure and clarity of organizational goals that impinge on preferences and choices, and the uncertainty or amount of information about the methods and processes by which tasks are to be accomplished and goals are to be attained. Goals may be fuzzy or clear, and organizational groups may disagree about their relative importance. There is therefore *goal ambiguity or conflict* about *what* organizational goals to pursue. Uncertainty may arise because organizational tasks or problems are technically complex, and there is not enough detailed information about cause–effect relationships or appropriate approaches to be adopted. There is therefore *technical uncertainty* about *how* goals and objectives are to be achieved. In Fig. 5–1 we locate the four models of organizational decision making along the two dimensions of goal ambiguity/conflict and technical uncertainty. On the horizontal axis, when goal ambiguity/conflict is low, decision making tends to take the form of problem solving that is guided by a clear set of goals and preferences. Conversely, when goal ambiguity/conflict is high, chance and contest become important contin-

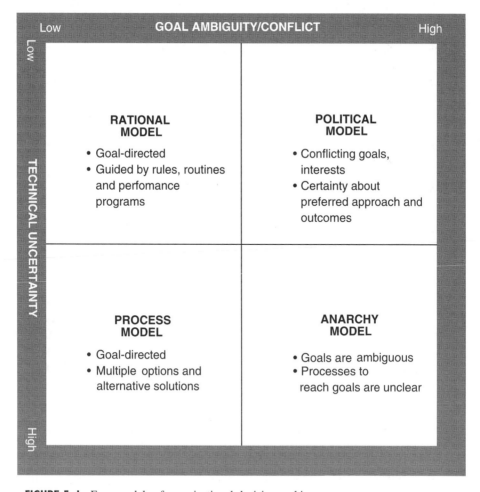

FIGURE 5–1. Four models of organizational decision making

gencies, with factors such as timing, influence, and effort influencing the choice of actions and decisions. On the vertical axis, when technical uncertainty is low, decision making tends to be relatively well structured, guided by rules and routines, and engaging well-defined participants and interests. Conversely, when technical uncertainty is high, decision making tends to be a dynamic process marked by frequent changes and unexpected interruptions. For now, the figure serves to preview the orientations and contingencies that characterize each decision mode, and the reasons for their placement should become clearer as we discuss each model in turn.

III. RATIONAL MODEL

The implications of the individual's bounded rationality for organizational decision making are further developed in March and Simon (1993,1958) and Cyert and March (1992,1963). The overarching theme is that the basic features of organization structure and function are derived from the characteristics of human problem-solving processes and rational human choice. As we noted earlier, because of the limits of the human mind and the complexity of the problems to be dealt with, decision making in organizations requires "simplifications." An important simplification is the use of action or ***performance programs:***

> . . . an environmental stimulus may evoke immediately from the organization a highly complex and organized set of responses. Such a set of responses we call a *performance program,* or simply, a *program.* For example, the sounding of the alarm gong in a fire station initiates such a program. So does the appearance of a relief applicant at a social worker's desk. So does the appearance of an automobile chassis in front of the work station of a worker on the assembly line . . . Most behavior, and particularly most behavior in organizations, is governed by performance programs. (March and Simon 1993,1958, 162–63)

Programs may specify one or more of the following: work activities, product specifications, and pacing rules. March and Simon hypothesize that programs will contain activity specifications in preference to product specifications when the activities but not the product quality and quantity are readily observed and supervised, and when the relations between activities and output are highly technical or specialized. Conversely, a program will contain more product specifications when the outputs but not the activity pattern are easy to observe, and when the activity output relations are commonsense or known through standard training. Finally, pacing rules are specified when other members need to synchronize or coordinate their activities with those of a particular member or group.

Performance programs are not intended to be completely rigid, but do provide scope for discretion, especially in terms of variation in the form of the performance program and the source from which it is acquired. The performance of a program may depend on the attributes of the environmental stimulus (such as the location of an alarm signal), and on supporting data from other sources (such as what resources are on hand). March and Simon (1993,1958) state that the amount and type of discretion available to an individual is a function of the performance program and the extent to which the program specifies activities and outcomes. For example, the choice of a course of action after a search depends on what has been found during the search, and the subsequent application of a selected strategy to specific circumstances requires discretion. The program may also reside in the individual's memory as a result of apprenticeship or experiential learning, so that its recall and use are again discretionary.

In a similar vein, Cyert and March (1992,1963) describe how organizations rely heavily on ***standard operating procedures*** for making decisions. For them, standard operating procedures are the memory of the organization, which provide stability for the organization and direction for the execution of recurring activities and decisions. Decision rules and procedures are based on three general principles. First, avoid uncertainty. The organization minimizes the need for predicting an uncertain future by adopting methods such as using short-term feedback to trigger action, and enforcing standardized decision rules. Second, maintain the rules. The organization tends to retain a set of decision procedures for as long as it can, to shun the complex task of process redesign. Third, use simple rules. Simple rules are often elaborated by individuals using their judgment to take into account the conditons and requirements of specific cases or problems.

Cyert and March (1992,1963) distinguish four major types of procedures: task performance rules, continuing records and reports, information-handling rules, and plans and planning rules. *Task performance procedures* specify methods for accomplishing the tasks assigned to a member or a group. Task performance rules are invoked at many levels of the organization, and are just as likely to regulate the decision making of engineers and managers as the choice behavior of operators and counter staff. Cyert and March observed that in most organizations strategic decisions about pricing, output, inventory, and sales are fixed by simple operating rules, so that complex decisions involving great uncertainty are reduced to simple problems with minimum uncertainty. Task performance rules are important because they encode past organizational learning, and because they help to ensure that the activity of each subunit is consistent and coordinated with the work of the other subunits. *Records and reports* are maintained by the organization for the purposes of control and prediction. Records such as financial statements or cost reports have a control effect because organizational members assume that the records are being kept for a purpose and that someone will review or check the records at some stage. Records are also used as a database of past events, performance, and results to predict the future, making the simplifying assumption that cause–effect relations interpreted for the past will also hold for the future. Records also reflect the organization's model of the world, so much so that what records are maintained influence what aspects of the environment the organization notices, and what alternatives will be considered by the organization. *Information-handling rules* define the organization's communication system "in order to provide reasonable certainty that relevant information will be available at the proper place at the proper time. . ." (Cyert and March 1992,1963, 123). Information-routing rules specify who will communicate to whom about what, and often define "proper" channels of information flow that reflect the administrative hierarchy and technical specialization of the organization. Information-filtering rules specify what information is to be generated and transmitted, which are based again on the specialization and point of view of the particular member or group, and can influence the formation of organizational expectations significantly. *Plans and planning rules* serve the general purpose of deriving an intended allocation of resources among the alternative activities of the organization, typically presented in the form of budgets or expenditure statements. Cyert and March argue that by being simultaneously a goal, schedule, theory, and precedent, a plan, like other standard operating procedures, helps to reduce the uncertainty of dealing with a complex world.

Cyert and March (1992,1963) view the organization as an adaptively rational system that is constrained by environmental uncertainty, problems of multiple goals and interests, and limitations in its information-processing capabilities. An organization is not monolithic, but acts like a continually shifting multiple-goal coalition. Managers, workers, shareholders, unions, suppliers, customers, bankers, tax collectors, and so on all have a stake in the firm, but their goals or preferences about what should be done differ. Organizational goals are set by a negotiation process that occurs among members of the *dominant coalition.* An organization consists of various groups, each seeking to further its own interests or goals, without any single group being able to completely determine what goals the organization should pursue. Group members thus look for allies in those groups whose interests are similar, and they negotiate with those groups whose interests are divergent but whose participation is essential. Each negotiated agreement between groups places constraints on what the organization can regard as an acceptable course of action: the goals themselves become complex preference statements which summarize the multiple conditions that any acceptable choice must meet. It is not surprising then that managers spend much of their time managing the coalition, as decisions cannot be made without taking into consideration all the diverse and often conflicting interests.

The decision-making model developed by Cyert and March is composed of four concepts: (1) quasi-resolution of conflict, (2) uncertainty avoidance, (3) problemistic search, and (4) organizational learning.

The goals of an organization act as independent constraints imposed by the members of the organizational coalition. The organization becomes a social concourse of intersecting interests in which a number of strategies are exercised to resolve conflict. These methods may not actually achieve consensus, but they enable the organization to continue to operate despite unresolved divergencies. The devices for the ***quasi-resolution of conflict*** are: local rationality (whereby a subunit solves problems rationally within its own specialized domain); acceptable level decision rules (whereby rules that are acceptable to all interests are used, rather than rules that are optimal overall); and sequential attention to goals (whereby the organization attends first to one goal, then to another, in sequence).

Organizations act to ***avoid uncertainty*** by focusing on the short term and attempting to control the environment. They use decision rules that emphasize short-run reaction to short-run feedback rather than trying to anticipate long-run uncertain events. They arrange for a negotiated environment through the imposition of plans, standard procedures, industry tradition, and contracts on the environment (Cyert and March 1992,1963, 167). For example, environmental uncertainty may be negotiated or controlled by the adoption of industry wide practices established through trade associations, standards organizations, informal agreements, and so on. Prices, markups, costing procedures, and other variables may then be decided according to agreed-upon norms.

Problemistic search is the means by which organizations determine what choices are thought to be available. Search is "motivated" in the sense that the occurrence of a problem initiates the search for ways to solve it, and that once a solution is found, the search stops. Search is "simple minded" in the sense that when a problem occurs, the search for a solution is concentrated in the neighborhood of the problem symptom and in the neighborhood of the current alternative. Search is "biased" in that it is influenced by the special training or experience of the organizational groups, the differences in the goals and aspirations of participants, and the communication biases that reflect unresolved conflict within the organization (Cyert and March 1992,1963).

Finally, ***organizational learning*** takes place in the decision-making process through the adaptation of goals, attention rules, and search rules. Goals are adapted by assessing past performance and experience, and evaluating these results with those of other comparable organizations. Attention rules are adapted as the organization learns to pay greater notice to some aspects of the environment, and so to attend more closely to some criteria and to ignore some other criteria. Search rules are adapted when the organization fails to find a viable solution using a certain search strategy or, conversely, when it discovers an attractive alternative by searching a particular way.

Figure 5–2 indicates how the four concepts are linked together in a decision-making model. Beginning at the left, the organization observes feedback from the environment. If the uncertainty is high, the organization negotiates with the environment to reduce uncertainty (uncertainty avoidance). Organizational members attend to one goal at a time, and evaluate performance and goal attainment using acceptable decision rules (quasi-resolution of conflict). If a goal is not being achieved, members activate a problem-driven search. The search first proceeds locally, and when this is unsuccessful, the search is

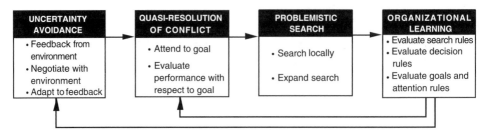

UNCERTAINTY AVOIDANCE	QUASI-RESOLUTION OF CONFLICT	PROBLEMISTIC SEARCH	ORGANIZATIONAL LEARNING
• Feedback from environment • Negotiate with environment • Adapt to feedback	• Attend to goal • Evaluate performance with respect to goal	• Search locally • Expand search	• Evaluate search rules • Evaluate decision rules • Evaluate goals and attention rules

FIGURE 5–2. Rational model of organizational decision making (adapted from Cyert and March 1992, 1993,175)

expanded to include more "remote" sources and alternatives (problemistic search). After the search is completed, the organization evaluates its search rules and decision rules (organizational learning). If the goal is seen as being achieved, the organization adapts to the environmental feedback with standard decision rules (again, uncertainty avoidance), and then evaluates its goals and attention rules (organizational learning). (This sequence is presented in Cyert and March 1992,1963, 175.)

IV. PROCESS MODEL

Process models of organizational decision making focus on the stages, activities, and dynamics of choice behaviors. One of the best known decision process models is that developed by Mintzberg, et al. (1976) based on their analysis of twenty-five strategic decision processes in various commercial and government organizations. The decisions ranged from an airline choosing new aircraft to a radio station firing a star announcer to a hospital introducing a new form of treatment. Although all the decisions were characterized by high levels of ambiguity, novelty, and movement, Mintzberg and associates were able to discern the phases and routines that suggest an underlying structure of the decision-making processes. Reflecting the complexity and open-endedness of strategic decisions, the model has a large number of elements: three central decision phases, three decision support routines, and six sets of dynamic factors.

The three central decision phases are identification, development, and selection (Fig. 5–3). The *identification phase* recognizes the need for decision and develops an understanding of the decision issues. Identification consists of decision recognition routines and diagnosis routines. In the decision recognition routine, problems, opportunities, and crises are recognized and initiate decisional activity. The need for a decision is defined as an information need: "a difference between information on some actual situation and some expected standard" (Mintzberg, et al. 1976, 253). These standards are based on past experience, projected trends, standards used in comparable organizations, people's expectations, and theoretical models. Mintzberg and associates suggest

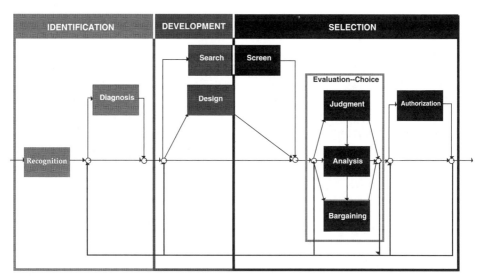

FIGURE 5–3. Process model of strategic decision making (Reprinted from "The Structure of "Unstructured" Design Processes" by Mintzberg, Raisinghani, and Théorêt published in *Administrative Science Quarterly,* vol. 21, no. 2 by permission of *Administrative Science Quarterly.*)

that stimuli accumulate in the minds of decision makers until they reach a threshold for action or decision. The amplitude of each stimulus depends on the individual's assessment of the source, interest level, perceived payoff, workload, and so on. In the diagnosis routine, management seeks to comprehend the stimuli initiating decision as well as the cause–effect relations relevant for the decision situation. It is primarily an information-seeking activity, involving "the tapping of existing information channels and the opening of new ones to clarify and define the issues" (Mintzberg et al. 1976, 254). The *development phase* leads to the development of one or more solutions to a problem or crisis, or to the elaboration of an opportunity. Development consists of search routines and design routines. Four types of search routines are identified: memory search by scanning the organization's existing memory; passive search by waiting for unsolicited alternatives; trap search by activating search generators (such as letting suppliers know what the firm is planning to buy); and active search by directly seeking information about alternatives. As suggested by Cyert and March (1992,1963), search appears to progress from the local to the remote, proceeding from memory and passive search to the less accessible sources of trap search and active search (Mintzberg et al. 1976). Design routines involve either developing a custom-made solution or modifying an existing ready-made alternative. Designing a custom-made solution tends to be a complex and iterative process by which vague starting ideas gradually converge on a specific solution. Whereas organizations attempting a custom-made solution pursue only one fully developed alternative, those choosing ready-made solutions typically select from multiple alternatives. The *selection phase* evaluates the alternatives and chooses a solution for commitment to action. Selection consists of screen routines, evaluation–choice routines, and authorization routines. Screen routines eliminate what is infeasible, thereby reducing the number of alternatives to be considered. Evaluation–choice routines use judgment, bargaining, or analysis to arrive at a choice. In judgment, an individual makes the choice in her own mind. In bargaining, choice is made by a group of decision makers with conflicting goals and interests, with each participant exercising judgment. In analysis, alternatives and their consequences are evaluated against a set of criteria so as to determine the best-performing option, and the final choice is made by judgment or bargaining. Authorization routines define a path through the organizational hierarchy for a decision to obtain internal and external approval, and to secure resources for implementation.

The central decision phases of identification, development, and selection are shown in Fig. 5–3. Theoretically, the simplest decision could just involve two routines: recognition and then evaluation–choice, as shown on the horizontal axis. In practice, most decisions require the development phase, during which ready-made solutions (modified) are searched or custom-made solutions are designed. Development typically takes up the bulk of the time and resources of the decision process, and tends to be iterative, going through multiple search and design cycles. While selection may be the final phase, it is not uncommon for new cycles back to the development or identification phase to be restarted from the evaluation-choice or authorization routines when, for example, a better alternative is desired or a redefinition of the decision situation is necessary.

The entire decision process is facilitated by three ***decision support routines:*** decision control routines, decision communication routines, and political routines (Mintzberg et al. 1976). *Decision control routines* guide the decision process and consist of decision planning, which determines the boundaries of the decision space, the selection of participants, scheduling constraints, resource commitments, and so on; and switching, which directs the decision maker's attention to the next step or the appropriate routine to activate. *Decision communication routines* gather as well as distribute information as part of the decision process. They consist of exploration, or the general scanning for information and passive review of what becomes available; investigating, or the focused search and research for information on a specific issue; and disseminating, or the distribution of information about the progress of the decision process to interested parties. *Political routines* are important in strategic decision processes, and can take the form of bargaining, persuasion, or co-optation. Bargaining is used among stakeholders who have some control over the choices being made to negotiate arrangements of mutual advantage. Persuasion is used to move someone over to a different position by reasoning, influence, or, as Mintzberg et al. suggest, by disseminating information early in the development and selection phases. Co-optation is used to preempt later resistance by inviting potential objectors to participate early in the decision process, such as during the development phase.

The most prominent feature of strategic decision processes is their dynamic, open-ended character. A number of dynamic factors continuously change the tempo and direction of the decision process: "They delay it, stop it, restart it. They cause it to speed up, to branch to a new phase, to cycle within one or between two phases, and to recycle back to an earlier point in the process . . . the process is dynamic, operating in an open system where it is subjected to interferences, feedback loops, dead ends, and other factors" (Mintzberg et al. 1976, 263). Six sets of *dynamic factors* influence the decision process—interrupts, scheduling delays, feedback delays, timing delays and speedups, comprehension cycles, and failure cycles. Interrupts are due to environmental forces, and may be caused by internal disagreement, external forces that block the decision process, or the appearance of new options late in the process. Scheduling delays are deliberately introduced by managers to separate and slow down the activities of the decision process so that they may have the time to attend to a variety of other tasks. Feedback delays arise when decision makers await the results of or feedback on actions previously taken. Timing delays and speedups are used by managers to time decisions so that they can tie in with or take advantage of some other circumstance or event. Comprehension cycles are sometimes needed to grapple with complex issues—managers cycle between routines in order to better understand a problem, assess the available alternatives, and reconcile multiple goals and preferences. Failure cycles happen when an acceptable solution could not be found, in which case the decision maker may cycle back to the development phase, relax the evaluation criteria, or delay the decision.

Overall, the value of the process model is in defining the phases and activities that lend structure to the apparent chaos that characterizes strategic decision processes. By clarifying the activities, routines, and dynamic factors that determine the speed and trajectory of the decision process, the process model provides a framework by which organizations can better manage the dynamic, open-ended flow of decision activities, and can anticipate and take advantage of the interruptions, the blockages, and the introduction of new options that are inherent features of strategic choice making.

V. POLITICAL MODEL

In analyzing decision making during the Cuban missile crisis of 1962, Allison (1971) first applied the rational actor model and the organizational process model but concluded that both models gave a limited explanation of the decision process that took place. What is needed is a political model that explicitly addresses how actions and decisions are also the results of the bargaining among players pursuing their own interests and exercising their available levers of influence. In Allison's political model, the metaphor of decision making is game playing, in which players with positions, stands, and influence, make their moves according to rules and their bargaining strengths. Actions and decisions may then be analyzed by answering a sequence of four questions:

1. Who are the players?
2. What are the players' stands?
3. What are the players' relative influence?
4. How are the players' stands, influence, and moves combined to yield decisions and actions?

Who are the players? They are the individuals whose interests and actions have an impact on the organizational decision-making process. Individuals become players by occupying positions that provide them with the authority and access to channels that can produce significant action. Players occupy positions that give access to action channels, but positions also define what the players are allowed to do and what they are obliged to do. Positions can confer advantages as well as handicaps, and positions can also impose obligations for the performance of certain tasks.

What are the players' stands? Each player's stand is determined by her perceptions of an issue; her goals, interests, and stakes; and her reactions to deadlines and events. Perceptions of what an issue is about are unavoidably parochial, colored by the position from which that question is considered (Allison 1971). What the players perceive as desirable outcomes is influenced by personal, departmental, organizational, and national goals and interests. Organizational members may come to believe that the health of their own group is vital to the interests of the organization, and the health of the group depends on maintaining influence and securing the necessary resources and capabilities. The overlapping of organizational, group, and personal interests together constitutes the individual's stakes for which the decision "game" is played, and it is these stakes that define the individual's stand on the issue (Allison 1971). Deadlines and events such as budgets or major announcements often bring issues to a head and require busy players to take stands. Players see different faces of an issue, depending not only on their goals and interests, but also on stituational elements such as deadlines and the channels in which an issue is raised.

What are the players' relative influence? This is a question of power, which Allison believes is the consequence of the individual's bargaining advantages, her skill and will in using bargaining advantages, and other players' perception of the first two elements (Allison 1971). He identifies several sources of bargaining advantages, including:

---

formal authority and responsibility (stemming from positions); actual control over resources necessary to carry out action; expertise and control over information that enables one to define the problem, identify option, and estimate feasibilities; control over information that enables chiefs to determine whether and in what form decisions are being implemented; the ability to affect other players' objectives in other games, including domestic political games; personal persuasiveness with other players (drawn from personal relations, charisma); and access to and persuasiveness with players who have bargaining advantages drawn from the above (based on interpersonal relations, etc.). (Allison 1971, 169)

How are the players' stands, influence, and moves combined to yield decisions and actions? In order to express their stands and assert influence, players have to be in positions that are connected to action channels, which are the formal, routinized means of taking action on a specific kind of issue. Issues are typically identified and framed within an established action channel, and action channels then structure the decision game by determining which players can play, their points of entrance, and their relative advantages and disadvantages for that game (Allison 1971). Rules define how the game is played in three ways. They establish positions, the power of each position, and the action channels. They limit decisions and actions, disallowing some forms of behaviors. They legitimize certain moves such as bargaining, persuading, or forming coalitions, while disapproving other moves. In the political model, actions and decisions are produced as political resultants—political because decisions and actions emerge from the bargaining by individual members along regularized action channels; and resultants because decisions and actions are outcomes of the compromise, conflict, and confusion of the players with diverse interests and unequal influence (Allison 1971).

On October 16, 1962, President John F. Kennedy was informed that the Soviet Union had installed offensive missiles in Cuba. During the ensuing thirteen days of the Cuban missile crisis, the major players included the U.S. president (John F Kennedy), the secretary of state (Dean Rusk), the secretary of defense (Robert McNamara), the secretary of treasury (Douglas Dillon), the special assistant for national security affairs (McGeorge Bundy), the presidential counsel (Theodore Sorensen), the attorney general (Robert Kennedy), the Joint Chiefs of Staff, and the chief of the CIA (John McCone). Each player saw a different face of the issue posed by the Soviet deployment of missiles on Cuba. Kennedy was incensed, especially since the policy of his administration had been aimed at relaxing tension and building trust between the two countries. McNamara saw the specter of nuclear war and argued that the missiles did not affect the strategic balance of power. He maintained that "a missile is a missile" and that "it makes no great difference whether you are killed by a missile from the Soviet Union or Cuba" (Hilsman 1967, 195). Robert Kennedy was concerned that, should the United States decide to launch an aggressive attack on Cuba, his brother's name would be discredited in history, since a sudden attack would be like a "Pearl Harbor in reverse" (Sorensen 1963, 684). To the Joint Chiefs of Staff, the missile deployment provided the occasion for removing the Castro communist threat from the Western Hemisphere, and they advocated a massive air strike, leading to an invasion and the overthrow of Castro. Despite the diversity of stands and perceptions, by the second day of the crisis, the Executive Committee handling the crisis had converged on two military alternatives: the air strike or the blockade. President Kennedy wanted a forceful, decisive response to bolster his leadership and confidence in his leadership (particularly after the fiasco of the failed invasion of the Bay of Pigs a year before). Under attack from other members of the Executive Committee, McNamara came to concede that the missile deployment did affect the balance of power. In the end, the nonmilitary option was abandoned more because of the intragovernmental balance of power than because of logical argument (Allison 1971). At first, President Kennedy favored a surgical air strike to destroy the missile bases alone, but this alternative was blocked by several factors. McNamara remained firmly against the air strike, while Robert Kennedy continued to press his Pearl Harbor analogy. Together with Sorensen, the three men, comprising the President's most trusted advisers, were united in a "triple alliance" coalition against the air strike. The players who supported the air strike, the Chiefs of Staff, chief of CIA, secretary of state, and others, were not the people the President considered his natural allies. McNamara introduced the information that a surgical air strike was militarily impractical in the view of the Joint Chiefs of Staff, that any military action would target all military installations in Cuba, leading to an invasion (Kennedy 1969, 34). The Air Force was apparently preparing for a massive air attack instead, for which, the Air Force admitted, "there could be no assurance that all the missiles would have been removed" (Sorensen 1963, 684). It was probably this that swayed the President over to the option of a blockade. The rest of the Executive Committee had to be persuaded, and Robert Kennedy and Sorensen were given the task. Robert Kennedy was particularly effective in encouraging uninhibited discussions, although the words of one participant may also be telling: "We all knew little brother was watching; and keeping a little list of where everyone stood" (Abel 1966, 58). On the evening of October 18, President Kennedy informed the Executive Committee that he was in favor of the naval blockade. Nevertheless, the advocates of the air strike continued to press their arguments over the next three days. The Joint Chiefs of Staff intercepted the President the next day to make their case again, and on Sunday the Air Force made a last plea for a massive air strike. But the President stayed his course—while a blockade may not remove the missiles, an air attack could not completely destroy the missiles either. On Monday, October 22, Kennedy announced to the world the U.S. decision to blockade Cuba to counteract the missile buildup in Cuba. Allison (1971) summarizes: "The decision to blockade thus emerged as a collage. Its pieces included the President's initial decision that something forceful had to be done; the resistance of McNamara, Robert Kennedy, and Sorensen to the air strike; the relative distance between the President and the air-strike advocates; and an inaccurate piece of information [McNamara's information that the surgical air strike was militarily impractical]" (pp. 206–7).

Since organizational goals and objectives are negotiated among groups of participants, it is unlikely that any allocation of resources will meet with general agreement. The divergence of goals and the contention for scarce resources make organizational decision making inherently a political process. Pfeffer and Salancik (1974) examined the effect of organizational power on decisions to allocate funds between twenty-nine departments at the University of Illinois at Urban-Champaign. In the absence of politics, a rational criterion that might guide resource allocation would be the instructional workload of each department. The study's data showed that in addition to workload, the proportional allocation of general funds was also significantly related to three measures of a department's power, namely, its membership on the university research board, its power ranking by department heads, and the number of persons on committees. The findings support the study's hypothesis that "organizational decision making, particularly with respect to decisions that allocate resources within the organization, are political in nature and that to understand resource allocation within organizations considerations of relative power of subunits, as well as of bureaucratic criteria, are necessary" (Pfeffer and Salancik 1974, 138). Pettigrew (1973) studied a large manufacturing organization and found a vivid example of how the ability to control information flow was used as a source of decision-making power. In the course of evaluating a large-scale capital investment decision, a senior manager who was positioned at the junction of the information flows between his subordinates, the vendors, and the company board, "was able to exert biases in favour of his own demands and at the same time feed the board negative information about the demands of his opponents" (Pettigrew 1973, 232). In public policy decisions it is not uncommon for preferred outcomes to be selected first, and then for information to be gathered and presented to justify the desired alternative and outcome. Meltsner's (1976) study of policy analysts made the differentiation between two categories of information sought by decision makers: information used to *make* decisions and information used to *support* decisions that have already been made (pp. 72–79).

VI. ANARCHIC MODEL

While the rational and process models conceptualize decision making as structured sequences of goal-directed problem solving, actual choice behaviors in organizations can sometimes appear random and disconnected, determined more by available solutions, interested participants, and existing decision situations. Cohen, March, and Olsen (1972, 2) draw the contrast:

> Although organizations can often be viewed conveniently as vehicles for solving well-defined problems or structures within which conflict is resolved through bargaining, they also provide sets of procedures through which participants arrive at an interpretation of what they are doing and what they have done while in the process of doing it. From this point of view, an organization is a collection of choices looking for problems, issues and feelings looking for decision situations in which they might be aired, solutions looking for issues to which they might be the answer, and decision makers looking for work.

Departing from orderly models of organizations, Cohen, March, and Olsen (1972) suggest an alternative view of organizations as ***organized anarchies,*** in which decision situations are characterized by problematic preferences, unclear technology, and fluid participation. First, the *preferences* used in decision making are ill-defined and inconsistent, comprising more a loose collection of ideas than a structured set, in which preferences may have to be discovered rather than being known beforehand. Second, the organization's *technology* is unclear in that its processes and procedures are not well understood by its members, and the means of achieving desired ends are not readily identifiable. Third, *participation* is fluid as people vary in the amount of time and effort that they give to different activities. These features are present to an extent in any organization at least part of the time, but Cohen and associates suggest that they are most evident in public, educational, and illegitimate organizations.

Within an organized anarchy, decisions are the outcomes of four relatively independent streams of problems, solutions, participants, and choice opportunities. *Problems* are points of dissatisfaction with current activities or performance that require attention. *Solutions* are products or ideas proposed by somebody (or group) for adoption—or, as Cohen and associates put it, they are answers actively looking for a question. Solutions exist independently of problems. Members may be attracted to an idea and push for it as a logical choice regardless of the problem. *Participants* come and go in a decision situation, depending on other demands on the participants' time. Participants also bring along with them their own preferences and perceptions about how to recognize or define a problem or solution. *Choice opportunities* are occasions when an organization is expected to make a decision, such as when awarding contracts, hiring staff, and allocating budgets. Choice opportunities provide a setting for the streams of problems, solutions, and participants to meet up. Cohen, March, and Olsen (1972) suggest that "one can view a choice opportunity as a garbage can into which various kinds of problems and solutions are dumped by participants as they are generated. The mix of garbage in a single can depends on the mix of cans available, on the labels attached to the alternative cans, on what garbage is currently being produced, and on the speed with which the garbage is collected and removed from the scene" (p. 2). In other words, a decision situation is like a ***garbage can*** into which various kinds of problems and solutions are dumped by participants as they are generated. A decision then happens when problems, solutions, participants, and choices coincide. When they do, solutions are attached to problems, and problems to choices by participants who happen to have the time and energy to do it. Which solutions are attached to which problems is a matter of chance and timing, depending on which participants with what goals happen to be on the scene, when the solutions and problems are entered, as well as "the mix of choices available at any one time, the mix of problems that have access to the organization, the mix of solutions looking for problems, and outside demands on the decision makers" (Cohen, March, and Olsen 1972, 16).

In an interesting study of decision making by editors in the college textbook publishing industry, Levitt and Nass (1989) concluded that the garbage can model fit well many aspects of the choice behavior. Interviews with editors of the ten best-selling introductory textbooks in physics and sociology found the editors consistently describing their work in gambling terms ("a lottery with bad odds," "a crapshoot") and that decision making was best described as "guesswork, intuition, and opinion." A sociology editor expresses this feeling of ambiguity and confusion: "Editors can become schizophrenic. You think a manuscript is good and it doesn't make money. Then you get a manuscript that you think is bad, and it makes money—but not always" (quoted in Levitt and Nass 1989, 192). In textbook publishing, decision situations are characterized by ill-defined preferences, unclear technology, and fluid participation. Preferences are ill defined because interpreting and differentiating between success and failure is highly equivocal and malleable. For example, one editor stated that a physics book which sold poorly was still considered a success because "it was important for the company to have an entry, any entry, in the physics market" (p. 193). The organizational technology is unclear because the connections between means and ends are unclear. There are no specifiable procedures or formula for producing a successful textbook, and editors often work in disciplines in which they were not trained. Participation is fluid because editors change departments and publishing houses relatively frequently. Levitt and Nass observed that "it is part of the occupational culture of editors that being fired (even more than once) is no indication of incompetence" (p. 195). Besides, the gestation period of textbooks is three to five years, with projects often being handed down to new successors. As predicted by the garbage can model, timing is an important element in deciding about projects. For example, introductory texts sell better in their second or later editions, but the decision to do this depends on whether the publisher is planning a new entry into that market segment. Serendipitous or random events often play a significant part in the acquisition of manuscripts, so that textbook editors recognize the importance of maintaining strong links with academics. Problems, solutions, and participants also track each other through time as, for example, when academics in the artificial intelligence field claim that they would teach introductory AI courses if there were a suitable text, whereas editors counter that such texts would be produced if there were courses (Levitt and Nass 1989). Despite the disorderly decision process, the textbooks produced as outcomes show significant levels of homogeneity in terms of the ordering of contents and topics. It was as though a lid was being placed on the garbage can. Levitt and Nass (1989) showed that textbook homogenization was the result of the forces of coercive, mimetic, and normative isomorphism (DiMaggio and Powell 1983). Thus established paradigms define the essential contents and topics that should be included (normative isomorphism); editors imitate successful textbooks produced by others (mimetic isomorphism); and the organizational structures of publishing houses often mirror that of the higher education institutes who are their customers (coercive isomorphism).

Cohen and associates suggest that in the garbage can model, decisions are made in three different ways: by resolution, by oversight, and by flight. *Resolution* is decision making to resolve problems by working on them over time. Resolution is the standard mode of choice behavior according to rational principles. *Oversight* occurs "if a choice is activated when problems are attached to other choices and if there is energy available to make the new choice quickly" (Cohen, March, and Olsen 1972, 8). In oversight, a choice is adopted quickly and incidentally to other choices being made. Decision by *flight* occurs when the problems leave the choice—the original problem has flown away as it were, leaving a choice that can now be made, but the decision resolves no problems. In organized anarchies, choice by flight and oversight may be more common than decision by resolution. For example, Cohen and associates observe that university decision making often does not resolve problems, but choices are made by flight or oversight. A university, unable to deal with an unproductive faculty member who is protected by tenure, may one day find that the problem has disappeared because the member has decided to relocate to another city (decision making by flight). Again, a department struggling to recast its role finds the decision made by oversight when it is merged with a larger department and its purpose is then defined as a component of the new parent's mission. Cohen, March, and Olsen (1972) stress this relative independence of problems and solutions:

A major feature of the garbage can process is the "partial decoupling" of problems and choices. Problems are worked upon in the context of some choice, but choices are made only when the shifting combinations of problems, solutions, and decision makers happen to make action possible. Quite commonly this is after problems have left a given choice arena or before they have discovered it (decisions by flight or oversight). (p. 16)

Although an anarchic model of decision making may seem unproductive, the garbage can process is not dysfunctional, for it can produce decisions under uncertain and conflictual conditions when goals are ambiguous, problems are poorly understood, and decision makers vary in the amount of time and energy they give to issues. Cohen and March (1986) present several case studies of decision making mainly at educational institutions in Denmark, Norway, and the United States, which illustrate many of the ideas presented in the garbage can model. These studies include the location decisions of a new Norwegian medical school, reorganization in the University of Oslo, ideology and management of a Danish free school, and structural changes at a medium-size American university. Other researchers have also analyzed government organizations using the garbage can model as framework, including Sproull, et al. (1978), Pinfield (1986), and Kingdon (1984,1995). Sproull, Weiner and Wolf (1978) found the organized anarchy model useful in analyzing the early years of the new National Institute of Education (NIE), created within the U.S.

Department of Health, Education and Welfare in 1972. The NIE's goals were ambiguous and expressed in general terms ("to seek to improve education"); the technology was unclear—education R&D was then regarded as one of the least mature of the social science research efforts; and participation was fluid, with many changing sets of external and internal actors. In the three decision processes that were analyzed (developing conceptual framework, designing a planning process, and creating an annual budget), a decision was made only after a large number of cycles had occurred, when closure was forced by external deadlines, with the final decision being the result of a top manager making somewhat arbitrary judgments: "As decision processes continued without closure, they became receptacles into which were dumped the latest important issues. Attempting to resolve the latest issue within the particular process inevitably changed the focus of the decision. Certain issues were never resolved . . . . They tended to appear and reappear in all the decision contexts" (Sproull, Weiner, and Wolf 1978, 200). Pinfield (1986) found the garbage can model helpful in understanding the decision-making process of the Canadian federal government as it worked toward a set of policies to manage its corps of senior governmental executives. The model elucidated the sequence of events, the effects of changes in participants, the evolution of problems, and the timing of these changes, but neglected how the content of issues can link decision streams, and how participation is channeled by hierarchy and specialization. Kingdon (1984,1995) analyzed policy making in the areas of health and transportation at the U.S. federal government level, and found the garbage can model useful in describing the process. Policy making may be conceived as "three process streams flowing through the system—streams of problems, policies, and politics. They are largely independent of one another, and each develops according to its own dynamics and rules. But at some critical junctures ["policy windows"] the three streams are joined, and the greatest policy changes grow out of that coupling of problems, policy proposals, and politics" (Kingdon 1995, 19).

VII. INFORMATION SEEKING AND USE IN ORGANIZATIONAL DECISION MAKING

Decisions are commitments to action. Organizational actions are justified in relation to goals and objectives, and are predicated on information and beliefs about how the methods or strategies selected will lead to desired outcomes. The four models of decision making may be contrasted on the basis of their assumptions about goal ambiguity and congruence, and technical uncertainty or complexity, as was shown in Fig. 5–1. The *rational model* assumes goals have sufficient clarity and agreement for the decision making to be goal directed, and for coalitions to be formed to enable choices to be made. Technical or procedural uncertainty is managed by designing rules, routines, and performance programs that guide or simplify decisions. The *process model* is a close relative of the rational model, and likewise assumes a basic level of goal clarity and consensus. Technical uncertainty is, however, higher as decision makers grapple with problems complicated by multiple options and alternative solutions. As a result, the decision process tends to be dynamic and open ended. The *political model* focuses on the effects of conflicting goals on decision making as various players with different stands and influence combine their moves to yield decisions. Technical uncertainty is low, to the extent that within their domains, each player is clear about the group's favored alternatives and the outcomes the group would prefer to bring about. The *anarchic model,* as its name suggests, describes decision situations where both goals and procedures are ambiguous. Participants dump their solutions and problems into choice situations, which act as receptacles where solutions are attached to problems, depending on timing, interest, outside forces, and so on.

From an information perspective, the four models of decision making are also characterized by distinctive approaches in their acquisition and use of information. We show this in Fig. 5–4, which compares their information behaviors according to the **breadth or intensity of the information seeking** (vertical axis) and the **control or directedness of the information use** (horizontal axis). In the *anarchic mode,* information seeking in the form of purposeful search is at a low level in the sense that solutions and alternatives are uncoupled from problems, and information leaves or enters decision situations with a certain amount of randomness. Information use is just as uncontrolled, where solutions are attached to problems through happenstance and individual interest, and decisions are made by flight and oversight more often than by rational resolution. In the *rational mode,* information seeking increases in breadth, but is initially limited to local searches in the neighborhood of symptoms or current solutions, and are driven by the appearance of well-defined stimuli or problems. Information use is relatively controlled, being guided by the principle of selecting an alternative that is good enough to pass minimally acceptable criteria. In the *political mode,* although information seeking may be selective and biased in favor of information that supports preferred options, information gathering intensifies for two possible reasons: information to support a favored alternative is accumulated by a broad scan covering several sources, including expert or well-regarded sources; and information is checked and verified in some detail to increase its credibility and to ensure that it will withstand adversarial scrutiny. Information use is highly controlled and directed as a political tactic to justify preferred outcomes. Information is selectively processed, so that information that contradicts assumptions or expectations is ignored or reinterpreted. In the *process mode,* information seeking is probably the most intense, partly because information gathering is spread out over time and iterates through many cycles, and partly because a substantial amount of search is required during the development phase of the process. Information use is focused, as repeated cycles of information processing converge on a solution that is a specific answer to a specific problem, and which has to be presented to and authorized by upper management.

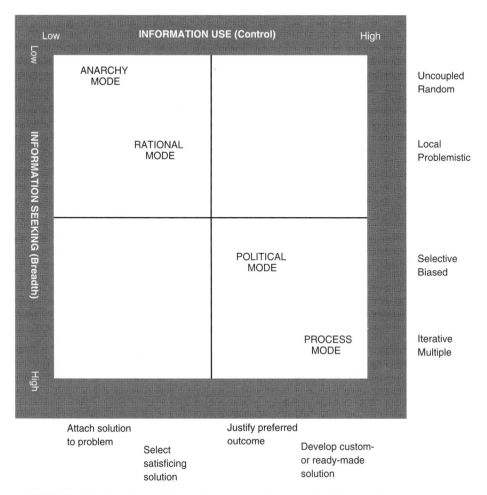

FIGURE 5–4. Information seeking and use in organizational decision making

In the following subsections we elaborate on the gathering and use of information in the context of organizational decision making, once again applying the chapter 2 framework of examining (1) information needs, (2) information seeking, and (3) information use, in terms of cognitive needs, affective responses, and situational dimensions. A summary outline of the ensuing discussion is given in Table 5–1.

Information Needs in Organizational Decision Making

Organizational decision making requires information to reduce uncertainty in at least three ways. First, information is needed to frame a choice situation.

TABLE 5–1. Information Needs, Seeking, and Use in Decision Making

	Information Needs	*Information Seeking*	*Information Use*
Decision making	• Determine problem frame and boundaries • Clarify preferences and rule appropriateness • Information about alternatives, outcomes, preferences	• Guided by heuristics, habits • Search is problem driven • Satisficing criteria	• Limitations in human information processing • Structured by routines and rules • Many issues compete for attention
Cognitive needs	• Phases of decision process: intelligence, design, choice, review • Identification and development needs	• Multiple managerial decision roles • High-velocity decision making	• Cognitive simplifications and biases • Selective information processing
Affective responses	• Stress due to complexity, risk, multiple interests, aspirations • Affective factors in problem formulation	• Conflict model of decision making: unconflicted adherence or change, defensive avoidance, hypervigilance, vigilance	• Pressure to conform in group think • Over commitment in escalation situations
Situational dimensions	• Programmed and non programmed decisions • Tactics to frame decision problems	• Types of decision processes: sporadic, fluid, and constricted • Structure, incentives, and information access	• Information-handling rules: routing rules and filtering rules • Uncertainty absorption

Boundaries are drawn to delimit a problem space in which solutions are to be searched, participants are to be solicited, and influence is to be wielded. The framing of a problem to a large extent determines the types and content of information that would be needed in order to be able to make a decision. Second, information is needed to define preferences and to select rules. Multiple goals and interests are clarified, reconciled, and expressed as choice criteria. Rules are activated by matching information that describes familiar situations with learned responses. Third, information is needed about viable alternatives and their projected outcomes. In some modes of decision making, a great part of the information-seeking effort is on identifying, developing, and evaluating alternative courses of action. Information needs then depend on whether alternatives already exist, whether existing solutions may be customized or modified, or whether new solutions have to be discovered.

In the next three subsections we examine decisional information requirements in terms of cognitive needs, affective responses, and situational dimensions.

Information Needs and Cognitive Needs: Information needs vary according to the *stages of the decision-making activity.* Simon (1977) identifies four phases: intelligence, design, choice, and review. The *intelligence phase* involves searching the environment for conditions calling for decision, where "executives and their staff spend a large fraction of their time surveying the economic, technical, political, and social environment to identify new conditions that call for new actions" (Simon 1977, 40). Research has found that environmental scanning by business organizations tends to be focused on market-related sectors of the environment. Information about customers, competitors, and suppliers are the most intensively gathered. In industries where other environmental forces such as technology, demographics, or regulatory policies have a strategic impact on the industry, scanning these sectors also becomes a high priority (Choo 1995a). The *design phase* involves seeking information in order to invent, design, or develop possible courses of action that can address a decision situation. Here the information needs are to locate, elaborate, and analyze alternatives in terms of their outcomes and contributions to organizational objectives. The *choice phase* is when a particular course of action is selected from the courses that have been developed. Choice may be influenced by information about the context in which the decision is to be taken, such as the mix of other decisions and problems that are being considered at the same time, and forthcoming events and deadlines that may affect the success or perception of the decision. The *review phase* involves "assessing the outcomes of past actions as part of a repeating cycle that leads again to new decisions" (Simon 1977, 40). Learning from past actions requires having the information to infer cause–effect relationships between decisions and outcomes that may be separated in time and space.

Simon's first three phases are the precursors of the identification, development, and selection phases derived by Mintzberg, et al. (1976) from their empirical analysis of twenty-five strategic decision processes. The *identification phase* is similar to Simon's intelligence activity. For Mintzberg and associates it is information need that drives the decision need, so that decision making is initiated by a difference between information on some actual situation and some expected standard. The breadth and content of information needed depend on whether the decision situation is perceived as a problem, opportunity, or threat. Problem decisions typically require information from several sources and stimuli in order to enable decision makers to read the situation and weigh the options before taking action. Opportunity decisions generally attempt to take advantage of some particular idea or innovation, or some set of circumstances, so as to improve on an already secure position. The idea may have been nestling in the decision maker's mind for some time, waiting for an appropriate time and setting to be translated into action. Crisis decisions on the other hand are reactive, requiring decision makers to respond to some pressing, perhaps threatening, stimuli or event. Information needs and information seeking may be narrowly pursued to enable prompt and effective measures to be taken. After a decision situation is recognized as a problem, opportunity, or crisis, the next step is "the tapping of existing information channels and the opening of new ones to clarify and define the issues" (Mintzberg, et al. 1976, 254). Each decision situation is unique and has to be diagnosed on the basis of information that describes the situation's more pertinent dimensions. In the *development phase* information is required about possible solutions. Mintzberg and associates categorize solutions as being ready-made solutions, custom-made solutions, and solutions modified from ready-made options. Information to identify and evaluate a ready-made solution is typically more structured and better defined than the broader, more tentative information required to develop a new solution or modify an existing one. In the *selection phase,* information is required to compare the relative values of the various developed alternatives. Additional information may be necessary to answer specific concerns or fill in particular information gaps. Where such concerns are not adequately met, the selection phase may define new information needs and initiate a new cycle of identification and development activities.

Information Needs and Affective Responses: At least four aspects of organizational decision making can evoke strong affective responses in participants. First, the *complexity* of the problem and the lack of clarity about its structure (that is, the alternatives, outcomes, and preferences) induce uncertainty leading to feelings of doubt and confusion. Second, most consequential decisions involve an amount of *risk* because of the inability to control or predict the future. The larger this perception of risk, the greater the feeling of stress. Where the risks are seen as necessary or worth taking, information may be sought on how better to manage or limit these risks. However, if the decision maker is risk averse, uncertain options might be discounted or avoided altogether. Third, organizational choice typically faces a *multiplicity of interests* and stakeholders, requiring bargaining, coalition building, and negotiation among interested parties. When political "pulling and hauling" is intense or confrontational, feelings of frustration or impotence may lead decision makers to steer away from unpleasant or conflict-laden situations and outcomes. Fourth, a gap between *personal aspirations* and those set by the organization may generate feelings of dissatisfaction or disappointment. For example, a decision maker disagreeing with organization-defined premises may feel that having to be constrained by them would compromise personal integrity.

The recognition and elaboration of a problem situation requiring decision, as in the intelligence phase or identification phase of the decision-making models described by Simon and Mintzberg and associates, respectively, affect the ensuing information seeking and processing by specifying the sets of solutions and information that are to be considered relevant. *Problem formulation* is sensitive to the perceptions and affective responses of the individual decision makers participating in the process. An analysis of strategic problem formulation by upper level managers of *Fortune* 500 companies in six industries clarified the influence of affective factors (Lyles 1987). The study found that the managers used three sets of subjective criteria to form their attitudes as well as affective and cognitive responses to the problem formulation process. These subjective criteria are clarity, politicality, and complexity. *Clarity* refers to the managers' perception that the problem formulation process is clear and understandable. The analysis found that a clear process was perceived to be one in which several views were debated followed by a synthesis that is approved by consensus. *Politicality* "represents an affective side of the process which suggests that the process is pleasant when it is relaxed and apolitical" (Lyles 1987, 271). Where the process involves strong debate between opposing values or gathering support of the powerful, the process was perceived as "tense, unpleasant, and political." A similar study conducted earlier (Lyles and Mitroff 1980) had found that fear and political power were recurring themes affecting how individuals formulated problems. Specific causes included the fear of retaliation by the politically powerful (for example, the fear of uncovering an error by senior management), the desire for the acquisition of power, and the use of political power to influence problem formulation. *Complexity* "represents a view of a complex process that is dynamic, tense and emotional because the problem is important and has widespread consequences" (p. 271). A process is perceived as complex when participants hold different views of the problem situation, and there is a continued disagreement about the nature of the problem.

Information Needs and Situational Dimensions Simon (1977) positions decisions along a continuum between two polar decision types—*programmed and nonprogrammed decisions.* This range may also be used to differentiate decision situations and their information-processing needs. Decisions are programmed to the extent that they are repetitive and routine, so that a definite procedure has been worked out for handling them. The decision situation is simplified by a set of common expectations, a system of subgoals, and well-defined information requirements and channels for processing the decision. Programmed decisions lend themselves to decision support technologies such as computer-based transaction processing and mathematical modeling. Decisions are nonprogrammed to the extent that they are novel, unstructured, and unusually consequential. The decision situation is ill structured and novel, requiring participants to use their judgment, intuition, and creativity. Nonprogrammed decisions tend to be made according to rules of thumb or learned heuristics, both of which are influenced by the training and background of the decision makers. Simon's separation of decision types may be elaborated by the problem dimensions identified by Taylor (1986). Just as decisions fall between programmed and nonprogrammed, their problem dimensions would fall between the well structured and ill structured, simple and complex, specific goals and amorphous goals, initial state understood and not understood, assumptions agreed and not agreed upon, assumptions explicit and not explicit, and familiar pattern and new pattern. Each dimension implies information needs, so that, for example, well-structured problems may require hard, quantitative data; specific goals require data for operationalization and measurement; and familiar pattern problems are handled with procedural and historical information.

The perception of information needs depends on how the decision problem is initially framed or formulated. While we looked at the effects of individual attitudes in the last subsection, the application of specific types of tactics creates a broader context by introducing external ideas, targets, and new norms. From an analysis of 177 decision cases collected from mostly high-level managers in organizations across the United States and Canada, Nutt (1992) concluded that the types of *tactics used to frame decision problems* not only shaped information needs and sources, but also influenced decision success. Four problem formulation tactics emerged from the study: idea tactics, problem tactics, target tactics, and reframing tactics. *Idea tactics* were the most frequently used, where an idea from outside the decision process is introduced into a decision situation as a solution. Ideas may originate from "the decision maker's visions and beliefs, educational activities, the media, the literature, vendors, joint-venture opportunities, the notions of key people, and staff proposals" (Nutt 1992, 527). These ideas are then elaborated, tested, and refined through the decision process. *Problem tactics* begin by identifying the problem and, based on this identification, exploring and analyzing the problem's distinctive features in order to develop a remedy. *Target tactics* specify desired objectives or directions expressed as performance improvements, cost reductions, and so on. Subsequent decision making then searches for alternative solutions, and selects the solution most likely to meet the target. *Reframing tactics* highlight the need for action by introducing new norms that magnify the problem and amplify the importance of acting to rectify it. New norms may be derived from "the experiences of competitors, breakthroughs by innovation, developments described in the literature, and in other ways" (Nutt 1992, 529), and are justified by citing their origins. The study also found that reframing, although the least frequently used, was the most successful tactic in that using the tactic led to all of the decisions being implemented, in the shortest average time, with the best results. Conversely, idea tactics were more frequently used, but much less successful. Nutt (1992) suggests that decision makers prefer idea tactics because they reduce uncertainty, because decision makers believed that implementing their own visions constituted good leadership, and because the tactic was economical as "time and money was not spent in idea finding, just idea testing" (Nutt 1992, 537).

Information Seeking in Organizational Decision Making

Information seeking during organizational decision making is guided by the habits and heuristics that the individual decision maker has acquired as a result of training, education, or experience. At the same time, organizations design and institutionalize rules and routines to structure search and choice behaviors based on premises derived from organizational goals and task objectives. Information seeking is therefore a function of individual preferences, institutional values, and the choice situation's attributes. As an activity, information seeking is problem-driven—it begins when a problem (including the problem of how to exploit an opportunity) is attended to and recognized as requiring decision and action. Search seems to respect a hierarchy of information sources, a hierarchy ordered by proximity to a problem or its symptoms, and by the perceived traits of sources, such as their accessibility or credibility. Information search stops when the first good enough solution is found (rational decision model), or when ample evidence is gathered to support a preferred option (political decision model), or when courses are developed or investigated sufficiently to be presented for final evaluation (process decision model). In the anarchic decision model, information is continually generated and dumped into decision situations, but they are initially uncoupled from the problems being considered. Interested participants may then attach information about solutions or problems to choice situations, but which solutions become linked to which problems depends on factors such as temporal sequence, individual interest, and the current mix of solutions and problems.

Information Seeking and Cognitive Needs: How managers as decision makers seek information is influenced by the range of roles the manager plays in the organization. Based on direct observation of managers at work, Mintzberg (1973) developed three sets of ***managerial roles:*** interpersonal roles, informational roles, and decisional roles. The manager plays three *interpersonal roles.* By virtue of the formal authority invested in a manager, he takes on the role of a figurehead, representing his organization in formal and social matters. As a leader, he defines the relationships with his subordinates through staffing, motivating, and so on. Finally, as a liaison, he interacts with peers and external persons to gain information and favors. The interpersonal roles give the manager access to many internal and external sources of information. As a result, the manager becomes the nerve center of organizational information. He acts in three *informational roles.* As monitor, he seeks and receives information about the organization and the environment. As disseminator, he transmits special information into his organization. As spokesman, he disseminates the organization's information out to the environment. The unique access to information combined with status and authority places the executive at the focal point of the organization where decisions are made. Four *decisional roles* are discerned. As entrepreneur, the executive searches for problems and opportunities, and uses information to initiate and design controlled change in the organization through "improvement projects," which exploit an opportunity or solve a problem. As disturbance handler, the executive deals with unexpected but important events for which there is no clear programmed response. Such stimuli may arise from conflicts between subordinates, loss of resources, and difficulties between one organization and another. As resource allocator, the executive controls the distribution of all forms of organizational resources by scheduling time, programming work, and authorizing decisions made by others in the organization. Finally, as negotiator, the executive engages in major, non-routine negotiation and communication activities with other organizations or individuals. Negotiation is regarded as "resource trading in real time," in which someone in authority commits the quantity of resources at stake. The three sets of ten managerial roles form an integrated whole, where "the manager is an input–output system in which authority and status give rise to interpersonal relationships that lead to inputs (information), and these in turn lead to outputs (information and decisions). One cannot arbitrarily remove one role and expect the rest to remain intact. . . . It is the manager's informational roles that tie all managerial work together—linking status and the interpersonal roles with the decisional roles" (Mintzberg 1973, 58,71).

Time scales have shrunk in today's organizational environments. Technologies and market forces now compel organizations to respond in hours and days where before they had weeks and months. How do managers seek and use information in *high-velocity environments?* Eisenhardt (1989, 1990) studied the information behaviors of top management teams in twelve microcomputer firms that were operating in "high-velocity" environments where market and technology are moving so rapidly that the information available is poor, mistakes are costly, and recovery from missed opportunities is difficult. In such dynamic environments the ability to make fast decisions was found to be linked to strong performance. Contrary to expectations that fast decision makers would limit their information gathering and analysis to save time, the study found that fast managers used as much, and sometimes more, information than do their slower counterparts. However, fast managers concentrated on real-time information about current operations and current environment that is reported with little or no time lag, whereas slow decision makers relied on planning and future-oriented information. Real-time information is gathered in several ways: fast managers tracked operational measures of performance, shared information in frequent operational meetings, and sought advice from experienced, trusted managers. Again, surprisingly, fast managers used the information to develop a larger number of alternatives than the slower decision makers. However, they analyzed the information quickly by comparing the alternatives with each another, rather than examining each alternative in depth. Fast managers have learned information strategies to accelerate their decision making without compromising decision quality.

Information Seeking and Affective Responses: Although organizations may attempt to regulate decision making by rules and routines, the engagement of human actors and human wills ensures that the decision process will kindle a range of emotional responses that shape and turn information seeking and use. Janis and Mann (1977) maintain that decisional conflicts are likely whenever consequential choices are made, and they arise because the decision maker simultaneously experiences the opposing tendencies to accept and reject a course of action. Decisional conflicts are sources of stress, which vents itself in feelings such as apprehensiveness, a desire to escape from the choice situation, and self-blame. Janis and Mann developed a *conflict model of decision making* that examines the distinctive patterns by which individuals cope with the stress of decision situations. The model is based on a series of questions that are raised in sequence by every decision maker. Faced with information suggesting a need for change, the decision maker asks herself these four questions:

1. Are the risks serious if I do not change?
2. Are the risks serious if I do change?
3. Is it realistic to hope to find a better solution?
4. Is there sufficient time to search and deliberate?

(Janis and Mann 1977)

If the risks of not changing are not serious (1), the individual behaves as before with no sense of conflict *(unconflicted adherence).* In this case the individual is indifferent toward information, taking only casual notice of messages about an unworrisome issue. If the no-change risks are or may be serious, then the second question asks what are the risks of taking on change (2). If the risks of effecting change are not serious, then the individual will carry out the change action, again with no feeling of conflict *(unconflicted change).* As before, the individual is nonchalant about information, since change is uncontentious. However, if the risks of effecting change are or may be serious, the individual becomes emotionally aroused as she starts to search earnestly for information about solutions or ways to avoid making a choice. The next question asks, for each of the contemplated alternatives, if there is hope of finding a better solution by furthering the information search (3). If it is unrealistic to hope for a better solution, and if the present alternatives are unacceptable or unsatisfactory, the individual will cope by avoiding cues that aggravate anxiety or other painful feelings about being trapped in a hopeless situation *(defensive avoidance).* The individual thus becomes close minded and biased in her information seeking. However, if it is realistic to hope to find better solutions, the next question asks whether there is sufficient time to search and deliberate (4). If there is too little time available to search for a better solution, as when the individual is given a deadline that is too tight or she can see the danger closing in, the individual enters a state that Janis and Mann call *hypervigilance,* a feeling of being trapped with little time left to find a safe way out. An extreme form of hypervigilance is panic, in which the individual makes a snap decision, often by simply following what others are doing. The individual shows indiscriminate openness to all information, failing to discern the relevance of messages, and eventually becoming overloaded by information. However, if there is sufficient time to search and deliberate, the individual feels confident about finding a safe or workable solution, and exercises care and discriminating openness in her information seeking *(vigilance).* The model therefore implies that vigilant information seeking and processing requires four conditions to be met: awareness of serious threat if no change is taken; awareness of serious risk in acting to change; hope or confidence that a satisfactory solution can be found; and sufficient time to search and evaluate (Janis and Mann 1977).

Information Seeking and Situational Dimensions: The amount and breadth of information seeking in decision making varies according to the task and organizational demands that constrain or direct the process. From a database of 136 strategic decisions, Hickson et al. (1986) were able to categorize decisions based on process variables which included information-seeking attributes. These attributes concerned the number of sources used, variability in the quality of information, use of external sources, and the amount of effort spent in acquiring information. (Other process variables described the nature of interaction, flow disruptions and impedances, process and gestation time, and the authority level at which decision ends.) The analysis showed that there were three kinds of decision processes: sporadic processes, fluid processes, and constricted processes (Hickson et al. 1986). *Sporadic decision processes* are protracted, informal, and spasmodic, taking over a year or two to come to a conclusion, but not before they have come up against many obstacles and disruptions that delay progress. Work is concentrated in short bursts of activity, and information gathering is characterized by the use of multiple sources, variability in information quality, and informal personal contacts. In sporadic processes, decision makers will find that "not all the information they get can be relied upon, so they and their staff will have to sift out that which they feel they have confidence in, and that which is better ignored. They will be drawn into bursts of activity in corridors and offices, in between the delays, when the matter is on everyone's mind and answers to questions are demanded there and then, until the excitement dies down as other things become even more pressing . . . " (Hickson et al. 1986, 118). In contrast, *fluid decision processes* move along swiftly at a steady pace and make use of formal channels. Work is handled by committees and project groups, requiring decision makers to attend a greater number of meetings, but "far from getting in the way, these formally-arranged proceedings seem to facilitate a rapid conclusion . . . " (p. 120). In fluid processes, fewer sources of expertise are consulted, and there is also less variability in the level of confidence in their views. *Constricted decision processes* are more narrowly channeled and are more restrained than the other two processes. Meetings and committees are still the mode, but there are fewer of them. Information seeking still involves multiple sources, but less effort is expended in acquiring information. These processes do not generate as much bustle because there is clarity about what information is required, and how that information may be found. A constricted process "does not stir up so much activity as the other types of processes do. The pertinent facts and figures are already in being or can be put together easily, and to get hold of them it is only necessary to pick up the phone and ask whoever has them at his or her fingertips, or could make a routine calculation" (p. 122).

Information availability and access are influenced by many institutional characteristics, notably the *organizational structure* that regulates the flow of information, and the *incentive systems* that impute value and preference to the pursuit of certain goals and information. Hierarchy and specialization are traditional means for organizations to increase their information-processing capacity in order to match task performance requirements (Galbraith 1973), but in some situations, hierarchy and specialization may impede or distort information flow. For example, O'Reilly, Chatman, and Anderson (1987) pointed out that "subordinates attempt to present themselves in a favorable light to those above them in the hierarchy and are willing to suppress certain important pieces of information while transmitting unimportant information if it reflects favorably on themselves" (p. 612). In a well-known study, Pettigrew (1972) wrote about how a senior manager occupying a strategic position in the organizational structure was able to influence the board of directors decision to purchase a large computer system through artfully gatekeeping the information reaching the directors. Besides structure, incentive systems influence information use by encouraging the transmission of certain types of information while discouraging the transmission of other types. Incentive systems also influence decision making by drawing decision makers attention to a few highly rewarded outcomes while excluding other important, possibly superior alternatives (O'Reilly, Chatman, and Anderson 1987).

Information Use in Organizational Decision Making

Organizational decisions are made by individuals or groups of individuals. Although human information processing has attained a high degree of adaptive versatility by learning rules of thumb that reduce mental effort, these same short-cuts can systematically limit and bias information processing in some situations. Moreover, humans seek to maximize or maintain order, consistency, and self-interest when evaluating choices, and this may lead them to strongly favor particular outcomes, to the extent that they may deliberately avoid, hide, or discount information that does not support their preferred alternatives. Decision making in groups can introduce additional social forces, including pressures to conform to group norms or to preserve group cohesiveness, which when accentuated can warp information use and processing. The situation is further exacerbated when decision makers carry heavy work and information loads, and try to juggle multiple demands and agendas at the same time. Many simultaneous, competing claims on their attention confuse and weaken their ability to allocate time and energy according to some appreciation of the relative importance of issues. Organizations attempt to compensate for limitations in human information processing by establishing rules and preferences that structure the decision process. These rules and premises define the saliency of information, provide criteria for evaluating information about alternatives, specify channels and patterns of information sharing and communication, and designate modes of record keeping.

Information Use and Cognitive Needs: In an earlier section we reviewed the *cognitive simplifications* that humans use in making judgments and decisions. While these heuristics do reduce mental effort, they can also introduce errors and biases. For example, people overestimate the frequency of events they can recall more easily; they weigh concrete information or vivid events more heavily than abstract information; they seek and use information that is consonant with their views; they generalize from unrepresentative small samples; they are sensitive to the order of information, adding importance to items that appear early or recently; and so on (Piatelli-Palmarini 1994; Hogarth 1987; Tversky and Kahneman 1974). Many of these biases may be amplified in organizational decision situations, as when the subject matter is complex, the information is ambiguous, or when time pressure or information overload forces decision makers to curtail their analysis. Choice behavior in organizations is rarely completely rational, for objective rationality is diminished by the limitations of human information processing, the multiplicity of subgoals and partisan interests, the linking up of problems and solutions by people, and the structure of decisional procedures and rules. Organizations may emphasize the attributes of the decision process over the attributes of the decision outcomes, so that *process rationality* dominates: "Explicit outcomes are viewed as secondary and decision-making becomes sensible through the intelligence of the way it is orchestrated" (March 1978, 8). This institutional push for uniformity and conformity can condition cognitive performance and reduce decision makers' capacity to recognize and respond to new information. The Challenger accident was not so much the result of defective decision making as the consequence of institutional and social pressures to preserve conformity (Vaughan 1996).

Besides heuristics and shortcuts, human decision makers in organizational settings are also biased by their tendency to selectively seek out and use information that confirms their beliefs or supports their desired outcomes. This *selective processing* does not imply that decision makers abbreviate their information search, but rather, decision makers seek out more information than is required, and use this information to increase their confidence in their choices (O'Reilly 1983). In organizational decision situations surrounded by high levels of uncertainty, "preferences for outcomes may be the least ambiguous component of the decision process, more certain than the definition of the problem, the range of feasible alternatives, or the probabilities associated with various alternatives" (O'Reilly 1983, 109). Decision makers may therefore reduce uncertainty by focusing on information that helps them achieve desired outcomes. In a study of policy analysts, Meltsner (1976) made the distinction between information that is used to make decisions and information that is used to support decisions that have already been made. Thus decision makers would hire external consulting groups to do evaluation studies not for the purpose of discovering better alternatives, but to garner expert support for options already chosen. Based on her own research and those by others in the field, Feldman (1989) observes that "bureaucratic analysts work in a situation characterized most of the time by a lack of attention by decision makers or policy makers. Many reports they write are not read; many contracts they set up are not used; much expertise they acquire is not called upon. Decisions about policies seem to be made on the basis of politics and personal loyalties rather than the information and expertise that the analysts have to offer" (p. 93).

Information Use and Affective Responses: Based on an analysis of well-documented fiascoes in policy decision making (including the Bay of Pigs invasion, the attack on Pearl Harbor, and the escalation of the Vietnam War), Janis (1982) attributed the errors to a tendency of people working in highly cohesive groups to seek concurrence to such an extent that it interferes with the vigilant processing of information. Janis (1982) coined the term **"groupthink"** to refer to "a mode of thinking that people engage in when they are deeply involved in a cohesive in-group, when the members' strivings for unanimity override their motivation to appraise alternative courses of action realistically" (p. 9). The symptoms of groupthink are divided into three types. First, group members share a feeling of invulnerability, which leads to optimism and a willingness to take risks. Second, group members are close minded, collectively rationalizing or discounting aberrant information and maintaining stereotyped views of opposing parties as weak and ineffectual. Third, group members press toward uniformity, sustaining a shared impression of unanimity through self-censorship as well as direct pressure against dissenting views. As a result of these affective illusions of invulnerability and solidarity, the group's seeking and use of information are compromised, and decision making becomes defective. Specifically, members fail to survey alternatives and objectives adequately; do not examine risks of preferred choice or reappraise alternatives that were initially rejected; search for information poorly; process information in a biased, selective way; and do not make contingency plans (Janis 1982). Groupthink is more likely when decision makers are members of a cohesive group, when organization structure insulates the group or lacks norms to require methodical procedures, and when the decision situation is highly stressful due to external threats. External threats draw the group even closer, with members increasing their reliance on the group for social and emotional support, thereby heightening the desire to seek concurrence and consensus.

In some situations decision makers become increasingly locked into losing courses of action. Why do decision makers positively evaluate and continue a course of action when the objective facts indicate that withdrawal is necessary to reduce further losses? Organizations often face such dilemmas in *escalation situations,* "where things have not only gone wrong, but where potential actions aimed at curing the problem can actually deepen or compound the difficulty" (Staw and Ross 1987, 40). A classic example of escalation is when an organization continues to pour resources into an ailing project rather than pulling the plug. (Two real-world case studies on escalation situations concern the world exposition [Expo 86] in Vancouver [Ross and Staw 1986], and Long Island Lighting Company's decision to build a nuclear power plant [Ross and Staw 1993].) Staw and Ross (1987) identify a number of project, psychological, social, and structural determinants that induce escalation and overcommitment. Among the psychological and social variables are prior reinforcement, self-justification, self-inference, and a desire to save face. Prior reinforcement (or the reinforcement trap) occurs when decision makers have received reinforcement from benefits achieved early in a course of action, and the deterioration is slow and irregular. Decision makers stay on a failing course because they expect success in the end or because the behavior has been ingrained. In self-justification, decision makers "justify an ineffective course of action by increasing their commitment to it, . . . in the hope of turning the situation around or saving their original decisions from being a failure" (Staw and Ross 1987, 51). In self-inference, individuals tend to become committed to a course when their earlier actions supporting the course have been explicit, volitional, visible, irrevocable, repeated, and significant (Staw and Ross 1987; Salancik 1977; Kiesler 1971). In face-saving, decision makers persist because they do not want to admit to themselves that they have made an error, much less expose their mistakes to others. In organizations where error-free decision making is valued, managers may attempt to hide their mistakes or postpone their discovery.

Information Use and Situational Dimensions: An important category of any organization's standard operating procedures are its *information-handling rules.* The rules specify the organization's communication system that directs and constrain the flow and use of information. In particular, the information-handling rules define the characteristics of the input information taken into the organization; the rules for distributing and condensing the input information; the rules for distributing and condensing internally generated information; and the characteristics of the information leaving the organization (Cyert and March 1992,1963, p. 127). As a result of these rules, not everyone in the organization seeks or receives all of the information the organization uses. Instead, certain organizational units or individuals will be given the responsibility for gathering particular information based on their having regular contact with the information source or having special expertise in collecting the information. The choice of who is to gather which information can be significant because the individual who encounters the information initially is also the first to evaluate its relevance, determine its routing, and in general to screen, condense, or highlight the information or some aspect of it. Cyert and March make clear that standard operating procedures direct information flow by determining *routing rules* and *filtering rules.* In routing information, many organizations follow the principle that "it is appropriate to process information through the hierarchy defined in terms of task specialization" (p. 129), since information needs are presumably tied to task specialization. In filtering information, each functional department (finance, personnel, production, sales) will introduce biases according to the idiosyncrasies of its specialization or view of the world. Routing and filtering rules interact to affect the seeking and availability of information: "What makes the routing rules important is their linkage with filtering at various communication relay points and the fact that there are dead ends in the routes. Information is condensed and summarized as it goes through the organization and some information never reaches some points" (Cyert and March 1992,1963, 130). The progressive summarization of information as it travels up the levels of an organization is a well-known phenomenon. (Recall how at NASA the amount of documentation on the space shuttle's flight readiness progressively shrank as the documentation was reviewed at higher levels.) March and Simon (1993,1958) call this information condensation *uncertainty absorption,* which takes place when "inferences are drawn from a body of evidence and the inferences, instead of the evidence itself, are then communicated. The successive editing steps that transform data obtained from a set of questionnaires into printed statistical tables provide a simple example of uncertainty absorption" (p. 186). While uncertainty absorption may reduce uncertainty and information load, the recipient is generally unable to judge its correctness but must rely on the confidence level in the source and the transformation process. As March and Simon quipped, the "facts" communicated may be disbelieved, but they can only rarely be checked (p. 187).

Stinchcombe (1990) points out that an organization will grow toward those locations where information for resolving uncertainty is chiefly located. The organization has to be "where the news breaks, whenever it breaks" (p. 3), where news is the first appearance of some information about how the future is going to be in an area important for the organization. Stinchombe believes that "information about the uncertain future becomes progressively available *in distinct social locations,* depending on what sort of uncertainty it is. What resolves the uncertatinty of particular actors, then, is the *earliest available information* that will show what direction the actor ought to be going because of the way the future of the world is, evidently, turning out" (p. 2). He suggests that information seeking and processing is at the core of the structure of organizations, so that the structure will reflect the kinds of uncertainties faced, the information sources that best address these uncertainties, and the need to capture and pass on information to the decision-making units in a timely manner.

VIII. SUMMARY: THE MANAGEMENT OF ORGANIZATIONAL DECISION MAKING

Organizations are networks of decisions, decision makers, and decision making. Decisions result in commitment to courses of action. Decisions facilitate action taking by defining and elaborating purpose and by allocating and authorizing resources. Although concurrent decision flows generate multiple action streams dispersed in time and location, the institution as a whole must move toward coherent goals, and to do so through strategies that are consistent and coordinated. Because the organization's actions and purposes interact with many elements of the environment over long time horizons, decision makers face great complexity and uncertainty in trying to understand what the issues are, identify feasible alternatives, appraise probable outcomes, and clarify and order preferences. A completely rational decision would require information beyond the capability of the organization to collect, and information processing beyond the capacity of humans to execute. As we saw in this chapter, organizations cope by designing and implementing rules and routines to simplify and guide choice behavior so that it is consistent and coordinated, at least at some minimal level. This perfectly rational idea contains the seeds of three paradoxes. First, structured decision premises and processes over time propagate cultural values of uniformity and consistency. While these values are necessary to maintain an organization's legitimacy and credibility, in some decision situations (as when stress, uncertainty, and complexity levels are high), overzealous pursuance of conformity can constrict information use and cause decision makers to fail to register vital information. Defective decisions can be the result, as was the case in the Challenger accident. Second, standard decision procedures encapsulate and operationalize what the organization has learned from experience. While standard procedures are intended to enable more systems in the organization to function at a higher level of learned intelligence, their promulgation can have an opposite effect when uncritical adherence to tradition discourages innovation and improvisation, and blocks the unlearning of outmoded assumptions. Third, an organization is not a monolith subscribing to a universal set of preferences and values. Goals and objectives do not line up in well-aligned hierarchies, but are constantly being shuffled by bargaining and coalition building. Choices are sometimes made based more on the forces of compromise and competition than on a reasoned assessment of the relative merits of outcomes. Understanding and resolving these paradoxes will be part of the conceptualization of organizational knowing presented in the next two chapters.

6

THE KNOWING ORGANIZATION I— THEORY AND PROCESS

'Tis written: "In the beginning was the Word!"
Here now I'm balked! Who'll put me in accord?
It is impossible, the Word so high to prize,
I must translate it otherwise
If I am rightly by the Spirit taught.
'Tis written: In the beginning was the Thought!
Consider well that line, the first you see,
That your pen may not write too hastily!
Is it then Thought that works, creative, hour by hour?
Thus should it stand: In the beginning was the Power!
Yet even while I write this word, I falter,
For something warns me, this too I shall alter.
The Spirit's helping me! I see now what I need
And write assured: In the beginning was the Deed!
  —Johann Wolfgang von Goethe 1808, *Faust; Part One* translated by
  George Madison Priest

"Why," said the Dodo, "the best way to explain it is to do it."
  —*Lewis Carroll 1865,* Alice's Adventures in Wonderland

Smallpox is the only major human disease to have been eradicated. Epidemics of smallpox had inflicted humankind throughout history, and as recently as 1967, some ten to fifteen million cases were still occurring annually in more than thirty endemic countries (Fenner et al. 1988). Of these some two million died and millions of survivors were left disfigured or even blind. Smallpox spreads by tiny droplets of aerosolized virus that are discharged from the mouth and nose of infected victims. Within two weeks of inhaling the virus, the viremia would have caused fever, muscular pain, infection of skin and internal organs, and the characteristic appearance of rash on the face and body.

The rash papules swell and become filled with pus. Scabs form in the second week and leave pitted scars after they fall off. There is no treatment for smallpox once it has been contracted. The more serious strain of the smallpox virus (variola major) causes fatality in 20 to 40 percent of those not vaccinated.

On January 1, 1967, the World Health Organization (WHO) launched the Intensified Smallpox Eradication Programme. At that time the plan was to rely entirely on mass vaccination of susceptible persons in endemic countries—the problem was defined as one of ***mass vaccination.*** The mass vaccination strategy had eradicated smallpox successfully in programs in Western Europe, North America, Japan, and other areas. The WHO Expert Committee on Smallpox in 1964 had recommended that the goal should be to vaccinate 100 percent of the population, based on the observation in India that smallpox persisted in some areas despite vaccinations reported to be an 80 percent or more of the population. (Then 80 percent was assumed to be the acceptable target of a well-conducted vaccination program.) A report by the WHO director-general in 1966 supported this thinking: "Eradication can be accomplished in a comparatively simple and straightforward manner by rendering immune, through vaccination, a sufficiently large proportion of the population so that transmission is interrupted. In a highly endemic area this requires almost 100 percent coverage of the population" (WHO 1966, 107). In hindsight, one might have asked whether the sample size of successful vaccination campaigns was adequate, whether results obtained in insulated areas (such as tests on the island of Tonga) could be replicated elsewhere, and to what extent campaigns in Europe and North America were helped by better controlled conditions (Hopkins 1989). The same expert committee which had recommended total vaccination had also "ignored the information from field studies in India itself, which showed that the proportion successfully vaccinated fell far short of 80% because of the use of subpotent vaccines and the frequent revaccination of the most easily accessible groups" (Fenner et al. 1988, 484). A review of the programs conducted after 1967 suggests that mass vaccination alone could have eliminated smallpox in South America and most African countries, but not in the densely populated countries of Bangladesh, India, Indonesia, and Pakistan (Fenner et al. 1988).

A 1966 outbreak in Nigeria started the evolution of a new strategy. In western Nigeria, where over 90 percent of the population had been vaccinated, another smallpox outbreak had occurred, apparently originating in a religious group that had resisted vaccination. Vaccine supplies were delayed, forcing program staff to quickly locate new cases and isolate infected villages, which could then be vaccinated with the limited supplies. A reporting network using the available radio facilities was established to locate new cases. Containment teams moved swiftly to isolate infected persons and to vaccinate susceptible villages. The Nigerian experience demonstrated that an alternative strategy of ***surveillance and containment*** could break the transmission chain of smallpox, even when less than half the population was eventually vaccinated (Hopkins 1989). In 1970 a major epidemic had begun in the Gulbarga district of Karnataka in southwestern India, claiming over 1300 victims (including 123 deaths) in more than 1000 villages and five municipalities. To prevent the epidemic from spreading to more populated areas, "prompt detection of all cases in an area of two million people was required. All available health personnel, not just smallpox health workers, were mobilized for a weeklong house-to-house search of the area. By carefully focusing containment vaccination around each newly discovered case, they eliminated smallpox from the district within weeks" (Brilliant 1985, 27). The Gulbarga experience was India's first real success with surveillance and containment, and showed that it could work even in a densely populated country. The new strategy evolved gradually and was accepted slowly as local campaigns controlled outbreaks with their own variations of surveillance and containment. In India, for example, when in 1973 a village-by-village search in Uttar Pradesh and Bihar identified 10,000 new cases, surveillance first shifted to a house-to-house search, and then to market surveillance: smallpox disappeared in some nineteen months before the strategy was ever fully worked out (Hopkins 1989). In Bangladesh, surveillance based on passive reporting was eventually supplemented by three systems of surveillance—market surveillance, infected village surveillance, and house-to-house surveillance. House-to-house searches were made much more effective by preceding them with presearch meetings that also examined feedback from prior searches (Fenner et al. 1988). In Nepal surveillance teams were supervised by assessment teams who planned the itineraries, concentrating on high-risk areas, schools, tea shops, factories, brick kilns, weekly markets, fairs, and so on. As in India, "watchguards" were posted at every infected house around the clock to prevent patients from leaving the house, and monetary rewards were offered for information leading to the discovery of new outbreaks (Fenner et al. 1988). Financial incentives, sometimes amounting to several months' wages, were presented in several countries to reward reporting of new smallpox cases. Even health workers were eligible for the rewards, and were encouraged to bypass their superiors to report cases. Disincentives were also used to force people to receive vaccination, as in some Indian cities where people were threatened with the loss of their food ration cards or with having the names of their family members erased (Hopkins 1989).

The initial definition of the problem as mass vaccination was a classic symptom of a confusion between ends and means. The goal of the program was the complete eradication of smallpox, and mass vaccination was a means to achieve that end. With the epidemiological experience available in 1966, the choice of mass vaccination as a strategy appeared rational. However, by limiting its attention to methods to vaccinate as many people as possible, and by measuring performance according to how many vaccinations were given, the program was focusing on methodology and not necessarily on goal attainment. National governments also favored mass vaccination partly because it was a highly visible display of government action, and partly because of the substantial investments already made in creating the vaccination infrastructure (including jobs and salaries). Fortunately the smallpox campaign learned quickly from its experiences in Nigeria, India, and elsewhere and was able to recast the problem and evolve a new surveillance–containment strategy through experimentation and innovation in the field. The then director of the WHO program commented on the shift soon after it occurred: "In the development of the global program, it thus seemed more logical to reconsider the strategy in terms of the actual objective, 'eradication of smallpox,' and to determine how best to interrupt completely transmission of the disease rather than to focus attention solely on methods to vaccinate all people" (Henderson 1972, 1). The process of institutional learning and local adaptation was central to the campaign's success: *"Indeed, that process, more than any other element in the campaign, is the key explanatory factor of the ultimate success of the program"* (Hopkins 1989, 74; italics in original). The surveillance and containment strategy was not a single policy deliberately planned for or even envisioned by WHO. Instead, it comprised a broad array of measures that emerged over time from the local practices of field teams who had to invent procedures that not only blended with local customs and conditions, but were also genuinely effective in providing early detection and enforcing isolation and control. What eventually eliminated smallpox was the combined approach of using mass vaccination to reduce disease incidence so that detection and containment could eliminate the remaining endemic foci (Brilliant 1985).

To achieve the large-scale vaccination in the program required high-volume production of potent, reliable vaccines, and an efficient, inexpensive means of delivering the vaccine. Three major technological innovations greatly facilitated the smallpox eradication program by addressing these needs. Perhaps the most significant was the development of the capacity to mass-produce high-quality freeze-dried vaccine in many countries. Edward Jenner had discovered as long ago as 1796 that humans inoculated with cowpox became immune to smallpox. An earlier 1959 WHO smallpox program had depended on a liquid vaccine that had to be used within 48 hours and was easily contaminated. The new freeze-dried vaccine, which had the potency and stability needed for mass vaccination, was developed mainly at the Lister Institute in London using modest resources. The first apparatus for heat-sealing the ampoules of freeze-dried vaccine on a production scale was built from a child's toy construction kit (Hopkins 1989). The final production method was subsequently made freely available. Since the quality of the vaccine was crucial, WHO took the important step of establishing two regional vaccine reference centers in Canada and the Netherlands to test and ensure vaccine quality. WHO continued with many activities and services to improve vaccine quality, including organizing a vaccine production seminar, consultation, fellowship training, detailed production manuals, equipment blueprints, and so on (Hopkins 1989). Within a few years after the program started, several countries achieved self-sufficiency in vaccine production, with nearly sixty countries participating in the production of freeze-dried vaccine (Fenner et al. 1988).

Apart from the vaccine, the program also had to solve the problem of developing an efficient technique of introducing the smallpox vaccine into humans. The traditional vaccination technique was to scratch a drop of the vaccine into the superficial skin layers, employing a rotary lancet or a needle, which sometimes resulted in serious wounds. The scratch method was clearly inadequate for large-scale vaccinations that were to be accomplished in compressed time frames. Starting in 1963, the U.S. National Communicable Disease Center had led field tests of a jet injector that was hydraulic powered, foot actuated, and portable. The jet injector could do over 1000 vaccinations in an hour, and in field tests more than 100,000 persons were successfully vaccinated in several countries. The jet injector was deployed to good effect in West Africa, but was too expensive a device for house-to-house vaccination in densely populated countries.

The third major technological innovation was the bifurcated needle. The new freeze-dried vaccine required a different method of presenting single doses of the vaccine. Because the vaccine had to be reconstituted each time and dispensed in tiny quantities, the traditional method of storing liquid vaccine in capillaries was no longer tenable. In developing a new solution, Benjamin Rubin of Wyeth Laboratories worked with Gus Chakros of the then Reading Textile Machine Company in needle design. It occurred to Rubin that a prolonged needle with a loop would provide both the capillarity activity and the scarification action required (Hopkins 1989). He suggested the use of a sewing needle in which the loop end was ground into a prolonged fork, creating two bifurcated prongs. A piece of wire suspended between the prongs was designed to hold a constant amount of vaccine by capillarity. By 1968 the bifurcated needle had replaced traditional methods in most countries, and by 1970 it was in use everywhere. The new needle conserved vaccine and was so easy to use that a local villager could be trained in 10 to 15 minutes to reconstitute vaccine and to perform effective vaccination (Fenner et al. 1988).

Although the freeze-dried vaccine, the jet injector, and the bifurcated needle were milestones in the smallpox campaign, the program would not have succeeded without the ingenuity and creativity with which the field staff surmounted a host of local problems. Important innovations such as smallpox recognition cards, watchguards, rewards, rumor registers, and containment books all came from fieldworkers (Brilliant 1985). Managers and supervisors encouraged the creative solving of problems as they arose, and adopted an attitude of supporting problem-oriented practical experimentation in the field. New techniques or improvements of existing procedures were then disseminated through surveillance newsletters and periodic review meetings.

Staff training was another major component of the campaign. Epidemiologists from various backgrounds and nationalities, including academic epidemiologists, had typically never worked in rural villages, and so required special training. In India, part of the training program included two simulation exercises. The first was a hypothetical outbreak that required the trainee to trace the source of infection, locate all contacts, and carry out containment operations. An example scenario involved an infectious disease hospital as a source of infection. Academic epidemiologists were incredulous, but realized when they reached the field that poorly guarded hospitals were notorious for spreading the disease they were trying to control. In the second exercise, the trainee played the role of the chief of a state smallpox program who had to watch against infection from neighboring areas, investigate sources of infection, and make sense of conflicting reports. Following the exercises, the entire training group then went out to a nearby village with a chickenpox outbreak and proceeded to vaccinate and contain the infection. The field training was highly practical and was conducted not by a ranking administrator but by a junior paramedical assistant who had intimate knowledge of village-level epidemiology.

At the strategy level, the smallpox eradication program of 1966 was guided by a plan that embraced two complementary approaches: *mass vaccination campaigns,* which employed freeze-dried vaccine of assured quality to substantially reduce the incidence of smallpox in endemic areas, and *surveillance systems,* which detected and reported cases early enough to permit the containment of outbreaks and the analysis of occurrence patterns so that appropriate vaccination and surveillance activities could be taken. The WHO program functioned in a collegial structure of many independent national programs, each developing its own administrative traditions and adapting to local social and cultural conditions. As a result, programs differed greatly from one country to another, as well as from one time period to another. Specific country programs were designed locally and jointly by the country staff and their WHO counterparts, whose roles again varied somewhat from country to country. The most effective counterparts were those who actively took part in field operations, and passive advisers who did not travel out of the cities were encouraged to leave the program (Hopkins 1989). The contribution of the WHO staff was significant:

As working counterparts, WHO staff with prior experience in other smallpox eradication programmes transmitted confidence in the feasibility of eradication and were better able to introduce new methods; they frequently served to provide continuity and sustain momentum in programmes when the national leadership changed; and it was sometimes easier for them than for their national counterparts to approach the more senior health officials in the country to seek additional support or changes in policy. (Fenner et al. 1988, 1361)

To foster a common understanding of the principles and procedures underlying the global program, WHO produced a comprehensive manual entitled *Handbook for Smallpox Eradication Programmes in Endemic Areas.* The handbook provided detailed information about all important aspects of the campaign, including an account of the clinical features of smallpox, laboratory diagnosis methods, and the operational approaches for conducting vaccination campaigns and containment programs.

Unambiguous standards of performance were stipulated from the outset and refined as the program advanced. Mass vaccination campaigns were expected to result in more than 80 percent of the population in each area having a vaccination scar. Independent assessment teams could easily ascertain the proportion of the population with such a scar. As campaigns improved, the target rates of coverage were raised to 80 percent of those under 15 years old and 80 percent of those under 5 years old. Furthermore, for primary vaccinations, a take-rate ("acceptance rate") of 95 percent or better was set as the standard. Both sets of targets shared the desirable attributes that they were attainable in well-executed campaigns under normal conditions, and that they could be easily measured and monitored soon after a campaign was concluded. From 1974 standards for surveillance and containment were added: 75 percent of outbreaks should be discovered within two weeks of the onset of the first case, containment of the outbreak should begin within 48 hours of its discovery, and no new cases should occur more than 17 days after containment had begun. Fenner et al. (1988) concluded that "the various standards were of the greatest value when the data were promptly collected, analysed and used as management guides for programme action. The knowledge by those collecting the information that their data were being promptly put to use contributed greatly to the development of the system and to better performance" (p. 1354). However, toward the end of the program, a proliferation of standards generated high volumes of data which could not be absorbed. It was clear that "a few indicators of overall performance, closely followed, were more valuable than a broad spectrum of indicators expressing the measure of many different aspects of programme execution" (p. 1355).

Each national program developed its own set of standard operating procedures that were tuned to the local task environment. In India, Operation Smallpox Zero was launched in 1975 with a closely specified set of rules and procedures (Brilliant 1985). Village-by-village searches were changed to house to house. In one state capital room-to-room searches were done to prevent an epidemic from spreading. Every case of rash with fever was recorded, monitored, and treated as smallpox until proven otherwise. A rumor register was maintained at the Primary Health Center. Uncertain diagnoses were followed with containment by default. Four watchguards were posted at infected homes. All villages within 10 miles of a case of known or suspected smallpox were searched. Everyone inside a one-mile radius was vaccinated. Market searches were intensified. Medical officers were posted to live in infected villages. The stringent procedures paid off. The average size of an outbreak fell to fewer than five cases down from seven cases six months before. The number of infected villages fell by 40 percent each month.

An important innovation which preceded Operation Smallpox Zero was the use of the infected rural village or urban neighborhood as an assessment index and, in effect, as a decision premise for allocating resources. A village in which any case of smallpox was recent enough to be potentially infective was labeled a "pending outbreak" and placed on the pending lists of active outbreaks maintained at the smallpox control offices. If no new cases were found at the end of the pending outbreak period (four to six weeks), the outbreak was removed from the lists with fanfare. Brilliant (1985) wrote that pending outbreaks were

> . . . an ideal management tool because for every outbreak, regardless of size, the same resources—a jeep, vaccine, proformae, gasoline, and containment staff—were needed to search every house in the village or mohalla [urban neighborhood] . . . This index of program performance was the lighthouse that guided the smallpox staff through the rough and stormy seas of the smallpox cycles. Since efficient resource allocation was the most pressing management decision, the use of pending outbreaks was an excellent management control—provided all the outbreaks were found. (Brilliant 1985, 54)

Throughout the program, the pursuance of clear and stringent rules and standards concerning vaccination, detection, and containment was matched by an equally fervent spirit of innovation and experimentation in the implementation of those procedures. Many people in WHO today believe that the program had bent many rules, and, indeed, many at WHO viewed the smallpox program negatively because it ran outside the regular WHO system. Hopkins (1989) recounts how one WHO official commented that if the India campaign were successful, he would "eat a tire off a jeep." When the last case was reported, Donald Henderson, director of the smallpox program, sent that person a jeep tire. There were many instances of cutting corners. Obtaining cash for the program required voluminous paperwork, and often cash flowed simply on the director's assurance that funds would be forthcoming. The regional finance officer in India often had to cover such advances, but considered them as "an act of faith well justified." In Bangladesh, traditional steps in the health service hierarchy were bypassed when the mobile surveillance teams drew personnel from their other regular assignments and gave them authority and powers that exceeded their service ranks. In India, relations in the joint WHO–government of India central command became characterized by an open, informal atmosphere developed from months of working closely in the field and office. Junior staff frequently leaped over formal hierarchical levels in order to expedite action, so much so that nearly every senior Indian health official cited "level jumping" as one of the reasons for the program's success. At the core of the campaign in India (as well as in many other countries) was a logic of learning by experimenting and sharing that learning quickly:

> Task implementation in smallpox was a dynamic process, constantly recycling lessons learned through hundreds of natural experiments in remote villages. As fast as these innovations could be shared at monthly progress review meetings in each state, they were disseminated at the next presearch meetings to the most peripheral PHC [Primary Health Center] levels. (Brilliant 1985, p. 92)

WHO had recognized early on the critical role of concurrently evaluating the performance of the various campaigns by independent teams so that deficiencies could be discovered and remedied while the campaigns were still active. Evaluation and assessment procedures constantly evolved in response to new experience and lessons learned from the field. Evaluation measures were kept flexible so that they could be changed to fit each local environment. Initial output-based measures such as the number of people vaccinated proved not useful and were replaced by outcome-based measures such as trends in the incidence of smallpox. More specific indicators were used at lower levels. In India, for example, attention shifted to pending outbreaks (infected villages where the infection could spread) in 1974; the focus then changed to the outcome of surveillance searches in 1975; and finally search efficiency was stressed in the closing years of the campaign. A sensitive feedback and control system was thus established, relying on the extensive, accurate, and rapid collection of data from the field. Field data were rapidly analyzed and acted upon in order to influence the campaigns while they were still in progress. The smallpox program excelled in careful planning and administration, creating hierarchical levels of control and reporting systems that were nevertheless simple enough for the field teams to understand. Regular feedback was provided through periodic review meetings at all levels for the analysis of failures and resolution of problems. Summaries of the program's progress also appeared regularly in the *WHO Weekly Epidemiological Record,* and special papers were published on the results of research and operational methods (Hopkins 1989).

In 1977 the last case of smallpox was reported in Somalia. For the first time, a major disease has been completely vanquished. Dr. H. Mahler, WHO director-general, described the smallpox eradication program as "a triumph of management, not of medicine." It is said that at a meeting in Kenya in 1978 the then director-general, on announcing the end of smallpox, had turned to Donald Henderson, who had directed the smallpox program, and asked him which was the next disease to be eradicated. Henderson reached for the microphone and said that the next disease that needs to be eradicated is bad management (Hopkins 1989).

Our retrospective analysis of the organizational processes of the smallpox eradication program suggests that the melding of sense making, knowledge creating, and decision making into continuous cycles of interpretation, innovation, and adaptive action underpinned the program's success. In *sense making,* the program was able to unlearn its past beliefs about the nature of smallpox and to redefine the problem of eradication. Many assumptions about the epidemiological nature of smallpox were proven wrong in the field. For example, data and experience from the field showed that smallpox did not spread as swiftly as first expected, that swabbing the vaccination area was unnecessary, and that adult females were much less susceptible to the disease. The problem was poorly defined at the start of the program, when the desired goal of eliminating smallpox was confused with the generally accepted means of mass vaccination. The initial belief was that smallpox could be eradicated simply by vaccinating all or nearly all persons in an endemic area. An outbreak in Nigeria, where vaccine supplies were short and replenishments were delayed, led fieldworkers to make do with selective vaccination, guided by detection and investigation, and followed up by isolation measures. These responses worked and showed the value of a hybrid strategy of surveillance, containment, and selective rather than comprehensive vaccination. Here was an instance of enacted learning, in which field teams acted on the environment (by locating cases and outbreaks), changed its configuration (by separating out infected homes and villages), and made it possible to deal effectively with the environment (by vaccinating and containing only the infected areas).

One of the most important elements of the program's success was its "capacity to interpret experience and to weigh evidence with the maximum degree of openness, and to respond to that experience and evidence" (Hopkins 1989, 127). Thus, while procedures, standards, and indicators were specified and measured, the program at the same time maintained a "creative but insistent iconoclasm," to guard against the reification of assumptions and modes of operation:

> The management of the smallpox campaign proved itself willing and able to recognize that means and ends had been confused in the original problem definition; to experiment with the new strategy of surveillance–containment and to enthusiastically adopt it as the guiding strategy; to adopt a simple technology in the form of the bifurcated needle when a more complex technology—the jet injector—could not do the job; and to constantly search for effective, direct means of assessment. (Hopkins 1989, 127)

As a global endeavor concurrently developing in more than fifty countries, the smallpox program evolved campaigns that were tailored to a wide range of cultures, traditions, and local practices. This diversity was held together by a unifying core of shared visions and beliefs. At the heart of the campaign was the common belief that the total eradication of smallpox was an attainable goal, that the eradication had to be done urgently, and that this was a noble, inspiring mission. One of the participants in the Indian campaign called this "management by inspiration," which was the result of:

1. A common goal that was attainable in the near future
2. A sympathetic group of coworkers who shared and encouraged belief in the goal
3. An emergencylike work situation (the program was often referred to as being on a war footing) with the concomitant increase in output and unification that such disaster situations invoke

(Jones 1976; cited in Brilliant 1985, 141–42)

In *knowledge creation* the development of the freeze-dried vaccine and the methods for presenting the vaccine answered the needs of the comprehensive vaccination program. The freeze-dried vaccine was more potent, stable, and portable than the traditional liquid vaccine; it was economical to administer and could be mass-produced. Vaccinating entire villages by novice or temporary fieldworkers also meant that the method of delivering the vaccine had to be efficient and easy to learn. The bifurcated needle invention scored highly on both criteria. These innovations had their beginnings in the tacit knowledge and personal observations of individuals working with modest tools and resources. The freeze-dried vaccine ampoules were first produced using a toy construction kit. Benjamin Rubin developed the concept of a bifurcated needle from considering a sewing needle. Compared with the jet injector, the bifurcated needle was a very simple "low-tech" device, but it was the one that became universally adopted.

Just as important as the technological innovations was the ability of the participants from various nationalities and backgrounds to work together in quickly developing innovative solutions to solve problems as they arose. Local fieldworkers drew upon their knowledge of local customs and practices to come up with practical measures that encouraged reporting and facilitated detection. Foreign staff, on the other hand, were often more effective in making contact with and persuading bureaucrats to change policies or approve resources. In India, an informal joint leadership team developed at the top management level of the campaign. Within the smallpox high command, as it was known,

. . . the titles and offices merged into an informal leadership partnership which, with its members trusting and liking each other, provided the impetus and the inspiration for eradicating smallpox from India. At the highest level, this shared sense of purpose expressed itself in true international collaboration. Sharing train rides together back and forth from infected areas, attending monthly progress review meetings in every state in India, jointly making plans, assessing organizational tactics and strategy, and watching the incidence of smallpox wane or wax with the success of the efforts to overcome it led to a very unusual solidarity among the central command.

The organizational charts and the charts of institutional roles fail to convey the sense of personal dedication and leadership that characterized the program participants who became emotionally tied to the success of the campaign. (Brilliant 1985, 96–97)

This open, two-way collaboration was possible because the participants shared the vision they were all working toward an important, inspiring goal that was attainable, but which required urgent, determined action.

Decision making in the smallpox campaign was nestled in a hierarchy of rules, routines, objectives, and indicators that became the management tools for controlling the operational strategies of mass vaccination, surveillance and containment, and assessment. A clear definition of the problem led to the development of specific operational procedures, which included quantitative performance targets and unambiguous evaluation measures. For mass vaccination, the targets were to reach at least 80 percent of the population and to achieve a 95 percent take-rate. For surveillance and containment, 75 percent of outbreaks were to be detected within two weeks of the first case, and containment should then begin within 48 hours.

Many of the targets were set, at least initially, based on limited information and on what was possible to achieve, and had a 'satisficing' quality about them. For example, the belief that mass vaccination was the best strategy was derived less from rigorous epidemiological analysis than from a "simplistic search" of recent vaccination experiences, which concentrated on the overall success of these experiences but ignored certain other aspects (such as their isolated locations or well-controlled conditions). The 80 percent mass vaccination target was set because it was what experience had shown that a well-run vaccination program could accomplish.

Targets and indicators were continually elaborated and broken down into secondary objectives and guidelines for execution at the village or municipal level, and it was in the field that the viability of the procedures and targets was tested. Adaptive organizational learning took place whenever existing goals and targets were not being met, and new searches (for solutions, not smallpox) were initiated to find out why. This would typically involve a better understanding of the local customs or conditions that might have impeded progress, or analyzing patterns and trends of disease incidence in order to improve operational planning. New procedures incorporating new rules and targets emerged, and when they proved effective, the methods were rapidly disseminated in the program. The cycles of learning and adaptation repeated, so that standard procedures, targets, and indicators evolved continuously to fit the specifics of the local task environment, and often became more stringent as the programs advanced and as more experience and knowledge accumulated.

Control was central to the program: control of the quality of the vaccine; control of the operational procedures and targets to carry out mass vaccination, surveillance, and containment measures; control of the reporting procedures to ensure that reliable information was available in time to solve problems as they arose; and control of the assessment procedures to provide an independent and realistic evaluation of a campaign as it was being implemented. The specification of a structure of rules and routines that provided management control was particularly vital in an international program being waged by numerous countries in very different parts of the world. One principle underlying the design of control was to seek simplicity: "Simple devices, simple procedures, and simple instructions are especially critical in programs where large numbers of people are involved in tasks that demand disciplined performance—as good epidemiology does. Uncomplicated technology and straight-forward procedures lend themselves far more effectively to success in high pressure situations under difficult conditions" (Hopkins 1989, 129). Yet, paradoxical as it may seem, control was effective because it kept an open heart and an open mind. Procedures and rules, though carefully defined at a general level, were interpreted and elaborated into field tactics and targets by adjusting them to a complex variety of indigenous cultures, religions, health systems, and governmental structures (Brilliant 1985). Experimentation and improvisation were encouraged as necessary tactics of learning and getting things done. Shortcuts that bypassed standard procedures, simplifications that cut costs or saved time, and people who skipped over formal levels in the hierarchy were all tolerated and recognized as legitimate responses justified by their ends.

Finally, the smallpox program was also a triumph of effective *information management.* The surveillance system, containment system, and assessment system, which were central to the program, were all, in essence, information systems. Information needs were clearly defined and derived from specified procedures and targets. Soon after its inception, the program avoided the trap of going only for easy-to-collect data about program inputs (such as the number of vaccinations), which measured effort not results, and moved its focus to data about program outcomes (trends of the disease incidence). Information gathering was comprehensive, involving participants at all levels of the program, including local villagers and community leaders. A long-standing problem was the gross underreporting of smallpox cases. Incentives were offered to encourage reporting, and these were designed to capture accurate data, rather than data that people thought the program managers wanted to see. Since accurate and timely information reporting lies at the heart of the containment strategy, a major organizational step was the separation of the surveillance and containment functions in order to avoid a conflict of interests:

Health workers are expected to demonstrate good results. Like all humans, they tend to find evidence which supports expectations, and to avoid evidence that doesn't. Workers responsible for controlling a disease [the containment function] will tend to understate its incidence [the surveillance function]. The separation of surveillance and control functions proved to be important. (Siffin 1977, 1)

Information use was sensitive and expeditious. Data collected were analyzed to discern patterns of incidence and spread, sometimes employing sophisticated methods from operations research. Unbiased minds used the data to test hypotheses which challenged existing beliefs. Where warranted by the information, shifts in strategy and operations were willingly implemented. Significant findings and innovations were promptly disseminated and shared with others in the program through periodic review meetings, conferences, and newsletters and other publications. Effective information management was the glue that held together the cycles of interpretation, innovation, action, and feedback, which moved the program toward its remarkable achievement.

I. CONCEPTUALIZING ORGANIZATIONAL KNOWING AS THEORY AND PROCESS

Organizations use information in three strategic modes: to make sense of its environment, to create new knowledge, and to make decisions. Sense making creates a framework of shared meanings and purpose, which gives identity and value to the activities of the organization. Sense making also frames the perception of problems or opportunities that the organization needs to work on. Dealing with problems and opportunities often creates occasions for decision making, and when the problems are complex and novel, they may require the creation of new knowledge. Knowledge creating depends on the tacit knowledge of individuals and groups, and on the knowledge links and alliances that they and the organization have developed internally and externally with other partners. The results of knowledge creating are new innovations or an expansion of the organization's capabilities. Decision making is structured by rules and routines, and guided by preferences that are based on a shared understanding of the purpose and goals of the organization. Where new capabilites or innovations are available, they introduce new alternatives and enlarge the problem search space. Decision making selects a course of action that is expected to perform well (or well enough) along the dimensions of the preferences. The processes of sense making, knowledge creating, and decision making constitute the main information activities of what we will call a knowing organization.

In this chapter we approach our conceptualization of organizational knowing in three stages. First, we reflect on organizations as theories of action, theories that provide the norms, strategies, and assumptions which underlie an organization's task and social behaviors. Second, we enumerate the properties of organizational knowing as a social process that is mediated and situated in a socially distributed activity system. Finally, we examine the general structure of organizational knowing in terms of the levels and cycles of feedback and learning, in which organizational knowing takes place.

The Organization as Theory of Action

Organizational members collectively perform complex tasks in complex environments. Individual behaviors and organizational practices are defined by a framework of goals, expectations, and learned methods, a framework that, in effect, serves as a theory of action. Argyris and Schön (1978) define an organization's ***theory of action*** as including its:

- Norms for corporate performance (for example, norms for margin of profit and for return on investment)
- Strategies for achieving norms (for example, strategies for plant location and for process technology)

- Assumptions which bind strategies and norms together (for example, the assumption that maintenance of a high rate of return on investment depends on the continual introduction of new technologies)

(Argyris and Schön 1978, 14–15)

An organization's theory of action may be deduced in two ways. First, an examination of the formal documents of an organization, such as its organizational charts, policy statements, job descriptions, and archives, yields an *espoused theory,* which the organization wishes to project to the outside world and to its members. Second, an observation of the actual behaviors of the organization may suggest that members act according to a different set of rules and assumptions, reflecting an alternative *theory-in-use,* which may not be consistent with the espoused theory. Argyris and Schön suggest that the theory-in-use is often tacit, and may remain tacit because its incompatibility with espoused theory is undiscussable, or because members are not able to articulate the elements of the theory-in-use. Nevertheless, each person in the organization constructs a partial representation of the theory-in-use of the whole, a "private image," in order to understand how her or his activity and identity relate to the overall organizational context. These private images make references to shared representations of organizational theory-in-use—"public maps" such as those depicting work flow, operating procedures, and compensation standards.

An organization learns by constructing, testing, and restructuring its theories of action. Individuals are frequently the agents of changing organizational theory-in-use:

> They act on their images and on their shared maps with expectations of patterned outcomes, which their subsequent experience confirms or disconfirms. When there is a mismatch of outcome to expectation (error), members may respond by modifying their images, maps, and activities so as to bring expectations and outcomes back into line. (Argyris and Schön 1978, 18)

Organizational learning takes place when members respond to changes in the environment by detecting errors and correcting the errors through modifying strategies, assumptions, or norms. The altered strategies, assumptions, or norms are then stored in the organization's memory, becoming part of the private images and public maps. Two modes of organizational learning are possible. Learning is *single loop* when the modification of organizational action is sufficient to correct the error without challenging the validity of existing norms. In other words, the central features of the current organizational theory-in-use are preserved. It is single loop because a single feedback loop between detected outcomes and action is adjusted so as to keep performance within the range set by organizational norms (Fig. 6–1). The goal of single-loop learning is therefore to increase organizational effectiveness within current norms for

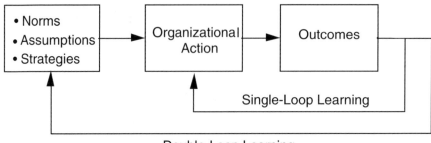

FIGURE 6–1. Single- and double-loop learning

performance (maintaining current objectives for product quality, sales, or task execution).

There are occasions when attempting to correct deviations within existing norms may not work, revealing instead conflicting requirements. Consider a firm whose current norms include pursuing high growth in sales and maintaining predictabililly in its operations. A new innovation from the research laboratory holds the promise of generating substantial sales but would require the firm to adopt new production methods and enter unfamiliar markets. A conflict arises between the existing norms of high sales and predictability. In this case, error correction requires the restructuring of the organizational norms themselves, which in turn necessitates a restructuring of strategies and assumptions associated with these norms. Learning here is *double loop* because a double feedback loop connects error detection not only to organizational action but also to the norms (Fig. 6–1). The goal of double-loop learning is therefore to ensure organizational growth and survivability by resolving incompatible norms, setting new priorities, or restructuring norms and their related strategies and assumptions. While single-loop learning is adaptive and is concerned with coping, double-loop learning is generative learning and creates new private images and public maps. The smallpox eradication program provides another example of double-loop learning: responding to new evidence from the field, the program restructured its norm or objective from carrying out mass vaccination to eradicating the disease itself. The new priority required new strategies and assumptions, which were quickly developed (again by learning from field practices), stored in organizational memory, and disseminated (through newsletters, publications, meetings).

There are three aspects of Argyris and Schön's discussion of organizational learning that are especially germane to our conceptualization of organizational knowing. First, *all organizations develop and subscribe to their own theories of action.* Theories of action enable organizations to accomplish complex tasks by establishing expectations of levels of performance, identifying methods and procedures to achieve those levels of performance, and postulating cause–effect relationships that in effect explain why what they are doing works. Second, *every organization maintains two versions of its theory of action.* The espoused theory is that by which the organization projects and explains itself publicly to outsiders and internally to its members. It is useful for encoding past learning and experience, sustaining legitimacy, and inducting new staff. The espoused theory contains the formal, the explicit, and the codified, and is therefore related to the recorded memories, the explicit knowledge, and the written-down rules and procedures that we encountered in our discussion of sense making, knowledge creating, and decision making. The theory-in-use, on the other hand, is that which is revealed in the actions and behaviors of the organization and its members. It is important because it provides the basis for all individual action and how the action relates to that of others. The theory-in-use is inherently informal, tacit, and often uncodifiable, and is therefore related to the enactments, tacit knowledge, and heuristics and shortcuts that we saw organizations employ as they make sense, make knowledge, and make decisions. Third, *each organization must continually construct, test, and restructure its theory of action if it is to learn and adapt (and thus survive) in a changing environment.* Again, there are two modes of learning. In single-loop learning, the organization corrects for anomalies in performance by adjusting its actions without causing any change to its theory of action (its norms, assumptions, and strategies). In today's complex and dynamic environments, single-loop learning is insufficient, and few organizations can continue to operate by clinging on to an unchanging theory of action. In double-loop learning, adapting to anomalies involves restructuring the norms themselves, which in turn requires their associated strategies and assumptions to be modified. A new theory of action emerges. True organizational learning therefore requires members to reach back to their assumptions and beliefs, objectively appraise their content and validity in the light of current conditions and new evidence, restructure or reject norms and aspirations that are no longer viable, and reconfigure new objectives and relearn new methods to achieve them.

There are two other asides that will parallel our subsequent elaboration of organizational knowing. Argyris and Schön make the interesting observation that double-loop learning is necessarily conflictual, requiring participants to expose and confront their conflicts in order to understand and resolve them. As we will elaborate, the activities of sense making, knowledge creating, and decision making each generate their own internal tensions, and the general process of organizational knowing involves navigating points of balance through these fields of strain.

Furthermore, Argyris and Schön also point out that while their model focuses on error detection and error correction,

---

. . . there is a domain of organizational knowing which lies, as it were, between error detection and error correction. In order to function as agents of organizational learning, individuals must set problems, construct models of organizational situations, and frame interpretations of error and anomaly. Their models, pictures, problem settings and interpretations display characteristic strategies for naming, framing, grouping, and describing the phenomena of organizational life. . . . we believe that [these] modes of organizational knowing are centrally involved in processes of organizational learning. An organization's capacity to correct error depends, in considerable measure, on its members' ways of constructing the problems reflected by error. (Argyris and Schön 1978, 317)

This allusion to the additional modes of framing and interpreting problem situations suggests a difference in scope between organizational knowing and organizational learning: organizational knowing begins with an analysis of how sense making, by bracketing experience and enacting situations, drives the dynamics of organizational knowing and adaptation.

Organizational Knowing as Social Process

The use of the "knowing organization" instead of, say, the "knowledge organization" in this book is an attempt to move from a conceptualization of knowledge as object or thing that has to be acquired toward a broader view of knowing as an ongoing process of social construction and collective action that is embedded in organizational tasks, relationships, and tools. Organizational knowing combines sensing, knowing, and doing into continuous cycles of interpretation, innovation, and initiating action. Since knowing is bound up with individual and collective doing—doing that actuates mental, material, and social resources (including language, tools, and roles)—we analyze organizational knowing from the point of view of activity theory, as processes that develop in *socially distributed activity systems* (Engeström 1991; Blackler 1993, 1995). Activity theory, with its foundations laid by the Russian psychologist Vygotsky (1978), sought to avoid the dichotomies between thought and action, and between individuals and society, that characterized Western theory. Acitivity theory examines the nature of practical activities in terms of their social origins and the structure of activity systems in which people collaborate, and explores the relationships between thought, behavior, individual actions, and collective practices (Blackler 1993). In a contemporary reading of the theory, Engeström applies its principles to an analysis of human activity systems. Engeström (1991) states that "an activity system comprises the individual practitioner, the colleagues and co-workers of the workplace community, the conceptual and practical tools, and the shared objects as a unified dynamic whole" (p. 267). The first triangle in Fig. 6–2 shows Engeström's conceptualization of the human activity system. A central feature of the system is the way that *multiple mediations* modulate interactions between the elements: tools and concepts mediate the interactions between the individual and her context; traditions, rituals, and rules mediate between the individual and her community; and a division of labor mediates between the community and the actions of its members (Engeström 1991; Blackler 1993). It is within this framework of mediated interactions between subject, object (of activity), and community that the activity system develops coherence, partly by predefining goals according to its rules and division of labor, and partly by recreating and modifying goals through the actions of participants. An activity system does not exist alone, but interacts with a network of other activity systems. It may, for instance, receive rules and instruments from the management activity system and produce outcomes for customer activity systems. The intrusion and internalization of external forces cause imbalance and induce conflict in the activity system: "The activity system is constantly working through tensions and contradictions within and between its elements. In this sense, an activity system is a virtual disturbance- and innovation-producing machine" (Engeström 1991, 269). The appearance of tensions provides the occasion for change and inquiry, as participants engage the contradiction in collective interpretation and negotiation in order to arrive at new ways of knowing and doing.

The second triangle in Fig. 6–2 shows Blackler's (1993) application of Engeström's model to represent organizations as activity systems. For the organizational setting, Blackler shows members as agents [subjects], working and interacting with colleagues and other groups [community], according to routines so as to produce outcomes [object of activity]. The mediating elements of instrument, rules, and division of labor are replaced, respectively, by tools and concepts, explicit and implicit rules, and organization and role structures. Organizations are therefore mediated systems in which active agents engage in collective activities (Blackler 1993).

To summarize, using the principles of activity theory and human activity systems as developed by Engeström (1991), five key properties of organizational knowing may be identified:

1. *The concept of activity.* People do not just think, they act on the world and they do this collectively. "Activity" is a highly appropriate concept for organization theory. It draws attention to the social origins of motives and helps to explain the overall coherency of different actions.

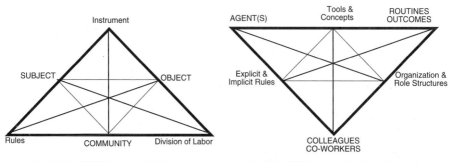

Engeström's (1991) Human Activity Model   **Blacker's (1993) Organizational Activity Model**

FIGURE 6–2. Human activity and organizational activity models (Reprinted from "Knowledge & the Theory of Organizations" by Blackler published in *J. Management Studies,* 1993 by permission of Blackwell Publishers Ltd.)

2. *The nature of activity systems.* Mediating mechanisms, such as tools, language, social rules, and the division of labor, transform the relationships between individuals, communities, and shared endeavor. Such factors are interwoven in a complex web of mutual interactions.

3. *Active participation.* Novices learn by participating in activities and activity systems. This is a creative, interpretative process. Such learning is likely to be tacit rather than explicit. Collective learning occurs when communities construct new conceptions of their activities and develop new activity systems.

4. *The significance of history.* Activities are socially and historically located. They evolve over time.

5. *The prevalence of incoherence and dilemma.* Incoherence, inconsistency, conflict, and dilemma are integral features of activity systems. They offer major opportunities for personal and collective learning.

(Blackler 1993, 875)

Blackler points out how compatible these properties are with the suggestion that "meaning is enacted, acquired through social participation, is negotiated, and is manifest in the doing as much as in the deciding" and with the view that "behavior is characterized by improvisation and creativity rather than by detailed preplanning, and that knowhow is not just a feature of individuals but is distributed within a community" (p. 875).

The objectification of knowledge sees it as a "thing" that is universal and permanent, and which could be achieved by transferring it from experts, buying equipment or rights, or studying books and manuals. It asks the question, "What knowledge does the organization need to acquire?" An activity view of knowing sees knowing as being tied to doing, and doing as leading to the making of sense in the context of the organization and its environment. It asks a different question, "How are systems of knowing and doing changing, and how should the organization respond?"

Rather than studying knowledge as something individuals or organizations supposedly have, activity theory studies knowing as something that they do and analyzes the dynamics of the systems through which knowing is accomplished. Recast in this way, knowing in all its forms is analyzed as a phenomenon which is: (a) Manifest in systems of language, technology, collaboration and control (i.e. it is *mediated*); (b) Located in time and space and specific to particular contexts (i.e. it is *situated*); (c) Constructed and constantly developing (i.e. it is *provisional*); and (d) Purposive and object-oriented (i.e. it is *pragmatic*). (Blackler 1995, 1039; emphasis added)

Furthermore, since different elements of a social system vary in their significance and their access to power, knowing is also ***contested.*** Tersely, then, organizational knowing is mediated, situated, provisional, pragmatic, and contested.

Organizational knowing is mediated. Organizational knowing is a property of organizational activity systems, which consist of individuals acting as agents, colleagues and groups, and routines or objects of activity. Knowing is the outcome of interactions between these three elements. The interactions are not direct, but are mediated through formal and informal rules, roles, and structural relationships, and the use of tools and technology (Fig. 6–2). Rules, roles, and technologies may be predefined by the organization, but may also emerge from the practices and conversations of the participants. New forms of collaboration, communication, and control are being shaped by new economic and organizational structures and by the use of information and communication technologies. Thus computer-based information systems mediate between individuals and their routines for seeking and using information. Communication technologies alter traditional roles and relationships within and between work groups and entire organizations.

Organizational knowing is situated. It is located in space and time, and it interacts with the physical and social particulars of the setting in which activity takes place. People's actions are constrained as well as prompted by their immediate physical and social surroundings, which orient or position them to exploit some contingencies of the task environment, while avoiding others (Suchman 1987). At the same time, their actions modify the environment, and by doing so create new avenues of interaction. Organizational knowing also depends on people's interpretation of the context in which they work, including their perception of and feelings toward the community of practice in which they belong and develop skills (Brown and Duguid 1991).

Organizational knowing is provisional. New knowing is always tentative, as theory and hypotheses are continuously constructed, tested, and restructured. Routines, rules, and roles are not timeless, but are constantly revised and reconfigured. The intrusion of forces from outside an activity system and the subsequent attempts at assimilation and internalization can induce tensions and contradictions. New ways of knowing and doing emerge as a result of resolving these tensions through dialogue, experimentation, and collective inquiry. The new knowing is still fluid, to be refined again by the next cycle of change.

Organizational knowing is pragmatic. It produces action that is oriented toward goals, directed at the object of the activity. Collective action is driven by the conceptions people have of the object of their activities (Blackler 1995). Again, information technologies are affecting how people perceive and relate to their objects of work, but the effects vary depending on the role assigned to technology. On the one hand, computerized information systems are known to obscure work content or increase the distance between the individual and the work object. On the other hand, information systems have the capacity to "informate" work environments, offering richer views of their work and opportunities to develop intellective skills (Zuboff 1988).

Organizational knowing is contested. Since knowledge is often used as a power resource, organizational knowing is laced with political overtones. Activity systems are social systems, and different elements of the social system vary in their ability to exert influence. Thus issues such as access to information, tools, and training, as well as participation in committees, dialogues, and decision making, become potential loci of conflict. Conflicts are also to be expected within and between the new generation of symbolic analysts (Reich 1991) and problem solvers, and the established ranks of professionals and managers (Blackler 1995).

The General Structure of Organizational Knowing

There have been many attempts to model the process of organizational change at a general, systemic level. March and Olsen (1976) sketch a general representation of organizational choice, which has become an archetypal model of organizational learning and adaptation. The model, shown in Fig. 6–3, shows the complete cycle of organizational choice as a closed loop of four connections:

1. The cognitions and preferences held by individuals affect their behavior.
2. The behavior (including participation) of individuals affects organizational choices.
3. Organizational choices affect environmental acts (responses).
4. Environmental acts affect individual cognitions and preferences.

(March and Olsen 1976, 13)

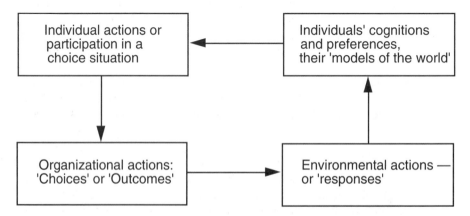

FIGURE 6–3. Complete cycle of organizational choice (March and Olsen 1976, 13)

Although March and Olsen feel that the model is "too simple and too seductive," it does display two general structural features that are useful for subsequent model building. First, organizational choice and adaptation take place across multiple levels—in this case the three levels of individual, organization, and environment. March and Olsen's model shows that environmental responses are interpreted through the eyes of individuals' minds, implies the role of action or enactment in ambiguous situations, and suggests that organizational action leads to environmental response (although the same action may have different responses at different times). Second, the process is a closed cycle involving detection, response, feedback, and adaptation. Detection and recognition of a need for choice depends on the individuals' "models of the world" that define saliency and the allocation of attention. Response is both individual (the individual participates in a choice situation) and collective. Feedback may be unclear, since it may be difficult to trace outcomes to organizational actions. Adaptation occurs when the individual observes events, changes beliefs in the light of experience, and presumably improves behavior on the basis of this feedback.

March and Olsen's conceptual model is implicit in many subsequent studies. For our purposes, we highlight the model developed by Meyer (1982) based on his field study of how voluntary hospitals in the San Francisco area responded to a crisis. In May 1975 a major malpractice insurer abruptly ended the group coverage of 4000 northern California doctors, offering to reinsure them at new rates, which were nearly four times higher. Hospital anesthesiologists went on a strike that was supported by most surgeons and referral physicians, causing alarming declines in hospital admissions, occupancy levels, and cash flows. The strike lasted one month, during which some hospitals lost more than half a million dollars. Based on an analysis of nineteen hospitals affected by the strike, including detailed case studies of three that showed surprising adaptations, Meyer developed a model of how organizations adapt to severe environmental jolts. As shown in Fig. 6–4, when the jolt occurs, organizations select and attend to stimuli according to their theories of action. Theories of action are composed of the organization's strategy, norms, and assumptions, in other words, its strategy and ideology. Organizational response is mediated by the routines and action programs that are part of its structure, and constrained by the amount of slack, or financial, personnel, as well as knowledge resources that the organization possesses. Organizational outcomes may lead to resilience or retention. Resilience occurs when the organization absorbs the jolt's impacts and reduces deviations. Retention occurs when new causal relationships are discovered, and the theory of action is restructured.

The model may be illustrated with one of Meyer's three case studies. Community Hospital (a pseudonym) had a reputation for being innovative, pioneering new services in outpatient surgery and ambulatory care, setting up a sexual-assault harassment center, and using computers and television to communicate with satellite family-care centers. Organizationally, Community Hospital was a loose federation of diverse groups which coalesced around

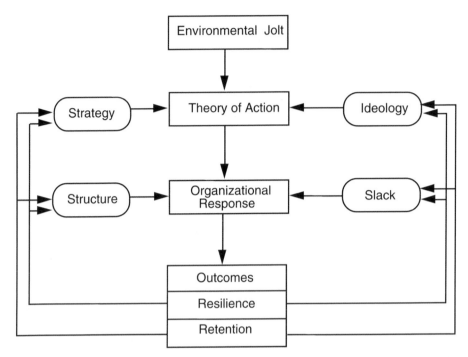

FIGURE 6–4. Organizational adaptation cycle (Reprinted from "Adapting to Environmental Jolts" by Meyer published in *Administrative Science Quarterly,* vol. 27 no. 4 by permission of *Administrative Science Quarterly.*)

particular programs or patient groups. One physician described the hospital as a chaotic place that reminded him of a mob. Meyer added that it was "an ideologically charged mob that valued innovation, pluralism, and professional autonomy" (Meyer 1982, 526). Work was coordinated and resources were allocated through informal, ad hoc agreements, which were "legitimated by shared values and cultivated by Community's administrator, who purposefully avoided codifying procedures, restricting information flows and freezing relationships between subunits" (p. 526). Community Hospital was able to anticipate the insurance crisis early and adapt to the strike action comprehensively and quickly. The administration saw the possibility of a strike two months before it happened. The administrator, the chief of surgery, and the head of outpatient services jointly developed a scenario that projected the consequences of the strike, including a loss of all surgical patients and half the medical patients, occupancy dropping to 40 or 50 percent, and outpatient services increasing 50 percent. The scenario was distributed to all departmental heads six weeks before the strike, and the heads were required to analyze the impact and work out contingency plans. When the strike hit and occupancy sank to 40 percent, departments implemented their contingency plans with little alteration. Cost cutting was so effective that the hospital actually made money during the strike. After the strike, occupancy returned to normal levels, and staff that had been laid off returned to work. Meyer's analysis of the case using his model showed that "Community's leaders perceived the jolt as an upheaval in the environment, and they interpreted the upheaval as an opportunity for a drill, testing members' adaptive flexibility. The pluralistic ideology gave rise to an ad hoc coalition that constructed accurate projections of the strike's impact on the hospital. Supervisors planned for this contingency adroitly because authority was customarily delegated to foster novel solutions to unfamiliar problems" (p. 531). Meyer's model is also interesting in that it attempts to bring together elements of sense making (theory of action as interpretative lens), knowledge creating (professional expertise as organizational slack), and decision making (contingency planning as organizational response).

II. ORGANIZATIONAL KNOWING

Organizations process and use information in the three arenas of sense making, knowledge creating, and decision making. Organizational knowing emerges when the three modes of information use are connected to each other to constitute a larger network of processes that continuously generate meaning, learning, and doing. In this section a model of the knowing organization is developed in two stages. First, we compare sense making, knowledge creating, and decision making and highlight properties and relationships that are important in organizational knowing. Second, we present two overlapping sets of linkages that connect sense making, knowledge creating, and decision making—one set is based on the cognitive, affective, and action-based resources that are employed in each mode, and the other is based on the outcomes and outputs of each mode of information processing. In the next chapter we probe a number of dichotomies that characterize the processes of organizational knowing, and suggest that the confrontation, interpretation, and collective resolution of these tensions is the key to adaptive learning. Finally, we examine the role of information management in supporting organizational knowing.

Three Modes of Information Use

Chapter 3, 4, and 5 analyzed how organizations use information to construct meaning, create knowledge, and make decisions. The principal processes, modes, and relationships in each of these arenas of information use are summarized in Table 6–1.

Sense making is precipitated by a change or difference in the environment that creates discontinuity in the flow of experience engaging the people and activities of an organization (Weick 1979b). These discontinuities provide the raw data from the environment which have to be made sense of. The sense making recipe is to interpret the environment through connected sequences of enactment, selection, and retention (Weick 1995). In enactment, people ac-

TABLE 6–1. Comparison of Sense Making, Knowledge Creating, and Decision Making

Model	Process	Modes	Interactions/Resources
Sense Making	Environmental Change → Enactment, seclection, retention → Enacted interpretations "Looking backward": Retrospective sense making	• Belief-driven processes • Action-driven processes	
Knowledge Creating	Knowledge-gap situation → Tacit, explicit, cultural knowledge → Knowledge conversion, building, linking → New knowledge "Looking across many levels": Multilevel learning from individuals, groups, organizations	• Knowledge conversion • Knowledge building • Knowledge linking	
Decision Making	Choice situation → Alternatives, outcomes, preferences → Rules, routines → Decisions "Looking ahead": Goal directed, future oriented	• Rational • Process • Political • Anarchic	

tively construct the environments which they attend to by bracketing, rearranging, and labeling portions of the experience, thereby converting raw data from the environment into equivocal data to be interpreted. In selection, people choose meanings that can be imposed on the equivocal data by overlaying past interpretations as templates to the current experience. Selection produces an enacted environment that is meaningful in providing cause–effect explanations of what is taking place. In retention, the organization stores the products of successful sense making (enacted or meaningful interpretations) so that they may be retrieved in the future.

Organizational sense making can be driven by beliefs or by actions (Weick 1995). In belief-driven processes, people start from an initial set of beliefs that are sufficiently clear and plausible, and use them as nodes to connect more and more information into larger structures of meaning. People may use beliefs as expectations to guide the choice of plausible interpretations, or they may argue about beliefs and their relevance to current experience, especially when beliefs and cues are contradictory. In action-driven processes, people start from their actions and grow their structures of meaning around them, by modifying the structures in order to give significance to those actions. People may create meaning in order to justify actions that are visible, deliberate, and irreversible (committing actions), or they may create meaning in order to explain actions that have been taken to induce changes in the environment (manipulating actions).

A general metaphor for sense making is that of people and organizations "looking backward," retrospectively making sense of events and actions that have already taken place by enacting and selecting meaningful interpretations. Sense making is the outcome of the dynamic, ongoing interactions between three elements: beliefs, enactments, and interpretations. People's *beliefs* shape their perceptions of what is significant and should be attended to. Their beliefs and expectations influence their *enactments,* that is, how they bracket data and act or create features of the environment to attend to. Enacted *interpretations* of successful sense making are stored and, in turn, reinforce or modify beliefs. The three elements are placed in a triangle in Table 6–1, both to reflect their interdependent three-way relationships and to remind us that these relationships are played out in activity systems of actors, communities, and routines, mediated by concepts, roles, and rules. (See Blackler's and Engeström's representations of activity systems as triangular relationships in Fig. 6–2.)

Knowledge creating is precipitated by a situation that identifies gaps in the existing knowledge of the organization or the work group. Such knowledge gaps stand in the way of solving a technical or task-related problem, designing a new product or service, or taking advantage of an opportunity. An organization possesses three kinds of knowledge: tacit knowledge embedded in the expertise and experience of individuals and groups; explicit or rule-based knowledge codified in organizational rules, routines, and procedures; and cultural knowledge expressed in the assumptions, beliefs, and norms used by members to assign value and significance to new information or knowledge. New knowledge is created by knowledge conversion (Nonaka and Takeuchi 1995), knowledge building (Leonard-Barton 1995), and knowledge linking (Badaracco 1991; Wikström and Normann 1994). In *knowledge conversion* (Nonaka and Takeuchi 1995) the organization continuously creates new knowledge by converting between the personal, tacit knowledge of individuals who develop creative insight, and the shared, explicit knowledge by which the organization develops new products and innovations. Tacit knowledge is shared and externalized through dialogue that uses metaphors and analogies. New concepts are created, and the concepts are justified and evaluated according to their fit with organizational intention. Concepts are tested and elaborated by building archetypes or prototypes. Finally, concepts which have been created, justified, and modeled are moved to other levels of the organizaton to generate new cycles of knowledge creation. In *knowledge building* (Leonard-Barton 1995) the organization identifies and nurtures activities that build up knowledge which strengthens the organization's distinctive core capabilities, enabling them to grow over time. These knowledge-building activities are: shared problem solving, experimenting and prototyping, implementing and integrating new processes and tools, and importing knowledge. Individuals with diverse signature skills work together on solving a problem. Through experimentation and prototyping, the organization extends its existing capabilities and builds new ones for the future. Successful implementation of new tools and processes requires users and technology to mutually adapt and to complement each other. Knowledge about the technology as well as the market is imported from outside the organization and absorbed. In *knowledge linking* (Badaracco 1991) the organization forms intimate learning alliances with other organizations in order to tranfer knowledge that is embedded in the specialized relationships, work cultures, and operating styles of the partner organization. Wikström and Normann (1994) see an organization as a knowledge-creating value star at the center of many incoming flows of knowledge from suppliers, customers, and other partners. Knowledge is transformed into value not only within the organization, but also through knowledge-based interactions with its customers, suppliers, and other partners.

A general metaphor for knowledge creation is that of "looking across many levels," since new knowledge is created by sharing and shifting knowledge across many organizational levels, including individuals, groups, and other organizations. New knowledge is the outcome of the continuous interaction between the three categories of organizational knowledge: cultural knowledge, tacit knowledge, and explicit knowledge. As we noted, *cultural knowledge* supplies the assumptions and beliefs with which people explain reality and recognize the importance or value of new knowledge. New knowledge may be tacit, explicit, or derived from external sources. *Tacit, informal knowledge* often provides the creative impetus that drives the beginning of a new idea or concept, whereas *explicit, formal knowledge* is in a form that can be tested and implemented in models or prototypes. Knowledge creation comes about through the constant cross leveling and cross pollination of tacit and explicit knowledge in a context established by the organization's cultural knowledge.

Decision making is precipitated by a choice situation, an occasion in which the organization is expected to select a course of action. Completely rational decision making involves identifying alternatives, projecting the outcomes of each alternative, and evaluating the alternatives and their outcomes according to known preferences or objectives. These information-gathering and information-processing requirements are beyond the capabilities of any organization or any individual. Depending on the level of goal ambiguity or goal conflict, and the level of technical uncertainty, an organization copes by adopting one of four modes of decision making. In the *boundedly rational mode,* when goal and technical clarity are relatively high, choice is simplified by performance programs (March and Simon 1993,1958) and standard operating procedures (Cyert and March 1992,1963), which execute the search and decision rules and routines that the organization has learned. In the *process mode* (Mintzberg, Raisinghani, and Théorêt 1976), when goals are strategic and clear, but the technical methods to attain them are uncertain, decision making becomes a dynamic process marked by many interruptions and iterations. Nevertheless the process shows a general structure: it begins with the recognition and diagnosis of the problem, followed by the development of alternatives through searching for ready-made solutions or designing custom-made ones, and ends with the evaluation and selection of an alternative that has to be authorized or approved. In the *political mode* (Allison 1971), when goals are contested by various interest groups and technical certainty is high within groups, decisions and actions are the results of the bargaining among players pursuing their own interests and manipulating their available instruments of influence. Political decision making may then be likened to game playing, in which players take up positions, stands, and influence, and make their moves according to rules and their bargaining strengths. In the *anarchic mode* (Cohen, March, and Olsen 1972), when goal and technical uncertainty are both high, decision situations consist of relatively independent streams of problems, solutions, participants, and choice opportunities. A decision happens through chance and timing, when problems, solutions, participants, and choices coincide; and when solutions are attached to problems, and problems to choices by participants who have the time and energy to do so.

A general metaphor for decision making would be that organizations are "looking ahead," since most choice behavior is goal directed, and being (at least intendedly) rational implies attempting to project future outcomes in order to make a choice at the present time. Decisions are the results of dynamic interactions between three elements: preferences, routines, and rules. Individuals, groups, and organizations possess *preferences* and premises which guide the way they perceive and frame decisions, and evaluate and choose between alternatives. Preferences are embedded into or are worked out through various forms of organizational *routines,* including those that support task performance, political bargaining, and moving a decision process along. Choice behavior is also guided by *rules* that specify appropriate behavior, the allocation of attention, participation in choice situations, as well as the wielding of political influence. When existing patterns of behavior fail to perform, the organization modifies its decision, search, and attention rules in an attempt to adapt.

The making of meaning, knowledge, and decisions is sometimes differentiated as being the work of disparate groups in the organization. Making sense of the external environment may be thought of as the primary function of upper management, whose principal managerial roles include disseminating and interpreting information from outside the organization, as well as maintaining liaisons with and representing the organization to the outside world (see, for example, Mintzberg 1973). The creation of technical knowledge is thought to be the specialized work of trained experts, frequently to be found toiling in research and development laboratories or product engineering departments. Knowledge is thus objectified as a proprietary resource of technical specialists. Decision making that moves the daily operations of the organization is thought to be the charge of the functional staff working in areas such as production, sales, finance, and personnel. In order to ensure efficiency and coordination, decisions are as much the product of policies, procedures, and plans as they are acts of human choice.

Each of the three information-processing modes is generally assumed to require its own information needs and uses, and to employ resources and processes unique unto itself. The needs and resources in each mode do not, or do not have to, connect with the resources used in the other modes. In this book we identify three levels of needs and resources common to all modes of organizational information processing: cognitive, affective, and situational. Information use in each mode is the result of interweaving cognitive, affective, and action-based resources to address information needs in these three domains. (Action-based resources are revealed or brought forth in the performing of an activity or task: they reflect situational needs, since the physical and social features of the setting prompt and constrain courses of action.) Thus upper managers as sense makers would draw upon their beliefs, aspirations, and past actions and outcomes to develop interpretations of environmental change. Technical staff as knowledge workers can produce new knowledge because they have acquired specialized know-how and intuition through years of training and practice, and they have developed the capacity to select, evaluate, and absorb new ideas from other specialized sources. Functional staff make decisions by relying on preferences, values, policies, and routines, which are relatively stable in the short run in order to reduce uncertainty and ambiguity. The overall impression is that the resources of sense making beliefs, technical knowledge, and decision rules are each distinctive with regard to their respective modes of information use.

In the model of the knowing organization being presented here, sense making, knowledge creating, and decision making are socially distributed activities that bridge many levels and functions in the organization. Thus sense making is collective, the result of communal dialogue that leads to the sharing of interpretations. The invention of new knowledge takes place not just in the laboratories, but also every time a person on the shop floor or in the field discovers a new way to solve a problem and shares it with others. Decision making receives inputs and influences from many sources in the organization, and is contingent on situational specifics such as who provides information to the decision, who are consulted, and who participates in the choice making.

Organizational Knowing Emerges from Sense making, Knowledge Creating, and Decision Making

Organizational knowing is the emergent property of the network of information-use processes through which the organization constructs shared meanings about its identity and activity; discovers, shares, and applies new knowledge; and initiates patterns of action through search, evaluation, and selection of alternatives. Although an organization processes information in the three modes of sense making, knowledge creating, and decision making, organizational knowing occurs when *the three modes of information genera-* *tion and use are linked together in a single, broader process by which the* *organization socially constructs meaning, learning, and doing.* Each mode of information use engages its distinctive cognitive, affective, and action-based (situational) needs and resources. Organizational knowing occurs when the resources in each mode of information use mesh with and complement the resources of the other modes. Organizations act on as well as adapt to the environment. The organization may act in response to or in anticipation of change in the environment, and it may also act to alter some aspect of the environment in order to make sense of it. Change introduces tension and con-tradictions, but it is precisely the confrontation and resolution of these tensions that provide the occasions for generating new understanding. Organizational knowing occurs when change-induced tensions are managed and exploited as opportunities for new knowing and doing. Coping with change may be local and piecemeal (or it may even be avoided altogether by, for example, denying or hiding the problem), or it may involve a basic restructuring of assumptions and norms that leads to new goals and strategies (double-loop learning).

Our discussions in this book suggest that for sense making, knowledge creating, and decision making to be integrated into one larger canvas of orga-nizational knowing, two related sets of linkages would be necessary. The first set is created by managing the cognitive, affective, and action-based resources employed in each mode of information use so that, where appropriate, they reinforce and enrich each other, and, where required, their divergences serve as starting points for new knowing and doing. The second set is created by establishing a continuous flow of information between the three modes, so that the outcome of information processing in one mode becomes the essential context and input to the information processing of another mode.

Consider the resources employed in each mode of information use, as summarized in the Interactions column of Table 6–1. The three triads repre-senting the interacting resources are of the general form illustrated in Fig. 6–5.

Affective, cognitive, and action-based (or "active") needs and resources

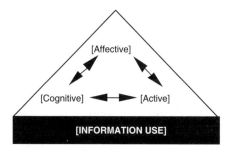

FIGURE 6–5. Cognitive, affective, active resources in information use

interact to influence the content and trajectory of information use. Affective resources are based on emotions which direct attention toward the favorable or the expected (or away from the unfavorable or dangerous), and help assign value and significance to information, events, and actions. Cognitive resources are activated in mental or intellectual activity as people attempt to reason, argue, or negotiate about the substance or significance of information. Action-based or active resources are those that are revealed or brought forth by doing, by performing shared tasks, or by carrying out a pattern of organizational responses. Their content is mediated by the particulars of the internal situation or the external environment in which that action or task is being executed.

In sense making, the resources represented by beliefs, interpretations, and enactments combine to construct meanings that make sense of the organization's environment. In knowledge creating, the resources of organizational values or intent, explicit knowledge, and tacit knowledge interact to generate and evaluate new knowledge and capabilities. In decision making, preferences, rules, and routines formalize organizational goals and learning so as to enable intendedly rational courses of action to be selected. If we look across these three modes, and connect the affective resources of each, we have a set of beliefs, values, and preferences, which propagate the assumptions, expectations, norms, criteria, and objectives by which organizational members determine the saliency of information and assess the value of alternatives. Viewed collectively, these beliefs, values, preferences, assumptions, and norms are elements of the ***organization's culture.*** Figure 6–6 suggests that the beliefs and mental models used in sense making, the norms and criteria (cultural knowledge) applied in knowledge creating, and the preferences and premises that guide decision making are all cut from the same cloth of the organization's culture. In the short term, beliefs, norms, and preferences that reinforce each other help the organization to perform, but in the longer term, contradictions and inconsistencies point to the need for change and adaptation.

If we likewise connect the cognitive resources from each mode of information use, we have a set of interpretations, explicit knowledge, and rules that are produced by the organization's sense making, knowledge-creating, and decision-making activities. Interpretations are often communicated to explain actions or events. Explicit knowledge is knowledge that has been formally

FIGURE 6–6. Organizational culture in information use

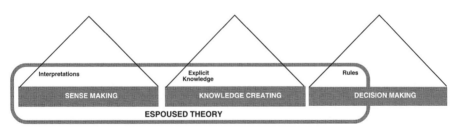

FIGURE 6–7. Espoused theory in information use

codified or documented. Rules are officially sanctioned and are reinforced by reward systems. Collectively, stored interpretations, documented knowledge, and institutionalized rules are elements of the ***espoused theory of action*** of the organization (Fig. 6–7). We suggest that espoused interpretations, codified knowledge, and formalized rules are all part of the public face of the organization, important for encoding and transferring learned experiences and for legitimizing its actions and existence to its internal and external constituencies. The organization uses resources from its espoused theory of action (stored interpretations, recorded knowledge, and institutionalized rules) to reason, argue, negotiate, present, and explain actions and events to external and internal stakeholders.

Finally, if we connect the action-based resources from each mode, we have a set of enactments, tacit knowledge, and routines. Enactments are actions imposed by the organization on the environment in order to help make sense of it. Tacit knowledge is developed by performing a task or immersing in a practice over time. Routines or action programs specify a general framework that simplifies performance in familiar situations, but within these routines individuals also use heuristics and shortcuts to improvise and deal with the specifics of each case. Taken together, enactments, task knowledge, and action routines are elements of the organization's ***theory-in-use*** (Fig. 6–8). We suggest that enactments, tacit expertise, and performance routines are all part of the corpus of organizational know-how that organizational members draw upon to make the organization work. The organization uses resources from its theory-in-use (enactments, tacit knowledge, and action routines) to make meaning and take action.

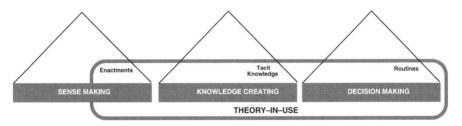

FIGURE 6–8. Theory-in-use and information use

As Argyris and Schön (1978) have emphasized, the espoused theory and theory-in-use are often inconsistent with each other, but this inherent contradiction is a necessary feature so that the organization may learn by constructing, testing, and restructuring its theories of action. Deeper, double-loop learning requires the organization not only to take remedial actions to correct errors, but also to reexamine the validity of its basic norms and assumptions critically, and to be prepared to modify existing strategies as a result. Error detection and error correction are mediated by a third "domain of organizational knowing" (Argyris and Schön 1978, 317), which supplies strategies for "naming, framing, grouping, and decribing the phenomena of organizational life." In our discussion here, organizational culture, by specifying beliefs, norms, and preferences, construct the environment in which inconsistencies between espoused theory and theory-in-use are worked out. Thus espoused theory and theory-in-use are both situated in the context of the organization's culture.

III. THE KNOWING CYCLE

The model of the knowing organization so far is largely a static description. To understand its dynamics, we need to consider the interactions between organizational culture, espoused theory, and theory-in-use. Although many patterns of interaction are possible, we focus on an archetypal configuration that we call "the knowing cycle," mainly because it illustrates clearly how sense making, knowledge creating, and decision making can work together to enable organizational learning and adaptation. In the knowing cycle, a continuous flow of information is maintained between sense making, knowledge creating, and decision making, so that the outcome of information use in one mode provides the elaborated context and the expanded resources for information use in the other modes, as shown in Fig. 6–9.

Through sense making, organizational members enact and negotiate beliefs and interpretations to construct shared meanings and common goals. *Shared meanings and purpose* are the result of sense making, and they constitute the framework for explaining observed reality, and for determining saliency and appropriateness. Shared meanings and purpose help to specify a shared *organizational agenda,* a set of issues that people in the organization agree on as being important to the well-being of the organization. While they may not agree about the content of a particular issue, and may adopt diverse positions on how it should be resolved, nevertheless there is collective recognition that these issues are salient to the organization. Shared meanings and purpose also help to define a collective *organizational identity,* or perhaps, more accurately, a set of multiple identities, since an organization assumes different identities in different situations. Defining an organizational identity establishes norms and expectations about the propriety, accountability, and legitimacy of the organization's choices and behaviors. A framework of shared meanings and purpose is therefore used by organizational members to assess

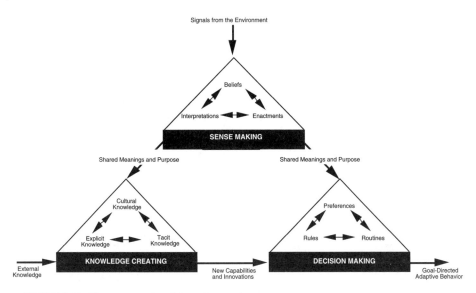

FIGURE 6–9. The organizational knowing cycle

(Note: Arrows in the figure do not imply one-directional sequence or causality. Figure depicts an interdependent and interacting network of information processes.)

consequentiality and appropriateness, and to reduce information ambiguity and uncertainty to a level that enables dialogue, choice, and action making. Where messages from the external environment are highly equivocal, shared meanings reduce ambiguity by helping members to select plausible interpretations. Where messages from the external environment are highly incomplete, shared meanings reduce uncertainty by supplying assumptions and expectations to fill in the voids. Shared meanings need to be continuously updated against new events and conditions. By allowing ambiguity and diversity in interpretations, an organization can constantly monitor its shared meanings against the environment to ensure that they are still valid.

Within the framework of its constructed meaning, agenda, and identity, the organization exploits current specializations or develops new capabilities in order to move toward its vision and goals. Movement may be blocked by gaps in the knowledge needed to bridge meaning and action. Gaps in knowledge may be about something that is lacking (such as a material with the desired properties, or a technique to perform an action); or they may be about something that is obstructing the way ahead (such as a problem to be solved, or an obstacle to be overcome). When the organization experiences gaps in its existing knowledge or limitations in its current capabilities, it initiates knowledge seeking and creating, set within parameters derived from an interpretation of the organization's goals, agendas, and priorities. Organizational members individually and collectively fabricate new knowledge by converting, sharing, and synthesizing their tacit and explicit knowledge, as well as by cross-linking knowledge from external individuals, groups and institutions. The outcome of knowledge creating is **new capabilites and innovations** that enhance existing competencies or build new ones; generate new products, services, or processes; or extend the range of viable organizational responses to a problem situation. The value of new knowledge is assessed locally by its ability to solve the problem at hand, as well as generally by its ability to enhance the organization's capabilities in the long run. New knowledge enables new forms of action but also introduces new forms of uncertainty. The risks and benefits of untested innovations and unpracticed capabilities are compared and evaluated by invoking rules and preferences in the process of organizational decision making.

Shared meanings and purposes, as well as new knowledge and capabilities converge on decision making as the activity leading to the selection and initiation of action. Shared meanings, agendas, and identities select the premises, rules, and routines that structure decision making. New knowledge and capabilities make possible new alternatives and outcomes, expanding the repertoire of available organizational responses. By structuring choice behavior through premises, rules, and routines, the organization simplifies decision making, codifies and transmits past learning, and proclaims competence and accountability. Rules and routines specify "rational" criteria for the evaluation of alternatives, "legitimate" methods for the allocation of resources, and "objective" conditions for distinguishing between normal states and novel situations that may necessitate the search for new rules.

Over time the organization has learned and codified a large number of rules and routines, so that choosing which rules to activate for a specific choice-making scenario is itself problematic. Shared meanings and understandings about the nature and needs of a particular situation are used to guide rule activation. Shared interpretations help select which rules to apply by answering the questions: "What kind of situation is this?" and "What rules do we have for dealing with this type of situation?" Shared interpretations may also select rules according to the criterion of appropriateness: "What kind of organization are we? What would be appropriate behavior for an organization like ours in a situation like this one?" Sometimes shared interpretations indicate that the situation is novel, where none of the learned rules seem to apply. When rules break down, the organization attempts to make new meaning in time to initiate action, effectively prototyping new rules to prompt choice making. The end result of this interaction between shared meaning (in interpretations and understandings) and shared learning (in rules and routines) is the execution of a pattern of actions that simultaneously constitutes the organization's attempt to move toward current goals and maintain current identity, as well as its attempt to adapt to changed conditions in the environment. In this sense, the outcome of decision making is **behavior that is both goal directed and adaptive.**

While each organization adjusts its behavior to perceived changes in the environment, its responses are diluted and diffracted by the concurrent actions of other actors that participate in the same arena. Thus each organization is reacting to the actions of other organizations that are also reacting to it. The resultant meshwork of interactions configures new patterns and new conditions that pose fresh ambiguities and uncertainties. A continuous stream of new events and equivocal cues necessitates iterative cycles of information processing. Where meanings or purpose change as a result of reinterpreting the environment, or where rules or routines are altered as a result of acquiring knowledge and understanding, the organization is adapting to variation and feedback in its environment.

The World Health Organization's smallpox eradication program exemplifies several of the defining properties of organizational knowing. As we described at the beginning of this chapter, the program continuously reinterpreted its objectives based on current evidence from the field, developed innovations and new knowledge that were instrumental in allowing the program to achieve its objectives, and implemented actions and procedures that afforded a high degree of control but also allowed room for local adaptation. This ongoing cycle of interpreting, innovating, and initiating action that enabled adaptive learning was the result of integrating the organization's sense-making, knowledge-creating, and decision-making activities. In sense making, the program was held together at its core by a shared sense of purpose. The common goal of eradicating smallpox, perceived as attainable, inspiring, and urgent, unified the diversity of national and local cultures that participated in the program. The shared purpose was amplified by detailed information about the epidemiology of the disease, laboratory diagnosis methods, operational approaches for vaccination and containment, health education, and a host of related subjects, all of which were published in the WHO smallpox handbook, the program's magna carta. Knowledge creating both in the research laboratories and in the field produced key innovations and new knowledge about the incidence of the disease that were pivotal to the program. One plank of the eradication strategy was mass vaccination, which required a new form of vaccine that would be potent, reliable, economical, and easy to administer. The innovations of the freeze-dried vaccine and the bifurcated needle for presenting the vaccine answered these needs. The other plank was the surveillance and containment of smallpox outbreaks, which required local knowledge about indigenous customs and practices, and how these may be taken advantage of in enforcing detection and isolation. This was where the knowledge of field workers was vital in inventing innovative measures that were genuinely effective because they leveraged local cultures and customs. The smallpox program established a system of rules, procedures, standards, and targets to regulate decision making in the implementation and concurrent evaluation of the various campaigns. The rules and routines provided for measurement and control, but at the same time, the formal system coexisted with an informal network of practices and relationships that deviated from the set norms, but were crucially effective in overcoming particular obstacles and expediting action. The results of each campaign were objectively assessed by independent teams, even as the campaign was in progress, thus providing feedback in time for corrective action. New experiences and practices learned by campaigns in other locales and countries were promptly disseminated through review meetings, conferences, and newsletters. In the smallpox program, the cycles of adaptation and learning depended on an unimpeded flow of accurate, timely, and actionable information that brought in current news about trends of disease incidence, the effectiveness of operational approaches, and new techniques and measures discovered in the field. Information needs were clearly understood and well defined, information gathering was thorough and efficient, and information use was managed so that analysis and interpretation of new data were accomplished in time to influence the course of action.

This chapter has examined the theory and process underlying the knowing organization. The next chapter describes the tensions that are inherent in these processes, and how the dynamics of balancing these tensions enable the knowing organization to be effective in the short term, and adaptive over the long term.

7

THE KNOWING ORGANIZATION II—
BALANCING TENSIONS AND
MANAGING INFORMATION

The growth of our knowledge is the result of a process closely resembling
what Darwin called "natural selection"; that is, the **natural selection of
hypothesis:** our knowledge consists, at every moment, of those hypotheses
which have shown their (comparative) fitness by surviving so far in their
struggle for existence; a competitive struggle which eliminates those
hypotheses which are unfit. . . . From the amoeba to Einstein, the growth of
knowledge is always the same: we try to solve our problems, and to obtain,
by a process of elimination, something approaching adequacy in our tentative
solutions.
—Karl Popper, 1979, Objective Knowledge: An Evolutionary Approach,
p. 261

Organizations are socially distributed activity systems of people, communities,
and activities that interact according to shared theories of action. Interactions
between individuals, groups, and patterns of action are mediated through rules,
roles, and tools that are partly predefined by the organization, but also grow
naturally from the social and technical practices of the activity system. New
forms of knowing and doing emerge when tensions between the old and new,
between change and stability, are confronted, interpreted, and resolved. New
forms of knowing and doing modify or create new theories of action, which
over time become ingrained in the rules, roles, and tools and concepts that
mediate interactions in the organization.

In our model of organizational knowing, sense making, knowledge creating, and decision making are linked by three constructs: (1) the framework of
shared meanings and purpose, developed by collective sense making, through
which members perceive and interpret reality; (2) the creation of new capabilities and innovations, developed through the conversion and linking of organi-

zational knowledge, which extend the repertory of organizational responses; and (3) the initiation of action, selected through formal and informal decision rules and routines, which move the organization toward its goals. While the three constructs hold the knowing cycle together, each construct is also characterized by its own contradictions, which contain the seeds for change and learning. In developing shared meanings, the organization balances the tension between ambiguity and clarity, and between diversity and consensus. In the creation of new knowledge, the organization shifts between the tacit and the explicit, and between the advantages of exploration and those of exploitation. In deciding and initiating action, the organization treads between improvisation and control, and between evolution and design. We examine these tensions in the following sections.

I. TENSIONS IN SENSE MAKING

Ambiguity and Clarity in Sense Making

The central problem in sense making is to reduce ambiguity. Ambiguity is the lack of clarity, but this opaqueness has more to do with the confusion of multiple, plausible meanings than with the absence of sufficient quantities of information. The lack of meaning drives sense making, while the lack of certainty drives information gathering: "In the case of ambiguity, people engage in sensemaking because they are confused by too many interpretations, whereas in the case of uncertainty, they do so because they are ignorant of any interpretations" (Weick 1995, 91). Ambiguity is perceived, and something is judged to be ambiguous when it appears to be unclear, complex, or paradoxical: "Ambiguity is perceived when a lack of clarity, high complexity, or a paradox makes multiple (rather than single or dichotomous) explanations plausible" (Martin 1992, 134).

Ambiguity permeates every aspect of the organization, obfuscating its goals, experience, and actions. March and Olsen (1976) identify four kinds of organizational ambiguity: the ambiguity of intention, the ambiguity of understanding, the ambiguity of history, and the ambiguity of organization. Ambiguity of intention results when the organization has inconsistent or ill-defined objectives. Ambiguity of understanding exists when there is lack of clarity about the technologies and processes of the organization, and when the environment is difficult to interpret. Cause and effect are disconnected, so that the organization is unable to link its actions to their consequences. Ambiguity of history exists when what has happened in the past is difficult to specify or comprehend. Recollection may be incomplete or distorted, and it may not be possible to define accurately what happened, why it happened, and whether it had to happen. Ambiguity of organization arises because participants vary the amount of attention and energy they devote to an issue, and their attention varies from issue to issue and from time to time. Together the four kinds of ambiguity relate to "what the organization intends to do, what is appropriate for the organization to do, what the organization has done in the past and why, and who in the organization is responsible for what the organization does" (Feldman 1991).

The task of sense making is therefore to reduce ambiguity and increase clarity sufficiently so that people can construct meaning about their identity and role in the organization, and about the actions and purpose of the institution. People reduce ambiguity by segmenting current streams of experience into smaller packets for attention, and then selecting or enacting interpretations to impose meanings. They spin webs of meaning by starting from some beliefs or actions that are sufficiently clear. Beliefs lead to expectations, and expectations draw together pieces of information that fit. Information contradictory to beliefs is reconciled through argumentation. Actions are taken to make things happen so that meaning can be more easily constructed. Conversely, meanings may be constructed to justify visible actions people are already committed to. Taken together, sense making processes driven by beliefs and actions restructure the organization's theory of action, clarifying ambiguity and explaining deviances: "The task of organizational inquiry is then to specify vague information, to clarify ambiguity, to prune excessive information, to enrich sparse information, to make untestable propositions testable, so that error or anomaly can be linked to inadequacies in organizational theory of action" (Argyris and Schön 1978, 57).

Balancing ambiguity with clarity is the essence of managing organizational sense making. Clarity, consistency, and certainty are prerequisites for collective identity and coordinated action. However, organizations cannot, and do not attempt to eliminate ambiguity completely. By retaining a certain level of ambiguity, the organization provides the white space within which members can play, experiment, and improvise. When ambiguity is excessively high, people are confused and anxious because they lack an understandable frame of reference to interpret their work and actions for the organization. On the other hand, when ambiguity is unduly suppressed, people become complacent and unwilling to experiment or change, shielded as they are from the need to adapt. Each organization finds its own balance between ambiguity and certainty, the particular locus depending on the business of the organization, its relationships with other institutions and stakeholders, its external environment, and its cultural ethos.

Diversity and Consensus in Sense Making

Sense making constructs a framework of shared meanings and purposes that makes possible concerted action. Shared meanings and interpretations provide the social order, temporal continuity, and goal-directed clarity for people to sustain and relate to their organizational activities. As a cognitive framework, it supplies criteria for selecting and evaluating information. Where information is lacking or ambiguous, shared meanings and assumptions fill in the gaps or lower equivocality sufficiently for people to be able to act. As a framework of goals and values, it supplies concepts for understanding past actions, and benchmarks for judging new initiatives.

The sharing of meaning is assisted by the sharing of experience. What is being shared are the actions and conversations that constitute the experience, as well as the opportunity to talk about that experience soon after it occurred so that people can collectively develop a common vocabulary to encode the experience and render it meaningful (Weick 1995). An alternative approach is to avoid altogether summarizing or labeling the shared experience, but to accept the shared experience for what it is. To evoke the mind set and shared meanings associated with the experience, it is sufficient to recount the experience in detail (without summarizing or labeling it). Shared experiences may thus be made sensible by equivalent, though not necessarily similar meanings:

> If I act on the basis of my understanding of that common experience, and you act on your different understanding of that same experience, we remain tied together by the common origin of those understandings. If each of us is quizzed separately as to why we did what we did, our answers flow from the same experience. That commonality is what binds us together and makes it possible for each of us to understand the sense that the other has made. (Weick 1995, 189)

The construction of shared meaning in organizational life makes use of myths, symbols, rituals, and stories, which comprise the *"instruments of meaning"* by which people understand the history of their actions and their place in it (March 1994). Myths are real or fictional stories, characters, or actions that embody the organization's ideals and sensibilities. For example, many organizations maintain creation myths of how they were founded, complete with mythic heroes (technical wizards, financiers), events (competition, market uncertainty), and explanations (superhuman effort, carving a market niche). Symbols are things, signs, or behaviors that link organizational experience to feelings and values. Thus meetings symbolize thought, language symbolizes status and power, and mission statements symbolize solidarity. Rituals are ceremonial activities that preserve traditions and sustain meanings. The development of a business plan is an example of a common ritual that signals the legitimacy of the meanings and interpretations that are linked to it. Stories are narratives that elaborate on explanations of what has happened, what is happening, or what might have happened. Much of what people know about the world comes from stories supplied by friends, relatives, teachers, journalists, and officials. Stories are powerful sense making devices because they posit a causal sequence of events that lead to an outcome, and because they provide a rich, multilayered representation of an episode that evokes understanding and empathy.

People in organizations construct shared meanings by tapping into common mental models or communal knowledge bases in order to establish sufficient cognitive consensus for collective, purposeful action. Developing consensus is aided by a number of communication behaviors that allow a diversity of interpretations or perspectives to cohabitate or to be reconciled. The nature and extent of the consensus is a function of the organization's culture, particularly the degree to which the culture is integrated, differentiated, or fragmented (Martin 1992). In an integrated culture there is organizationwide consensus, and members share basic assumptions and common concerns that are consistently represented and enacted in organizational "instruments of meaning" (myths, symbols, rituals, stories). In a differentiated culture, the organization consists of several subcultures differentiated by their areas of interest, their work or professional practices, and their power and influence. Consensus is localized within subcultures, while conflict due to differing interpretations between subcultures is normal. In a fragmented culture, organizations are webs of individuals who form loose and temporary coalitions to tackle specific issues and concerns. Consensus is transient and tied to particular issues, and a different cluster of individuals and interests is formed to deal with each issue.

The tension between consensus and diversity is dynamic, and organizations adjust the locus of balance constantly. Organizations recognize that the amount and nature of consensus vary at different points in time, in different parts of the organization, and with respect to different kinds of issues. An organization's culture combines elements from the integration, differentiation, and fragmentation perspectives: the expression of consensus and diversity at any instant is understood by invoking all three perspectives. Some manifestations of beliefs and meanings are interpreted similarly throughout the organization (integration), other issues show up as inconsistencies separated by subcultural differences (differentiation), while other issues still induce a diversity of personal interpretations, which then coalesce in temporary coalitions (fragmentation) (Martin 1992).

Although some order and stability are essential for purposeful, sustained action, organizations do not operate in isolation, but must constantly amend their assumptions and interpretations in response to what other organizations are doing and how the environment is changing. Adaptive learning requires the organization to have the capacity to challenge old assumptions, and compose fresh meanings. New sense making flourishes in an organizational environment where divergent points of view exist side by side, and where diverse interpretations intrude into each other's domains to challenge and to persuade.

II. TENSIONS IN KNOWLEDGE CREATING

The Tacit and The Explicit in Knowledge Creating

All organizational knowledge is rooted in tacit knowledge. Tacit knowledge is difficult to verbalize or codify using language or symbols. It is difficult to decompose into elements, steps, or rules because tacit knowledge is distributed in the totality of the individual's action experience. It is action centered, relying on the tactile cues registered by the human body interacting with its environment. It is situated so that its expression varies according to the physical and social particulars of the setting in which it is being applied. Although it is hard to learn, tacit knowledge is regularly transferred through imitation, identification, and learning by example. Apprentices learn their craft by identifying with and copying their masters; professionals acquire expertise and norms of behavior through periods of internship; and new employees are immersed in on-the-job training. In these instances, tacit knowledge is made observable through patterns of actions and behaviors, and it is made understandable through rich modes of discourse that include the use of analogies, metaphors, exemplars, models, and stories. Although tacit knowledge is personal, the learning and demonstration of that knowledge is a social activity that takes place in pairs, groups, or communities tied together by a shared set of practices. Communities of practice enable knowledge creation by specifying roles and relationships, defining a realm of discourse and inquiry, and identifying tools and objects for manipulation.

Yet as long as tacit knowledge remains the private property of individuals or select groups, the organization cannot multiply its value in at least two important modes. First, the organization is limited in its ability to amplify that knowledge to gain economies of scale or strategic advantage:

> Unless able to train large numbers of individuals or to transform skills into organizing principles, the craft shop is forever simply a shop. The speed of replication of knowledge determines the rate of growth; control over its diffusion deters competitive erosion of the market position. For a firm to grow, it must develop organizing principles and a widely-held and shared code by which to orchestrate large numbers of people and, potentially, varied functions. (Kogut and Zander 1992, 390)

Large management consulting companies, such as the firm studied by Orlikowski (1988), are keenly aware of the leverage potential of the tacit knowledge of their consulting staff, and many of them have established systems, methodologies and tools to transform the personal knowledge of individuals into organization wide assets.

Second, the organization is unable to sustain cycles of new knowledge generation that depend on the continuous conversion of tacit and explicit knowledge, and on the amplification of this knowledge across many levels of the organization (Nonaka and Takeuchi 1995). Knowledge conversion takes place when people share, externalize, combine, and internalize their knowledge. Knowledge expansion takes place when new ideas and concepts move to other parts of the organization to spark new cycles of knowledge creation.

Explicit knowledge is knowledge that is made manifest through language, symbols, objects, and artifacts. Histories, statutes, patents, software codes, chemical formulas, mathematical models, business plans, and statistical reports are all examples of explicit knowledge. Knowledge conversion between the tacit and the explicit is facilitated by the use of multiple means of inquiry and communication, such as deduction, induction, dialectic reasoning, contradictions and paradoxes, metaphors, analogies, and war stories (Nonaka and Takeuchi 1995). When knowledge is made explicit by articulating it in a language, it can provide a focus for joint reflection, and it becomes possible to distribute and debate the knowledge (Sveiby 1996).

Knowledge made explicit and communicable through formalization or codification is a necessary transformation in many organizational processes. Decision-making processes often make use of formal, written down knowledge in order to justify, persuade, and explicate the selection or rejection of courses of action. Tacit knowledge can be unpersuasive in complex situations marked by high levels of uncertainty. Recall our discussion of the Challenger accident in chapter 5, when the engineer knowledgeable about O-rings could not convince NASA decision makers to believe his tacit assessment that the rings would not seal in the cold temperatures on the morning of the launch. Even when in the last analysis, choice is made by a decision maker using her intuition and instinct, such a choice is usually made to appear legitimate or rational by a trail of visible knowledge and arguments.

The dichotomy between tacit and explicit knowledge has been so often emphasized that we need to remind ourselves that the two are not only complementary to each other, but are in many ways interdependent. In an organization the exercise of one form of knowledge almost always requires the presence and utilization of the other form of knowledge. Thus the exercise of tacit knowledge typically makes references to plans or blueprints, entails the handling of tools and equipment, and involves carrying out a conversation with other people, all of which embody various levels of explicit knowledge. Conversely, the application of explicit knowledge often requires individuals who can interpret, elaborate, demonstrate, or instantiate the formal knowledge with respect to a particular problem setting. Behind every formal knowledge system in an organization is an informal support structure that is just as important and necessary for the organization to function properly. Some of the most useful sources of knowledge in an organization are those that combine the tacit and the explicit, that articulate the judgmental or the conjectural, and that reveal the hidden or the nonobvious. Examples would include market forecasts, future scenarios, technology projections, user product evaluations, feasibility studies, mock-ups and prototypes, and computer simulations.

Exploration and Exploitation in Knowledge Creation

Exploration and exploitation are complementary modes of organizational learning. Exploration is learning through discovery or experimentation that leads to the finding of new goals and untapped opportunities. Exploitation is learning through specialization and the amassing of experience within the scope of existing goals and activities. Both forms of learning are necessary. To be viable in the short term, an organization needs to be efficient—to be good at what it does, to be able to lever on its present skills and capabilities. This is the realm of exploitation, the productive utilization of existing knowledge. Exploitation is achieved by accumulating experience in a limited number of activity domains, and by increasing proficiency through repeated practice and the formalization of task-related knowledge. However, to be viable in the longer run, an organization also needs to be able to develop new capabilities, to absorb or create new concepts or technologies. This is the realm of exploration, the pursuit of new knowledge. Exploration is inherently a messy process. Many attempts at discovery or experimentation that transgress the bounds of current competences or the norms set by existing routines might well prove to be unrewarding, but this is a necessary cost of learning. A few of the deviations from standard practice will be promising enough to point to new ideas and directions which the organization can turn into usable knowledge. Thus organizations "engage in exploration—the pursuit of new knowledge, of things that might come to be known. And they engage in exploitation—the use and development of things already known. An organization that engages exclusively in exploration will ordinarily suffer from the fact that it never gains the returns of its knowledge. An organization that engages exclusively in exploitation will ordinarily suffer from obsolescence. The basic problem confronting an organization is to engage in sufficient exploitation to ensure its current viability and, at the same time, to devote enough energy to exploration to ensure its future viability" (Levinthal and March 1993, 105).

The balance between exploration and exploitation, while necessary is problematic. Within each of the realms of exploitation and exploration, internal dynamics create self-reinforcing tendencies to concentrate organizational attention and resources on one over the other. The more common imbalance is for exploitation to displace exploration. The principal reason is that the returns to exploitation are more certain, more immediate, and closer in space than are the returns to exploration (March 1991). There are also economies of experience to be gained: past exploitation in an activity domain makes future exploitation in the same domain even more efficient. Furthermore, exploitation in organizations is transferred between individuals and different parts of the organization through the use of rules, procedures, and standard practices. This routinization improves the reliability of individuals and organizations, but reduces variability and exploratory deviation. The overall effect is to increase competence in existing domains and to raise the opportunity cost of exploration. Levinthal and March (1993) describe this result as *"the traps of distinctive competence,"* or *"the success trap."*

The self-reinforcing nature of learning makes it attractive for an individual or organization to sustain current focus. The result is that distinctive competence is accentuated, and organizations become specialized into niches in which their competences yield immediate advantage. . . . [However,] establishing preeminence involves exploration. Exploration is, on the average, unfruitful, but it is the only way to finish first. . . . Exploitation generates clearer, earlier, and closer feedback than exploration. It corrects itself sooner and yields more positive returns in the near term. As a result, the primary challenge to sustaining an optimal mix of exploration and exploitation is the tendency of rapid learners and successful organizations to reduce the resources allocated to exploration. (102, 107)

The reverse of the success trap is a situation in which an organization is caught in a spiral of constant change and exploration. The organization experiments with some new idea or technology, the experiment fails, and the organization moves on to another new innovation, which again fails. Frequent failure is unsurprising, partly because good new ideas are hard to come by, and partly because individuals and organizations need time and experience to learn how an innovation could be made to work well in their particular settings. Not only does a persistent cycle of exploration and failure not deliver alternatives that are or are perceived to be promising, it also absorbs energy and resources that would otherwise be available for exploitation.

Organizations also build inventories of competences (Feldman 1989) and *inventories of knowledge,* (Levinthal and March 1993), which they draw upon in order to respond swiftly and effectively to changes in the environment. Thus organizations develop contingency plans; store knowledge about products, markets, technologies, and social and political conditions; and maintain contacts with analysts, consultants, and other colleagues. When the environment is highly fluid, it becomes difficult to define and maintain desirable knowledge inventories: "By the time knowledge is needed, it is too late to gain it; before knowledge is needed, it is hard to specify precisely what knowledge might be required or useful" (Levinthal and March 1993, 103). There is again a tendency to concentrate on knowledge in current markets and technologies which have well-understood, short-term payoffs. However, developing knowledge that transcends existing specializations expands the organization's internal capacity to adapt to change, as well as its capacity to assess, absorb, and apply new knowledge from outside (Cohen and Levinthal 1990).

An organization can control the balance between exploration and exploitation by adjusting aspirations, beliefs, feedback, incentives, and socialization or selection processes (Levinthal and March 1993). An organization can break loose from the success trap of focusing narrowly on existing competences by raising aspirations to levels that induce exploration or new knowledge creation, or by introducing feedback that exaggerates the high value of exploration. For example, if aspiration levels are tied to the best performers in an industry, then individuals may perceive themselves as performing substantially below the standard, and are more likely to take risks and to explore. In this case aspiration levels are managed to increase the tolerance for risk taking. A parallel approach is to reduce the perception of risk that is involved in exploration. For example, confident individuals in a successful organization with a "can do" culture may underestimate the risk of actions they have taken and the risk they presently face. Symmetrically, an organization can break out of a failure cycle of repeated explorations and failures by lowering aspirations, or by introducing a particularly good alternative. When indiviudals perceive themselves as operating above or close to aspiration levels, they become risk averse and refrain from exploitation. In other words, modest success is associated with risk aversion (March and Shapira 1987).

Organizations may deliberately modulate the efficiency and accuracy of their feedback structures in order to avoid overly narrow exploitation. Thus organizations may purposely forget past lessons, overlook old solutions, and generally manage communication and feedback about current practice so as to increase the probability of experimentation. At the same time, organizations may offer incentives to encourage exploration. For example, large economic rewards and monopoly property rights may be the trophies to be won as a result of successful exploration.

Organizations tend to promote people who have been successful in the past and to select or socialize new recruits according to the traits, beliefs, and practices of these successful individuals. To strengthen exploration, organizations may provide safety nets for exploratory failures, celebrate the lessons learned from failures, and slow down the process of socialization and acculturation.

III. TENSIONS IN DECISION MAKING

Improvisation and Order in Decision Making

The unfolding of organizational decision making is thought to require a clarity of purpose and a clarity of procedure. The particular mode of organizational choice making thus depends on the level of clarity about the organizational goals that define rational behavior, and on the level of clarity about the organizational methods and techniques that enable goal attainment. Clarity can be increased by designing structures of rules, routines, roles, and premises that introduce order and control in the decision making process. An orderly structure helps to maintain focus on important goals and preferences, and to justify choice behaviors and outcomes based on criteria of consistency competence, and accountability. However, an organization that overemphasizes order and control in the name of rationality ignores two essential aspects of the link between decisions and the actions they select. First, choice is as much a process for discovering goals as it is for acting on goals (March 1976). Second, rules cannot completely absorb the variation and the surprise that render the details of each choice situation unique, and on the critical occasions when order collapses, organizational members must somehow fabricate new order in time to take action (Weick 1996).

March (1976) suggests that organizations from time to time need to suspend their pursuit of rational order and controlled consistency in order to discover new goals and purposes. To escape the logic of received rules, an organization would deliberately but temporarily relax these rules to explore the viability of alternative rules. By acting playfully the organization defers the requirement of consistency and encourages experimentation and improvisation. The organization replaces its technology of reason with a technology of foolishness by challenging its conventions about the nature of goals, intuitions, hypocrisy, memory, and experience (March 1976). Goals are to be treated as hypotheses to be tested during decision processes—experimenting with alternative goals makes it possible to discover "complicated and interesting combinations of good values" that would otherwise have not been imagined. Intuition is to be treated as real, allowing it to show us "some possible actions that are outside our present scheme for justifying behavior." Hypocrisy is to be treated as a transition and not a vice, since a preoccupation with penalizing hypocrisy would inhibit change and deter experimentation. Memory is to be treated as an enemy, and to be replaced occasionally with the ability to forget previous responses or to overlook what others are already doing in the organization. Finally, experience is to be treated as theory that could be changed retrospectively as the organization experiments with alternative histories—histories that "need to be rewritten rather continuously as a base for the retrospective learning of new self-conceptions" (March 1976, 79).

Weick (1996) differentiates between the ordered world of strategic rationality in decision making where questions and answers are clear, and the confusing world of contextual rationality where questions and answers are vague. When the choice situation suddenly changes from the expected to the unexpected or the incomprehensible, the ordered world of strategic rationality can break down because rule and role systems no longer make sense. Weick (1996) argues that the collapse of role systems need not result in disaster (as it did in the case he was analyzing to illustrate contextual rationality, when thirteen firefighters were killed in the Mann Gulch forest fire of 1942) if the organizational participants develop skills in improvisation. Weick elaborates:

By improvisation, I mean bringing to the surface, testing, and restructuring one's intuitive understandings of phenomena on the spot, at a time when action can still make a difference. Improvisers remain creative under pressure precisely because they have the ability to bring order out of chaos. Thus, when situations unravel, they can proceed with whatever materials are at hand. . . . If organizations paid more attention to improvisation, it would be possible, when one organizational order collapsed, to invent a substitute immediately. (Weick 1996, 145)

The capacity to improvise allows organizational members to balance against being either overconfident or overcautious, and to maintain the open-minded curiosity necessary for prudent decision making and organizational learning:

> . . . what organizations miss—and what explains why most fail to learn—is that ignorance and knowledge grow together. . . . In a fluid world, wise people know that they don't fully understand what is happening at a given moment, because what is happening is unique to that time. They avoid extreme confidence and extreme caution, knowing that either can destroy what organizations need most in changing times, namely, curiosity, openness, and the ability to sense complex problems. The overconfident shun curiosity because they think they know what they need to know. The overcautious shun curiosity for fear it will only deepen their uncertainties. Both the cautious and the confident are close minded, which means that neither make good judgments. In this sense, wisdom, understood as simultaneous belief and doubt, improves adaptability. (Weick 1996, 148)

Crossan et al. (1996) describe the need for an organization to improvise and learn through practice and performance in order to respond to an environment that is unpredictable and constantly changing. Using the theater as analogy, the improvising organization manages the unique role of story development as strategy, cast as organization members, ambiance as culture, and audience as customers. As in a theater in which actors largely improvise, the organization would develop its strategy or narrative in incremental steps; cultivate trust and promote communication and flexibility among its members or cast; create a culture of commitment, risk taking, and innovation; and work with stakeholders to create the future (Crossan et al. 1996). Improvisation does not replace but builds upon traditional practice and performance:

> Successful improvisation requires a strong skill base in traditional practice and performance skills. . . . Successful improvisation rests upon strong development of core skills, whether in theater, music, or business. Communication within a team and with the audience is the greatest asset improvisers have for spontaneous performance. This skill, developed through practice and performance, requires that the performer have a flexible attitude in order to adapt to the demands of the audience, fellow workers, and leader. It is not enough to listen to the customer, observe changes, and sense the potential; the performer must also respond, both in language and action, to those changes. Ultimately, the success of the group depends upon the skills of each individual. (Crossan et al. 1996, 30)

The difference between improvisation and control in decision making, and exploration and exploitation in knowledge creating may be summarized as follows. Improvisation is the restructuring of current experience in order to produce new understandings in time to influence action and choice making. Control in decision making is the structuring of past, learned experience into rules and preferences in order to ensure consistent, rational choice behavior. Thus, both improvisation and control represent alternative modes of structuring organizational experiences that support decision making. Exploration and exploitation on the other hand represent alternative modes of organizational learning through discovery or experimentation (exploration), and through specialization or accumulation of experience (exploitation), both of which support the creation of new knowledge.

Evolution and Design in Decision Making

Rules and preferences in decision making induce the generation and selection of alternatives that take advantage of the organization's available learning in a delineated domain of activity. At the same time there will always be individuals or small groups who step outside of the present scope of the organization to experiment with new initiatives. These initiatives bear a higher risk of failure, but also offer the prize of new learning and new capabilities. Rules and preferences confer design and focus, but experimentation and entrepreneurship are necessary for the organization to adapt over the long term. In the arena of strategic choice making, Burgelman (1991) suggests an evolutionary framework of analysis, in which processes of variation, selection, and retention operate on internally generated courses of action:

> An organization is viewed as an ecology of strategic initiatives which emerge in patterned ways, and compete for limited organizational resources so as to increase their relative importance within the organization. Strategy results, in part, from selection and retention operating on internal variation associated with strategic initiatives. Variation in strategic initiatives comes about, in part, as the result of individual strategists seeking expression of their special skills and career advancement through the pursuit of different types of strategic initiatives. Selection works through administrative and cultural mechanisms regulating the allocation of attention and resources to different areas of strategic initiative. Retention takes the form of organizational level learning and distinctive competence, embodied in various ways—organizational goal definition, domain delineation, and shared views of organizational character. (Burgelman 1991, 240)

Burgelman distinguishes between two types of strategic choice making processes—induced processes and autonomous processes. *Induced processes* concern the variation, selection, and retention of courses of action that fall within the current scope of the organization's goals, strategies and capabilities. *Variation* occurs when courses of action are brought forward by managers that are induced by pressures from the existing, regular structure of incentives, rewards, and career advancement opportunities in the organization. *Selection* of initiatives is through both administrative mechanisms and cultural mechanisms. Administrative mechanisms include rules, routines, and reward systems that underlie activities such as strategic planning and resource allocation. Cultural mechanisms include norms and rituals that make reference to existing key values, premises, and preferences. Together, administrative and cultural mechanisms constitute what Burgelman labels the organization's "structural context." In this structural context, strategic choice making "depends on widely dispersed and routinized decision criteria that winnow out arguments and narrow a firm's strategic focus. It is clear from Burgelman's arguments that strategic decisions . . . are shaped by organizationwide administrative selection systems that have become part of the company's planning process" (Porac, Meindl and Stubbart 1996, p. xx). *Retention* takes place when the organization expresses its strategy in rules and preferences that guide the selection of action, and induces more initiatives that are in line with the prescriptions. Over time, rules and preferences join decisions and actions to produce distinctive patterns of organizational competences, define realms of desirable organizational activity, and maintain organizational identity and character.

Autonomous processes concern the variation, selection and retention of initiatives that emerge outside of the current scope of the organization, but provide potential for new learning. *Variation* exists because at any time in an organization, some individuals or groups would be attempting to get the organization to move into activities that are outside the perimeters of its current strategy (Burgelman 1991). Although autonomous processes may seem riskier than induced initiatives, some managers may engage in autonomous initiatives because they believe they have the skills and capabilities needed to succeed in these new initiatives, or because they see their access to existing career opportunity structures as being limited and wish to explore alternative avenues. *Selection* occurs when the organization attempts to define a "strategic context" for the new initiatives by finding resources from outside the regular resource allocation procedures, demonstrating viability through entrepreneurial manoeuvers, mobilizing upper management support, developing new skills, and setting the stage for a revision in organizational strategy. *Retention* takes place as the organization alters its conceptions about the organization's distinctive competence, and reappraises the significance of the new activities in its action domain. Such changes may cumulatively lead to a new, ex post vision about the organization's goals and capabilities. This new vision, when formally ratified into the organization's "structural context" of administrative and cultural inducements, then becomes part of the basis for induced processes.

To illustrate and analyze the dynamics of autonomous processes, Burgelman drew on several episodes from his field study of Intel Corporation, including Intel's decision to exit the DRAM (dynamic random -access memory) market and concentrate on the microprocessor market, the evolution of its EPROM (erasable programmable read-only memory) business, and its experience with the ASIC (application specific integrated circuits) business. Here's an account of how the company entered the RISC (reduced instruction set computing) processor business:

> [At that time,] Intel's deliberate corporate strategy was not to enter the RISC business, but rather to focus on the extremely successful x86 architecture. Les Kohn had been attempting to get Intel into the RISC processor business since he joined the company in 1982. . . . His solution was to disguise his product. Andrew Grove, Intel's CEO, mentioned that Kohn sold the design to top management as a co-processor, rather than a standalone processor. . . . By the time top management realized what their "co-processor" was, Kohn, with the help of two other champions, had already lined up a customer base for the standalone processor, a base he suggested was different than the companies who purchase the 486 chips: in Kohn's own words, "a lot of customers who before did not even talk to Intel." Thus Kohn could argue that he was broadening Intel's business rather than cannibalizing it. During 1989 Intel's top management decided to amend the corporate strategy to incorporate the RISC chip business. (Burgelman 1991, 246–47)

In summary, structural and strategic contexts complement each other and together constitute the internal selection processes operating on the choice of strategic initiatives or courses of action. In induced processes, the organization uses its structural context of administrative rules and routines, as well as cultural preferences and norms, to induce, design, and direct new initiatives so that they build on past successes and existing capabilities. The structural context from time to time needs to be revised to respond to the selective pressures of the external environment. In autonomous processes, the organization facilitates the activation of a strategic context (resources, entrepreneurship, managerial support) in order to allow new initiatives to evolve and demonstrate their adaptive value for the organization. Whereas induced processes suggest planning and design, autonomous processes suggest experimentation and entrepreneurship within a context that recognizes and selects initiatives which bestow adaptive advantage. Thus, the organization designs its rules and structures to heighten its focus on strategic intentions and core competences, while at the same time creating an internal ecology that allows the organization to evolve through experimentation, entrepreneurship, variation, and selection.

Although they overlap considerably and the processes they represent complement each other, it may nevertheless be helpful to highlight some differences between evolution and design in decision making, improvisation and control in decision making, and exploration and exploitation in knowledge creating. Evolution follows the biological model of increasing variation in initiatives, including initiatives that move beyond the current organizational scope, and then allowing evolutionarily "fit" initiatives to be selected and retained as new goals and strategies. On the other hand, the design of decisional rules and routines seeks to reduce variation, encouraging initiatives that lie within the organization's existing domain of activity or ecological niche. This evolutionary perspective may be contrasted with improvisation that restructures current organizational experience in order to react to new situations, and with control that structures past organizational experience in order to act in familiar situations. It may also be differentiated from exploration that learns new knowledge and goals through discovery and experimentation, and from exploitation that promotes learning through specialization and accumulation of experience.

Summary

Sense making depends on the social construction of shared understandings. Ambiguity needs to be reduced to understand what is happening with sufficient clarity, but a residual equivocality provides the necessary room for learning and adaptation. Consensus about a basic set of shared meanings and purposes enables coordinated activity, but divergent perspectives and interpretations promote variation and robustness. Knowledge creation depends on the collective experiences of multiple participants sharing their tacit know-how and explicit knowledge. Exploitation of existing expertise yields economies of scale and specialization, but exploration of new areas leads to the development of new capabilities required for long-term survival. Decision making depends on organizational rules and preferences that preserve past learning and ensure future viability. Routines structure choice making, but individuals exercise improvisation and initiative to generate variation and surprise so that the organization can discover new goals or cope with unfamiliar situations.

IV. INFORMATION MANAGEMENT IN THE KNOWING ORGANIZATION

Much of the information that impinges on an organization is nuance and innuendo, more a potential than a prescription for action. To become strategic, information must be galvanized into understanding and knowledge that can guide action. This transfiguration of information into learning, insight, and commitment to action is the goal of information management. Information management is often equated with the management of information resources, the management of information tools and technologies, or the management of information policies and standards. While each of these functions is necessary, we also need a unifying framework that binds these functions together. Information resources, technological tools, and policy standards constitute the technical infrastructure of information management. Over this infrastructure, the generation and transformation of information in an organization are shaped by the organization's culture; by the organization's interpretation of its purpose and agenda; and by its specification of rules, routines, and roles. Ultimately, information and meaning are forged in the thoughts, feelings, and actions of individuals.

A Process Model of Information Management

Just as we have conceptualized organizational knowing as the emergent quality of a network of information use processes, we now suggest that information management be viewed as the management of a network of processes that acquire, create, organize, distribute, and use information. In an important sense, the knowing organization is an organization that is skilled at marshalling its information resources and capabilities, transforming information into understanding and insight, and deploying this knowledge through initiatives and patterns of action so that the organization learns and adapts to its changing environment. This book has analyzed organizational information use in terms of information needs, information seeking, and information use. To develop information management strategies it may be helpful to elaborate the information processes that comprise these broad categories. We analyze information management as a continuous cycle of six closely related processes: (1) identification of information needs; (2) information acquisition; (3) information organization and storage; (4) development of information products and services; (5) information distribution; and (6) information use (Choo 1995a; Davenport 1993; McGee and Prusak 1993). The outcome of effective information use is adaptive behavior—the selection and execution of a pattern of actions that is directed at goals, but that also responds to current conditions of the environment. The organization's responses interact with the actions of other organizations in the environment, generating new signals and messages to attend to, thereby sustaining new cycles of information use.

In the following subsections we examine each of the six information processes from the perspective of an information management function whose responsibility is to plan and design information systems, services, processes, and resources. Figure 7–1 shows the process model of information management that we will present.

Identification of Information Needs: Information needs arise from the problems, uncertainties, and ambiguities encountered in specific organizational situ-

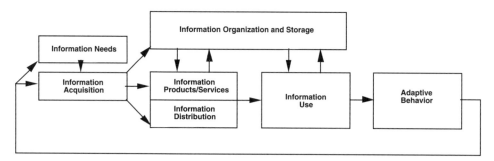

FIGURE 7–1. Process model of information management (Reprinted with the permission of Information Today, Inc., Medford NJ from the book *Information Management for the Intelligent Organization: The Art of Scanning the Environment,* 1995, p. 24.)

ations and experiences. Such situations and experiences are the interactions of a large number of factors that relate not just to subject matter, but also to contextual factors such as organization culture, task constraints, goal clarity and consensus, degree of risk, professional norms, amount of control, and so on. As a result, the determination of information needs does not stop at asking: "What do you want to know?" but also addresses questions like: "Why do you need to know it? What does your problem look like? What do you know already?" What do you anticipate finding? How will this help you? How do you need to know it?" and "In what form do you need to know it?" (MacMullin and Taylor 1984). Thus we are not only concerned with the meaning of information, but also with the conditions, patterns, and rules of use, which render information meaningful to specific individuals in specific situations.

During sense making, the requirement is for information that reduces ambiguity in the messages indicating change in the environment. The main question is, "What is going on in the environment?" and the need is for information that provides plausible answers or interpretations. During knowledge creating, information is required to specify gaps in existing knowledge, capability, or understanding; and to identify sources or methods for filling these gaps. Here information needs center on three questions: "What do we know already? What new knowledge is feasible and may be found or developed?" and "What kinds of new knowledge are advantageous?" During decision making, information is required to frame a problem situation in order to set boundaries, select preferences, and constrain search. Information needs focus on questions such as "What type of problem is this? What outcomes do we prefer?" and "Where do we look for solutions?"

The first step in developing an information management strategy is to accurately appraise the information needs of the various groups and individuals in the organization. *Information needs are contingent, dynamic, and multifaceted, and a sufficiently complete specification is only possible within a rich representation of the total information use environment.* Taylor's (1991) delineation of the information use environment identifies factors that go beyond subject matter, by which users judge the value or usefulness of the information they receive. These factors are grouped into four categories: sets of people; structure of problems faced by these sets of people; work or social settings; and resolution of problems. *Sets of people* are defined in terms of their information behaviors, and Taylor identifies four classifications: the professions (including managers), entrepreneurs, special-interest groups, and special socioeconomic groups. Each set of people or information users has its own characteristics (e.g., education, media use, social networks, attitudes) that explain differences in information behavior. Each set of people is concerned with a distinct *class of problems,* created by the requirements of its profession, occupation, or life style. Problems change all the time as new information is obtained and as the user changes position and perception. Four attributes of the *work setting* influence information behavior: attitude toward information, task domain, information access, and past history and experience. Finally, each set of people has a different perception of what constitutes the *resolution of a problem.* Eight classes of information use are defined, as well as several information traits that can be related to problem dimensions to determine information usefulness (see chapter 2). Taylor's framework suggests a systematic way of analyzing the information requirements of an organization: identify the groups of information users in the organization, recognize the kinds of problems they typically handle, examine their work and social settings, and understand the ways in which they consider a problem to have been resolved.

Information Acquisition: Information acquisition has become a critical but increasingly complex function in information management. Information acquisition balances two opposing demands. On the one hand, the organization's information needs are wide ranging, reflecting the breadth and diversity of its concerns about changes and events in the external environment. On the other hand, human attention and cognitive capacity are limited so that the organization is necessarily selective about the messages it attends to. The first demand suggests that the range of sources used to monitor the environment should be sufficiently numerous and varied as to reflect the span and sweep of the organization's interests. While this suggests that the organization should tap a broad range of human, textual, and on-line sources, in order to avoid information saturation, this information variety must be controlled and managed. *The selection and use of information sources has to be planned for, and continuously monitored and evaluated just like any other vital resource of the organization.*

In systems theory the principle of requisite variety (Ashby 1956) suggests that the internal control mechanisms of a living or social system must be as varied as the environment in which it is trying to survive. A system with the requisite control variety can deal with the complexity and challenges of its environment. A system that tries to insulate itself from environmental variety will become highly unstable. In other words, "only variety can absorb variety" (Beer 1974, 30). According to Beer, an organization is a dynamic system that is characterized by its variety or the number of possible states of the system. The number of possible states grows daily because of the number of new possibilities generated by the environment through the interaction of markets, technology, education, and so on. To maintain stability, the organization needs to absorb this variety. There are two general strategies, which may be combined: the first is to amplify variety in the organization, the second is to attenuate variety from the environment. In the context of information management, requisite variety suggests an important first principle in information acquisition: *the selection of sources to monitor the external environment must be sufficiently numerous and varied as to reflect the span and sweep of the external phenomena.* An organization that commits itself to a handful of "established" journals and newspapers to sense the environment is probably attenuating variety to an undesirable degree. An organization can improve its ability to absorb variety in several ways: take advantage of specialized knowledge possessed by librarians and other information professionals; outsource the monitoring of specific issues that are of special importance or for which internal expertise does not exist; and use information technology to both amplify and attenuate variety. Information technology can amplify variety through, for example, systems that let users profile their information needs and then retrieve relevant documents automatically from multiple databases. The same systems can also attenuate variety by adapting to users' preferences over time, progressively fine-tuning the criteria used to trawl external information.

An effective way of managing information variety is to involve as many persons in the organization as possible in the gathering of information, effectively creating an organizationwide information collection network. People, not printed sources or electronic databases, will always be the most valuable information sources in any organization. Human sources filter and summarize information, highlight salient elements, interpret ambiguous aspects, and in general provide richer, more satisfying communication about an issue. The management of information acquisition requires a plan for promoting the collection and sharing of information by human sources in the organization. This involves identifying individuals with specialized expertise, training, experience, or access to important information; creating the channels and routines for reporting and collating information; and establishing the norms and incentives for sharing information.

The simultaneous pressures for amplifying and attenuating information variety may be experienced to varying degrees during sense making, knowledge creating, and decision making. Sense making implies scanning the environment broadly through a variety of sources that reflect the range of the organization's concerns. However, in order to make sense of the environment, information variety is attenuated by bracketing certain signals, ignoring other messages, and relating the information to beliefs or actions. During knowledge creating, amplifying information variety (such as foraging in other fields to look for solutions or concepts) is often a precondition of creative brainstorming, while information attenuation (such as limiting search to a selected market need) helps to focus the development effort. During the rational mode of organizational decision making, rules, routines, and preferences attenuate information variety (by, for example, designating sources, kinds of information to be collected, and the amount of search) in order to simplify the search and choice activities.

Information Organization and Storage: Part of the information that is acquired or created is physically organized and stored in archives, computer databases, file systems, and other information systems in order to facilitate information sharing and retrieval. The way information is stored reflects the organization's perception and representation of its environment, including its labeling of entities, specifying of relationships, tracking of transactions, and measurement of performance. Stored information represents a significant and frequently consulted component of the organization's memory (Stein 1995;

Walsh and Ungson 1991). Information is retrieved from this knowledge base to facilitate debate, discussion, and dialogue, as well as to answer questions, interpret situations, or solve problems. Here again organizations have to balance two opposing conditions: organizations may be threatened by amnesia if they neglect to develop and manage an adequate institutional memory; on the other hand, inflexible adherence to organizational memory can block experimentation and entrepreneurship.

Sense making involves the retrieval of retained interpretations of past enactments in order to select past successful interpretations that might be used to make sense of current experience. Retained interpretations are in the form of "connected summaries" or "cause maps" that organizational members maintain in their minds. Members invoke these interpretations through retrospective accounts, stories, or some form of narrative, which allow earlier events to be reexperienced. Sense making discourse may be enriched by the use of stored information in the form of photographs, drawings, handwritten notes, or audio recordings that provide a more vivid rendering of past experience. Traditionally organizations regard information in such media as being too ephemeral or unstructured for systematic storage. Recent years have seen a growing awareness of the value of informal information resources which cannot act only as "instruments of memory" (March 1994), but also as tokens of tacit knowledge and traces of triggered assumptions. The organization, storage, and retrieval of textual, pictorial, audio and other forms of unstructured data are important issues in information management. *Information storage systems are increasingly called upon to provide the flexibility to capture hard and soft information, support multiple user views of the data, link items that are functionally or logically related, and allow users to explore patterns and connections.*

Knowledge creation may be expected to use information storage systems in two principal modes: to locate sources of expertise within the organization, and to retrieve reports of past work on similar problems. The first requirement suggests that a directory of internal experts and an inventory of individual skills or project experience be maintained as part of the organization's stored knowledge base. The second requirement implies that due care be given to designing a classification system that would provide both thoroughness and flexibility in retrieving past research and project documentation. A well indexed system provides access to the organization's accumulation of explicit knowledge and can accelerate the knowledge creation process. The use of explicit and tacit knowledge is complementary and interdependent. The practice of tacit know-how often involves the use of plans, blueprints, documents, and printed tools. Conversely, the reading and interpretation of explicit knowledge often require the personal input of knowledgeable individuals. Organizations build "inventories of knowledge" (Levinthal and March 1993) in order to enhance their ability to respond effectively to environmental changes. Thus organizations develop and store contingency plans; knowledge about markets, products, technologies, and economic and political conditions; and information on key contacts. A knowledge inventory that is broad ranging and that complements internal capabilities can extend the scope of the organization's knowledge acquisition options, and increase the depth of its knowledge assimilation capacity.

Decision making in organizations often generates a trail of records that is maintained in a file system. In general, information may be retrieved from the storage system to review results and rationales of past decisions, and to clarify issues such as the existence of precedents, the composition of decision making groups, and the appropriate procedure for a choice situation. Decision making in organizations is sensitive to the need to appear rational and accountable, so the maintenance of a stored history of decisions is recognized as necessary. Two factors complicate information retrieval. First, decisions in organizations often impact each other so that for example, a decision by one group may affect choices available to another group, or a decision in one unit may change the attractiveness of an option to another unit. Second, assumptions and premises driving past decisions may not be readily apparent from the stored record. For these reasons, flexible methods to access, represent, and link information are again needed to retrieve both the context and the subtext necessary for understanding and evaluating past decisions. Flexibility might be increased by, for example, providing capabilities for users to search the full text of stored records, retrieve information using concept hierarchies, and annotate and cross-reference related documents.

Information Products and Services: A primary function of information management is to ensure that the information needs of organizational members are being met through a balanced diet of information products and services. Users want information not just to give answers to questions (What is happening here?) but also to lead to actions that solve problems (What can we do about this?). Moving from question answering to problem solving means moving from a subject-based orientation in which providing information about a topic is a sufficient goal to an action orientation in which information has a focus and format that can enable decisions and actions. To be relevant and consequential, information products and services would be designed to address not only the subject area of the problem but also the specific contingencies that affect the resolution of each problem or each class of problems. Taylor (1986) suggests *a value-added approach, in which information systems, products, and services are developed as sets of activities that add value to the information being processed in order to assist users to make better decisions and better sense of situations, and ultimately to take more effective action.* Value-added activities are those that signal, enhance, or otherwise strengthen the potential usefulness of messages in the system. Taylor identifies six categories of value-added activities that enhance information products: ease of use, noise reduction, quality, adaptability, time savings, and cost savings.

Ease of use reduces the difficulty in using the product or service, and includes: adding browsing capability to let users scan an information space;

presenting and arranging data to facilitate scanning and selection; assisting users in getting answers and in gaining understanding and experience with the system; dividing or grouping subject matter; and making physical access easier.

Noise reduction is achieved by excluding unwanted information, including information of conceivable value, and focusing information where appropriate on specific items or facts. Noise reduction includes the values added by applying intellectual technologies, such as indexing systems or database management systems, to assist users to narrow the information universe to a set of potentially useful data; setting up pointers to related information, thereby expanding user information options; helping users to find exactly what is wanted by ranking output or providing signals on attributes such as language and level of subject treatment; and selecting input information that is likely to be of interest to the user population.

Quality is a user perception of the general excellence of the information product or service, and includes the values added by the error-free transfer of information; completeness of coverage on a topic or subject; recency of data and access vocabularies; trust a user has in the consistent quality performance of the service; and inclusion of signals about the soundness or otherwise of the data.

Adaptability refers to the ability of the service to be responsive to the needs and circumstances of users in their work environments. Most of the adaptability value is added by human intermediaries because they can reshape information to better fit user problem settings. Adaptability includes the values added by providing products and services that meet the specific needs of a person in a particular situation with a particular problem; supporting a variety of ways for users to work interactively and flexibly with the data; presenting the most lucid data, explanations, hypotheses, or methods from among several within quality and validity limits; and increasing goodwill and visibility through activities such as organizing seminars, editing speeches and papers, and so on.

Finally, *time savings* and *cost savings* are the perceived values of the service based on the speed of its response and the amount of dollars saved for the users. The value-added approach provides a framework for designing information products and services that takes into account the information use environment of organizational members.

Information Distribution: Information distribution is the process by which information is disseminated and routed in the organization so that "the right information gets to the right person in the right time, place, and format." A wider distribution of information can yield many positive consequences: organizational learning becomes more broadly based and more frequent; retrieval of information becomes more likely; and new information can be created by piecing together disparate items (Huber 1991). The objective of information distribution is to promote and facilitate the information sharing that is vital to organizational sense making, knowledge creating, and decision making.

During sense making, the environment is scanned and information is bracketed for interpretation. Plausible interpretations are constructed through face-to-face discourse by enacting the environment, exchanging information about equivocal areas, and selecting past interpretations. During knowledge creating, particularly in the context of solving problems or developing innovations, people work in project teams that combine a variety of expertise and specializations. They share information intensively in group dialogues, tap knowledge from outside the team or organization, and discover new concepts through the use of analogies and metaphors. During formal decision making, the flow of information is regulated by rules and routines that may, for example, determine who has access to information or who can request information, and stipulate what information is to be created at which stage and for whom. While rules structure the overall process, the choice making itself would also involve bargaining, negotiation, and persuasion between individuals and factions.

All three modes of information use exhibit common information-sharing requirements. First, people use rich channels of communication in face-to-face discourse to focus on issues, deal with vagueness and uncertainty, resolve differences, and stimulate creativity. Second, people need a continuous flow of information from the outside to clarify ambiguities, fill in gaps, update interpretations, and obtain feedback. Each of these requirements is an objective of managing information distribution.

Rich channels of information transfer are desirable, but may be difficult to achieve in an organization whose members, expertise, and information resources are geographically dispersed. Computer mediated communications such as electronic mail, on-line discussion groups, video conferencing, and network-based information repositories may provide alternative information-sharing methods to support remote collaboration. Each of these channels is capable of providing some degree of informality, feedback, and spontaneity that can simulate rich communication.

A steady flow of relevant information from outside the group or organization would have to be maintained to keep the group abreast of current developments. Such information has to be made meaningful by linking it with specific problem contexts. This is generally a two-step process. First, gatekeepers and informational boundary spanners, as well as information professionals with a firm grasp of the organization's business, could scan, filter, and introduce important external information into a group. Second, group members discuss and debate among themselves the significance of the new information by analyzing its impact on the local context of the problem or project being addressed.

Information Use: Information use is the dynamic, social process of inquiry and construction that results in the making of meaning, the creation of knowledge, and the selection of patterns of action. Organizational information sustains multiple meanings, each representation being the result of the subjective cognitive and affective interpretations of individuals or groups. When in use, organizational information continuously vacillates between the fine grained and the broad brushed, between components and the whole, between immediate instances and general policies. In the activity of knowledge creation, organizational information is transformed into the tacit, explicit, and cultural knowledge that constitute the cognitive fabric of the organization. For much of its life, organizational information cannot be objectified or reified, but resides and grows in the thoughts, feelings, and actions of individuals.

As a result, information use for the construction of meaning and understanding requires information processes and methods that provide for a high degree of flexibility in information representation and that facilitate the vigorous exchange and evaluation of multiple representations among individuals. Labeling or naming of concepts and categories has to be relevant to the users' interpretive discourse, and be flexible and easy to change. Information is needed about specific events and instances as well as about new theories and hypotheses that dispute current beliefs and expectations. Assumptions made should be surfaced for discussion and review. Information is to be shared easily but without loss of cognitive richness. Through the exchange and interpretation of information, and through its blending of tacit and explicit knowledge, the organization is able to develop new meanings and new capabilities to guide action.

Information is sought and used throughout the decision-making process. Mintzberg, Raisinghani, and Théorêt (1976) found that strategic decision processes may be divided into the identification phase, the development phase, and the selection phase (see chapter 5). Their analysis suggests that the intensity of information use varies according to the decision phase, with the greatest amount of information resources being consumed during the development phase, when information is used to work out solutions or elaborate opportunities. Information use is also intense during the early stages of the identification phase, and again during the early stages of the selection phase. Information is used in qualitatively different ways during the three decision phases. In the identification phase, information is used to help frame the problem situation and detect causal relationships. The main purpose is to provide enough *comprehension* of an issue so that the decision process can start. In the development phase, alternatives and solutions have to be found or generated, and options have to be described in sufficient detail. Development usually begins with a vague image of the ideal solution, which is then progressively fleshed out into one or more specific alternatives. Because the process is iterative and cyclic, information gathering is greatest during development. Here the main purpose is the *design* of viable solutions. In the selection phase, the outcomes of various alternatives are predicted, and the criteria for choosing alternatives will have to be defined, clarified, and reconciled. Further research and analysis may be needed to filter out weak options, or to embellish the case for feasible

options. The main goal now is rational *evaluation* using the best available
information, so that the decision is acceptable and can be authorized for action.
The complexity and variability of decision making suggest that the information
manager or an information specialist may need to participate proactively in
important decision processes. The participant would be sensitive to the open,
dynamic nature of the choice process, and be well prepared to address the
different kinds of information needs that characterize each decision phase.

Information use results in the making of meaning, knowledge, or decisions. In each case, the use of information is a social process of inquiry that
is fluid, reciprocal, and iterative. The inquiry cycles between the consideration
of parts and the whole, and between the consideration of practical specifics
and general assumptions. Participants clarify and challenge each other's representations and beliefs, and choices may be made by personal intuition or political bargaining rather than by rational analysis. The challenge before information management is to design and create organizational information structures
and processes that are as flexible, energetic, and permeable as the processes of
human inquiry and decision making that they are attempting to support.

Summary

The key to understanding organizations as information use systems is to recognize the twin information-based anomalies that confront every organizational
activity—ambiguity and uncertainty. All organizational activity is inherently
ambiguous. Current actions are based on what the organization has done in
the past, or, more specifically, they are based on a retrospective interpretation
of the significance and rationale of its past actions. Current messages about the
external environment are also interpreted according to beliefs and expectations
developed from a reflective reading of past experience. Unfortunately information about the past invariably supports more than one plausible interpretation,
and it is this equivocality that gives rise to ambiguity. In principle, organizations would then clarify important ambiguities by intensifying scanning, communication, and the active testing of hypotheses. In practice, organizations
simplify their information seeking by relying on a number of heuristics. During sense making, organizational members selectively attend to a few parts of
the environment, and grow larger structures of meaning around information
derived from beliefs or recent actions. During knowledge creating, they impute
value and usefulness to untested, tentative formulations of new concepts. During decision making, they imbue choices and actions with purposiveness and
legitimacy by working through practices that project reasoned competence.

All organizational activity is also inherently uncertain. Whereas ambiguity
occurs at the intersection of looking back at the past in order to understand
the present, uncertainty arises when the organization peers into the future in
order to act in the present. Current actions are based on what the organization

projects about the future in terms of predicted consequences and the expected values of those outcomes. Unfortunately the future cannot be controlled or specified in the present, so that information about the future is never complete or completely accurate. In principle, organizations would fill information gaps or improve information reliability by intensifying search, analysis, and the development of in-depth knowledge. In practice, organizations again simplify their information seeking with heuristics. During sense making, organizational members plug gaps in their meaning making with assumptions and expectations. During knowledge creating, they rely on insight or intuition or else attempt to inject new expertise from external sources. During decision making, they make up for missing information by exercising fiat and judgment in a manner influenced by their preferences and premises.

Much more research is needed to understand how tools, resources, and people may be combined synergistically in well-managed information processes. All too rarely do we make the necessary distinction between the management of information and the management of information tools and resources. A failure of managing tools and resources is a failure of artifact. A failure of managing information is a breakdown of organizational function and purpose. Organizations may become debilitated by internal rivalry between groups that lack a common understanding of where the organization is heading as a single community. Organizations may become unable to draw upon the personal expertise and knowledge of their members. Organizations may make poor decisions even when well-equipped and well-intentioned minds are brought to bear on a problem. These are some of the well-known symptoms related to poor management of information. Tools and resources can help in these situations, but they must be designed and deployed with a broader understanding of how information is created and used in organizations.

Our discussions in this section point to a number of general principles that can serve as a framework for the management of information processes:

- Information needs are contingent, dynamic, and multifaceted, and a sufficiently complete specification is only possible within a rich representation of the total information use environment.

- The selection and use of information sources for information acquisition has to be planned for, and continuously monitored and evaluated just like any other vital resource of the organization. Information variety is to be managed so that information collected reflects the range and complexity of the environment without overwhelming users with too much information.

- Internal information storage systems are invaluable extensions of the organization's memory. Such systems are increasingly being called upon to provide the flexibility to capture hard and soft information, support multiple user views of the data, link items that are functionally or logically related, and allow users to explore patterns and connections.

- Information products may be designed using a value-added approach, in which information systems, products, and services are developed as sets of activities that add value to the information being processed in order to assist users to make better decisions and better sense of situations, and ultimately to take more effective action.

- Information distribution promotes information sharing and retrieval. To deal with ambiguity and uncertainty, people generally prefer rich channels of communication, which allow them to focus on issues, seek clarification, resolve differences, and stimulate creativity. They also need a continuous flow of information from the outside to monitor current developments, update interpretations, fill in gaps, and obtain feedback.

- Information use for the construction of meaning and understanding requires information processes and methods that provide for a high degree of flexibility in information representation and that facilitate the vigorous exchange and evaluation of multiple representations among individuals.

V. CODA

Organizational knowing is the collective property of the network of information use processes through which people in organizations construct shared meanings, discover new knowledge, and become committed to courses of action. Organizational knowing emerges when the three information use processes—sense making, knowledge creating, and decision making—are integrated in an ongoing cycle of interpreting, learning and doing. At the core of these processes are the patterns of roles, relationships, rules, and resources that make information meaningful and useful. What the organization's participants know depends on how they come to know what they know, as well as on how they make use of what they know.

The nurturing of organizational knowledge is a particular challenge because organizational knowledge is fluid, contested, situated, and therefore hard to control or direct. Thus that which is held to be true, valid, or useful at one point in time, could be, or could have been, regarded as anachronistic, provisional, or uninteresting at another time. Organizational knowledge is interpreted knowledge, and the interpretations differ according to the people who are perceiving, participating, and responding to the particulars of a specific situation. Organizational knowledge is situated and mediated—it is brought forth in the doing of tasks and the using of tools in physical and social settings; and moderated through the relationships that link individuals and groups, and the structures that tie the organization to its external environment.

The relevance of organizational knowledge is revealed through the systems of meaning that the organization uses to assign merit and significance to new information and knowledge. The value of organizational knowledge is manifested in how it extends the organization's range of capabilities and choices. The effectiveness of organizational knowledge is unveiled over time in its ability to nourish the growth and renewal of the organization.

The knowing organization provides a background of stable definitions of identity, renderings of reality, and patterns of behavior. Against this background, there is a foreground where individuals are capable of creating meanings, discovering knowledge, and making choices. It is this interplay between a sturdy, orderly background and a vigorous, surprising foreground that animates organizational learning and adaptation. The knowing organization thus evolves knowledge across three planes. It constructs knowledge as shared meanings about what the organization can perceive as reality; it develops knowledge as expanded competences about what the organization can do; and it nurtures knowledge as learned behaviors about what the organization can achieve.

REFERENCES

Abel, E. 1966. *The Missile Crisis.* Philadelphia, PA: Lippincott.

Aguilar, F. J. 1988. *General Managers in Action.* New York, NY: Oxford University Press.

Allen, T. 1969. Information Needs and Uses. In *Annual Review of Information Science and Technology* vol. 4, ed. C. A. Cuadra, 2–29. Chicago, IL: Encyclopaedia Britannica.

Allen, T. J. 1977. *Managing the Flow of Technology: Technology Transfer and the Dissemination of Technological Information within the R & D Organization.* Cambridge, MA: MIT Press.

Allison, G. T. 1971. *Essence of Decision: Explaining the Cuban Missile Crisis.* Boston, MA: Little Brown.

Argyris, C., and D. A. Schön. 1978. *Organizational Learning: A Theory of Action Perspective.* Reading, MA: Addison-Wesley.

Ashby, W. R. 1956. *An Introduction to Cybernetics.* London, UK: Chapman & Hall.

Auerbach Corporation. 1965. *DOD User Needs Study, Phase I.* 1151-TR-3.

Auster, E., and C. W. Choo. 1993. Environmental Scanning by CEOs in Two Canadian Industries. *Journal of the American Society for Information Science* 44, no. 4:194–203.

Badaracco, J. L. 1991. *The Knowledge Link: How Firms Compete through Strategic Alliances.* Boston, MA: Harvard Business School Press.

Baden-Fuller, C., S. Pitt, J. Stopford, and D. Taylor. 1987. *Sustaining Competitive Advantage Against Low Cost Imports: The Lessons from the High Quality British Knitwear Producers.* Working paper, Center for Business Strategy, London Business School.

Bartlett, F. C. 1932. *Remembering.* Cambridge, UK: Cambridge University Press.

Bates, M. 1971. *User Studies: A Review for Librarians and Information Scientists.* U.S. Department of Health Education & Welfare.

Beer, S. 1974. *Designing Freedom.* Toronto, Ontario, Canada: CBC Publications.

Belkin, N. J. 1980. Anomalous States of Knowledge as a Basis for Information Retrieval. *The Canadian Journal of Information Science* 5 (May): 133–43.

Belkin, N. J., R. N. Oddy, and H. M. Brooks. 1982. Ask for Information Retrieval: Part 1. Background and Theory. *Journal of Documentation* 38, no. 2:61–71.

Bell, T. E. and K. Esch. 1987. The Fatal Flaw in Flight 51-L. In *IEEE Spectrum* 24, no. 2:36–51.

Bettis, R. A., and C. K. Prahalad. 1995. The Dominant Logic: Retrospective and Extension. *Strategic Management Journal* 16, no. 1:5–14.

Blackler, F. 1993. Knowledge and the Theory of Organizations: Organizations as Activity Systems and the Reframing of Management. *Journal of Management Studies* 30, no. 6:863–84.

———. 1995. Knowledge, Knowledge Work and Organizations: An Overview and Interpretation. In *Organization Studies* 16, no. 6:1021–46.

Boisot, M. H. 1995. *Information Space: A Framework for Learning in Organizations, Institutions and Culture.* London, UK: Routledge.

Bougon, M., K. Weick, and D. Binkhorst. 1977. Cognition in Organizations: An Analysis of the Utrecht Jazz Orchestra. *Administrative Science Quarterly* 22: 606–31.

Brilliant, L. B. 1985. *The Management of Smallpox Eradication in India.* Ann Arbor, MI: University of Michigan Press.

Brockeriede, W. 1974. Rhetorical Criticism as Argument. *Quarterly Journal of Speech* 60, no. 4:165–74.

Bronowski, J. 1968. Honest Jim and the Tinkey Toy Model. *The Nation,* (March 18): 381–82.

Brontë, C. 1968. *Jane Eyre.* ed. by Q. D. Leavis. Harmondsworth, UK: Penguin.

Brown, J. S. 1993. Session II—Papers Submitted by, presentation by, main themes generated by John Seely Brown. In *Proceedings of Learning in Organizations Workshop* (Western Business School, London, Ont., Canada, June 21–23, 1992), eds. M. M. Crossan, H. W. Lane, J. C. Rush, and R. E. White, 81–115. London, Ont.: University of Western Ontario.

Brown, J. S., and P. Duguid. 1991. Organizational Learning and Communities-of-Practice: Toward a Unified View of Working, Learning, and Innovation. *Organization Science* 2, no. 1:40–57.

Brown, J. S. and E. S. Gray. 1995. The People Are the Company. *Fast Company,* no. 1 December: 78–82.

Burgelman, R. A. 1991. Intraorganizational Ecology of Strategy Making and Organizational Adaptation. *Organization Science* 2, no. 3: 239–62.

Caplan, N., A. Morrison, and R. J. Stambaugh. 1975. *The Use of Social Science Knowledge in Policy Decisions at the National Level.* Ann Arbor, MI: University of Michigan, Institute for Social Research.

Carroll, L. ©1865. *Alice's Adventures in Wonderland.* New York, NY: Macmillan.

Chandler, Jr., A. D. 1962. *Strategy and Structure: Chapters in the History of the American Industrial Enterprise.* Cambridge, MA: MIT Press.

Chang, S. J., and R. E. Rice. 1993. Browsing: A Multidimensional Framework. In *Annual Review of Information Science and Technology* vol. 28, ed. M. E. Williams, 231–76. Medford, NJ: Learned Information.

Chen, C. 1982. Citizens' Information Needs—A Regional Investigation. In *Information Needs of the 80s,* ed. R. Stueart, 77–94. Greenwich, CT: Jai Press.

Chen, C., and L. B. Burger. 1984. *Assessment of Connecticut Citizens' Information Needs and Library Use Study.* Hartford, CT: Connecticut State Library.

Chen, C., and P. Hernon. 1980. Library Effectiveness in Meeting Information Consumers Needs. In *Library Effectiveness,* ed. Library Administration and Management Association Library Research Round Table, 49–62. Chicago, IL: Library Administration and Management Association.

Choo, C. W. 1993. Environmental Scanning: Acquisition and Use of Information by Chief Executive Officers in the Canadian Telecommunications Industry. Ph.D. diss. University of Toronto.

Choo, C. W. 1994. Environmental Scanning by Canadian CEOs. *Proceedings of the 22nd Annual Conference of the Canadian Association for Information Science* (Montréal, May 25–27), ed. A. Tabah, 446–64. Montréal, Que.: Canadian Association for Information Science.

————. 1995a. *Information Management for the Intelligent Organization: The Art of Scanning the Environment.* Medford, NJ: Information Today.

————. 1995b. Information Management for the Intelligent Organization: Roles and Implications for the Information Professions. In *Proceedings of the 1995 Digital Libraries Conference* (Singapore, March 27–30), 81–99. Singapore: SNP.

Choo, C. W., and E. Auster. 1993. Scanning the Business Environment: Acquisition and Use of Information by Managers. In *Annual Review of Information Science and Technology,* vol. 28, ed. M. E. Williams, 279–314. Medford, NJ: Learned Information.

Clemons, E. K., and M. Row. 1988. A Strategic Information System: McKesson Drug Company's Economost. In *Planning Review* 16, no. 5:14–19.

Cohen, M. D., J. G. March. 1986. *Leadership and Ambiguity.* 2nd ed. Boston, MA: Harvard Business School Press.

Cohen, M. D., and P. Bacdayan. 1994. Organizational Routines Are Stored as Procedural Memory: Evidence from a Laboratory Study. *Organization Science* 5, no. 4:554–68.

Cohen, M. D., J. G. March, and J. P. Olsen. 1972. A Garbage Can Model of Organizational Choice. *Administrative Science Quarterly* 17, no. 1:1–25.

Cohen, W. M., and D. A. Levinthal. 1990. Absorptive Capacity: A New Perspective on Learning and Innovation. *Administrative Science Quarterly* 35, no. 1 (March): 128–52.

Collins, J. C. and J. I. Porras. 1994. *Built to Last, Successful Habits of Visionary Companies.* New York, NY: HarperBusiness.

Cowper, W. 1973. *The Task.* "A Scolar Press facsimile." Reprint of the 1785 ed. published by J. Johnson, London. = [Menston, UK =]: Scolar Press.

Crane, D. 1971. Information Needs and Uses. *Annual Review of Information Science and Technology,* ed. C. A. Cuadra, 3–39. Chicago, IL: William Benton.

Crawford, S. 1978. Information Needs and Uses. In *Annual Review of Information Science and Technology,* ed. M. E. Williams, 61–81. White Plains, NY: Knowledge Industry Publications.

Crossan, M. M., R. E. White, H. W. Lane, and L. Klus. 1996. The Improvising Organization: Where Planning Meets Opportunity. *Organizational Dynamics* 24, no. 4:20–34.

Culnan, M. J. 1983. Environmental Scanning: The Effects of Task Complexity and Source Accessibility on Information Gathering Behavior. *Decision Sciences* 14, no. 2:194–206.

Cyert, R. M., and J. G. March. 1963. *A Behavioral Theory of the Firm.* Englewood Cliffs, NJ: Prentice-Hall.

————. 1992. *A Behavioral Theory of the Firm.* 2nd ed. Oxford, UK: Blackwell.

Daft, R. L., and R. H. Lengel. 1986. Organizational Information Requirements: Media Richness and Structural Design. *Management Science* 32, no. 5:554–71.

Daft, R. L., J. Sormunen, and D. Parks. 1988. Chief Executive Scanning, Environmental Characteristics, and Company Performance: An Empirical Study. *Strategic Management Journal* 9, no. 2:123–39.

Daft, R. L., and K. E. Weick. 1984. Toward a Model of Organizations as Interpretation Systems. *Academy of Management Review* 9, no. 2:284–95.

Damasio, A. R. 1994. *Descartes' Error: Emotion, Reason, and the Human Brain.* New York, NY: Grosset/Putnam.

Davenport, T. H. 1993. *Process Innovation: Reengineering Work Through Information Technology.* Boston, MA: Harvard Business School Press.

Daveport, T. H., R. G. Eccles, and L. Prusak. 1992. Information Politics. *Sloan Management Review* 34, no. 1:53–63.

de Geus, A. P. 1988. Planning as Learning. *Harvard Business Review* 66, no. 2:70–74.

Dervin, B. 1983a. Information as a User Construct: The Relevance of Perceived Information Needs to Synthesis and Interpretation. *Knowledge Structure and Use: Implications for Synthesis and Interpretation,* eds. S. A. Ward and L. A. Reed, 153–84. Philadelphia, PA: Temple University Press.

———. 1983b. An Overview of Sense-Making: Concepts, Methods, and Results to Date. Paper presented at the International Communication Association Annual Meeting; Dallas, TX, May 1983. Available: Brenda Dervin, Department of Communication, Ohio State University, Columbus, OH 43210.

———. 1992. From the Mind's Eye of the 'User': The Sense-Making Qualitative–Quantitative Methodology. In *Qualitative Research in Information Management,* eds. J. D. Glazier and R. R. Powell, 61–84. Englewood, CO: Libraries Unlimited.

Dervin, B., and K. Clark. 1987. Asking Significant Questions: Alternative Tools for Information Need and Accountability Assessments by Libraries. Report to California State Library.

Dervin, B., and M. Nilan. 1986. Information Needs and Uses. In *Annual Review of Information Science and Technology,* ed. M. E. Williams, 3–33. White Plains, NY: Knowledge Industry Publications.

Dill, W. R. 1962. The Impact of Environment on Organizational Development. In *Concepts and Issues in Administrative Behavior,* eds. S. Mailick and E. H. Van Ness, 94–109. Englewood Cliffs, NJ: Prentice-Hall.

DiMaggio, P., and W. W. Powell. 1983. The Iron Cage Revisited: Institutional Isomorphism and Collective Rationality in Organizational Fields. *American Sociological Review* 48, no.2: 147–60.

Donnellon, A., B. Gray, and M. G. Bougon. 1986. Communication, Meaning, and Organized Action. *Administrative Science Quarterly* 31 no. 1 (March): 43–55.

Douglas, M. 1986. *How Institutions Think.* Syracuse, NY: Syracuse University Press.

Drucker, P. F. 1993. *Post-Capitalist Society.* New York, NY: HarperCollins.

Duncan, R. B. 1972. Characteristics of Organizational Environments and Perceived Environmental Uncertainty. *Administrative Science Quarterly* 17, no. 3:313–327.

Eden, C. 1992. On the Nature of Cognitive Maps. *Journal of Management Studies* 29, no. 3: 261–85.

Eisenhardt, K. M. 1989. Making Fast Strategic Decisions in High-Velocity Environments. *Academy of Management Journal* 32, no. 3: 543–76.

———. 1990. Speed and Strategic Choice: How Managers Accelerate Decision Making. *California Management Review* 32, no. 3:39–54.

Ellis, D. 1989a. A Behavioural Approach to Information Retrieval System Design. *Journal of Documentation* 45, no. 3:171–212.

———. 1989b. A Behavioural Model for Information Retrieval System Design. *Journal of Information Science* 15, no. 4/5 (Special Issue): 237–47.

Ellis, D., D. Cox, and K. Hall. 1993. A Comparison of the Information Seeking Patterns of Researchers in the Physical and Social Sciences. *Journal of Documentation* 49, no. 4:356–69.

Engeström, Yrjo. 1991. Developmental Work Research: Reconstructing Expertise through Expansive Learning. In *Human Jobs and Computer Interfaces,* eds. M. Nurminen and G. Weir, 265–90. North-Holland, Netherlands: Elsevier.

Feldman, M. S. 1989. *Order without Design: Information Production and Policy Making.* Stanford, CA: Stanford University Press.

———. 1991. The Meanings of Ambiguity: Learning from Stories and Metaphors. In *Reframing Organizational Culture,* eds. Peter J. Frost et al., 145–56. Newbury Park, CA: Sage.

Feldman, M. S., and J. G. March. 1981. Information in Organizations as Signal and Symbol. *Administrative Science Quarterly* 26, no. 2:171–86.

Fenner, F., D. A. Henderson, I. Arita, Z. Jezek, and I. D. Ladnyi. 1988. *Smallpox and Its Eradication.* Geneva, Switzerland: World Health Organization.

Festinger, L. 1957. *A Theory of Cognitive Dissonance.* Stanford, CA: Stanford University Press.

Fineman, S., ed. 1993. *Emotion In Organizations.* London, UK: Sage.

Finney, M., and I. I. Mitroff. 1986. Strategic Plan Failures: The Organization as Its Own Worst Enemy. In *The Thinking Organization: Dynamics of Organizational Social Cognition,* eds. H. P. Sims, Jr., D. A. Gioia, and Associates, 317–35. San Francisco, CA: Jossey-Bass.

Fiol, M. C. 1994. Consensus, Diversity, and Learning in Organizations. *Organization Science* 5, no. 3: 403–20.

Galbraith, J. R. 1973. *Designing Complex Organizations.* Reading, MA: Addison-Wesley.

Galer, G., and K. van der Heijden. 1992. The Learning Organization: How Planners Create Organizational Learning. *Marketing Intelligence & Planning* 10, no. 6:5–12.

Garud, R., and M. A. Rappa. 1994. A Socio-Cognitive Model of Technology Evolution: The Case of Cochlear Implants. *Organization Science* 5, no. 3:344–62.

Garvey, W. D. 1979. *Communication: The Essence of Science.* Oxford, UK: Pergamon Press.

Geertz, C. 1973. *The Interpretation of Cultures.* New York, NY: Basic Books.

Gerstberger, P. G., and T. J. Allen. 1968. Criteria Used by Research and Development Engineers in the Selection of an Information Source. *Journal of Applied Psychology* 52, no. 4:272–79.

Ghoshal, S. 1988. Environmental Scanning in Korean Firms: Organizational Isomorphism in Practice. *Journal of International Business Studies* 19, no. 1:69–86.

Giddens, A. 1984. *The Constitution of Society: Outline of the Theory of Structuration.* Oxford, UK: Polity Press.

Gioia, D. A. 1986. Symbols, Scripts, and Sensemaking: Creating Meaning in the Organizational Experience. In *The Thinking Organization: Dynamics of Organizational Social Cognition,* eds. H. P. Sims, Jr., D. A. Gioia, and Associates, 49–74. San Francisco, CA: Jossey-Bass.

Gioia, D. A., A. Donnellon, and H. P. Sims, Jr. 1989. Communication and Cognition in Appraisal: A Tale of Two Paradigms. *Organization Studies* 10, no. 4:503–29.

Gioia, D. A. and H. P. Sims, Jr. 1986. Introduction. *The Thinking Organization: Dy-*

namics of Organizational Social Cognition, eds. H. P. Sims, Jr., D. A. Gioia, and Associates, 1–19. San Francisco, CA: Jossey-Bass.

Goethe, J. W. von. ©1808, 1952. *Faust: Parts One and Two.* Translated by George Madison Priest. Chicago, IL: Encyclopaedia Britannica.

Goldstein, J. 1994. *The Unshackled Organization: Facing the Challenge of Unpredictability Through Spontaneous Reorganization.* Portland, OR: Productivity Press.

Harter, S. P. 1986. *Online Information Retrieval: Concepts, Principles, and Techniques.* Toronto, Ont: Academic Press.

———. 1992. Psychological Relevance and Information Science. *Journal of the American Society for Information Science* 43, no. 9:602–15.

Hayek, F. 1945. The Use of Knowledge in Society. *American Economic Review* 35, no. 4:519–30.

Haynes, R. B., K. A. McKibbon, C. J. Walker, N. C. Ryan, D. F. Fitzgerald, and M. F. Ramsden. 1990. On-Line Access to MEDLINE in Clincal Settings. A Study of Use and Usefulness. *Annals of Internal Medicine* 112, no. 1:78–84.

Hedberg, B., P. C. Nystrom, and W. H. Starbuck. 1976. Camping on Seesaws: Prescriptions for a Self-Designing Organization. *Administrative Science Quarterly* 21, no. 1:41–65.

Henderson, D. A. 1972. Smallpox Surveillance in the Strategy of Global Eradication, Inter-regional Seminar on Cholera and Smallpox, Malaysia and Singapore, November 11–18. WHO/SE/72.8.

Herner, S. 1954. Information-Gathering Habits of Workers in Pure and Applied Science. *Industrial and Engineering Chemistry* 46:228–36.

Herner, S., and M. Herner. 1967. Information Needs and Uses in Science and Technology. In *Annual Review of Information Science and Technology,* vol. 2, ed. C. A. Cuadra, 1–34. New York, NY: Interscience.

Hewins, E. T. 1990. Information Need and Use Studies. In *Annual Review of Information Science and Technology,* vol. 25, ed. M. E. Williams, 145–72. New York, NY: Elsevier.

Hickson, D. J., R. J. Butler, D. Cray, G. R. Mallory, and D. C. Wilson. 1986. *Top Decisions: Strategic Decision-Making in Organizations.* San Francisco, CA: Jossey-Bass.

Hilsman, R. 1967. *To Move a nation; The Politics of Foreign Policy in the Administration of John F. Kennedy.* Garden City, NY: Doubleday.

Hogarth, R. M. 1987. *Judgement and Choice: The Psychology of Decisions.* 2nd ed. New York, NY: John Wiley.

Hogarth, R. M., and S. Makridakis. 1981. Forecasting and Planning: An Evaluation. *Management Science* 27, no. 2:115–38.

Hopkins, J. W. 1988. The Eradication of Smallpox: Organizational Learning and Innovation in International Health Administration. *The Journal of Developing Areas* 22, (April): 321–32.

———. 1989. *The Eradication of Smallpox: Organizational Learning and Innovation in International Health Administration.* Boulder, CO: Westview Press.

Huber, G. P. 1991. Organizational Learning: The Contributing Processes and the Literature. *Organization Science* 2, no. 1:88–115.

Huff, A. S., ed. 1990. *Mapping Strategic Thought.* Chichester, UK: John Wiley.

Ingrassia, P. J. and J. B. White. 1994. *Comeback: The Fall and Rise of the American Automobile Industry.* New York, NY: Simon & Schuster.

Isenberg, D. J. 1984. How Senior Managers Think. *Harvard Business Review* 62, no. 2:81–90.

———. 1986a. The Structure and Process of Understanding: Implications for Managerial Action. In *The Thinking Organization,* eds. H. P. Sims, Jr., and D. A. Gioia, 238–62. San Francisco, CA: Jossey-Bass.

———. 1986b. Thinking and Managing: A Verbal Protocol Analysis of Managerial Problem Solving. *Academy of Management Journal* 29, no. 4:775–88.

———. 1987. The Tactics of Strategic Opportunism. *Harvard Business Review* 65, no. 2:92–7.

Janis, I. 1982. *Groupthink: Psychological Studies of Policy Decision.* Boston, MA: Houghton Mifflin.

Janis, I. and L. Mann. 1977. *Decision Making: A Psychological Analysis of Conflict, Choice, and Commitment.* New York, NY: Free Press.

Jones, T. S. 1976. Smallpox Eradication: A Study of Motivation. Unpublished manuscript.

Kahneman, D., P. Slovic, and A. Tversky, eds. 1982. *Judgement Under Uncertainty: Heuristics and Biases.* Cambridge, UK: Cambridge University Press.

Katz, R., and T. J. Allen. 1982. Investigating the Not Invented Here (NIH) Syndrome: A Look at the Performance, Tenure, and Communication Patterns of 50 R&D Project Groups. *R&D Management* 12, no. 1:7–19.

Kefalas, A., and P. P. Schoderbek. 1973. Scanning the Business Environment—Some Empirical Results. *Decision Sciences* 4, no. 1:63–74.

Kelly, G. A. 1963. *A Theory of Personality: The Psychology of Personal Constructs.* New York, NY: W. W. Norton.

Kennedy, R. F. 1969. *Thirteen Days: A Memoir of the Cuban Missile Crisis.* New York, NY: W.W. Norton.

Kingdon, J. W. 1984. *Agendas, Alternatives, and Public Policies.* Boston, MA: Little, Brown.

———. 1995. *Agendas, Alternatives, and Public Policies.* 2nd ed. New York, NY: HarperCollins.

Kiesler, C. A. 1971. *The Psychology of Commitment.* New York, NY: Academic Press.

Kleiner, A. 1989. Consequential Heresies: How "Thinking the Unthinkable" Changed Royal Dutch/Shell. [Available from the author.]

———. 1994. Creating Scenarios. In *The Fifth Discipline Fieldbook,* eds. P. Senge, A. Kleiner, C. Roberts, R. Ross, and B. Smith, 275–78. New York, NY: Doubleday.

Kogut, B., and U. Zander. 1992. Knowledge of the Firm, Combinative Capabilities, and the Replication of Technology. *Organization Science* 3, no. 3:383–97.

Kotter, J. P. 1982. What Effective General Managers Really Do. *Harvard Business Review* 60, no. 6:156–67.

Kremer, J. M. 1980. Information Flow among Engineers in a Design Company. Ph.D. Diss., University of Illinois at Urbana-Champaign.

Kuhlthau, C.C. 1988. Developing a Model of the Library Search Process: Cognitive and Affective Aspects. *Reference Quarterly* 28, no. 2:232–42.

———. 1991. Inside the Search Process: Information Seeking from the User's Perspective. *Journal of the American Society for Information Science* 42, no. 5:361–71.

————. 1993a. A Principle of Uncertainty for Information Seeking. *Journal of Documentation* 49, no. 4:339–55.

————. 1993b. *Seeking Meaning: A Process Approach to Library and Information Services.* Norwood, NJ: Ablex Publishing.

Lakoff, G. and M. Johnson. 1980. *Metaphors We Live By.* Chicago, IL: University of Chicago Press.

Lave, J., and E. Wenger. 1991. *Situated Learning: Legitimate Peripheral Participation.* Cambridge, UK: Cambridge University Press.

LeDoux, J. 1996. *The Emotional Brain: The Mysterious Underpinnings of Emotional Life.* New York, NY: Simon & Schuster.

Le Guin, U. K. ©1969. *The Left Hand of Darkness.* New York, NY: Harper and Row [1980].

Leonard-Barton, D. 1995. *Wellsprings of Knowledge: Building and Sustaining the Sources of Innovation.* Boston, MA: Harvard Business School Press.

Lester, R., and J. Waters. 1989. *Environmental Scanning and Business Strategy.* London, UK: British Library, Research and Development Department.

Levinthal, D. A., and J. G. March. 1993. The Myopia of Learning. *Strategic Management Journal* 14 (Special Issue, Winter): 95–112.

Levitt, B., and C. Nass. 1989. The Lid on the Garbage Can: Institutional Constraints on Decision Making in the Technical Core of College-Text Publishers. *Administrative Science Quarterly* 34, no. 2:190–207.

Lin, N., and W. D. Garvey. 1972. Information Needs and Uses. In *Annual Review of Information Science and Technology* vol. 7, ed. C. A. Cuadra, 4–37. Washington, DC: American Society for Information Science.

Lindblom, C. E. 1959. The Science of Muddling Through. *Public Administration Review* 19, no. 2:79–88.

Line, M. B. 1971. The Information Uses and Needs of Social Scientists: An Overview of INFROSS. *Aslib Proceedings* 23, no. 8:412–34.

Line, M. B., J. M. Brittain, and F. A. Cranmer. 1971. Investigation into Information Requirements of the Social Sciences Research Report No. 2: Information Requirements of Social Scientists in Government Departments. University Library, University of Bath, Bath, UK.

Lipetz, B. A. 1970. Information Needs and Uses. *Annual Review of Information Science and Technology,* vol. 5, ed. C. A. Cuadra, 3–32. Chicago, IL: Encyclopaedia Britannica.

Lord, R. G., and R. J. Foti. 1986. Schema Theories, Information Processing, and Organizational Behavior. In *The Thinking Organization: Dynamics of Organizational Social Cognition,* eds. H. P. Sims, Jr., D. A. Gioia, and Associates, 20–48. San Francisco, CA: Jossey-Bass.

Lyles, M. A. 1987. Defining Strategic Problems: Subjective Criteria of Executives. *Organization Studies* 8, no. 3:263–80.

Lyles, M. A., and I. I. Mitroff. 1980. Organizational Problem Formulation: An Empirical Study. *Administrative Science Quarterly* 25, no. 1:102–119.

MacMullin, S. E., and R. S. Taylor. 1984. Problem Dimensions and Information Traits. *Information Society* 3, no. 1:91–111.

March, J. G. 1976. The Technology of Foolishness. In *Ambiguity and Choice in Organizations,* eds. J. G. March and J. Olsen, 69–81. Bergen, Norway: Universitetsforlaget.

———. 1978. Bounded Rationality, Ambiguity, and the Engineering of Choice. *Bell Journal of Economics* 9, no. 2:587–608.

———. 1991. Exploration and Exploitation in Organizational Learning. *Organization Science* 2, no. 1:71–87.

———. 1994. *A Primer on Decision Making: How Decisions Happen.* New York, NY: Free Press.

March, J. G., and Cohen. 1976.*Leadership and Ambiguity.* 2nd ed. Boston, MA: Harvard Business School Press.

March, J. G. and J. P. Olsen. 1976. *Ambiguity and Choice in Organizations.* Bergen, Norway: Universitetsforlaget.

March, J. G., and Z. Shapira. 1987. Managerial Perspectives on Risk and Risk Taking. *Management Science* 33, no. 11, (November): 1404–18.

March, J. G., and H. A. Simon. 1958. *Organizations.* New York, NY: John Wiley.

———. 1993. *Organizations.* 2nd ed. Oxford, UK: Blackwell.

Marchionini, G. 1995. *Information Seeking in Electronic Environments.* Cambridge, UK: Cambridge University Press.

Markey, K. 1981. Levels of Question Formulation in Negotiation of Information Need during the Online Presearch Interview: A Proposed Model. *Information Processing & Management* 17, no. 5:215–25.

Martin, J. 1992. *Cultures in Organizations: Three Perspectives.* New York, NY: Oxford University Press.

Martin, J., and D. Meyerson. 1988. Organizational Culture and the Denial, Channeling, and Acknowledgment of Ambiguity. In *Managing Ambiguity and Change* , eds. L. R. Pondy, R. J. Boland, Jr., and H. Thomas, 93–125. New York, NY: John Wiley.

Martyn, J. 1964. *Literature Searching by Research Scientists.* London, UK: Aslib Research Dept.

———. 1974. Information Needs and Uses. In *Annual Review of Information Science and Technology* 9, ed. C. A. Cuadra, 3–23. Washington, DC: American Society for Information Science.

McCall, M. W., Jr., and R. E. Kaplan. 1990. *Whatever It Takes: The Realities of Managerial Decision Making.* 2nd ed. Englewood Cliffs, NJ: Prentice-Hall.

McCaskey, M. B. 1982. *The Executive Challenge.* Toronto, Ont: Pitman.

McCurdy, H. E. 1989. The Decay of NASA's Technical Culture. *Space Policy* (November): 301–10.

McGee, J. V., and L. Prusak. 1993. *Managing Information Strategically.* New York, NY: John Wiley.

Medawar, P. B. 1968. Lucky Jim. *New York Times Book Review* (March 28): 3–5.

Meltsner, A. J. 1976. *Policy Analysts in the Bureaucracy.* Berkeley, CA: University of California Press.

Menzel, H. 1966. Information Needs and Uses in Science and Technology. In *Annual Review of Information Science and Technology,* vol. 1, ed. C. A. Cuadra, 41–69. New York, NY: Interscience.

Merton, R. K. 1968. Making It Scientifically. *New York Times Book Review,* (February 25): 41–43.

Meyer, A. D. 1982. Adapting to Environmental Jolts. *Administrative Science Quarterly* 27, no. 4: 515–37.

Meyerson, D., and J. Martin. 1987. Cultural Change: An Integration of Three Different Views. *Journal of Management Studies* 24, no. 6:623–47.

Mick, C. K., G. N. Lindsey, and D. Callahan. 1980. Toward Usable User Studies. *Journal of the American Society for Information Science* 31, no. 5:347–56.

Mintzberg, H. 1973. *The Nature of Managerial Work.* New York, NY: Harper & Row.

Mintzberg, H., D. Raisinghani, and A. Théorêt. 1976. The Structure of "Unstructured" Decision Processes. *Administrative Science Quarterly* 21, no. 2:246–75.

Mitroff, I. I., and H. A. Linstone. 1993. *The Unbounded Mind: Breaking the Chains of Traditional Business Thinking.* New York, NY: Oxford University Press.

Morgan, G. 1986. *Images of Organization.* Newbury Park, CA: Sage.

Morris, R. C. T. 1994. Toward a User-Centered Information Service. *Journal of the American Society for Information Science* 45, no. 1:20–30.

National Library of Medicine. 1988. *Survey of Individual Users of MEDLINE on the NLM System.* Springfield, VA: U.S. Dept. of Commerce, National Technical Information Service.

Nelson, R., and S. Winter. 1982. *An Evolutionary Theory of Economic Change.* Cambridge, MA: Belknap Press.

Nisbett, R., and L. Ross. 1980. *Human Inference: Strategies and Shortcomings of Social Judgement.* Englewood Cliffs, NJ: Prentice-Hall.

Nishi, K., C. Schoderbek, and P. P. Schoderbek. 1982. Scanning the Organizational Environment: Some Empirical Results. *Human Systems Management* 3, no. 4:233–45.

Noble, D. F. 1984. *Forces of Production: A Social History of Industrial Automation.* New York, NY: Knopf.

Nonaka, I., P. Byosiere, C. C. Borucki, and N. Konno. 1994. Organizational Knowledge Creation Theory: A First Comprehensive Test. *International Business Review* (Special Issue).

Nonaka, I., and H. Takeuchi. 1995. *The Knowledge-Creating Company: How Japanese Companies Create the Dynamics of Innovation.* New York, NY: Oxford University Press.

Normann, R., and R. Ramirez. 1993. From Value Chain to Value Constellation: Designing Interactive Strategy. *Harvard Business Review* 71 no. 4:65–77.

Nutt, P. C. 1992. Formulation Tactics and the Success of Organizational Decision Making. *Decision Sciences* 23, no. 3:519–540.

Olsen, M. D., B. Murthy, and R. Teare. 1994. CEO Perspectives on Scanning the Global Hotel Business Environment. *International Journal of Contemporary Hospitality Management* 6, no. 4:3–9.

O'Reilly, C. A. 1983. The Use of Information in Organizational Decision Making: A Model and Some Propositions. In *Research in Organizational Behavior,* eds. B. M. Staw and L. L. Cummings, 103–39. Greenwich, CT: JAI Press.

O'Reilly, C. A., J. A. Chatman, and J. C. Anderson. 1987. Message Flow and Decision Making. In *Handbook of Organizational Communication,* eds. F. M. Jablin et al., 600–23. Newbury Park, CA: Sage.

Orlikowski, W. J. 1988. Information Technology in Post-Industrial Organizations. Ph.D. Diss., New York University.

Orr, J. E. 1990. Sharing Knowledge, Celebrating Identity: Community Memory in a Service Culture. In *Collective Remembering* , eds. D. Middleton and D. Edwards, 169–89. UK: Sage.

Paisley, W. 1968. Information Needs and Uses. In *Annual Review of Information Sci-*

ence and Technology, vol. 3, ed. C. A. Cuadra, 1–30. Chicago, IL: Encyclopaedia Britannica.

Pelz, D. C. and F. M. Andrews. 1966. *Scientists in Organizations: Productive Climates for Research and Development.* Revised ed. Ann Arbor, MI: Institute for Social Research, University of Michigan.

Perrow, C. 1986. *Complex Organizations: A Critical Essay.* 3rd ed. New York, NY: McGraw-Hill.

Pettigrew, A. M. 1972. Information Control as a Power Resource. *Sociology* 6, no. 1:187–204.

———. 1973. *The Politics of Organizational Decision Making.* London, UK: Tavistock Institute.

Pfeffer, J., and G. R. Salancik. 1974. Organizational Decision Making as a Political Process: The Case of a University Budget. *Administrative Science Quarterly* 19, no. 2:135–151.

Piatelli-Palmarini, M. 1994. *Inevitable Illusions.* New York, NY: John Wiley.

Pinelli, T. E. 1991. *The Relationship between the Use of U. S. Government Technical Reports by U. S. Aerospace Engineers and Scientists and Selected Institutional and Sociometric Variables.* Washington, DC: National Aeronautics and Space Administration.

Pinfield, L. T. 1986. A Field Evaluation of Perspectives on Organizational Decision Making. *Administrative Science Quarterly* 31, no. 3:365–88.

Plotkin, H. C. 1994. *Darwin Machines and the Nature of Knowledge.* Cambridge, MA: Harvard University Press.

Polanyi, M. 1962. *Personal Knowledge towards a Post-Critical Philosophy.* Chicago, IL: University of Chicago Press.

———. 1966. *The Tacit Dimension.* London, UK: Routledge & Kegan Paul.

Popper, K. R. 1979. *Objective Knowledge: An Evolutionary Approach.* Oxford, UK: Clarendon.

Porac, J. F., J. R. Meindl and C. Stubbart. 1996. Introduction. In *Cognition within and between Organizations,* eds. J. R. Meindl, C. Stubbart, and J. F. Porac: ix–xxiii. Thousand Oaks, CA: Sage.

Porac, J. F., H. Thomas, and C. Baden-Fuller. 1989. Competitive Groups as Cognitive Communities: The Case of Scottish Knitwear Manufacturers. *Journal of Management Studies* 26, no. 4:397–416.

Porter, M. E. 1985. *Competitive Advantage: Creating and Sustaining Superior Performance.* New York, NY: Free Press.

Prahalad, C. K., and R. A. Bettis. 1986. The Dominant Logic: A New Linkage between Diversity and Performance. *Strategic Management Journal* 7, no. 6:485–501.

Presidential Commission on the Space Shuttle Challenger Accident. 1986. *Report to the President by the Presidential Commission on the Space Shuttle Challenger Accident,* vols. 1–5. Washington, DC: U.S. Government Printing Office.

Quinn, J. B., P. Anderson, and S. Finkelstein. 1996. Managing Professional Intellect: Making the Most of the Best. *Harvard Business Review* 74, no. 2:71–80.

Reich, Robert. 1991. *The Work of Nations: Preparing Ourselves for 21st Century Capitalism.* New York, NY: Simon & Schuster.

Rogers, E. M. 1983. *Diffusion of Innovations.* 3rd ed. New York, NY: Free Press.

Rosenbaum, H. 1993. Information Use Environments and Structuration: Towards an Integration of Taylor and Giddens. In *Proceedings of the 56th Annual Meeting of the American Society for Information Science,* ed. Susan Bonzi, 235–45. Columbus, OH: Learned Information.

———. 1996. Managers and Information in Organizations: Towards a Structurational Concept of the Information Use Environment of Managers. Ph.D. Diss., Syracuse University.

Rosenberg, V. 1967. Factors Affecting the Preferences of Industrial Personnel for Information Gathering Methods. *Information Storage and Retrieval* 3, no. 3:119–27.

Rosenbloom, R. S., and F. W. Wolek. 1970. *Technology and Information Transfer: A Survey of Practice in Industrial Organizations.* Boston, MA: Division of Research, Graduate School of Business Administration, Harvard University.

Ross, J., and B. M. Staw. 1986. Expo 86: An Escalation Prototype. *Administrative Science Quarterly* 31, no. 2:274–97.

———. 1993. Organizational Escalation and Exit: Lessons from the Shoreham Nuclear Power Plant. *Academy of Management Journal* 36, no. 4:701–32.

Sabel, C. F. 1982. *Work and Politics: The Division of Labor in Industry.* Cambridge, UK: Cambridge University Press.

Sackmann, S. A. 1991. *Cultural Knowledge in Organizations: Exploring the Collective Mind.* Newbury Park, CA: Sage.

———. 1992. Culture and Subcultures: An Analysis of Organizational Knowledge. *Administrative Science Quarterly* 37, no. 1:140–61.

Salancik, G. R. 1977. Commitment and the Control of Organizational Behavior and Belief. In *New Directions in Organizational Behavior,* eds. B. M. Staw and G. R. Salancik, 1–54. Chicago, IL: St. Clair.

Salancik, G. R., and J. Pfeffer. 1978. A Social Information Processing Approach to Job Attitudes and Task Design. *Administrative Science Quarterly* 23, no. 2:224–53.

Saracevic, T. 1970. The Notion of 'Relevance' in Information Science. In *Introduction to Information Science,* ed. T. Saracevic, 111–51. New York, NY: R. R. Bowker.

———. 1975. Relevance: A Review of and a Framework for the Thinking on the Notion in Information Science. *Journal of the American Society for Information Science* 26, no. 6:321–43.

Saracevic, T., et al. 1988a. A Study of Information Seeking and Retrieving. Part I: Background and Methodology. *Journal of the American Society for Information Science* 39, no. 3:161–76.

———. 1988b. A Study of Information Seeking and Retrieving. Part II: Users, Questions, and Effectiveness. *Journal of the American Society for Information Science* 39, no. 3:177–96.

———. 1988c. A Study of Information Seeking and Retrieving. Part III: Searchers, Searches, and Overlap. *Journal of the American Society for Information Science* 39, no. 3:197–216.

Schacter, D. L. 1996. *Searching for Memory: The Brain, The Mind, and The Past.* New York, NY: Basic Books.

Schamber, L. 1994. Relevance and Information Behavior. In *Annual Review of Information Science and Technology* vol. 29, ed. M. E. Williams, 3–48. Medford, NJ: Learned Information.

Schein, E. H. 1985. *Organizational Culture and Leadership.* San Francisco, CA: Jossey- Bass.

———. 1991. What Is Culture. In *Reframing Organizational Culture* , eds. P. J. Frost, L. F. Moore, M. Reis Louis, C. C. Lundberg, and J. Martin, 243–53. Newbury Park, CA: Sage.

————. 1992. *Organizational Culture and Leadership.* San Francisco, CA: Jossey-Bass.

Schön, D. A. 1983. *The Reflective Practitioner: How Professionals Think in Action.* New York, NY: Basic Books.

Schumpeter, J. A. 1934. *The Theory of Economic Development.* Cambridge, MA: Harvard University Press.

Schwartzman, H. B. 1987. The Significance of Meetings in an American Mental Health Center. *American Ethnologist* 14, no. 2:271–94.

————. 1989. *The Meeting: Gatherings in Organizations and Communities,* vol. 56. New York, NY: Plenum.

Schwenk, C. R. 1984. Cognitive Simplification Processes in Strategic Decision-Making. In *Strategic Management Journal* 5, no. 2:111–28.

Senge, P. M. 1990. *The Fifth Discipline: The Art & Practice of the Learning Organization.* New York, NY: Doubleday Currency.

Shrivastava, P., I. Mitroff, and M. Alvesson. 1987. Nonrationality in Organizational Actions. *International Studies of Management and Organization* 17, no. 3:90–109.

Shrivastava, P., and S. Schneider. 1984. Organizational Frames of Reference. *Human Relations* 37, no. 10:795–809.

Siffin, W. J. 1977. *Problem Analysis: Lessons from a Case of Smallpox.* Bloomington, IN: Program of Advanced Studies in Institution Building and Technical Assistance Methodology.

Simon, H. A. 1957. *Models of Man: Social and Rational.* New York, NY: John Wiley.

————. 1976. *Administrative Behavior: A Study of Decision-Making Processes in Administrative Organization.* 3rd ed. New York, NY: Free Press.

————. 1977. *The New Science of Management Decision.* Revised ed. Englewood Cliffs, NJ: Prentice-Hall.

————. 1987. Making Management Decisions: The Role of Intuition and Emotion. *Academy of Management Executive* 1, no. 1:57–64.

Sims, Jr., H. P., D. A. Gioia and Associates, eds. 1986. *The Thinking Organization: Dynamics of Organizational Social Cognition.* San Francisco, CA: Jossey-Bass.

Singley, M. K., and J. R. Anderson. 1989. *The Transfer of Cognitive Skill.* Cambridge, MA: Harvard University Press.

Skelton, Barbara. 1973. Scientists and Social Scientists as Information Users: A Comparison of Results of Science User Studies with the Investigation into Information Requirements of the Social Sciences. *Journal of Librarianship* 5, no. 2 (April): 138–156.

Smircich, L. 1983. Organizations as Shared Meanings. In *Organizational Symbolism* , eds. L. R. Pondy, P. J. Frost, G. Morgan, and T. C. Dandridge, 55–65. Greenwich, CT: JAI Press.

Snyder, M. 1984. When Belief Creates Reality. In *Advances in Experimental Social Psychology,* ed. L. Berkowitz, 248–305. Orlando, FL: Academic Press.

Sorensen, T. 1963. *Decision-Making in the White House: The Olive Branch and the Arrow.* Foreword by J. F. Kennedy. New York, NY: Columbia University Press.

Spender, J. C. 1989. *Industry Recipes.* Oxford, UK: Basil Blackwell.

Sproull, L. S., S. Weiner, and D. Wolf. 1978. *Organizing an Anarchy: Belief, Bureaucracy and Politics in the National Institute of Education.* Chicago, IL: University of Chicago Press.

Squire, L. R., and B. J. Knowlton. 1995. The Organization of Memory. In *The Mind, the Brain, and Complex Adaptive System,* eds. H. Morowitz, and J. L. Singer, 63–97. Don Mills, Oni.: Addison-Wesley.

Starbuck, W. H. 1992. Learning by Knowledge-Intensive Firms. *Journal of Management Studies* 29, no. 6:713–40.

Starbuck, W. H., and F. J. Milliken. 1988a. Challenger: Fine Tuning the Organization until Something Breaks. *Journal of Management Studies* 25, no. 4:319–40.

———. 1988b. Executives' Perceptual Filters: What They Notice and How They Make Sense. In *The Executive Effect: Concepts and Methods for Studying Top Managers,* ed. D. C. Hambrick, 35–65. Greenwich, CT: JAI Press.

Staw, B. M. and J. Ross. 1987. Knowing When to Pull the Plug. *Harvard Business Review* 65, no. 2:68–74.

Stein, E. W. 1995. Organizaiional Memory: Review of Concepts and Recommendations for Management. *International Journal of Information Management*15, no. 2:17–32.

Stinchcombe, A. L. 1990. *Information and Organizations.* Berkeley, CA: University of California Press.

Streatfield, D. R., and T. D. Wilson. 1982. Information Needs in Local Authority Social Services Departments: A Third Report on Project INISS. *Journal of Documentation* 38, no. 4:273–81.

Suchman, L. A. 1987. *Plans and Situated Actions: The Problems of Human–Machine Communication.* Cambridge, UK: Cambridge University Press.

Sutherland, S. 1992. *Irrationality: The Enemy Within.* London, UK: Constable.

Sutton, S. A. 1994. The Role of Attorney Mental Models of Law in Case Relevance Determinations: An Exploratory Analysis. *Journal of the American Society for Information Science* 45, no. 3:186–200.

Sveiby, K. E. 1996. *Tacit Knowledge.* Available from the author at: http://www.sveiby.com.au

Taylor, R. S. 1968. Question-Negotiation and Information Seeking in Libraries. *College & Research Libraries* 29, no. 3:178–94.

———. 1986.*Value-Added Processes in Information Systems.* Norwood, NJ: Ablex Publishing.

———. 1991. Information Use Environments. In *Progress in Communication Science,* eds. B. Dervin and M. J. Voigt, 217–54. Norwood, NJ: Ablex Publishing.

Thomas, J. B., S. M. Clark, and D. A. Gioia. 1993. Strategic Sensemaking and Organizational Performance: Linkages among Scanning, Interpretation, Action, and Outcomes. *Academy of Management Journal* 36, no. 2:239–70.

Tushman, M. L., and T. J. Scanlan. 1981. Boundary Spanning Individuals: Their Role in Information Transfer and Their Antecedents. *Academy of Management Journal* 28, no. 2:289–305.

Tversky, A., and D. Kahneman. 1974. Judgment under Uncertainty: Heuristics and Biases. In *Judgement Under Uncertainty: Heuristics and Biases,* eds. D. Kahneman, P. Slovic, and A. Tversky, 3–20. Cambridge, UK: Cambridge University Press.

Utterback, J. M. 1994. *Mastering the Dynamics of Innovation: How Companies Can Seize Opportunities in the Face of Technological Change.* Cambridge, MA: Harvard Business School Press.

van der Heijden, K. 1994. Shell's Internal Consultancy. In *The Fifth Discipline Fieldbook,* eds. P. Senge, A. Kleiner, C. Roberts, R. Ross, and B. Smith, 279–86. New York, NY: Doubleday.

————. 1996. *Scenarios.* New York, NY: John Wiley.

van der Wyck, R. W. A. and P. G. M. Hesseling. 1994. Scenario Planning As Learning: "Metanoia." Diss., Faculty of Economics, Department of Business Organization, Rotterdam; ,MA Thesis Faculty of Economics, Department of Business Organization. Rotterdam: Erasmus University.

Varela, F. J., E. Thompson, and E. Rosch. 1991. *The Embodied Mind-Cognitive Science and Human Experience.* London, UK: MIT Press.

Vaughan, D. 1996. *The Challenger Launch Decision : Risky Technology, Culture and Deviance at NASA.* Chicago, IL: University of Chicago Press.

von Hippel, E. 1988. *The Sources of Innovation.* New York, NY: Oxford University Press.

————. 1994. "Sticky Information" and the Locus of Problem Solving: Implications for Innovation. *Management Science* 40, no. 4:429–39.

Vygotsky, L. S. 1978. *Mind in Society.* Cambridge, MA: Harvard University Press.

Wack, P. 1985. Scenarios: Uncharted Waters Ahead. *Harvard Business Review* 63, no. 5:72–89.

Wallas, G. 1926. *The Art of Thought.* London, UK: J. Cape.

Walsh, J. P. 1995. Managerial and Organizational Cognition: Notes from a Trip down Memory Lane. *Organization Science* 6, no. 3:280–321.

Walsh, J. P., and G. R. Ungson. 1991. Organizational Memory. *Academy of Management Review* 16, no. 1:57–91.

Watson, J. D. 1968. *The Double Helix: A Personal Account of the Discovery of the Structure of DNA.* New York, NY: Atheneum.

Weick, K. E. 1979a. Cognitive Processes in Organizations. In *Research in Organizational Behavior,* ed. B. M. Staw, 41–74. Greenwich, CT: JAI Press.

————. 1979. *The Social Psychology of Organizing.* 2nd ed. New York, NY: Random House.

————. 1995. *Sensemaking in Organizations.* Thousand Oaks, CA: Sage.

————. 1996. Prepare Your Organization to Fight Fires. *Harvard Business Review*74, no. 3:143–48.

Weick, K. E., and R. L. Daft. 1983. The Effectiveness of Interpretation Systems. In *Organizational Effectiveness: A Comparison of Multiple Models,* eds. K. S. Cameron and D. A. Whetten, 71–93. New York, NY: Academic Press.

Weick, K. E., D. P. Gilfillan, and T. Keith. 1973. The Effect of Composer Credibility on Orchestra Performance. *Sociometry* 36:435–62.

Wenger, E. 1991. Communities of Practice: Where Learning Happens. *Benchmark* (Fall): 82–84.

WHO. 1966. *Official Records,* 151. A19/P&B/2, (March 28).

Wikström, S., and R. Normann. 1994. *Knowledge and Value: A New Perspective on Corporate Transformation.* London, UK: Routledge.

Wilensky, H. 1967. *Organisational Intelligence: Knowledge and Policy in Government and Industry.* New York, NY: Basic Books.

Wilson, S. R., M. D. Cooper, and N. Starr-Schneidkraut. 1989. *Use of the Critical Incident Technique to Evaluate the Impact of MEDLINE.* Palo Alto, CA: American Institutes for Research in the Behavioral Sciences.

Wilson, T. D. 1981. On User Studies and Information Needs. *Journal of Documentation* 37, no. 1:3–15.

————. 1994. Information Needs and Uses: Fifty Years of Progress? In *Fifty Years of*

Information Progress: A Journal of Documentation Review, ed. B. C. Vickery, 15–51. London, UK: Association for Information Management.

Wilson, T. D.,and D. R. Streatfield. 1977. Information Needs in Local Authority Social Services Departments: An Interim Report on Project INISS. *Journal of Documentation* 33, no. 4:277–93.

———. 1981. Structured Observation in the Investigation of Information Needs. *Social Science Information Studies* 1, no. 3:173–84.

Wilson, T. D., D. R. Streatfield, and C. Mullings. 1979. Information Needs in Local Authority Social Services Departments: A Second Report on Project INISS. *Journal of Documentation* 35, no. 2:120–36.

Wilson, T., and C. Walsh. 1995. *Information Behaviour: An Inter-Disciplinary Perspective.* Sheffield, UK: University of Sheffield, Department of Information Studies.

Winter, S. G. 1987. Knowledge and Competence as Strategic Assets. In *The Competitive Challenge: Strategies for Industrial Innovation and Renewal,* ed. D. J. Teece, 159–84. Cambridge, UK: Ballinger.

———. 1994. Organizing for Continuous Improvement: Evolutionary Theory Meets the Quality Revolution. In *The Evolutionary Dynamics of Organizations* , eds. J. A. C. Baum and J. Singh. New York, NY: Oxford University Press.

Zuboff, S. 1988. *In the Age of the Smart Machine: The Future of Work and Power.* New York, NY: Basic Books.

INDEX

The letters *t* and *f* following entries denote table and figure respectively.